COMMERCIAL EXPLOITATION OF INTELLECTUAL PROPERTY

Hilary E Pearson, MA, LLB

Barrister, Middle Temple
Simmons & Simmons, London

and

Clifford G Miller, BSc, ARCS

Solicitor of the Supreme Court of England and Wales
Simmons & Simmons, London

BLACKSTONE
PRESS LIMITED

First published in Great Britain 1990 by Blackstone Press Limited,
9-15 Aldine Street, London W12 8AW. Telephone 081-740 1173

© Hilary Pearson and Clifford Miller, 1990

ISBN: 1 85431 044 5

British Library Cataloguing in Publication Data
A CIP catalogue record for this book is available from the British Library

Typeset by Style Photosetting Ltd, Mayfield, East Sussex
Printed by Livesey Limited, Shrewsbury

Contents

1 Introduction   1

Why this book was written — How to use this book — What is intellectual property? — Why should you read this book?

2 Putting intellectual property to work   7

I The story — II The intellectual property — III Epilogue

3 Basic concepts   16

Property and ownership — Assignments and licenses — Contracts

4 Protection of ideas and information — confidentiality, commercial and technical information, secrets and know-how   24

Introduction — The law — Information — Information which is not publicly known — Circumstances imposing an obligation of confidentiality — The obligation is not to disclose or use — How long does the obligation last? — Employees

5 Protection of ideas and information — patents for inventions   41

Introduction — Recognising an invention when you see one — It is new and not obvious but is it patentable? — The right to apply for a patent — Applying for a patent — Describing inventions — Amending patents — Novelty and obviousness — Infringement — Duration of patent rights and a few possibilities for getting around them

6 Protection of form and appearance 95

Copyright works, designs, semiconductor chips and performances — Recognising what can be protected — Designs of products — Is it a copy of something else? — The rights protecting form and appearance — Rights in product designs — So you think you have something that might be protected — Who is the author? — Identifying the author — Can it qualify for protection? Is it a foreign work? — Does anyone own the rights? — Ownership of product designs — Has the period of protection expired?

7 Protecting image and reputation 178

Passing-off, trade marks and service marks — How marks and get-up work — Recognising what can be protected — Distinctiveness — Picking a registrable mark — Rights and infringement — Passing-off and the rights of the owner of goodwill — Criminal offences — No confusion – no infringement — Attacking a registration or application — Ownership of rights — Duration of rights — Licensing, franchising and character merchandising — Picking marks and get-up — Choosing company and business names

8 Remedies 222

Exercising your rights — What are you trying to achieve? — Getting what you need as quickly as possible — Remedies in intellectual property cases — Criminal offences

9 Competition law and intellectual property 235

What is competition law? — What has this to do with intellectual property? — Systems of competition law — UK competition law — EEC competition law — US antritrust law

10 Business approaches to using intellectual property 248

Intellectual property is useless if not used — The first step – what do you have in your tool-box? — Using intellectual property for competitive advantage — Sharing with others — Selling the intellectual property — Using other people's intellectual property

11 Heading off infringers (without going to court) 256

Prevention is better than cure — How to discourage infringement — Negotiating with infringers — Resolving disputes without going to court — The dangers of doing nothing

Preface

If a man write a better book, preach a better sermon, or make a better mouse-trap than his neighbour, tho' he build his house in the woods, the world will make a beaten path to his door.

(attributed to Ralph Waldo Emerson 1889)

Intellectual property is vital to success in obtaining and maintaining a competitive advantage in any industrial and commercial activity. In fact, the EC Community, Japan and the USA estimated that their industries lost $43bn to $61bn from inadequate foreign protection of intellectual property rights in 1986 and consequently they made an intellectual property rights agreement a top priority in the 1990 Uruguay round of GATT talks. Additionally, experts have estimated that up to 30 per cent of all public and private research expenditure in the EC Community of a total of 50,000 million ECU annually (nearly £70,000 million) is wasted on redundant work which could be avoided if appropriate and efficient use of patent information were to be made.

If any nation is to be able to compete at home or abroad it must be able to stop others copying its ideas, products and designs. Of all the industrialised countries, one stands out from its economic rivals in this respect. West German activity just in protecting inventions is remarkable. Per head of population West Germans make over three times as many European patent applications as the UK or the US and two and a half times as many per head as the Japanese and French.

The ability to prevent others copying is just one aspect of using intellectual property. It is also necessary to know how to copy lawfully to remain competitive without infringing the intellectual property rights of others.

We hope this book will help in raising the general level of knowledge and understanding of intellectual property in the UK and how to exploit such a potentially valuable asset. Our aim was to write a book for people who are motivated to learn about intellectual property but have no legal training. We hope we have achieved a measure of success in this aim. The non-lawyer, whether businessman, accountant, management consultant, scientist, engineer or artist, will find the principles of the law set out, with practical advice on the use of intellectual property. We have also endeavoured to make a complicated area of law as easy to understand as possible without sacrificing too much depth.

This book should also be useful as a work of first reference for the non-specialist lawyer and as an introductory text for the student. The specialist practitioner may find the explanation and layout of the chapter covering the new and old law of copyright, design, performer's rights and semiconductor chip protection particularly useful.

Certain subjects of a narrow interest are not covered in this book. We have not covered seed and plant variety protection nor the taxation aspects of intellectual property, (a subject that needs a book of its own). We have merely mentioned trading standards and consumer protection legislation, where relevant.

In order to produce a book of suitable brevity on such complex areas of law, examples have been omitted from some parts. Chapter 6 (Protection of Form and Appearance) covers five separate and complex areas of law. If there are areas where more examples would be helpful we should be pleased to hear about them. Any helpful comments on the structure and content of the book will be gratefully received. The chapters on the laws of confidentiality, patents, general copyright, rights in performances, copyright, design rights and registered design rights for products, semiconductor chip design protection and trade and service marks (chapter 4 to 7) are the responsibility of Clifford Miller. Chapter 2 and most of chapter 3, as well as the chapters on remedies and competition law (chapters 8 and 9) and part 2 of the book on methods of exploitation (chapters 10–15) are the responsibility of Hilary Pearson.

Acknowledgments

We have been greatly helped in this enterprise by several people, whose sole reward is to be publicly thanked in this preface.

A special word of thanks for his patient, good-humoured support and for generously allowing time to be devoted to the project goes to Kevin Mooney, solicitor, intellectual property lawyer and a senior partner of Simmons & Simmons, London. Without him, our paths would not have crossed, nor would we have discovered a mutual interest in writing a book of this nature.

Thanks are due to the following for their helpful comments and suggestions: first, the non-lawyers: Steven Callaghan, Chairman of Bauco (UK) Ltd and Managing Director of Industrial Supplies Consultants Ltd, Dr Michael Llewellyn-Williams, a Director of The Creative Business, and Mrs Patricia Wassell. The lawyers: Christopher Wadlow, solicitor and author of *Passing-Off*, Dr Gerald Kamstra, solicitor, and Alan Walls, European patent attorney and UK patent agent, (who are all colleagues at Simmons & Simmons, London office), Margaret Anderson of Houston, a Texas attorney and US patent attorney and, last but not least, Professor Peter Murphy of South Texas College of Law, Houston, an English barrister and American attorney and an accomplished author of textbooks on evidence and advocacy.

They are not to blame, however, for any errors.

Finally, thanks to our friends and publishers, Alistair MacQueen, Heather Saward and Jonathan Harris, for suggesting this endeavour and for keeping it on track despite delays.

Clifford Miller

Simmons & Simmons
London EC2M 2RJ

or

c/o Imperial College of Science,
Technology and Medicine
Continuing Education Centre
London SW7 2AZ

Hilary Pearson

Simmons & Simmons
London EC2M 2RJ

1 Introduction

WHY THIS BOOK WAS WRITTEN

The first thing we do, let's kill all the lawyers (*Henry VI Part 2*, Act IV, Scene ii).

Lawyers are not always held in high regard. So why are two lawyers trying to inform the public and dispel ignorance rather than maintaining traditional professional mystique?

There is, at least in part, an altruistic motive in writing this book. The general ignorance of intellectual property rights in industry and commerce actually does affect the competitiveness of our businesses, both at home and abroad.

It is hard to imagine a business that does not have some commercially valuable intellectual property, even if it is only the name the business trades under or the customer list. Despite the importance that intellectual property law therefore has for business, it is an unfortunate fact that it is rarely taught to those studying law, business, science and technology or creative arts. As a result, many of those most involved in creating and using intellectual property, the artists, scientists, engineers and business people, are often woefully ignorant of what their intellectual property rights are, what they protect, what their commercial value is and how they can be used.

Furthermore, the engineer, scientist and technologist engaged in industry may not have direct access to legal advice. The managing director may be the only person who decides to employ the services of specialist legal advisers and he or she may not realise when this is necessary. A case may need to be made out to justify the investment in obtaining legal advice.

The small business often cannot afford to consult a lawyer every time a problem arises. There are things that can be done on a day-to-day basis to identify, anticipate and avoid problems. With the proper information, a business can conserve its resources by only seeking professional advice when it is really needed. Further, an informed client is better able to use the lawyer's time effectively than he or she otherwise might.

While this book should provide you with the basic information you need to make informed decisions regarding intellectual property in your business, you must realise that in many circumstances it cannot substitute for proper advice from professionals specialising in the field of intellectual property law. Just as you would not do your own dentistry or perform your own heart surgery, you should consult a patent agent if you want to apply for a patent, or a solicitor with experience in intellectual property litigation if you want to sue an infringer. A little bit of experienced professional advice about potential intellectual property problems at the beginning of a project may be the best investment you can make.

HOW TO USE THIS BOOK

Chapter 2 puts intellectual property law in context. This is done by using the story of an imaginary product from an imaginary company. This product is followed through the typical stages from initial idea to full commercial production and marketing. Each stage is then analysed to see what protectable items have come into existence, and there is a discussion of the relevant intellectual property rights which could be used to get protection and maintain competitive advantage.

The rest of the first part of this book could be described as an intellectual property tool-box. Under the general headings of protection of ideas and information, protection of form and appearance, and protection of image, style and presentation, we look at each type of intellectual property law, examining what they are and how they work. Other areas of law that are involved in the exploitation of intellectual property, such as contract and competition law, and the legal remedies for infringement of intellectual property rights, are also covered.

We have done our best to make this law understandable, but you should be warned that this is a complicated subject. These chapters are not light bedtime reading. Also, we have tried to make the coverage as comprehensive as possible, so there may be sections that are of no relevance to your business.

The second part of the book is an instruction manual in the use of the tools described in the first part of the book. Various strategies for the use of intellectual property in business are described, and then ways to use intellectual property in furtherance of these strategies are described in detail. Here again, the subject can be complex, and these chapters may require some concentration to absorb the information.

WHAT IS INTELLECTUAL PROPERTY?

Intellectual property law is about legal rights. The owner of the intellectual property has certain exclusive rights recognised by law to control what is done with the intellectual property.

In England intellectual property includes copyrights, patents, designs, registered and unregistered trade marks and service marks, confidential information and other matter such as semiconductor chip designs. In other countries not all these intellectual property rights are recognised and in some there are additional intellectual property rights.

The subject-matter of intellectual property rights is, in general terms, the product of thought, creativity and intellectual effort. As will be seen later, intellectual property may not necessarily be the product of a fine intellect. Intellectual property law often operates to afford protection to the relatively mundane.

The following is a highly simplified summary of the subject-matter covered by each type of intellectual property:

- patents protect ideas

Patents are discussed in chapter 5.

- copyright protects form and appearance, not ideas

Copyright is dealt with in chapter 6.

- the law of confidentiality protects almost any kind of information (provided it can be considered confidential)

Confidentiality is the subject of chapter 4.

- trade mark and service mark rights protect names, logos and 'get-up' (appearance) used to identify businesses, products and services

Trade and service marks are covered in chapter 7.

- design rights (including protection for semiconductor chip designs) are very similar to copyright in that they protect form and appearance, not ideas

Design rights are discussed together with copyright in chapter 6.

WHY SHOULD YOU READ THIS BOOK?

With intellectual property, sometimes you must take positive steps to obtain the protection of the law or to avoid infringing the rights of others. If those steps are not taken, you can lose your right to protection or you may find you have a serious problem with infringement. Ignorance of the law could seriously endanger the health of your business.

You also need to know who owns the intellectual property rights that you use. As you will learn, this can be complicated and often far from obvious.

Proper protection for inventions, ideas, designs and trade and service marks can make all the difference between commercial success and failure. Take the example of Chester Carlson and the Haloid Corporation.

Chester Carlson was a physicist turned patent attorney who was irritated by a frequent occurrence in his daily work. However many carbon copies of a patent application were prepared there never seemed to be enough. The only way to obtain further copies was expensive photographic reproduction, or to have the whole document completely retyped and reproofed. In his spare time he worked on finding a practical method of quickly reproducing documents, and after considerable experimentation he developed the basic method of xerography, the form of photocopying which is now used universally. Carlson carefully patented each stage of the development.

Initially no one was interested in his idea. Finally, a small photographic paper company called the Haloid Co. was persuaded to invest in development of the first commercial xerographic copier.

The Haloid Corporation is now the multinational Xerox Corporation. This company's growth is the result of the active exploitation of Chester Carlson's invention and the vigorous defence of a strong patent position, allowing the company to remain several years ahead of its competitors while it developed the market.

In marked contrast, through ignorance of the law, none of the inventors got patents on one of the most important inventions of this century, maybe one of the most important inventions of all time — the digital programmed computer.

John Atanasoff, who built the first true working special-purpose electronic digital calculator, intended applying for patents, but although a patent application was drafted, it was never filed.

John Mauchly and J. Presper Eckert were responsible for building for the US Army the first true electronic computer, known as 'ENIAC', and a successor machine called 'EDVAC', which was the first computer to store programs internally in memory instead of being hard-wired or stored externally on cards. John von Neumann wrote an analysis of EDVAC's logical design, summarising all the thinking that had gone into it. This analysis was widely distributed and became the blueprint for the modern computer — what today is called the classic 'von Neumann machine'.

In the US, a patent application must be filed within one year of the first public disclosure or non-secret use of the invention. No patent was filed in the one-year period, so any right of Mauchly, Eckert and von Neumann to patent the stored-program computer was lost.

Although Mauchly and Eckert finally obtained a patent on ENIAC, in litigation the patent was held invalid on several grounds, among them that von Neumann's draft report on EDVAC also constituted a prior public disclosure of ENIAC, and that the true inventor was Atanasoff, not Mauchly and Eckert.

Trespassing on the intellectual property rights of others can have serious effects. Mr Britton worked as a sales representative for Normalec Ltd, with a sales territory that covered much of Yorkshire. For about five years he worked the territory, building up good relationships with customers for the light bulbs and electric fittings that his employer sold.

Then an entrepreneurial urge hit Mr Britton. He decided to set up his own company. Unfortunately, he made three fatal mistakes. He dealt in the same line of goods as his employer; he sold to the customers he had been visiting on behalf of his employer for the past five years; and he did it while still employed by Normalec. This meant that he broke his duty of loyalty to his employer, and he built up his business using confidential information that belonged to his employer — information about the names, locations and requirements of customers for electric bulbs and fittings.

Normalec only discovered all this after Mr Britton suddenly left his job. The new sales representative found he could make no sales at all, and all the business was going to Mr Britton's company. Normalec sued, and asked for an order pending trial (an interlocutory injunction) to immediately stop Mr Britton selling to its customers.

The judge gave Normalec its injunction. Then he went even further — he said that, because Mr Britton's business was built on the information that he had, in effect, stolen from his employer, his whole business in fact belonged to Normalec. So Mr Britton's mistakes regarding use of his employer's information cost him his job and his business.

A dramatic example of the advantages of intellectual property to its owner and of the dangers of infringement involves Polaroid, Kodak and instant photography.

Dr Land, the founder of Polaroid, invented 'one-step photography', in which negative and positive are produced simultaneously, within the camera, immediately after exposure. The original system was for black and white photographs, and it took many years to develop a system of colour instant photography. Polaroid protected this work by taking out a number of patents.

Kodak launched a major research project to try to come up with its own system of instant colour photography that would not be covered by Polaroid's patents. Despite enormous expenditures of time and money, this effort was unsuccessful.

When Kodak finally introduced its own instant photography system, after studying the Polaroid system, Polaroid sued for patent infringement. The trial judge found that several Polaroid patents were valid and were infringed by the Kodak system.

Kodak was forced to withdraw from the instant photography business, and had to compensate all those who had bought Kodak instant cameras, now made useless by lack of film. It will also have to pay a large sum in damages. Ignoring the patent rights of others had a very serious effect on an industry giant — it would have put a lesser company out of business.

We hope that by now our message has become clear — unless you have a basic understanding of intellectual property rights and how to protect them, you may either fail to obtain rights to which you would otherwise be entitled or you may lose the rights you have. Either way, ignorance of intellectual property law could lead to the loss of competitive business advantage for you or your clients.

2 Putting Intellectual Property to Work

I THE STORY

The idea is born

Our company, Household Goods plc, is a well-known manufacturer of domestic appliances. Sales have been flat for some time, and Far Eastern manufacturers have taken a significant share of the market for small domestic appliances. A meeting of research and marketing managers has been called to discuss what can be done to improve the company's business.

The domestic appliances marketing manager states that one product which has large and steady sales is the toaster. After all, most couples receive at least two as wedding gifts, and they tend to be thrown away and replaced when they break down. The research director points out that there have been no real developments in toaster design for many years, and that an improved toaster might be the product they are looking for. Everyone agrees that a big problem with toasters is that, when you need to make a lot of toast, after the first few slices the elements have become too hot, and the rest of the toast is either burned, or the bread pops out merely lukewarm without being toasted at all.

The head of small product development then has a brainwave. Why not design a system that will continually monitor the colour of the slice of bread, and feed that information to a chip that will turn the elements off and pop the toast when the desired colour is reached? It is agreed that research should be done on the feasibility of this idea.

Research and development

After considerable work and experimentation, the design team come up with a mechanism that reliably senses the colour of the bread in the toaster. A narrow beam of light is shone on to the bread and the reflected beam directed into a photoelectric cell. To allow for differences in reflectivity of various types of bread, the designers realise that the important factor in determining whether the toast is sufficiently browned is the change in reflectivity between the initial and final states of that particular slice. The signal from the photoelectric cell is therefore fed to a specially programmed chip, which constantly calculates the difference in reflectivity from the initial state.

By experiment, the team determine the required change in reflectivity to produce a selected range of doneness for all usual types of bread, such as white, brown and wholemeal, and a program is written to turn off the elements and activate the pop-up mechanism when the predetermined difference in reflectivity is reached.

During the course of this development, design drawings for all the parts are made. Flowcharts and programming for the software are prepared. A chip which can withstand the temperature fluctuations inside the toaster, and which is sufficiently rugged to operate reliably despite the type of handling that a toaster normally receives, has to be designed. The circuitry of the chip needed to carry out the operations of the software program is designed to operate efficiently and economically.

Product design

Once management is satisfied that it is possible to produce a sensing mechanism which would work in practice, a team of product designers is assigned to produce a design for the toaster. This team's task is to produce a design which will appeal to the toaster-buying public, which will accommodate and protect the sensing mechanism and which will be economical to manufacture. The team also decide that they will try to come up with a design sufficiently different from conventional toaster designs for it to be easily recognised by members of the public.

Working with the sensing mechanism developers, and creating large numbers of drawings both by hand and using computer-aided design (CAD), a design for the toaster evolves. Public reaction to the design is tested by market surveys in which potential toaster buyers are shown mock-ups of various toaster designs as well as actual toasters marketed by competitors. The final design gets a high approval rating and recognition level from those surveyed.

Having settled on the shape, the team then design the decoration. They come up with a design featuring golden ears of wheat drawn in a very modernistic manner, to convey the impression of traditional goodness in a high-tech setting.

Production engineering and testing

Once the product design is finalised, the next stage is to develop the commercial production process and extensively test the product.

Testing of the toaster reveals a problem. Slices of bread can have large holes in them which appear during the baking process. If the beam strikes the bread at the point where there is a hole, it is reflected off the metal plate on which the heating element is mounted. This intense reflection causes the chip to malfunction, immediately triggering the signal to turn off the element and pop up the untoasted bread. In some cases it is found that the signal from the photoelectric cell when this happens is so large that the chip is permanently damaged.

Eventually, a solution to the problem is found. The beam is made to scan a strip of the surface of the slice of bread sufficiently long to ensure that at least part of the scan will be on the bread. The signals are detected by an array of photoelectric cells, which feed into a circuit which filters out extreme peaks in signal strength caused when the beam passes through a hole in the bread and is reflected off the back plate.

Choosing a name

While the engineers are preparing to manufacture the toaster, the marketing department are making preparations for the launch of the product. Before publicity can be prepared and all the rest of the hoop-la that accompanies the introduction of a new product to the public set in motion, a name must be chosen. This name, the trade mark, will be of great importance in successfully marketing the product.

Marketing is having great difficulty coming up with a name. 'Spacetoast' was rejected early on as having drug culture overtones. 'Paf' was in favour for a while until the sales director for Europe, a Belgian, informed marketing that the word was colloquial French for drunk. Eventually two names were in contention, both with their ardent supporters. The camp supporting 'Nevaburn' urged that this name would sell the really innovative aspect of the toaster. The opponents, who favoured 'Golden Harvest', felt that their choice conveyed a classier, more appealing image of success and good nutrition. They also pointed out that it tied in with the design on the toaster casing, and would be more easily understood in the European market.

A search of the Register has shown nothing closely resembling 'Golden Harvest' in the class which includes toasters, although there are registrations for baked goods and canned fruit.

Eventually, 'Golden Harvest' was selected as the trade mark. Now the task is to build up the desired image for the mark as quickly as possible once the toasters hit the market.

Preparing for launch

The publicity campaign for the launch of the Golden Harvest toaster is in the hands of Household Goods plc's advertising agency, Imaginative Advertising Associates. Household Goods plc's marketing department have stressed that, although they want the great step forward in toaster design that this product represents featured, they do not want customers to be afraid that it would be too advanced for them to use easily.

Imaginative Advertising come up with a theme for television advertisements, which will be adapted for print advertising. The ad will open with a well-known clip from a silent movie comedy, then move into a scene with an actor who resembles the silent movie actor wrestling with a conventional type of toaster that keeps burning the toast, this scene being in black and white and with a typical silent movie music score. Into the scene comes a 'Golden Harvest' toaster, in colour. As the actor effortlessly produces a stream of golden toast from the toaster, the whole scene converts from black and white to colour, and the music becomes electronic. Three story lines are proposed, one using Charlie Chaplin, one using the Keystone Cops and the third using Mack Sennett.

The marketing department and senior management are very enthusiastic about these proposals. Imaginative Advertising are commissioned to make the commercials and produce accompanying print advertising. Using the basic theme, the marketing department plan various launch events. These include appearances at various large elecrical goods and department stores of the actors who appear in the ads, dressed as the silent film star. The campaign slogan is devised by a brainstorming meeting of the whole department with the people from Imaginative Advertising — 'Golden Harvest, modern technology making old-fashioned toast'.

As this is a fairy story, of course it has a happy ending. The Golden Harvest toaster is a great success. It takes a large share of the toaster market, and greatly increases Household Goods plc's profits. And, as Household Goods takes all the proper steps to protect what it has created, it is able to keep out imitators from its market. What are those steps? Read on.

II THE INTELLECTUAL PROPERTY

The idea is born

By the end of this meeting, we have an idea for a toaster with a new and, if it works, improved way of producing properly browned toast. As Household Goods plc is hoping that this will result in a smash-hit new product that will improve its sales and profits, it is clearly important to take proper precautions to protect this inventive idea. Ideas can be protected by treating them as confidential information or by patenting the invention.

At this stage, the idea is probably in too sketchy a form for a patent to be filed. No way of putting the idea into practice has yet been thought of. Indeed, it is not yet certain the idea can be made to work at all.

As patent protection is not really suitable at this stage, it is vital that the idea is kept secret so that it can be protected as confidential information. Those at the meeting must agree to keep the information confidential, and employees who are assigned to work on developing the product must do the same. The minutes of the meeting, and any other documents which reveal the idea for the new toaster should be marked and treated as confidential. It is particularly important to keep track of employees who know about this project, in case any of them leave to work for a competitor before the product is publicly launched. In the event of that happening, the departing employee would have to be particularly warned that this information is confidential and must not be imparted to the new employer. Visitors to Household Goods plc's premises where the development is going on should be kept away from anything that would disclose the existence or nature of the project.

Research and development

At this stage, a lot of potentially protectable items have come into being. Care must be taken, as protection could be lost if the wrong steps are taken. Further, some choices about mutually exclusive kinds of protection may have to be made.

The sensing mechanism

First, the design of the sensing mechanism: this is something that is potentially patentable. The first step is to investigate the patentability of the idea, by having a search for relevant prior art made. This job is most commonly done by a patent agent, aided by the company's design engineers who will probably have considerable knowledge of the literature on the subject. If any potentially troublesome patents are found in the search, a legal opinion is needed, both on the effect of these patents on the patentability of the toaster sensing mechanism and also on whether the planned design could infringe any of those patents.

The best time to consider applying for a patent is when there is an operative prototype. One advantage of applying for a patent at an early stage of development is that there is much less risk of loss of patent rights through a non-confidential disclosure. The risk of an unauthorised disclosure of the details of the design becomes more and more likely the nearer the product is to official launch. Early application may also get you ahead of a competitor who is working on a similar product. The main disadvantage of early application for a patent is that it is usually too soon to be able to ascertain the commercial importance of the invention, and thus to be able to determine whether the cost of applying for a patent will be justified. Further, the process of commercial production may lead to significant improvements in the design, which will require further patents for protection.

The alternative to patent protection is to keep the design a trade secret. For protection of the idea itself, patent and trade secret protection are true alternatives. The patent must contain details of the invention which are therefore made public as soon as the application is published, thereby removing the confidentiality necessary for trade secret protection. However, even when a patent is obtained, there may still be related information which can be protected by confidentiality. For example, a patentee is not required to disclose the exact details of commercial manufacture, which may be a very valuable trade secret.

A major factor in deciding between patent and trade secret protection is the readiness with which the design could be reverse engineered. Reverse engineering is the process of studying a product in order to determine how it works and how it was made. In general, reverse engineering of a publicly available product is legitimate. This means that any information which can be discovered by reverse engineering cannot be kept secret once the product is on the market. In the case of our toaster, reverse engineering would be fairly simple, so patenting is the only viable protection.

Other factors which can be weighed when choosing between patent and trade secret protection are:

1.   The high cost of patenting and the relative cheapness of maintaining secrecy, which need to be balanced in view of the likely commercial value of the invention.

2. Whether there is patentable subject-matter — certain technical re-quirements must be met for patentability, but for trade secrets all that is required is that the subject matter is not already known to the public.

3. Getting a patent involves making details of your invention known to the public — in the case of a product which can be reverse engineered to learn this information, this does not matter. However, in the case of a manufacturing process, it may be possible to keep the process a secret because it cannot be learned by reverse engineering the product which it produces, which is all that is available to the public. On the other hand, catching infringers of a process patent can be very difficult for the same reason. This means that trade secret protection may be preferable.

4. If you don't get a patent and your competitor does, you may be prevented from using your trade secrets because they infringe that patent.

The chip
There are a number of kinds of intellectual property which are relevant to protection of the chip and its programming, and they are not all mutually exclusive. To the extent that the circuitry and processing of the chip to make it sufficiently rugged for use in a toaster are patentable, again the choice is between patent and trade secret protection. The semiconductor industry uses some very sophisticated reverse engineering techniques which can determine circuitry, so it may be preferable to apply for patent protection for the circuit. On the other hand, it can be very difficult to determine the process of manufacture by reverse engineering.

The actual masks used to make the layers of the chip are protectable as semiconductor topographies.

The software
The program in the form of flowcharts and source code is not published, and these may be treated as both unpublished copyright works and confidential information. The status of the program as embodied in circuits in the chip is less certain; while the term 'computer program' is not defined in the Copyright, Designs and Patents Act 1988, a court may find it difficult to accept that an arrangement of transistors on a silicon substrate is a 'literary work'. However, an Australian judge has recently interpreted the Australian copyright statute, which was amended in 1984 to expressly make computer programs literary works, as covering such 'hard-wired' programs. The question whether a circuit design is protectable by design right does not at present have a clear answer, so it would be unwise to rely on this.

The drawings
The drawings themselves are protectable by copyright. This means, for example, that an employee who takes copies of one or more of these drawings with him on leaving the company could be forced to return or destroy the copies and any copies made from them by an action for copyright infringement. On the other hand, if the drawings are used by a rival to copy Household Goods plc's toaster sensing mechanism, that is an infringement of the design right in the design recorded in the drawing. Because this is a functional design,

registration as a registered design is not available. Of course, if the mechanism is patented, the competitor would also be infringing the patent.

The circuit drawings for the chip, and the drawings from which the masks for making the chip are made, are usually produced nowadays by computer-aided design (CAD). The Copyright, Designs and Patents Act 1988 does not specifically provide for protection of computer-generated drawings and two-dimensional designs, so there is at least a question about their protection. While it is unlikely that the courts would refuse to grant protection, Household Goods would be well advised to make print-outs of all these drawings and designs which will clearly be capable of protection.

Product design

The shape of the toaster

The drawings generated in the design process would themselves be protectable by copyright, as discussed above. The designs embodied in those drawings are protectable by design right. However, in this case, the design is not purely functional. While the shape of the toaster was in part dictated by the need to accommodate and protect the sensing mechanism, it also appeals to the eye, as shown by the market survey responses. The test for registrability after 1 August 1989, the date that the relevant parts of the Copyright, Designs and Patents Act 1988 came into force, is whether the appearance of the article is 'material'. This means that the design is registrable if people who purchase toasters normally take aesthetic considerations into account and it would make a difference to these people whether or not the design is applied to the article. While toaster purchasers are primarily concerned with getting a toaster that will toast without burning the bread, they are also likely to be concerned with the appearance of an article that is going to sit around their kitchens. The market survey should also help to prove that the appearance is material and therefore the design is registrable, assuming it is new.

One note of warning: although market surveys are most desirable to develop a successful design and to improve the chances of getting that design registered, they do carry a risk. Unless care is taken, Household Goods plc's plans can leak out to its competitors, thereby allowing them to make their own plans. This could considerably shorten the time after launch in which Household Goods will have the competitive advantage, time that it needs to build up its market share before competitive goods arrive. The surveys should convey no hint of the new sensing mechanism, and preferably should not even identify Household Goods as the source of the new toaster.

The advantage of seeking a design registration, if it is available, is that it gives a patent-like protection against the independent creation of a similar design. Design right merely affords protection against copying. It is also much simpler to prove the existence and ownership of a registered design.

Even though the design is distinctive over existing designs, so that once the toaster is in the market the public will be able to associate it with Household Goods, the distinctive shape will not be accepted for registration as a trade mark. Even the highly distinctive shape of the traditional Coca-Cola glass bottle has been refused registration.

The decoration
The modernistic design of golden ears of wheat on the sides of the toaster is surface decoration. Surface decoration is expressly excluded from design right protection. It would, however, be registrable as a feature or ornament which appeals solely to the eye, provided it meets the novelty requirements of the Registered Designs Act 1949. It would also seem to be protectable by copyright under the scheme of the Copyright, Designs and Patents Act 1988 because it is not protectable by design right.

Production engineering and testing

During the development of the commercial production process and testing of a product, it is often necessary to make minor changes to the design of the product. When this occurs, patents and registered designs should be examined to see whether the changes could take the manufactured product outside the scope of protection. This is unlikely if the patents and design registrations were drafted to give a proper scope of protection.

In the case of the toaster, solving the problem of malfunction caused by the beam hitting a hole in the bread required more than minor changes. The scanning and sensing mechanisms were substantially redesigned.

Where changes are more than minor, a number of problems can arise. First, there may now be a serious question whether the patent or registered design protection covers the new design. Second, a major change may move the product within the scope of some previous patent or registered design which the original design did not infringe. Therefore a major change like this one during testing and production engineering should trigger a new patentability study.

If the new design is outside the scope of the original patent application but is patentable, a new patent application covering the improvement must be filed. The original application cannot be amended to include the new material.

Choosing a name

The deliberations over a suitable trade mark show the importance of carefully selecting a mark to accord with the image you want to build up in the mind of your customers and potential customers. Even fairly tenuous negative connotations, like the drug culture overtones of 'Spacetoast', should be avoided.

When the goods are likely to reach a non-English speaking market, the meaning and image in the other language must also be looked at. This can be expensive, requiring the help of a native speaker. After all, most truly offensive words in any language are unlikely to be found in the average dictionary! Sometimes there is no alternative but to choose a separate mark, but this can considerably add to the expense of marketing in that country. Under European competition law, you should have a good reason for having different marks in different markets if you are going to be able to enforce them without incurring accusations that you are trying to divide up the market.

'Nevaburn' is likely to be refused registration because the Trade Marks Registry will regard it either as purely descriptive of the goods (if the toaster truly never burns the toast) or deceptive (if it ever burns it). Marks which are descriptive, including those which are merely a misspelling of a descriptive word or term, are generally not a good choice.

Preparing for launch

The proposed television advertisements raise some difficult questions of copyright law.

The film clips

Is anyone's permission needed to use the film clips? They are all US works, made before the US first joined an international convention giving reciprocal rights with the UK (27 September 1957). This means that they will not have copyright protection in the UK *unless* they were 'simultaneously published' in the US and in the UK or another country with which the UK had reciprocal protection at the time. In the case of works of US origin, the simultaneous publication often occurred in Canada. It may be very difficult to determine whether the necessary publication was made in order to gain protection in the UK, although in the case of commercially important films such as those proposed for use in these advertisements it is likely that the film studio arranged for such publication.

Even if protection was obtained, it must still be determined whether the copyright is still in existence. Assuming these films were made after 1 July 1912 but before the Copyright Act 1956 came into effect, the term of copyright is governed by the Copyright Act 1911. That Act did not have a copyright category for films, but they could be protected as dramatic works or as a series of photographs. Unfortunately, it is important to decide which category applies, as the term of protection for a dramatic work is the life of the director plus 50 years, whereas for a series of photographs it is 50 years from the end of the calendar year in which they were taken.

Even playing it safe by deciding to ask for permission to use the clips has its problems. Permission must be obtained from the copyright owner, and it may not be easy to determine who that is in the case of old works.

Imitating the stars

The second question is whether there will be any problems with using actors to imitate the silent film greats. The English courts have so far refused to acknowledge a 'right of publicity' owned by public figures who exploit their fame (or notoriety) for profit, although such a right is now well established in the US. The silent film stars involved are now all dead, so there can be no action for libel or similar personal torts. They have no moral rights, as the works were created before the Copyright, Designs and Patents Act 1988 came into force on 1 August 1989.

Ownership of copyright

The advertisements were thought up, written and made by Imaginative Advertising. Household Goods gave a general directive and paid for them. Who owns the copyright?

Unfortunately, the law is far from clear. Under both the Copyright Act 1956 and the Copyright, Designs and Patents Act 1988, the author of a film (who is the original owner of the copyright in it) is 'the person by whom the arrangements necessary for the making of the film were made'. There is no further explanation of this vague term, and no court decisions to help interpret it.

The only safe course of action for Household Goods to ensure that it owns the copyright in the advertisements is to get a contractual agreement from Imaginative Advertising that they will assign any rights that they may have to Household Goods. Further, the agreement should waive moral rights as far as possible.

III EPILOGUE

Our revels now are ended. These our actors,
As I foretold you, were all spirits, and
Are melted into air, into thin air
                              (*The Tempest,* Act IV, Scene i)

This story, our company and its product, may have been fictional, but the facts are close to real life. We hope you are beginning to see how intellectual property is relevant to all kinds of business, and how it can be used to advantage.

3 Basic Concepts

There are a few basic legal concepts that underlie all the topics that are discussed in the following chapters. An elementary understanding of these concepts will help in wrestling with the sometimes very complex subject of intellectual property law and its exploitation. What follows is a very basic discussion of some important concepts.

PROPERTY AND OWNERSHIP

There is a distinction between property and the things which can be property.

This distinction is fundamental to a proper understanding of intellectual property law. However, the ownership of things is so fundamental to our society and so much a part of our daily lives that this distinction is frequently overlooked.

Property is a concept, not a thing

In the absence of any legal rights or other social norms governing the possession and use of anything, there would still be things but there would be no property.

The term 'property' refers to something capable of ownership. 'Ownership' basically means rights to possess, use and dispose of property to the exclusion of others.

If you own land you have the exclusive legal right to keep out everyone except those you choose to invite to visit. If you own a car you have the exclusive legal right to stop someone else driving it without your permission. If you own copyright in a copyright work you have several legal rights, including the exclusive right to prevent anyone copying the work.

The medium is not the message

The lay person often fails to distinguish a physical item from the rights recognised by law in the item. The intellectual property rights in a physical item are independent of the item itself.

For example, someone who purchases a painting from an artist becomes the owner of the painting. The owner can sue to recover the painting from someone who wrongfully refuses to return it, including the artist himself. However, unless the owner has also purchased the copyright in the picture, he or she will not be able to sue someone else for making a copy of the picture without permission. The copyright is a right which is wholly independent of the right to possess or control a physical item, and ownership of copyright is similarly distinct from ownership of an item which embodies the copyright work.

Additionally, not only are intellectual property rights independent of the subject-matter to which they relate, they are also independent of each other and of any other property rights in a physical item.

To take an everyday example, imagine that your doctor has given you a prescription for a new antibiotic. When you pay the chemist for the capsules, they belong to you. The capsules themselves are your property. On the other hand, suppose the antibiotic inside those capsules is patented by the drug company. The fact that you have bought the capsules gives you no right to make the drug, a right given exclusively to the patent owner. Further suppose that the capsules are a new design, which is easier to swallow. The drug company may be able to stop other manufacturers from using capsules of the same shape, even for different drugs not covered by the patent. Now suppose that the capsules are half transparent and half coloured, and through the transparent half you can see the drug in the form of tiny spheres of two different colours. That colour scheme can be a trade mark, so that another manufacturer will not be able to use the same scheme, even for the same drug that he is free to make after the patent expires.

Ownership is not absolute

While the law usually gives high priority to ownership rights there may be an overriding public interest which prevails over private rights.

The rights conferred on the owner of intellectual property are not without limit. For example, some intellectual property rights are limited in time. Some activities which might amount to infringement are expressly or impliedly permitted by law. If you buy a product which is protected by patents, you have the implied right to repair it even if this might otherwise amount to patent infringement.

Some subject-matter can never be protected by intellectual property rights. Basic scientific discoveries cannot be patented, nor, in most countries, can methods of treating disease. Once an invention has been made openly and freely available to the public, it cannot be taken back again and patented. The common name for an object cannot be adopted as a protectible trade-mark for that object, and a trade-mark which becomes the generic name for the goods it denotes ceases to be the sole property of its owner.

ASSIGNMENTS AND LICENCES

During the rest of this book we will often refer to 'assignments' or 'licences' of intellectual property. To save having to explain these and related terms every time we use them, basic definitions are given here.

● assignment is the legal term for transfer of ownership

It covers all the ways in which ownership of property is transferred from one person to another, such as selling, swapping, and giving it away. It is particularly used to refer to forms of transfer that require a document to pass the property over. Intellectual property, an abstract concept, cannot be physically handed over, so a document is always need to transfer ownership. The person who is transferring ownership is known as the 'assignor', the recipient is called the 'assignee'.

Assignments of intellectual property are discussed in detail in chapter 14.

● a licence is permission to use

The law gives the owner of intellectual property certain exclusive rights. An exclusive right is simply a right to exclude others from doing certain things which use the intellectual property. The same is true of physical property — for example, you can stop anyone else driving your car. However, if you wish, you can let a friend drive your car while you are in it, or even borrow it for a while.

In the same way, you can give others permission to use your intellectual property. This licence can be limited, for example, to do only some of the things that the intellectual property carries the exclusive right to do, or to do them in a limited area. The person giving the permission is the 'licensor', the person receiving it is the 'licensee'.

Licences of intellectual property are dealt with in detail in chapter 13.

CONTRACTS

This book not only explains what intellectual property is, it is also intended to help you to make money from your intellectual property. This will often involve agreements with other people. Agreements are such a basic part of life in our society that the law has evolved detailed rules about them.

● a contract is an agreement which gives rise to legally enforceable obligations

Not all agreements are enforceable in this way; only those which satisfy the requirements laid down by the law for enforceability.

An agreement need not be in writing; it can be oral or even by conduct. For example, you pick up a loaf of bread at the supermarket, take it to the check-out, the price is rung up on the till and you hand over the money. You have just completed a legally enforceable contract, possibly without a word being said.

Formation of a contract

The basis of the English law of contract is the concept of a bargain. There must be:

● an offer from one party
● which is accepted by the other
● and there must be some value given in exchange for the obligation entered into — this value is known as 'consideration'.

These three elements will be considered in turn.

Offer

An offer is made when the person making the offer (the offeror) shows a willingness to enter a binding agreement on certain terms if and as soon as that offer is accepted by the person to whom it is addressed (the offeree). Clearly, an offer cannot be effective unless it is received by the offeree.

An offer should be distinguished from a communication which may lead up to a contract, but which does not show this intent to be immediately bound. Such a communication is known to lawyers as an 'invitation to treat'. For example, 'I will sell you my car for £500 cash' is an offer. 'I am thinking about selling my car; would you be interested in it for about £500?' is an invitation to treat.

Acceptance

An acceptance may be made verbally, or (where appropriate) by conduct. However, the acceptance must be unconditional; an 'acceptance' which stipulates different terms from the offer is, at common law, not an acceptance but a counter-offer. The original offeror is then at liberty to decide whether or not to accept the counter-offer.

In general, acceptance must be communicated to the offeror before a contract comes into existence. This is because it would clearly be unfair to hold the offeror to a contract which he did not know existed. On this basis, there are certain circumstances where fairness does not require direct communication, for instance, where it is the offeror's own fault that he did not receive the communication — he failed to read his mail or to check his telex machine. In general, the offeror cannot treat silence as acceptance.

Unless it indicates to the contrary, in general an offer can be withdrawn any time before acceptance. However, this withdrawal should be brought to the offeree's attention.

An offer is terminated by rejection, and 'rejection' includes the making of a counter-offer. An offer which is stated to be for a fixed time terminates on expiry of that time; in all other cases the offer remains open for a period which is reasonable in the circumstances. An offer may also lapse upon the occurrence of some specified condition, or upon the occurrence of some event which makes the offer impossible to perform. Once an offer is terminated, it cannot be accepted.

Consideration

In certain legal systems any serious promise is enforceable. This is not the rule in England, for all ordinary contracts.

- a promise is only enforceable as a contractual obligation if it is supported by consideration

What is meant by 'consideration'? The traditional definition is that it is some benefit to the promisor, or some detriment to the promisee. The word 'detriment' has nothing to do with whether there is a bad bargain, and is not used exactly in its normal sense. Perhaps a better definition is:

- consideration is the price paid for the promise

This fits in well with the English common law concept of contract as being a bargain. The common law does not enforce gratuitous promises. An exchange of mutual promises can be consideration for each other.

Although there must be consideration of some economic value to make the agreement enforceable, the law is not in general concerned with the adequacy of the consideration. A nominal consideration, in the sense that it is clearly worth much less than the value of the performance promised in return, may be used to make enforceable what would otherwise be a mere gratuitous promise. The exception to this is where the inadequacy of the consideration is the result of oppressive conduct, of a type legally recognised as such, on the part of the party benefiting from the inadequacy. A promise to do something that the promisor was already legally obliged to do is not valid consideration.

Varying a contract

After a binding contract has been entered into, the parties may wish to change one or more of its provisions. In order for these changes to be legally binding, they must be supported by some consideration. If the change potentially benefits both parties, then that is in itself sufficient consideration. However, when only one party can benefit from the change, there must be consideration given by the benefited party.

Whatever did they mean? Construing the contract

In order for there to be an agreement, there must be some common intent on the part of the parties to the agreement. This intent must be communicated through words. Unfortunately, words are not a precise instrument to convey what is in the mind. The courts, faced with the impossibility of determining directly what was in the parties' minds, have laid down the rule that:

- intention is to be determined by the reasonable interpretation of the words the parties have used to express that agreement

The law has also laid down rules to guide that interpretation. The advantage of having such rules is that the parties can put their agreement into words knowing with some certainty how a court will interpret them if they end up in a legal dispute over the contract.

If the language used by the parties is so vague or incomplete that the court is unable to determine anything more than an agreement to agree, then the entire contract is unenforceable. The courts will, however, do their best to make an enforceable agreement out of what they have before them if the parties clearly intended to enter a binding contract. Thus, the courts will imply terms that are common in the type of contract before them, or terms that seem to be reasonable in the circumstances, rather than invalidate the whole agreement. They will not do this, however, with terms that are vital to the agreement, such as the price of unique goods, or the description of land.

Rules of interpretation
The first and overriding rule of interpretation:

- if the words impart a clear, unambiguous meaning, then that is the meaning they must be given

The court-developed rules of interpretation given below only apply if the language used by the parties is ambiguous in meaning:

(a) The words used should be given their usual meaning unless they were clearly used in a technical sense. If the parties wish to ensure that a particular meaning will be given to a word, they should set out a clear definition of the word in their agreement.

(b) The words used should be interpreted in the context of the whole agreement and the circumstances in which it was made.

(c) If, out of two possible interpretations, one makes the agreement clearly unworkable or unenforceable, the court should choose the other.

(d) An ambiguity is construed against the party who was the cause of the ambiguity.

(e) Wherever possible, inconsistent clauses must be reconciled, although a provision which is totally inconsistent with the rest of the contract may be rejected.

(f) When a contract is printed, typewritten provisions prevail over printed provisions, and handwritten provisions prevail over both printed and typewritten provisions.

Where the contract is in writing, the court will try to interpret it solely from the words used. In general:

- the court will not consider evidence of intention outside the words of the agreement

This rule is known to lawyers as the 'parol evidence rule'. However, if the ambiguity cannot be resolved by study of the actual words used, the court will look at evidence outside the 'four corners of the contract' to determine intention. This may include evidence of negotiations leading up to the contract, and of the practical interpretation put on the contract by the parties themselves by the way they perform their obligations, if performance has commenced.

Implied terms

In addition to the terms which the parties expressly spell out in their agreement, other terms may be included by implication. Implied terms may be categorised as:

- those implied as a matter of fact
- those implied as a matter of law
- those implied by custom

Terms implied in fact
These are terms which a court will include to fill some obvious gap and which are needed to make a particular agreement workable.

- the court will only imply a term if it is obvious that the parties would have included it if they had thought about it

The term must not only be obvious, it must also be necessary to give the contract business efficacy. The court must not imply a term simply because it would improve the contract.

For a term to be implied in fact, it must not only have been obvious to both parties, but it must be clear that both parties would have agreed to it. Any term which is in the interest of only one of the parties will therefore not be implied.

Terms implied in law
Terms are implied in fact when a fictional intent of the parties is discerned. Terms are implied in law regardless of the intent of the parties. There are a very large number of such terms, many of them relating to particular types of contracts. Many are the result of the development of the common law, others are imposed by statute. They are generally imposed in the furtherance of some public policy, for example, to ensure that the parties to a contract treat each other with fairness and honesty, or to protect the economically weaker party. These terms are too numerous to be dealt with individually here.

Terms implied by custom
This particularly applies to commercial contracts. In particular trades and businesses there are often customary provisions which are common to everyone in the business. This can range from whole contracts, as in the case of architects and building contractors, to single provisions.

- when both parties knew of these terms at the time of contracting, such customary terms are implied unless

  — they are unreasonable, or

  — are expressly excluded, or

  — are inconsistent with the parties' own terms

Even if terms are not common to the trade, they may be implied if the parties have dealt with each other on a number of occasions, and on each previous occasion a particular term had been expressly included in the agreement.

Just sign here — standard-form contracts

We are all familiar with standard-form contracts. When we buy a car, buy furniture on credit, sign up for a package holiday or take out a bank loan, we are faced with a standard-form contract. If we want the goods or services, we have to sign and accept all the terms. Other transactions may involve a standard-form contract which we don't even sign; the ticket you get when you drive into a parking garage or leave clothes at the cleaners may include contractual terms. It is obvious that, with such contracts, the concept of freedom of contract on the consumer's part is illusory. The courts and the legislature in almost all jurisdictions have come to realise this, and have intervened to prevent the abuse of economic power which such forms can represent.

One of the most serious abuses of economic power is the use of such standard contracts to exclude or severely limit the liability of the stronger party under the contract. Fully negotiated contracts often include some limitation of the full contractual liability of one or both of the parties, but this is an acceptable mutual shifting of risks, often risks that can be insured against. In the case of such exemption clauses in standard-form contracts, such a clause may be wholly or partially invalid, either by statute or under judge-made rules.

First:

- an exemption clause will not form part of a contract which was not signed by the consumer unless it was clearly brought to his or her attention, or at least all reasonable steps were taken to do so

It cannot be on a notice posted in a place where the customer would not normally expect to find contractual terms.

Secondly:

- an exclusion clause in a standard contract will be very narrowly interpreted, and the slightest uncertainty construed against the party who imposes the standard form on the other

The courts are particularly reluctant to exempt such a party from the results of his own negligence, and only the clearest words will be interpreted as having this result.

In the United Kingdom, there has been extensive legislation in recent years controlling abuses of economic power, in particular, limiting the use of exclusion clauses in standard-form contracts. The most important piece of legislation in this respect is the Unfair Contract Terms Act 1977. This prevents exclusion of liability under certain terms implied into contracts for the sale of goods, at least in the case of buyers who are individual consumers. Similar provisions have been applied to the supply of services by the Supply of Goods and Services Act 1982 and the Supply of Goods (Implied Terms) Act 1973. Other statutory provisions limiting the use of exemption clauses are to be found in the Misrepresentation Act 1967, which prevents the use of clauses limiting liability for misrepresentation unless they are shown to be reasonable, and a number of other Acts relating to particular kinds of contracts such as leases and employment contracts.

Provisions other than exclusion of liability may also be oppressive. The standard form may purport to strip the weaker party of certain rights he would otherwise have, or to give certain extra rights to the stronger party. An example of the former can often be found in bank guarantee forms, of the latter in estate agents' contracts which provide for the payment of commission to the agent whether or not the sale is to a buyer whom he found. A number of specific abuses have been dealt with by legislation, in particular, those connected with consumer credit.

The above makes it clear that anyone proposing to use a standard-form contract in his business should have it carefully checked for enforceability by a lawyer knowledgeable in this area of the law. Similarly, anyone who has signed one of these contracts who now finds that the other party has defaulted but is claiming exemption for liability for such default because of a clause in the contract may not be without a remedy.

4 Protection of Ideas and Information — Confidentiality, Commercial and Technical Information, Secrets and Know-how

INTRODUCTION

In the commercial world, confidential information can be very valuable. Much business information may be of value to others in the same line of business. The business which has generated the information would obviously like to prevent its competitors from discovering and using this information. Additionally, it may be very important to an individual to prevent private personal information from being published in the press. This chapter deals with how such information can be legally protected.

This chapter explains

- the way the law of confidentiality operates
- what can be done to obtain and maintain protection for confidential matter
- what can be done to avoid infringing the rights of others
- how to minimise the risks involved in accepting disclosures of information in confidence

Despite being easily comprehensible the law of confidentiality raises some difficult issues.

The problem of control

Setting out to control who can have information and what they are allowed to do with it is likely to be a difficult task. Clearly, it is difficult to treat information as one person's exclusive property. If two or more people know the same information and carry it around in their heads, how is it that any one of them can truly be said to be able to control exclusively what use others make of the information and thus be considered to own it? If the information is a general concept or idea capable of being put to use in many ways, perhaps as part of a complex product, it may be difficult to challenge someone's claim to have thought up the idea independently or even to trace the use made of the information in any event.

There must be limits to the control

Allowing one person the exclusive right to control the use made of information could place intolerable burdens on everyone else. Clearly, there must be limits on the extent to which pure information can be controlled by individuals to the exclusion of others. The law of confidentiality does not give unfettered rights to control the use and disclosure of information.

THE LAW

The legal basis of the action for breach of confidence is obscure. As information is not property the courts were unable to rely upon property law to afford a remedy to anyone who went to law complaining of the misuse of information. Thus, various other legal concepts were either used or developed, including breach of contractual obligations not to misuse or disclose information, breach of trust and breach of confidence. Whatever the niceties of legal theory, what is important for practical purposes is that a form of protection exists. In order to obtain protection there must be:

- information
- which is not publicly known
- the recipient of the information must have become subject to an obligation to keep it confidential

An obligation to keep information confidential entails

- not disclosing or using the information
- without permission
- of the person to whom the obligation is owed

INFORMATION

Any kind of information can be protected

In theory almost any kind of information which is confidential can be protected under the law of confidence. The same law applies to secret industrial processes as applies to information about an individual's sex life and other personal information. Thus, although terms like know-how, trade secrets and confidential information are convenient labels for different kinds of information, the same law applies to them all.

During the life of a business much information is generated which is perhaps of a sensitive nature: new product plans, product costings, best materials to use, sources of materials, financial standing of the business, accounting information, employee records, credit ratings of customers, production information, manufacturing methods and processes, business methods and organisational structure, to name but a few types.

Sometimes certain kinds of information are referred to as 'know-how'. Know-how is not a special legal term. Know-how is neither well defined nor is it easy to define. It is often a term associated with technical information like confidential drawings, technical manuals, specifications and designs for products. However, it can equally be used in other ways such as in relation to how a business should be organised and run, where supplies can be obtained, who quotes the cheapest prices. If you find it convenient you can describe one kind of information as technical know-how and the other as commercial know-how. The bottom line for this area of the law is that they are treated in much the same way.

The law does not apply to all information equally. For example, where employees are concerned the law attempts to strike a balance between the employer's need to protect secret information and the employee's need to earn a living elsewhere by making use of the general skills and knowledge acquired whilst employed as an employee. However, anything that can truly be classed as a 'trade secret' should be protectable, regardless of circumstance, provided it has been kept secret.

In general it seems there may be some requirement of originality in relation to industrial or commercial technical information. Where people are skilled in particular fields it may not be just to prohibit them using relatively mundane information.

Confidential information must be distinguished from private information

Whether or not particular information about a person qualifies for protection as confidential information, it is well accepted that people should be entitled to have their privacy respected. However, English law recognises no general right to privacy. Under English law an individual must rely upon specific law such as the law of defamation, confidentiality, data protection and the like.

An example of the distinction between confidential information and private information is your name and address. Anyone's name and address is recorded in many places by a large number of different organisations, like banks, credit card companies, credit reference agencies, hospitals and other medical records, the taxation and vehicle licensing authorities. Although it is not impossible to keep a name and address confidential, it can be difficult to prove that it is not freely available from some source or other. Thus, a name and address may be private information but it is not always confidential and hence not always protectable by the law of confidentiality.

Must information be valuable?

There are indications in some decided cases that information must have some value in some way or another in order to be protectable. However,

● the value of information does not have to be financial

Additionally, the same information can have different value to different people. To a newspaper an exclusive story may mean more revenue in sales whereas to the people concerned it may mean fame and recognition or perhaps embarrassment, pain or humiliation.

Practical considerations

The intangible nature of information makes it difficult to control. The problem of control can be compounded by not taking sufficient care to fix the information in some manner so that it is reasonably well defined. If it is not clear exactly what the information sought to be protected is then it will be difficult or even impossible to protect.

Oral disclosures

There have been cases involving oral disclosures of information where the person making the disclosure has been successful in obtaining a finding that there has been a breach of confidence.

One case, known as the 'Rock Follies' case after the mid 1970s television series to which it related (*Fraser* v *Thames Television Ltd* [1984] QB 44) concerned an idea for a television series which was disclosed orally to the defendant. The defendant made use of the idea in producing and broadcasting a series based on it without the plaintiff's permission and in breach of confidence. There were many conflicts of evidence between the plaintiff's and defendant's witnesses. There was also a question over what exactly it was that had been disclosed and the defendant tried to cast doubt, among other matters, over the extent to which the idea had been formulated. It would certainly have made matters easier if there could have been no argument about what had been disclosed.

This exemplifies the need to ensure there is a clear and accurate record of what is disclosed in order to avoid this sort of uncertainty.

Practical advice

● in disclosing information, put it in writing or some other permanent form of record

● keep a copy of what is disclosed, and a record of when and to whom

● if an oral disclosure is made in confidence, confirm in writing what was disclosed and that it was given in confidence

Additionally,

● the recipient of oral confidential disclosures should make a careful written record of what was disclosed

This is protection against a later suggestion that further or other information was disclosed. Always bear in mind that in the event of court proceedings being taken, both parties' written records may, if relevant, have to be disclosed to the other — see chapter 12. If the person making the disclosure later confirms in writing his or her version of what was disclosed orally, check this carefully. If it is incorrect, it may be prudent to write a letter and say so. If there is going to be a dispute, it is better to have your version of the facts on record at an early stage.

In summary,

- information must be sufficiently identifiable by some means or another
- the mere fact that information has been disclosed orally does not affect whether it can be afforded protection under the law of confidentiality
- there are risks both for the disclosing party and for the recipient in not making a sufficient record of information disclosed orally

INFORMATION WHICH IS NOT PUBLICLY KNOWN

In the leading case of *Saltman Engineering Co. Ltd* v *Campbell Engineering Co. Ltd* (1948) 65 RPC 203 it was said by Lord Greene MR that:

> information, to be confidential, must . . . have the necessary quality of confidence about it, namely, it must not be something which is public property and public knowledge.

Other judges have used the expression 'public domain' in relation to information being 'in the public domain' and hence not confidential. As information is not recognised as a form of property it is not clear what is meant by 'public property'. It is also not clear what is meant by the phrase 'public domain'. Perhaps what is meant is that the information is freely available to the public. Unfortunately, this is circular. If the information is freely available to the public it cannot be confidential and if the information is confidential it cannot be freely available to the public. Clearly, none of these expressions give a clear test for what characterises the 'quality of confidence'.

There are two obvious tests

Where information is not freely available to the public and is held by one or more people and all of them treat it as confidential then it is confidential.

It is also quite plain that published information in books, magazines and the like is freely available to the public and hence not confidential. At least this is so for as long as the publications containing the information exist and can be obtained, say through a library, or sufficient numbers of people are still alive who have the information.

Information can be of a mixed nature, that is, some of the information may be derived from publicly available sources of information and the rest produced perhaps by deduction from public information or perhaps as a result of research and development effort or even individual creative thought. Where information is of a mixed nature this does not necessarily allow someone the right to make use of the publicly available part after receiving disclosure of all the information.

A report on the results of searches carried out on publicly available information and a list of references can be confidential. In essence what is protected is the non-publicly available information resulting from the effort involved in compiling the information. However, it may not be wise to consider the report and list of references in isolation from the publicly available information itself. Despite some information being from publicly available sources, there may be aspects which are not publicly available. A set or collection of compiled public documents might, because of their collection together, be of greater value as a result of the effort and judgment in selecting and compiling them. The individual pieces of public information may together enable conclusions to be drawn and decisions made which could not otherwise have happened.

In other cases it may be difficult to lay down hard and fast rules for demarking what is confidential information from what is not. Whether in any particular case a court will give protection to information alleged to be confidential is in the court's discretion. Thus, in borderline cases the decision is often based on the particular facts of the case.

This does not mean to say that protecting confidential information is a lottery. Bear in mind that for the purposes of adjudicating a dispute a decision must be made and in law that falls to be decided by the judge. Regardless of how hard a decision may be to make, the judge's job is to make it and to make it on a reasoned basis. Thus,

● taking measures in advance to protect information, such as by taking precautions to keep it confidential can, in a difficult case, have a considerable impact by influencing the court to take the route of protecting the information

Practical advice

From a knowledge of the legal principles concerned (or lack of them) it ought to be possible to devise some ground rules for establishing basic practical actions to take on a day-to-day basis.

First, consider the position of the holder of information. If the holder of information can demonstrate where the information originated from, that it did not come from some public source and that it has been kept confidential, then, subject to someone producing evidence to the contrary, the information must be considered at least prima facie confidential. Similarly, where someone is accused of misusing confidential information that person will want to be able to show that the information was at the time freely available to the public, or it was common knowledge or obtained independently from other sources or as a result of creative effort. This suggests that, whether you are the discloser or recipient of information alleged to be confidential, you should

● try in some way to record how it is that you have come to be in possession of particular information

In many cases it may be obvious how the information was derived by referring to contemporaneous documents. It may still be necessary to call witnesses to give oral evidence. If contemporaneous documentation is available, this often helps people to recall events played out years previously. In any event,

- adopt a procedure concerning the retention of documents and destruction of documents

In showing that information has been treated as and kept confidential, it is helpful to be able to demonstrate what measures have been adopted to protect confidentiality. It could be a standard procedure to keep certain types of information under lock and key and to limit disclosure to people who agree to keep the information confidential. Employees should be made aware of the whole question of confidentiality. Particular types or categories of information which are considered secret could be pointed out as examples of what is considered confidential information. The employees should then understand what is to be kept confidential by them.
Ensure

- confidential documents are marked as confidential

If the documents are not so marked this may not necessarily have any adverse effect under the law but it draws the attention of the recipient to the fact that the document is considered confidential. However,

- there can be disadvantages in marking too many documents as confidential

If documents are commonly marked confidential which are not really confidential or are only marginally confidential recipients may be less likely to take confidentiality seriously. Marking documents as confidential and disclosing them widely without taking any other measures could destroy the confidentiality of the information contained in the documents.

CIRCUMSTANCES IMPOSING AN OBLIGATION OF CONFIDENTIALITY

In summary, the ways that someone can become subject to an obligation of confidentiality are:

- expressly by a contractual obligation
- impliedly by a contractual obligation
- from the nature of the relationship between the discloser and recipient

Express contracts

The way a contractual obligation can arise has been discussed in chapter 3. As has been seen, a contract can be oral or the terms of the contract can be recorded entirely (or even partly) in writing. There is no great magic legal formula required to create a binding contract. A contractually binding obligation can arise where one person agrees to disclose information and the other agrees in return that it is to be treated as confidential. The contract could be concluded orally without anything being recorded in writing.

Using a written contract can make the process of proving what has been agreed much more certain. There are inherent difficulties in relying solely upon the evidence of witnesses based upon their recollections of what they thought was agreed. A written document (depending upon how well drafted and comprehensive it is) can also reduce the risks of misunderstandings.

Implied terms in contracts

It is possible for a term to be implied in a contract that the recipient of information is obliged to keep the information confidential. As has been mentioned in chapter 3, terms can be implied in contracts in several ways. The courts have long recognised that parties to a contract do not always expressly state in detail all of the terms of the agreement. The courts may imply terms into agreements in order to give them 'business efficacy'. However,

- a term will be implied *if and only if* the court finds that the parties to the contract *must have intended* the term to form part of the contract.

Often information of a confidential nature is disclosed without there being any express agreement about confidentiality. Technical information and prototype equipment may be disclosed to potential customers and manufacturers for the purposes of evaluating the information and prototypes with a view to purchase or manufacture.

When you are about to engage in sensitive business negotiations or any similar situation, clearly it is far better for all concerned to avoid uncertainty and potentially litigious situations by dealing expressly with the question of confidentiality

- make sure whatever contract there is covers the confidentiality question

- if there is no specific contract make one. Use a confidential disclosure agreement or create some other form of written record of the agreement, even if this is achieved simply by letter

Equitable obligations of confidentiality

Of all the principles of law under which an obligation to keep information confidential can arise, equity is probably the most significant and where the greatest risks can arise in the commercial world. The reason for this is that

- in equity the obligation to keep information confidential can arise simply by the fact that confidential information has been supplied

- there is no need for any contractual relationship

It is beyond the scope of this book to describe the nature and development of equity. In very general and simplistic terms, think of it as a concept of fair play recognised by the courts which can modify the effect of legal rights and obligations in certain circumstances. Lord Denning MR said in *Seager* v *Copydex* [1967] RPC 349 that:

. . . he who has received information in confidence shall not take unfair advantage of it. He must not make use of it to the prejudice of him who gave it without obtaining his consent.

How an obligation may arise in equity

In order to obtain some feel for how complex the consequences of the automatic imposition of an equitable obligation of confidentiality could be, consider the ways in which information might be supplied or obtained. There could be differing consequences, depending upon

- how the supplier of the information came by it,
- what the relationship of the parties to the disclosure is, and
- the manner in which disclosure is made

Supplier of the information

Starting with the source of the information there could be several kinds of source. Consider the following:

- the information is the supplier's confidential information, i.e., the supplier is the original holder of it
- the information could be someone else's confidential information
- the supplier could have obtained the information without any obligation of confidentiality being owed, either

(a)   because the information is not confidential;
(b)   because the information was confidential but was not disclosed in circumstances imposing an obligation of confidentiality at the time of the disclosure.

The information is the supplier's confidential information
There is no problem where the source of the information is an original holder of it. The recipient must either agree to keep the information confidential or ensure that the supplier of the information knows it is not going to be kept confidential or acknowledges that the information is not confidential.

The information is someone else's confidential information
A problem arises with the second situation if information is confidential but the supplier does not disclose this. The real difficulty is that if the recipient later discovers that the information is someone else's confidential information then from that moment on the recipient may become subject to the confidentiality obligation and could as a result become unable to use or disclose the information.

The consequences could cause difficulty where, say, the information is essential for use in a manufacturing process, and the recipient has invested heavily in establishing a manufacturing facility which relies upon the process, say, in an activity like steel making.

The supplier is not the original holder but is free to use the information
There is no problem with the third situation provided the recipient can be confident that the information is not or is no longer confidential information.

Practical advice

From the recipient's point of view, if it is practicable in the circumstances,

- obtain express confirmation from the supplier that the information is not confidential and, where reasonably possible, before accepting disclosure

It could be helpful to do this face to face, perhaps during negotiations in order to judge the supplier's reaction. This tactic will also help where the supplier turns out to be an original holder of the information. If an original holder of information confirms that the information is not confidential then no confidentiality obligation should arise.

From either party's point of view, for good measure,

- make a contemporaneous note of what is said so that there is a record for the future and, if appropriate, confirm the point by letter

Acting in good faith and paying for the information in some way or another might help. Unfortunately, the law of confidentiality is not well developed

- someone who purchases information in good faith and later finds it was disclosed in breach of confidence may still be in the same position as someone who has received a disclosure gratuitously

From the supplier's point of view,

- avoid giving any confirmation that information supplied is free from any prior confidentiality obligation

But, if this is unavoidable,

- check the position carefully first, and
- ensure any necessary protective qualifications are stated

Relationship between the supplier and the recipient of the information

Examining the nature of any relationship is not very helpful. It is possibly a poor basis for deciding whether an obligation should or should not exist. We all have relationships with everyone with whom we have any form of social or business connection, even if it is merely one of supplier and customer, such as might exist between a hairdresser and his or her customers (a relationship which the less discreet amongst us might hope gives rise to an obligation of confidentiality) or between a sales representative and prospective customer or between passing acquaintances in the street. At what point is the line drawn?

Consider the following extremes

- a perfect stranger supplies the information
- the information is supplied by someone who is already known to the recipient

If information is supplied by a perfect stranger then there is nothing about the relationship which ought to give rise to an obligation of confidentiality. But do not overlook the other circumstances in which an obligation of confidentiality might arise (considered later in this chapter). Where the suppier is known to the recipient there are problems. These can be split between two different situations

- where there is a special relationship between the supplier and recipient

- where there is no special relationship

Certainly, there are some relationships where it is established that an obligation of confidentiality arises, such as between doctor and patient, banker and customer, priest and parishioner. In these cases it is thought that people need to be secure in the knowledge that their private affairs disclosed to professional advisers and other similar kinds of confidant will be kept confidential. Do not assume, however, that there is a rigid demarcation which allows people to distinguish immediately between confidential and non-confidential relationships. In practice,

- if there is any doubt from the recipient's point of view, assume the relationship is a confidential one

Where there is no special relationship between the parties then no obligation to keep information confidential should arise from the nature of the relationship. However, again, do not overlook the other ways an obligation to keep information confidential could arise dealt with below.

Manner in which the disclosure is made

Quite often the way information is supplied can be a clue to whether the information is confidential. There may be no special relationship between the supplier and recipient of the information. Nothing may be said about confidentiality. There may be no express limitation placed on the recipient concerning the use or disclosure of the information.

There are two distinct situations to consider

- where confidentiality is expressly mentioned

- where nothing is said about confidentiality

Disclosure where confidentiality is mentioned
Consider the following situations and assume the recipient has no independent means either at all or for the immediate future of discovering whether the information is really confidential or not.

Where the recipient is told before disclosure that the information is confidential and accepts it on that basis, even if there is no contractual obligation of confidentiality, the recipient is bound to keep the information confidential unless or until it is shown not to be confidential information at all.

If the recipient is told about the confidentiality but makes clear before disclosure that the information will not be accepted on that basis then the recipient will not be bound by the obligation of confidentiality if the source is an original holder of the information. There is a problem where the source is not an original holder especially if the disclosure is in breach of confidence. The recipient will be bound by the obligation of confidentiality from the moment this is made known to the recipient.

If the recipient is told prior to disclosure about the confidentiality, accepts disclosure but does not say anything about whether the confidentiality is accepted the recipient is highly likely to be bound to keep the information confidential.

The recipient may be told after the disclosure that the information is confidential, perhaps quite some time after. The confidentiality obligation will depend upon who made the disclosure. If the disclosure was made by the original holder then whether the recipient will be bound to keep the information confidential may depend upon whether or not it is clear from the circumstances that the information was disclosed in confidence or clear from the nature of the information that it was confidential. If the supplier was already under an obligation to keep the information confidential, then the recipient will also be from the moment this is made known.

Nothing is said about confidentiality
Where nothing is said about confidentiality what can there be about the circumstances of a disclosure or the nature of the information disclosed that indicates it is to be kept confidential by the recipient? There is no easy answer to this question. There is some guidance in existing court judgments to help in arriving at an answer but the law is not well developed in this area.

One test of whether an obligation of confidentiality arises may be whether information is provided for a limited purpose. In effect, when information is disclosed to be used for a limited purpose the discloser is implicitly saying, 'This information is or I believe it to be confidential' or, 'Irrespective of any doubt about its confidentiality, you have to keep it confidential'. 'I am only allowing you to use it for a limited purpose and the law will, or I believe it will, protect my rights in the matter.' Although there may be no way of telling whether information itself is really confidential, the bottom line is that an obligation to keep it confidential arises in such circumstances unless it can be shown the information is not confidential.

Where information is not supplied for a limited purpose   Consider the following:

- the supplier freely discloses the information without necessarily being asked for it
- the information is supplied in response to a request
- the information is not freely given nor has it been obtained with the supplier's knowledge or consent

In the last example, information can be obtained without the knowledge or consent of the supplier in various ways. Perhaps the information has been obtained surreptitiously, by tapping a telephone, or by listening to a conversation where the conversants thought they were alone, or by questioning someone's young children or by reading over someone's shoulder in a train or bus.

In all of the above situations, how is the recipient supposed to know that the information is or is not confidential? Even in the case of telephone tapping, this can be important in deciding whether or not there is to be any obligation of confidentiality. Telephone tapping can after all be not illegal. It can be lawfully sanctioned for official purposes such as investigating crime and national security even though the subject of the tapping may not be involved in criminal activities.

Circumstances of disclosure and nature of information

The circumstances of the disclosure might indicate that the information is confidential. In *Fraser* v *Thames Television Ltd* [1984] QB 44, it was apparently accepted by each witness in the television and theatre business that it would be wrong to make use of another's idea without consent and the judge considered this moral obligation was a factor to be taken into account when deciding whether there was a legal obligation also.

If all else fails, whether information is to be treated as confidential may depend upon the nature of the information itself. The following situations are examples of where an obligation may arise by virtue of the circumstances of the disclosure

- the information might be, by its nature, commonly considered confidential, such as

  — details of a another person's medical condition, or

  — engineering drawings, which are commonly considered to be confidential by those engaged in engineering.

- the information is of a kind that will probably be considered confidential by someone but the way it is disclosed leads the recipient to believe it is not confidential

  — e.g., someone discusses a business or legal matter at a social function in the course of conversation.

All of the above situations are potential danger areas for both the supplier and recipient because of the inherent uncertainty in having to rely after the event on what a court might decide. The precautions and practical measures described in the earlier parts of this chapter may help to avoid or minimise the risks in relation to the first two situations.

THE OBLIGATION IS NOT TO DISCLOSE OR USE

The fact that the obligation not to disclose or use information is enforceable at law makes confidential information a commercial commodity. For example, an organisation may wish to buy in technology by obtaining a patent licence from ·the owner of the patent. The organisation may have sufficient knowledge and expertise to exploit the patented invention. However, if it has not and there is some particular confidential know-how that would save it time or money to get started, it is possible for the holder of the information to extract a fee for supplying it initially and further fees for allowing the organisation to use the information thereafter.

HOW LONG DOES THE OBLIGATION LAST?

Unless there is agreement to the contrary, an obligation to keep information confidential lasts as long as the information remains confidential. The recipient cannot simply avoid the consequences of the law by disclosing information to the world at large. The consequences are twofold

- wrongful disclosure by the recipient can still result in the recipient being prevented by law from using the information

- the recipient can be liable in damages resulting from the wrongful disclosure

Putting a time-limit on the obligation

Serious problems can arise if an agreement imposing an obligation of confidentiality on the recipient does not also deal with the question of how long the obligation lasts. A common problem arises where there is an agreement to keep information confidential, such as in the case of production or other manufacturing information. If, when the agreement comes to an end, the question of whether the information is to be kept confidential thereafter is not dealt with, then the recipient may find that the supplier of the information requires the recipient to stop using the information in the production or manufacturing process. This could obviously have disastrous effects for the recipient where the entire business depends upon continued use of the information which has been supplied.

It can be a risky practice to enter into limited-period confidential know-how licences where there will be continuing reliance on a supply of further information or where there is unlikely to be any other source of suitable information when the licence is drawing to a close.

Although UK or EEC competition law may provide a way out of such problems it will not do so in all cases. Thus, from the recipient's point of view

- put a time-limit on how long information should be kept confidential

- or at least get express agreement that the information can be freely used after expiry of the agreement

From the supplier's point of view, and subject to EEC and UK competition law restraints

- do not put any time-limits on the duration of an obligation to keep information confidential, or, if this is not commercially feasible, keep the recipient on the hook as long as you can — it may be worth it

EMPLOYEES

The problem for employees and confidential information can be summarised in two points

- employees who become ex-employees can know too much
- ex-employees still need to be able to earn a living

Employees learn much about the organisation and management of a business. They need information about the business in order to do their jobs. Some information can be mundane, some information is sensitive like pricing and some can be highly confidential like future product plans or unique manufacturing processes or product specifications. An employer may want to be able to exercise some sort of control over this sort of information after an employee has left.

Additionally, because employees handle all sorts of information daily, the distinctions between what is confidential and what is not confidential can become blurred.

Furthermore when employees become ex-employees they are usually still only qualified to do the same sort of work but somewhere else. If the 'somewhere else' is with a competitor of the former employer then problems can arise. On the one hand the ex-employee needs to be able to use general skills and knowledge acquired during former employments and on the other the former employer will want to stop any information being given to the competitor which may increase competition or damage business.

Thus, there are two main questions to address

- when does the ex-employee's obligation to keep information begin and when does it end?
- what information of a former employer can an ex-employee make use of when engaged with a competitor?

Imposing obligations on employees

An employee can be obliged to keep information confidential

- impliedly by law during the period of employment
- expressly by contract for the duration of employment
- expressly by contract for the period following termination of employment

Implied obligation of the employee

Even though nothing may be expressly agreed, orally or in writing, every employee owes the employer an obligation to act in good faith during the period of employment. This includes keeping confidential information confidential.

The case of *Normalec Ltd* v *Britton* discussed in chapter 1 shows that the consequences of breach of an employee's duty of good faith can be dire. In that case the employee used the employer's customer information to build up his own business, and built the business up *whilst still an employee*. The end result was that the court decided the employee should lose the whole business to the employer.

Note that the employee only owes the duty of fidelity whilst employed. The duty comes to an end on termination of employment. Additionally, the courts recognise a right of any person to use and to exploit for the purpose of earning a living all the skill, experience and knowledge at the employee's disposal, including that acquired in the course of previous employments. This does not mean the employee can make use of any information for personal benefit. It will be seen that trade secrets will still be protected but other information may not. However, the problem can be in deciding what is confidential and what is not.

Express obligation in a contract of employment
Instead of relying on an implied obligation it is better to have an express written agreement, such as in the employment contract. If the express agreement does not deal with the question of confidentiality after employment has ceased then the employee will be free to make use of all general skill, experience and knowledge acquired whilst in the employer's employ (other than trade secrets).   Thus,

- in any contract with an employee the employer should ensure the question of whether any obligation of confidentiality is to continue after cessation of employment is dealt with

However, this in itself is not enough

- firstly it does not prevent the employee working for a competitor
- secondly it does not deal with what information is to be treated as confidential

Restrictions on future employment

It is possible to include in an employee's contract a non-competition clause to be operative following cessation of employment. This requires

- the employer must have a legitimate interest to protect in imposing the obligation
- the restriction must not be unreasonable either in duration or geographical extent

The first of these requirements is normally easily fulfilled. If the employee cannot work anywhere else because of the restraint but there is no real justification for the protection for the employer then it can be unenforceable. Similarly, if the restriction is broader than is required to protect the employer's interests, either geographically or in relation to what kinds of work the employee can engage in then it may be unenforceable. Whether a clause is too broad in any particular case depends on the facts. Thus, for employers

- take care with drafting restraint clauses in employee contracts

and for employees

- read your employment contract carefully before you sign it

What information is to be treated as confidential

Where there is no express obligation
If there is no express contractual agreement, the employee is free to make use of any information unless it was clear it was a trade secret. It *Faccenda Chicken Ltd* v *Fowler* [1987] Ch 117, the Court of Appeal said that the following points should be taken into account in deciding whether or not any particular item of information was covered by the implied obligation

- if the employee regularly handled confidential information then he or she can be expected to recognise confidential information more readily than other employees
- the nature of the information — can it properly be classified as a trade secret?
- was it clear from the steps the employer took to protect confidential information that the information concerned was confidential?
- how easy is it to distinguish the information from other information supplied to the employee?

Where there is an express obligation
Where there is an express contractual obligation, there is still the problem of defining what information is to be kept confidential. A clause which is too broad or vague may be of little help. At the same time it may be difficult to define in a contract clause every kind of information that is to be kept confidential. Thus, contract terms are only part of a scheme of protection which must include day-to-day measures like those outlined earlier in this chapter.

Employees, confidentiality and ownership of intellectual property

The law of confidentiality may override the legal rules governing who is the owner of intellectual property rights.

In *British Syphon Co. Ltd* v *Homewood* [1956] RPC 225, Roxburgh J said:

> Now . . . would it be consistent with good faith, as between master and servant, that, he should in that position be entitled to make some invention in relation to a matter concerning a part of the plaintiffs' business and keep it from his employer, if and when asked about the problem, or even sell it to a rival and say: 'Well, yes, I know the answer to your problem, but I have already sold it to your rival'. In my judgment, that cannot be consistent with a relationship of good faith between a master and a technical adviser. It seems to me that he has a duty not to put himself in a position in which he may have personal reasons for not giving his employer the best advice which it is his duty to give if and when asked to give it.

Note that the above quotation does not apply to employees like the tea-boy or the toilet cleaner. It applies to 'technical advisers'. However, do not take the term 'technical adviser' too literally. The same principle could apply to a wide variety of employees whose ordinary duties necessarily involve the creation of various intellectual property rights.

5 Protection of Ideas and Information – Patents for Inventions

INTRODUCTION

Patents are about protecting inventions. It is difficult to define what amounts to an invention. For the moment think of inventions as new ideas with a useful practical application in a product or in a manufacturing process.

Some people have an image of inventors as stereotypical eccentric boffins and believe that inventions arise from brilliant scientific discoveries beyond the abilities of ordinary people. It is true to say that the paper-clip, the safety-pin and the zip-fastener are quite clever but these inventions are well within the bounds of comprehension of the average person. Some inventions for which patents are obtained are so seemingly obvious that it can be surprising that a patent has been obtained. Indeed, some so-called inventions turn out not to be patentable inventions and the patent can thus be invalid. However, by that time the patent may have done a good job for its owner and kept a host of competitors off the market.

Scope of patent protection

The protection afforded by a patent is extensive. Just keeping an infringing example of a patented product amounts to infringement. It may be no help disposing of it as disposal is also an infringement.

A patent is a monopoly given by the State to the proprietor, who is also called the patentee. The proprietor has the exclusive right to exploit the patented invention. This means that if others make a product which incorporates the invention, even if they are completely unaware of the existence of the patent they infringe the proprietor's rights.

Another important aspect of patent protection is that inventive concepts can often be implemented in a wide variety of ways. If someone produces a product which embodies the essential elements of a patented invention, again, even though the product is quite independently designed and may look quite different from the example of the invention described in the patent, infringement may still have occurred.

Patent protection versus the law of confidentiality

In the development of any new product, assuming the development is a reasonably organised affair, the product ideas and concepts are probably the first things to be created. In any event new ideas and ways of doing things may be devised during development.

The law of confidentiality is adequate as far as it goes for protecting things that can be kept secret but it has its shortcomings. Obviously, it is one thing to be able to maintain information about a new product as secret and protectable by law before the product goes on sale. Once the product goes on the market and is freely available to the public many of the things that were once secret are out in the public gaze. The law of confidentiality may then be of little, if any, help.

Additionally, it may be difficult keeping developments totally secret and away from competitors. Employees come and go. They sometimes go to work for competitors or set up in competition on their own. Although the law of confidentiality can help, as can suitable restrictions in employees' contracts, commercial reality and the art of the possible may dictate that the law is an impractical route to follow in keeping trade secrets secret for long.

There is also always the risk that competitors will come up with the same developments through their own efforts. Confidentiality is of no help in that situation.

When might patent protection be of the most importance?

If the concepts underlying the function or operation of the product are not protected by patents but are the things of greatest importance rather than the particular design, then the absence of patent protection can leave a manufacturer vulnerable to competition from differently designed products which operate on the same basic principles. Competitors may be able to produce their own versions of the product, independently designed but embodying the essential concepts of the product, soon after it goes on sale without copying the design of the product at all. Thus, the rights available for protecting design may be of little benefit in such circumstances in the absence of patent protection.

At what stage should patent protection be considered?

The research and development ('R & D') stage of product development is probably the very latest time when patents should be first considered. There are three particular reasons for this.

One reason for considering patents is that

- it can sometimes be pointless working on an idea or developing an invention if someone else already has valid patent rights covering it

As patents are registered rights it is possible to carry out extensive searches of the registers of patents, not just for UK patents but also for foreign patents, to find out if something has been patented before.

Where pre-existing patent rights are discovered it may be necessary to examine their validity to see if the patents can be attacked or whether it is possible to find another way of achieving the same result ('designing around' the patent). Examining validity and investigating ways of designing around require some understanding of how patents work if serious mistakes are to be avoided, such as misconstruing the description in the patent of the essential elements of an invention.

Another reason for considering patents at an early stage is that, as patents are published documents setting out how inventions work

- it is possible to find out what has been done by others in the past and to learn from what they have done

In other words, there is little point reinventing the wheel and at the same time it may be that what others have done may suggest other and better ways of achieving the same result without encroaching on pre-existing patent rights.

The third reason to start considering patents no later than the R & D stage is that

- if a totally new idea or invention is devised there is no prize for coming second in the patent race

The first person to apply for a patent for a patentable invention gets it. If someone else has applied for a patent just before the R & D department makes its application then the first person to apply takes priority over anyone else. The earlier patent application could well mark the end of an aspect of development work. It could be the end of plans for an entirely new product range; that is, unless the validity of the patent can be attacked or the patent can be designed around or rights can be aquired from the owner of the patent, at a price.

The patent owner normally has no obligation to give permission to anyone else to do anything that infringes the patent rights. There are some circumstances in which the proprietor of the patent rights can be forced to give permission (a licence) but these do not apply in all circumstances.

The current state of patent law

Before examining existing patent law a brief explanation of the current state of the law will put a few things in context.

Patents go back a long way, to the Statute of Monopolies 1624 and earlier. The term 'patent' means an open letter. The Crown could, by the exercise of its royal prerogative, confer rights on individuals. The patent or open letter was a means of doing so. The UK patent system thus has a long history and is well developed. Patents are now, however, conferred as a result of Parliamentary legislation rather than royal prerogative.

The main legislation currently governing patents is the Patents Act 1977 (the '77 Act'). This Act for the most part came into effect on 1 June 1978. Patents applied for on and after 1 June 1978 must satisfy the 77 Act requirements about what kinds of things are patentable inventions.

The predecessor to the 77 Act was the Patents Act 1949 (the '49 Act'). Patents granted under the 49 Act will still be around until 1 June 1998 as patents last, in general, for 20 years.

Although in broad concept what constitutes a patentable invention under the 77 and 49 Acts is much the same, the 49 Act has different rules about what inventions are patentable. These rules may still be significant if the validity of a 49 Act patent is attacked. An attack on the validity of a patent can be the strongest attack anyone accused of patent infringement can make.

For both 49 Act and 77 Act patents, what constitutes patent infringement is for all practical purposes exactly the same and is governed by the 77 Act rules.

International aspects of patents

There is a basic feature of patent protection which should be noted from the outset. Patents are national monopolies. A UK patent only affords protection in the UK. However, the law of many other countries is very similar in many respects and the basic concepts of UK patent protection are reflected in the patent systems of other countries. This has much to do with various international conventions and treaties (agreements between countries) which seek to harmonise laws and ensure nationals of signatory States are given the same treatment under the laws of other States as the nationals of those other States are themselves given.

One feature of the system of obtaining international protection is that if a patent application is made in one convention country the applicant has a year or sometimes more, depending upon the convention relied on, to make patent applications in other countries. These 'convention' applications retain priority over any later patent applications made by others.

There are three main international conventions which concern UK patent law — the European Patent Convention ('EPC'), the Patent Cooperation Treaty ('PCT') and the Community Patent Convention ('CPC').

The European Patent Convention

Of the three international agreements, the EPC has currently the most significance. There are several reasons for this.

The EPC is intended to establish a single procedure for the grant of patents. Thus, instead of applying for a patent in the UK Patent Office and additionally making separate applications in other countries, one application under the EPC can be made to the European Patent Office in Munich. The application can result in the grant of several patents, each covering a different country. Each patent granted is valid in that country only. Thus, it is possible to make one application to the European Patent Office for patents for all countries covered by the EPC. It is also possible to make patent applications in just a selection of the countries covered by the EPC.

For example, a patent application could be made for a patent to be granted in each of Germany, France and the UK, rather than all EPC signatory States.

The application, if successful, would result, for the UK, in the grant of a European Patent (UK), and likewise, for Germany and France, the grant of a patent valid in each of those countries.

Once the patent is granted, questions of validity and infringement of the patent are decided by the local national courts. In the case of the UK, the courts are the High Court and Patent County Courts. The only exception is that the grant of a European Patent can be opposed in the European Patent Office provided proceedings are commenced within nine months of official publication of the fact that the patent has been granted (EPC Article 99).

Another aspect of the EPC is that it is intended to establish standard rules governing patents in each of the EPC signatory countries. Germany, for example, has adopted as its national patent law legislation which is almost exactly the same as the EPC. The UK's 77 Act was drafted to accord with the provisions of the EPC. Although the 77 Act is not exactly the same as the EPC, in many respects, particularly the rules governing what kinds of inventions are patentable, it operates in a very similar way.

The Patent Cooperation Treaty

The PCT is not as extensive in its effect as the EPC. It is not possible to obtain a patent by applying to a PCT Patent Office.

The way the PCT works is that a patent application can be made to a PCT Patent Office. The PCT Patent Office checks that the application conforms to the rules and forwards a copy to the International Searching Authority and to the International Bureau.

The International Searching Authority carries out international searches to see how the invention compares with what has been done before. The International Bureau forwards a copy of the patent application to the relevant Patent Office of each of the countries in which the applicant has applied for a patent and the application is processed by the local patent office of the relevant country. Unlike the EPC, whether or not a patent is granted following a PCT patent application depends upon the local law of each country in which a patent is sought.

The Community Patent Convention

At the moment the CPC has very little significance. This is because it is not in effect yet. However, when it does eventually come into effect, it will be of greater significance than the EPC.

The CPC is intended to effect one common patent system for the whole of the EEC. This will mean that only one patent application is made and only one patent will be granted. The patent will cover the whole of the EEC, unlike the EPC, under which separate patents are granted for separate EEC States.

It is also intended that a uniform system of rules governing validity and infringement will be effected under the CPC for all EEC countries. The rules on what kinds of inventions are patentable will be the same as those under the EPC.

RECOGNISING AN INVENTION WHEN YOU SEE ONE

It is obviously important to have a conceptual grasp of what an invention is in order to be able to recognise whether patent protection may be available. However, most books on patent law do not start out by trying to explain what an invention is. It is difficult to do so. A basic lay person's 'common-sense' test could be that an invention is a clever idea that no one has ever thought of before. However, in the context of patent law relying on such a simple test alone can be misleading and it is necessary to take things further.

What for example is meant by a 'clever idea'? How clever does the idea have to be to be patentable? What appears clever to one person might not to another. The response to these questions might be that the idea has to have an inventive spark, some inspiration, a conceptual leap. However, in itself this is not useful for distinguishing what is clever from what is not.

Even if the tests to be applied to assess whether an idea is clever can be arrived at, what tests can be used to decide that no one else has ever thought of the idea?

Under the old law there were two fundamental tests to assess whether an invention (or in the legal jargon of the time 'any manner of new manufacture') was patentable. In simple terms these were

- whether the 'new manufacture' was new and if so
- whether it was obvious

Thus, rather than defining what an invention is, the approach adopted by the courts was to apply the tests of patentability to what the inventor alleged was an invention. The 77 Act does the same by defining an invention as being what the applicant or inventor claims is the invention (77 Act, s. 125(1)) and it then applies the tests of patentability to the claimed invention. Under the EPC the position is identical.

There are three vitally important aspects of the law's approach to what an invention is that need to be noted

- it is the inventor's responsibility to ensure the invention is specified adequately
- if what the inventor specifies as an invention does not pass the legal tests of patentability, this can be fatal for obtaining any protection for an invention
- it may be possible to amend the patent to cure a defective specification of an invention but it is not always possible to do so

The legal tests of patentability

Examine the 77 Act's basic criteria for what a patentable invention is. Under s. 1 of the 77 Act a patentable invention must:

- be new
- involve an inventive step

- be capable of industrial application
- not be excluded from protection under the 77 Act

These criteria are almost identical to the corresponding provisions in the EPC.

It is the first two of these criteria that need consideration in the light of the 'common-sense' test. The most conceptually important and difficult being that the invention must involve an 'inventive step' or, in the terms of the non-legalistic 'common-sense' test, that the invention must be a clever idea.

The 49 Act tests of patentability are similar in broad terms and will be compared in the following discussion.

Is it really such a clever idea? The basic test of inventiveness

The basic test of inventiveness in patent law is whether the invention is obvious. If it is obvious then it can hardly be said to be inventive. An obvious invention cannot be said in everyday terms to have any inventive spark, be inspired, or amount to a conceptual leap. In other words, applying the lay person's common-sense test, if the idea is obvious it is not really that clever after all. The next problem is how to decide what is obvious. The exact words of the 77 Act (with added emphasis) are that

- an invention shall be taken to involve an inventive step if it is not obvious *to a person skilled in the art, having regard to any matter which forms part of the state of the art*

So obviousness is judged (at least notionally) through the eyes of someone skilled in the relevant field having regard to what such a skilled person is taken to know about that field. (The position under the EPC is much the same.)

Has anyone ever thought of it before? Inventions must be new to be patentable

Under the second part of the 'common-sense' test of inventiveness the clever idea had to be one that no one had ever thought of before. The test the law applies is broadly similar. Under the 77 Act an invention has to be new in the sense that

- it has never been disclosed to the public in any way *anywhere in the world*

There is a difference between the common-sense test and the patent law test. Under the patent law test an invention can still be new even if someone else has thought of the invention before. What counts is whether, having thought of or devised the same invention previously, disclosure of the invention is made to the public. If the invention has not been previously disclosed then it can still be new in the patent law sense until it is disclosed.

The 49 Act patent law test for novelty was similar to the 77 Act test. However,

- disclosure to the public was only significant under the 49 Act *if it took place in the UK*

IT IS NEW AND NOT OBVIOUS BUT IS IT PATENTABLE?

Even if an idea satisfies the objective tests of inventiveness under patent law, there is still the question of whether it is capable of being the subject of a patent protection. This is where things start to get a little tricky.

Some ideas may be new and not obvious but because of their nature it could seem strange to prohibit the public at large from making use of them by granting one person monopoly patent protection.

Assume someone has invented a new colour scheme for decorating a house that happens to be particularly attractive but has no other notable qualities. If this were to be given monopoly patent protection as an invention one might wonder why and ask 'But what does it do? What practical use or benefit is there? Why should anyone else who later devises the same colour scheme be prevented from using it?' Alternatively others may think it appropriate that the colour scheme should be capable of obtaining monopoly patent protection perhaps because it improves people's environment or that inventive 'colour engineering' should be encouraged. What if the colour scheme had a useful application in that it had an effect of calming potentially violent people or it encouraged people to work more quickly?

The problem with the imaginary colour scheme is that it satisfies the common-sense test of being a clever idea that no one has ever thought of before. Should it be patentable? This raises the broader question, what is there that can be used as a test to distinguish inventions that should be patentable from those that should not?

The position under the 49 Act will be examined first followed by the position under the 77 Act. The position under the EPC will be referred to at the same time as the relevant provisions of the 77 Act are considered.

There are some differences between what is patentable under the 49 Act and the 77 Act, such as what is excluded from being a patentable invention. There is a practical reason for pointing out that these differences exist. It may be that, as part of a product development project, a patent investigation may reveal existing 49 Act and 77 Act patents and 77 Act patent applications

- it is as well to be aware that there are differences in the legal requirements of patent validity in order not to make a mistake about the grounds upon which the validity of the patents can be attacked

What was patentable under the 49 Act?

Under the 49 Act, to be patentable an invention had to be a 'manner of manufacture'. It may be helpful to summarise some of the tests the courts have applied in distinguishing inherently patentable inventions ('manufactures') from inherently unpatentable inventions under the 49 Act and earlier law.

- ideas are not patentable in themselves

- the idea has to be capable of application in or be embodied in a product or it must be capable of application in a method or process

● the invention must have some useful practical application or advantage

● the invention must result in some way in some physical state of affairs that is changed rather than, say, in an intellectual sense

● the invention must be of value economically in a broad commercial or industrial sense

● inventions of an intrinsically aesthetic or artistic nature or which are of value solely in an aesthetic or artistic sense are unpatentable

What is patentable under the 77 Act and European Patent Convention?

Under the 77 Act an invention cannot be patented unless it is capable of industrial application. The corresponding provision under the EPC is that the invention must be 'susceptible of industrial application' (Article 52).

The industrial application criterion is broadly similar to the requirement that an invention must be a 'manner of manufacture' under the 49 Act and earlier law.

The 77 Act test of what is capable of industrial application
Under the 77 Act an invention is to be taken to be capable of industrial application if it can be made or used in any kind of industry, including agriculture (77 Act, s. 4). This test is very broad. It is similar to the requirement under the old law that an inventive product, method or process must have some useful application or advantage in a practical sense and result in a changed physical state of affairs (rather than a change in a purely intellectual sense).

Agricultural inventions
Under the 49 Act and older law there was some uncertainty about whether methods used in agriculture, such as methods of improving the quality of land to obtain a better crop yield or of cultivating plants or of animal husbandry were inherently patentable. The 77 Act removes the uncertainty by making it clear that inventive agricultural methods are patentable.

Is it capable of industrial application if it does not work?
If something that is claimed to be an invention just does not or cannot work then it fails the test of being capable of industrial application under the 77 Act. The same might also apply if the invention has no use in a broadly commercial or industrial sense even if it does 'work'.

Remember

● it is up to the patentee to describe the invention

● if the description is broad enough to cover matter which cannot work as well as matter which can then the patent may be held to be invalid as not being useful

This was the position under the 49 Act and it may well prove to be the same under the 77 Act on the ground that the invention lacks industrial application.

What is not patentable

Although the courts have mostly avoided laying down exclusive fixed criteria
for judging what kinds of inventions are and are not patentable, certain kinds
of matter were, under the 49 Act and older law, inherently unpatentable.

The cases are of considerable assistance in understanding the principles of
what is patentable. In one way or another the special cases are examples of the
application of general principles of patentability.

The inherently unpatentable matter under the 49 Act and earlier law
included

- discoveries
- principles
- methods of agricultural cultivation (now patentable under the 77 Act)
- methods of medical treatment
- the presentation of information
- mere schemes or plans
- methods of testing (now patentable under the 77 Act)

There are two categories of things that are not patentable under the 77 Act

- things that are not patentable 'to the extent that' the invention relates to
  the thing 'as such'
- things that are not patentable at all

What is not patentable 'as such'?
The following list is taken from s. 1(2) of the 77 Act which sets out what is not
patentable 'as such':

- a discovery
- scientific theory or
- mathematical method
- a literary, dramatic, musical or artistic work or any other aesthetic
  creation whatsoever
- a scheme, rule or method for
    - performing a mental act,
    - playing a game or
    - doing business,
- a program for a computer
- the presentation of information

This list is identical to the list of inventions excluded from patentability under the EPC Article 52 and is similar in some but not all respects to the 49 Act list.

What might still save an excluded invention

The 77 Act includes the following important proviso in s. 1(2)

- but the foregoing provision [i.e., the above list of excluded inventions] shall prevent anything from being treated as an invention for the purposes of this Act *only to the extent that* a patent or application for a patent relates to that thing *as such*

It is this proviso which saves inventions, which might seem as if they fall within the excluded categories, from being unpatentable. (The EPC contains a very similar saving provision in Article 52(3).)

Discoveries

The exclusion of discoveries from patentability is quite logical

- a discovery is of no use until an application has been found for it

Assume the principle is discovered that a coiled metal spring stretches or contracts in direct proportion to the force exerted on it. This discovery is a pure principle, an idea. In itself it has no practical or technical advantage. However, if the discovery is applied in a practical way then it is a different matter. The spring balance is an application of a pure principle (discovery) and if it were new and not an obvious application it would be patentable.

Scientific theories

As with discoveries, a scientific theory itself is not patentable, but a practical application of the theory can be.

Mathematical methods

A mathematical method such as a method of performing calculations is not patentable as such. However, if a machine can be constructed so that it performs calculations in accordance with the method then the application of the mathematical method in the form of the machine so constructed could be patentable.

Aesthetic creations

Novels, paintings, songs and suchlike cannot be patented. As their principal value as creations lies in their aesthetic appeal, to admit them to the patent system would contravene basic principles of what a 'manner of manufacture' is. Applying the 'rule of thumb' tests, their value is not principally economic in a commercial and industrial context (even though some works of art command high prices but for reasons other than their utility) nor are they useful in a practical sense.

The protection afforded by the law to these kinds of creations lies under copyright and similar law.

Scheme, rule or method for performing a mental act, playing a game or doing business
This area of special cases probably can be considered as particular examples of the general rule that ideas, intellectual conceptions and the like are not patentable in themselves. There must be an application.

Inventing the rules for a new game does not make the rules of the game patentable. The process of playing the game does not have a practical result of value in the commercial or industrial sense. If the game requires some novel physical items in order to play it then the items may be patentable as items to be used in playing the game according to the rules.

Similarly, a particular method of organising a business or carrying on accounting activities is effectively an intellectual activity. There may be a practical result of value in a commercial sense but there is no result in the sense of some physical state of affairs that is changed. The notional state of a business reflected in its accounts might be changed but that is purely a conceptual state of affairs.

Computer programs
If a computer program is thought of as a sequence of instructions which are either written down on paper or stored in a coded form on a magnetic disk or tape then it is difficult to see how it could be patentable 'as such'. In itself it has no advantage or benefit. It only has an application when it is loaded into a computer and the computer is operated in accordance with the program.

What is not patentable is the computer program itself but the overall invention can be. The patentability of computer programs is an area in which the law is developing quickly and care needs to be taken.

Presentation of information
This category of excluded subject-matter is confusing. Does the word 'presentation' refer to the act of presenting information or to what the information looks like in a static sense like words on a page or a painting?

In one case, *Pitman's Application* [1969] RPC 646, a method of printing text so that words were represented in different type sizes and positions on a printed page was patentable. The essence of the invention lay in being able to convey to the reader of the text the correct stressing and inflexions of words and phrases according to the way they were printed. For example, stress was indicated by printing words in capital letters. Unstressed words and syllables were printed in lower-case type. Inflexion was indicated by printing the words in superscript or subscript text.

All that can be suggested in relation to this excluded class of inventions is that the rules of thumb be applied. If there is no new practical useful result or any changed physical state of affairs (e.g., a book created in a special way) and the invention lies in something akin to merely presenting intellectual information then it is likely to be unpatentable.

Surgery, therapy and diagnosis
In addition to the categories of matters excluded from patent protection 'as such', there is a further specific exclusion. An invention of a method of

treatment of the human or animal body by surgery or therapy or of diagnosis practised on the human or animal body shall not be taken to be capable of industrial application under the 77 Act (s. 4(2)).

There is a similar provision in the EPC.

It is important here to note that the exclusion is directed to methods of 'treatment' which are by 'surgery', 'therapy' or 'diagnosis'. Thus, anything that is not a method of treatment or which does not encompass surgery, therapy or diagnosis may not be excluded under these provisions from being capable or susceptible of industrial application. Cases under the 49 Act and old law may be helpful in understanding what is meant.

Under the old law the courts adopted the practice of refusing patents for inventions consisting of methods or processes for the medical treatment of human beings to cure or prevent disease. The rationale for doing so is somewhat obscure.

In an unreported English case under the old law, *Chamberlain's Application,* a process for permanently waving hair was allowed as patentable. This was not a method or process of preventing or curing disease. Thus,

- by analogy, under the 77 Act, although something may be a method of treatment of the human or animal body, provided it does not amount to a method of treatment by surgery, therapy or diagnosis in itself then it may be patentable

Drugs and pharmaceutical preparations

New drugs which can be used in methods of medical treatment are patentable. Essentially this is on the basis that the invention is the drug rather than a method or process for medical treatment

- the 77 Act expressly provides that the exclusion of methods of treatment by surgery, therapy or diagnosis does not prevent a product consisting of a substance or composition (e.g., a drug or medicine) being treated as capable of industrial application because it is invented for use in any such method (77 Act, s. 4(3)).

The unpatentable

Both under the old and the new law certain things are simply not patentable at all, whether or not they are inventive.

Under the new law s. 1(3) of the 77 Act provides:

A patent shall not be granted:

   (a)   for an invention the publication or exploitation of which would be generally expected to encourage offensive, immoral or antisocial behaviour;
   (b)   for any variety of animal or plant or any essentially biological process for the production of animals or plants not being a microbiological process or the product of such a process.

The EPC contains very similar provisions.

Inventions which are expected to encourage offensive, immoral or antisocial behaviour are not patentable. This is one area of patent law where the most interesting cases might be expected to be decided. However, either the Patent Office has a very broadminded approach to granting patents or those who might be expected to be inventive in the area of offensive, immoral or antisocial activity are not in the habit of applying for patents.

There are some very old cases concerning patent applications for gaming machines. The machines might have been suitable for use in unlawful gambling. However, the machines did not necessarily have to be used for gambling. The patent applications were allowed (*Pessers* v *Haydon & Co.* (1908) 26 RPC 58; *Walton* v *Ahrens* (1939) 56 RPC 195).

Things which might be considered at one time to encourage offensive, immoral or antisocial behaviour may not at another depending upon the generally accepted standards of behaviour prevailing. Thus, it is not wise to assume that something which might fall into this category of unpatentable inventions is in fact unpatentable.

Any variety of animal or plant
It is not possible at the moment to obtain patent protection for any new animal or plant. It is also not possible to obtain protection for any 'essentially biological' process for the production of animals or plants.

Plant varieties are protected under the Plant Varieties and Seeds Act 1964. This is not the same kind of protection as patent protection. This book will not be covering plant and seed variety protection.

Thus, if a previously unknown animal is discovered which has a useful application in the patent sense no patent can be obtained for the animal or any essentially biological process for the production of the animal. With modern techniques of genetic engineering it is possible to create a new kind of animal by altering the genes of existing creatures. These kinds of creatures cannot be patented at the moment.

In the United States it is possible to obtain patent protection for new varieties of animals. A patent has been granted in the US, for example, for a genetically engineered strain of mouse. There are also moves being made by the European Commission to change and harmonise law in Europe to permit patents to be granted for inventions consisting of or relating to plant, animal and living matter.

Biotechnology, microbiology and genetic engineering
The current exclusion of plant and animal varieties from patent protection does not mean biological processes and micro-organisms are not patentable. It also does not mean that genetically engineered matter and genetic engineering methods and processes are not patentable.

A biological process for producing butanol and acetone by fermenting grain was patentable (*Commercial Solvents Corporation* v *Synthetic Products Co. Ltd* (1926) 43 RPC 185).

Methods of producing antibiotics using micro-organisms are patentable (*American Cyanamid Co. (Dann's) Patent* [1971] RPC 425). Even strains of micro-organisms can be patented as was permitted in one case where the claim was to a micro-organism which was a pure culture of a natural (i.e., not man-made) micro-organism.

THE RIGHT TO APPLY FOR A PATENT

This section is concerned with who has the right to apply for a patent and will deal with the position of

- inventors
- employee inventors
- employers
- consultants or commissioned non-employee inventors

Only the 77 Act rules and those applicable under the EPC will be examined here as it is unlikely that ownership of patent rights in an existing 49 Act patent will be an issue for many people. However, just in case it ever is, be aware of the fact that the 49 Act rules of ownership are not the same.

The basic rule

Anyone can apply for a patent for an invention. The applicant does not have to be the inventor.

However, in the event of conflict, the basic rule for patent applications made under the 77 Act is that the person entitled to apply for a patent is

- the person who is entitled by law (e.g., under a contract) to the entire rights in the invention (whether by virtue of UK law, or, in the case of a foreign invention, foreign law)

Under the 77 Act this person could be

- the inventor (if the right to apply does not already belong to someone else, e.g., it was sold by the inventor)
- a person who has purchased the right to apply for a patent for the invention (whether the purchase was directly or indirectly from the inventor or from anyone else who is entitled by law to the right to apply)
- a person who has acquired the right to apply for a patent from any one of the above categories of people who was entitled to apply

The position is basically much the same under Articles 58 to 60 of the EPC. The inventor is primarily entitled to apply for a patent unless the right has been sold to someone else. Where the right to apply has been sold then the person who has acquired the right is entitled to apply. In the event of dispute the applicable law for determining who has become entitled is the local law of the country concerned.

Who is the inventor?

In order to track the entitlement to apply when it may have been bought and sold, it is necessary to be able to identify the inventor. The inventor is the person who actually devises the invention. If the invention is devised jointly, the inventor is not one person but all of the people who devised the invention.

However, where large teams of people are involved in developing or creating things where patentable inventions may result, it is not always easy to identify who, from the whole team, is to be considered the inventor or whether all of those engaged in the work are to be

- the position in such circumstances is best covered by express agreement as to who is to be entitled to apply for any patents

This is what normally happens in practice. Large teams of research and development personnel are usually engaged under employment contracts which address the question of patent rights or which are covered by the rules relating to employees set out later in this section. However, sometimes, some of the personnel are independent consultants. In either case, from the point of view of whoever is intended to be entitled to the rights, it is important to ensure that the question of ownership of the right to apply for patents is covered one way or another and that the contractual provision is enforceable.

Simultaneous invention
If several people, independently of each other, invent the same thing around the same time, they are each inventors and are each entitled to apply for a patent. However, they will not all get a patent. Only one patent will be granted.

Before you start to think that it is the first person to make the invention that gets the patent, stop, because you will be wrong. It is the first person to apply who gets the patent.

- if you delay applying for a patent you run the risk of someone else getting an application for the same invention filed first

Employees and employers

The rules relating to employee inventions are straightforward to understand but not necessarily so easy to apply in practice from the point of view of some categories of employee.

For the purposes of the EPC, the rules to be applied for determining whether it is the employee or employer who is entitled to apply for European patents are those in effect under the law of the country in which the employee is mainly employed. If the country cannot be ascertained then the rules to be applied are those in effect in the country in which the employer has the place of business to which the employee is attached.

For the UK, the local-law rules for determining whether the employer or employee is entitled to apply for a patent for an invention are primarily set out in section 39 of the 77 Act. Under these rules some but not all inventions belong to the employer. The first rule is that, regardless of what the employee's contract says, the employer will own the right to apply for the patent where the invention was made in the course of

- the employee's normal duties, or

● duties specifically assigned to the employee

However, in either case the circumstances must be such that an invention might reasonably be expected to result from the performance of the duties. Thus, where the tea-boy invents something during the course of his employment the employer will not necessarily own the invention.

The second rule is that the employer will own the invention where it was made

● during the course of the employee's normal duties and at the time, because of the nature of and the particular responsibilities arising under those duties, the employee has a special obligation to further the interests of the employer

The second rule is applicable to employees who may not necessarily be employed to invent, but because of their position they have a special obligation to their employer. There is no hard-and-fast rule demarking what kind of employee falls within the scope of the second rule. It is likely to apply to employees like managing directors and senior non-technical employees like senior sales managers, marketing managers and the like.

The third rule is that all other inventions belong to the employee. This rule will be considered below in relation to attempts by an employer to use the employee's employment contract to lay claim to the employee's rights to an invention.

Inventions made in an employee's own time
Note that none of the above rules refer to when an invention is made. Where an employer is likely to own the rights under the above rules, the employee cannot escape the consequences by trying to allege that the invention was made at home over the weekend or after 5.30 p.m.

Contracting out
Section 42 of the 77 Act is intended to prevent employers from trying to use employment contracts to get employees to sign away their rights in or to patents. The effect of s. 42 is to make certain terms in certain contracts unenforceable against the employee.

The kinds of terms to which the section applies are those which would otherwise diminish the rights an employee has, by virtue of the 77 Act rules, to apply for patents for inventions. The effect of s. 42 is that any provision the employer puts in the contract to diminish the employee's rights will be ineffective. The employee's rights will be unaffected.

The kinds of contracts to which the section applies are contracts dealing with any kind of rights the employee may have in or to patents and which are either

● employment contracts

● a contract entered into with someone other than the employer,
    — but at the employer's request (e.g., in the case of an employee consultant, working for outside clients of, say, a scientific or technical consultancy)

— or as part of an obligation to do so under the employee's contract of employment

Consultants

Consultants will be treated as inventors in their own right. The consultant will have the right to apply for any patents for inventions made during the course of consultancy activities. This is subject to three aspects

- express contractual agreement
- implied contractual agreement
- any equitable rights the client may have

With regard to the first of these aspects, the consultant can expressly agree who should own what rights. This is the preferred route to follow and should be done in a written contract rather than orally.

If the question of ownership of rights is not dealt with then the position is uncertain. The ownership of rights to apply for any patents would have to be implied by reference to whatever was implicitly agreed between the consultant and the client from all the circumstances.

The last situation may result in the client having a right to any patents as a result, say, of the operation of the law of confidentiality or some other equitable obligation.

Compensation for employee inventions

Employees are entitled to compensation from their employers arising from the exploitation of patent rights in two circumstances

- where the employee is the inventor but the patent rights belong to the employer
- where the patent rights belonged to the employee but have been transferred to the employer and the benefit the employee has received is inadequate

In either case the employee will be entitled to compensation if the requirements of s. 40 of the 77 Act are satisfied.

The first requirement is that the patent must have been of outstanding benefit to the employer. Unfortunately, it is not clear what this means and even if it were clear, how can something as vague as 'outstanding benefit' be measured?

The next problem for the employee is that the amount of compensation must be a 'fair share' of the benefit the employer has received from the patent. As a principle this is fine, but how is any court or anyone else to be expected to assess what or how much a 'fair share' is?

These questions have no definite answers and the position in any particular case is likely to depend on all the circumstances. In essence, only employees who have invented something outstanding are likely to benefit.

Employees employed by the Crown (e.g., government departments) or by a research council are covered by an additional provision. Where patent rights (including rights to apply for patents) are transferred to another body without charge or for a nominal charge, then the Crown or the research council is treated as if it received any benefit that other body derives for the purposes of applying the employee compensation rules. For these purposes a research council is a body which is a research council for the purposes of the Science and Technology Act 1965.

Where a collective agreement is negotiated by a trade union the compensation rules may not apply. The provisions applicable to collective agreements will be found in s. 40 of the 77 Act.

APPLYING FOR A PATENT

Introduction

This section is not going to deal in detail with how patent applications are made. However, there are some aspects of how patent applications are made and processed that it is helpful to know. Should you wish to learn more about applying for a patent, the UK Patent Office supplies at no charge some useful pamphlets. More information can be obtained from: Head of Marketing and Publicity, The Patent Office, State House, High Holborn, London WC1R 4TP.

In addition, a publication entitled *How to Get a European Patent* can be purchased from: The European Patent Office, Erhardtstrasse 27, D-8000 München 2, Federal Republic of Germany.

Another publication, *PCT Applicant's Guide,* can be purchased from: The World Intellectual Property Organisation, 34 chemin des Colombettes, CH-1211 Geneva 20, Switzerland.

The above publications may also be available for inspection in some reference libraries.

One of the most important things you should be aware of about patent applications is that

● the date of the first patent application is important in relation to obtaining patent protection internationally

The priority date

With a few special exceptions, the first person to apply for a patent for an invention will own the patent. The position is the same in most countries throughout the world. If only this rule governed the priority of applications then life could be inconvenient. Clearly, trying to ensure patent applications are lodged world-wide at the same time would be grossly inconvenient for anyone seeking to obtain international patent protection. Hence, there is the concept of the 'priority date' for a patent.

The priority date of a patent is, in simple terms, the date on which the first patent application is made regardless of the country in which the application is made. Where one or other of the international conventions applies the applicant for a patent can make subsequent patent applications in other countries and be treated as having made those subsequent applications on the priority date.

Note, however, that the priority does not last forever. The international applications must be made within a particular period after the priority date. This is usually 12 months but can be longer, depending upon which international convention applies to the application.

Where to apply

There are several different routes to take in applying for a patent. The different routes result from the various international agreements concerning patent protection. Although these are not the only methods, the three basic ways of applying for a patent are by

- an application made to the UK Patent Office for a UK patent

- an application made to the UK Patent Office or the European Patent Office for patents to be granted in all or a selection of the EPC countries

- an application made to the UK Patent Office or to one of the other PCT receiving offices for patents to be granted in the various PCT countries

Do not be over-concerned about which route to choose in applying for a patent. Which is the more advantageous can depend on the circumstances and can be discussed with your patent agent. (Although you do not necessarily have to use a patent agent it is advisable to do so, especially when it comes to drafting the patent specification.)

UK residents must apply in the UK first

It is important to note that

- it is a criminal offence under s. 23 of the 77 Act for any person resident in the UK to make, or cause to be made, an application for a patent outside the UK without having made an application for a patent in the UK Patent Office at least six weeks previously

The purpose of this provision is to maintain control over inventions the publication of which would be prejudicial to the defence of the realm. Note that the provision applies to 'residents': it is not restricted to British nationals or citizens.

UK procedure

The procedure under the 77 Act starts with the filing of the application. The application must meet certain formal requirements and the application is subject to an initial examination to ensure it meets the requirements. The application must contain at least an initial description of the invention. Where the invention relies on a micro-organism in order to work there are rules concerning how the micro-organism must be described in the description and for the deposit of a culture of the micro-organism so as to ensure it will be available to the public.

If the claims to the patent were not filed at the time of making the application, they must be filed within 12 months of the priority date or one month from the date of application whichever is later (see page 64 for an explanation of what the claims are).

The patent specification is published within 18 months of the priority date (see page 63 for what the patent specification concerns). This will mean that anyone else can carry out patent searches and, if they wish, can see the published application and obtain a copy of it from the relevant patent office.

The next step is for the substantive examination to be carried out to check that the invention complies with the requirements inventions must satisfy in order to be patentable. The request for this to be carried out must be made within six months of the publication of the patent specification.

If the invention meets the requirements for patentability a patent will be granted. Thus, with luck the whole process can be completed in around two years, but it normally takes very much longer, perhaps four years.

If the invention does not meet the requirements for patentability then a patent will be refused, but it is possible for an appeal to be made against the refusal of a patent application.

Third-party opposition
It is not possible for third parties to apply to the UK Patent Office to oppose the grant of a patent under the 77 Act. However, it is possible for third parties to make observations to the relevant patent office about the patentability of an invention.

The ability to make observations can be of considerable importance if there has been an application for a patent which, if granted, might affect the activities of some person. Naturally, there is no point making observations if there is nothing wrong with the application. However, sometimes the patent protection sought is broader than the invention justifies. Observations on patentability may result in the scope of the patent being more limited and this in turn may mean that the patent no longer poses any threat to the third party's activities.

Remember also that, although the patent office examiners have considerable expertise, it may be more apparent to a third party that an invention is obvious or a third party may have knowledge of some prior use or publication of the alleged invention or some other information that shows the invention is not new. Do not assume that the Patent Office will necessarily reject seemingly obvious or old inventions.

Observations on the validity of a patent can only be made before a patent is granted. There is no express provision permitting observations or oppositions to the grant on any other grounds (77 Act, s. 21).

EPC procedure

In broad terms, the procedure for patent applications under the EPC is similar to the procedure under the 77 Act. The application is checked for compliance with the formal requirements for patent applications. A European search is carried out and sent to the applicant. The European search is concerned with checking the invention is not obvious and that it is new. The patent specification is to be published within 18 months of the priority date and the European search report is meant to be published at the same time. Within six months following publication a request can be made for the invention to be examined for compliance with the criteria to be met by patentable inventions. If the criteria are met a patent will be granted. Thus, like the 77 Act, with luck, the process can take around two years but again it will take longer in practice.

If a patent is refused it is possible to appeal against the refusal.

Third-party opposition

Under the EPC it is possible to make observations to the European Patent Office concerning the patentability of a patent application, invention or patent.

Unlike the 77 Act, under the EPC it is possible to apply to oppose the grant of a patent for an invention. Opposition proceedings must be brought within nine months following official publication of the fact that the patent concerned has been granted. Hence they are of limited general applicability. However, they are an important route to choose in deciding to attack the grant of a patent because the only way each European patent can be attacked afterwards is by separate proceedings brought in each country for which a patent is granted.

Procedure under the PCT

In broad terms, the procedure for applying for a patent under the PCT is similar to the procedure under the EPC and 77 Act. There are some differences which can affect time-limits. However, the main difference is that, although international searches are carried out, the results of the searches are sent to the patent offices of the countries in which patents are sought. The decision on whether a patent is granted is made by the individual patent authorities in each country in which a patent is sought.

No observations or oppositions can be made against a PCT patent application. Whether or not observations or oppositions can subsequently be lodged in the local patent offices of each of the countries in which a patent is sought is a matter for the local patent law of those countries.

Points to note

Just because a patent is granted does not mean that it is valid. The examination carried out by the examiner of the relevant patent office is quite thorough. However, the examination cannot be expected to cover every possible point. Additionally, the examiner is not trying to stop people obtaining patents but just to ensure that the invention as described in the patent seems to meet the criteria for patentability and that the clearly unpatentable does not slip through.

If a patent is granted for the UK under the 77 Act or under the EPC, this does not mean that the patent is unchallengeable. It is possible to apply for revocation of a patent on various grounds.

Additionally, the EPC is only concerned with the law and the procedure to be followed leading to the grant of European patents, whether for the UK or for other EPC countries. Once a European patent (UK) has been granted, when it comes to challenging the patent, the grounds of attack to be applied are those set out in the 77 Act. The only exception is that opposition proceedings can be commenced in the European Patent Office, as noted above.

The position is the same for all other EPC countries. Once a European patent has been granted, the law to be applied to it is that in effect in the country concerned.

DESCRIBING INVENTIONS

Eureka, I've done it! But what is it?

Pretty well everything in patent law concerns the invention as specified in the patent. Thus, it is vitally important to understand how the invention is specified and how to interpret the specification. This applies whether you want to ensure you obtain the maximum protection for an invention or whether you want to assess whether someone else's patent prohibits you doing what you want to do. Additionally, if the invention is incorrectly specified this can be fatal to the validity of the patent and hence for protection for the invention.

The inventor does not have to say what is inventive

The inventor's obligation is to state what the essential features of the invention are and how to implement it. The inventor does not have to say what it is about the invention that is inventive. The inventor merely has to describe it. This is because it can often be extremely difficult to separate out the old from the new or to say which aspects of the essential features make the invention inventive. If it was a requirement that the inventor had to state what made an invention inventive the inventor would be running the risk of getting it wrong.

The patent specification

An example of a patent is set out in appendix 1. The patent is not too complicated to read. It illustrates how an invention is described in a patent. The patent concerns a way of creating a sufficiently sturdy structure in the ground to support posts like fence posts, signposts, goal-posts and suchlike.

The first striking thing about the invention described in the patent is that it is not about 'high technology'. It should also be noted that the invention is not limited in its application to things like goal-posts.

The three elements of a patent – the 'specification'
Take a look at the patent and you will see that it comprises three parts:

- the drawings
- a verbal description of the invention, and,
- the claims to the essential inventive elements comprising the invention. (The claims are at the end of the verbal description.)

The verbal description, together with the drawings and claims, is referred to as the 'specification'.

There are several ways things can go wrong with the specification and it might help to remember a fundamental point that people often overlook. When people talk about an invention in the context of a patent they do not always take care to distinguish which 'invention' they are talking about. There can in fact be three different 'inventions' for any patent

● there is the invention the inventor makes – the 'real' invention

● there is the 'invention' described in the description and any drawings

● there is the 'invention' which has the essential features set out in the claims

The purpose of the claims

In the simplest possible terms, the claims define the extent of the invention covered by the patent. The claims are the key to the extent of the patent monopoly. In other words,

● the claims need to specify the essential features of the invention and no more nor less

If the claims are too narrow then others may still be able to find ways of implementing the 'real' invention without doing or creating anything which could fall within the scope of the claims. Conversely, if the claims are too broad they may cover more than the 'invention' described in the verbal description and any drawings justifies.

The normal practice is to express the essential features in the broadest possible terms in order to obtain the widest possible protection. If, for example, the verbal description of an invention refers to part of a device being constructed using a nut and bolt to hold two parts together, in the claims this might be described as 'means for affixing' one part to the other. 'Means for affixing' would then cover gluing, welding, joining, riveting, using self-tapping screws and any other means.

In such a case it would be wise to ensure the description of the invention made it clear that the parts could be fixed together with a nut and bolt as just one way, among others, of attaching them. If there is any uncertainty over what 'means for affixing' covers, the description of the invention taken together with any drawings are available to put the broad wording of the claim into context.

There only needs to be one claim in a patent. However, it is extremely rare to see a patent with only one claim. Usually the first claim is the broadest in scope and the claims following the first narrow its scope by specifying additional features as being essential to the invention. The reason for having tiers of claims is to try to ensure the broadest protection is available but at the same time, in case the first or subsequent claims are invalid for some reason, the narrowing of the scope of what is claimed is intended to ensure that the narrower later claims may still prove to be valid.

Thus,

- each claim should be treated as setting out in its own right the essential features of a separate invention

Unless something has each essential feature of an invention set out in at least one claim to a patent, it cannot be covered by the patent. If a patent claim has four essential features and some device only exhibits three of them then the device is not covered by the patent. Thus, if the claims include things as essential features which are not really essential to the working of the invention then others may be able to get round the patent by leaving them out. However, just because a claim in a patent refers to a particular feature, it is not safe to assume, as will be seen later, that it is always to be considered an essential feature.

The purpose of the description
As the example of a patent in appendix 1 shows, patent claims in themselves are not easy to interpret without the aid of the verbal description and drawings. The purpose of the description and any drawings is to explain how the invention can be made, if it is a product, or how it is to be performed if it is a process.

The description and drawings may illustrate features which are not essential elements of the invention but which might incidentally be included in an example of the invention. These do not have to be set out in the claims.

The description of an invention in a patent cannot sensibly be expected to cover every different use of an invention or every way that an inventive device can be combined with other things. Thus, the invention described in the patent in appendix 1 might be used to support a beach umbrella, or a lamp post. It might have applications in the construction industry for temporarily holding structures in place whilst the foundations of the structures are more permanently fixed such as by concreting them. All of these different applications or combinations ought to be covered by the claims even though not specifically mentioned in the verbal description or drawings.

What can go wrong with the specification
Assuming the inventor has created an invention that is patentable, when it comes to describing the 'real' invention several things can go wrong. The claims could, for example, cover more than the 'real' invention justifies. This could be fatal to validity of the patent. The claims could also cover less which means that the scope of protection would be less than it should be. Additionally, the 'invention' described in the verbal description and drawings might not match the essential features of the 'invention' specified in the claims. This could also be fatal to validity if the scope of the claims is not justified on the basis of the verbal description. Essentially, there are two areas where defects in the specification can arise and the kinds of defects are different in each area. The areas are where

- the inventor has failed to specify properly the essential features of the 'real' invention in the claims

- the inventor has failed to describe properly the 'real' invention in the description and any drawings

Legal requirements for claims

Under the 77 Act, s. 14(5) the claims in the specification of an application for a patent must

- define the matter for which the patent applicant seeks protection
- be clear and concise
- be supported by the description
- relate to one invention or group of inventions which are linked so as to form a single inventive concept

These requirements are almost identical for patent claims of a European Patent. As the law stands at the moment, these requirements must be met by the claims in the specification of the patent application before a 77 Act or EPC patent can be granted. However, even if these requirements are not met when the application is made, but for some reason the patent is still granted, the only way in which it seems the patent can be attacked in the UK Courts for having defective claims is if the patent specification is considered not to

- disclose the invention in a manner which is clear enough and complete enough for the invention to be performed by a person skilled in the art (77 Act, s.72(1)(c))

The position is similar for opposition proceedings in the European Patent Office. Under the 49 Act the requirements that must continue to be met by existing 49 Act patents are

- the scope of the claims has to be sufficiently and clearly defined
- the claims have to be fairly based on what is disclosed in the specification

Are the claims defective

A fundamental defect in patent claims is that the essential features of the 'invention' specified in the claims turn out to cover something that is not a patentable invention. Although what can qualify as a patentable invention has been covered in the section entitled 'Recognising What Can Be Protected' do not assume you know everything just by reading that section. For example, if the claims adequately cover the essential features of an invention that does work, but also are broad enough to cover something that does not work, then the patent could be invalid on the basis that it does not satisfy one of the requirements of a patentable invention, namely that it is not capable of industrial application (unless it can be saved by amendment).

Example
In one case under the 49 Act the invention claimed was a method of manufacturing solid polymer foam of the kind that might be used for carpet underlay. The previous methods enabled foams of several inches thick to be

manufactured for use in products like vehicle seats, mattresses, pillows and foam sections used in upholstery. The description and claims of the invention did not state there was any limitation to the thicknesses of foams that could be produced. However, it was proved by experiments carried out for the purposes of trial that, although it was possible to manufacture thin foams using the process, it seems it was not possible to use the process to manufacture solid foams of even one inch thickness, and in any event it was not possible to manufacture foams of greater than three inches. Thus, the invention claimed by the patentee was not useful for the purpose of manufacturing solid foams generally and was held to be invalid. (*Dow Chemical* v *Spence Bryson* [1984] RPC 359.)

It can be seen from this that there may have been a real invention in a new way of manufacturing foams but of relatively thin section compared to that made by previous methods. The invention described in the patent was, however, for a method for manufacturing foams including those of the thicknesses that could be achieved under the earlier methods. The claimed invention could not possibly do what was claimed for it, even though it did work in some circumstances. In other words, the invention described in the patent may have been very clearly and completely disclosed but it just did not work as described.

Where the 'real' invention is a patentable invention, patent claims can otherwise be defective in three broad ways

- an inessential feature has been included or
- an essential feature is missing or
- that one or more of the essential features set out in the claims are vague

The first kind of defect in claims

Where a claim includes something that is not an essential feature of the 'real invention' the law sometimes makes allowances for the fact that the inventor or the patent agent who drafted the patent has used the wrong words and may have included some feature in the claims which is not really essential to the invention. The significance of having an inessential feature included in a claim is that it may then be easy for others to avoid infringement. Unless a court decides the feature is not really an essential part of the 'invention' specified in the claims all anyone else would have to do would be to make something having all of the features of the invention except for the one that is not really necessary to make the invention work.

In an important case under the old law it was said that:

The function of the claims is to define clearly and with precision the monopoly claimed, so that others may know the exact boundaries of the area within which they will be trespassers. Their primary object is to limit and not extend the monopoly. What is not claimed is disclaimed. The claims must undoubtedly be read as part of the entire document, and not as a separate document; but the forbidden field must be found in the language of the claims and not elsewhere. (*EMI* v *Lissen* (1939) 56 RPC 23.)

The point is that the court has to decide whether or not a feature of a claim is or is not to be considered essential. In interpreting patent claims under the old law and deciding whether of not a feature of a claim is essential the following principles taken from decided cases are a guide

- a patent specification has to be given a purposive construction rather than a purely literal one. The question is whether persons of the relevant practical knowledge and experience would understand that strict compliance with a particular descriptive word or phrase was intended by the patentee to be an essential requirement of the invention, so that any variant would fall outside the monopoly claimed, even though it could have no material effect upon the working of the invention

- where a feature in a claim is found by the court not to be considered essential to the invention and the defendant substitutes an equivalent for the non-essential feature then this still amounts to infringement

- if it seems from the specification that the patentee has chosen specifically to make something an essential feature of the invention then anyone who can make the invention without including the feature does not infringe

Whether a court will be persuaded that a specific feature of a claim is or is not essential is almost a lottery in borderline cases. It is not safe to assume that substituting something which does not fall within the wording of a claim will avoid infringement. Careful consideration needs to be given to a patent if such a course is being contemplated. Thus, the importance of getting the claims right should be obvious. Indeed, getting the verbal description of the invention right can also be extremely important as it can be important in ascertaining what is really essential to the invention.

Under the new law the scope of the invention specified in the claims must be interpreted in the light of invention described in the verbal description and any drawings (77 Act, s. 125(1)). Additionally, as a result of the UK being a signatory to the European Patent Convention ('EPC') there is another aspect to take into account. A provision applicable to the EPC also applies to interpreting UK patents (it is referred to as the Protocol on the Interpretation of Article 69 of the EPC). The essential test under the Protocol is that there must be 'fair protection' for the patentee as against a 'reasonable degree of certainty' as to how far a patent goes for everyone else.

In a recent case, before the Court of Appeal, concerning a 77 Act patent, (*Improver Corporation* v *Remington Consumer Products* [1989] RPC 69 (CA)), the court adopted the old 49 Act law approach (described above). The surprising aspect is that a German Court had come to the opposite conclusion to the UK Court. The German case concerned the same invention, the UK version of which was embodied in a product sold under the name Epilady. The defendant's version was sold in the UK under the name Lady Remington Smooth and Silky.

Both devices were designed to remove body hair. The plaintiff's version used a long coiled spring. The mechanism made the spring move in a curve so that the coils opened up on one side of the curve and closed as they moved off the curved portion. The coils of the spring were used to catch the hair and, as the coils contracted when reaching the other side of the curve, they caught the hair and pulled it out. The defendant's version did not use a coiled spring but instead used a long rubber-like material which was formed into a band or continuous loop and which had notches in it. The manner of operation was the same. The hair caught in the notches and was pulled out.

The key words of the patent claim were that the device was to have an 'helical spring'. The defendant's device did not have an helical spring but worked in much the same fashion. The UK Court considered that the defendant did not infringe because the use of an helical spring was to be considered an essential element of the invention specified in the claims. The German Court stated that solutions which the average person skilled in the art can determine due to his professional knowledge as being equally effective, based on considerations oriented to the invention described in the claims, will generally fall within the scope of the patent.

This approach is quite different to the UK approach. The question of whether the patentee clearly intended the wording of the claims to demark the scope of the invention (in this case only two examples of the invention implemented used a helical spring), is not considered. In the German Court the question seems to be simply whether the allegedly infringing variant on the invention is equally effective and was obvious to the average person skilled in the relevant field. In other words, under the German approach, getting the wrong words in the claim does not limit the scope of the invention to the exact words used. If someone else is able to make use of the same inventive concept in a way not foreseen by the person who drafted the patent claims this can still amount to patent infringement. Which approach, English or German, will eventually be applied throughout Europe's Courts remains to be seen. The clever money is likely to be on the German approach prevailing.

The second defect in claims

● one or more of the essential features set out in the claims are vague

There are two different consequences of a claim being vague. One aspect is that if the claim is too vague then the entire patent (or perhaps just the one claim) is invalid. The other is that if an apparently vague or ambiguous patent claim is found to be valid the court will necessarily have to declare which of two or more possible meanings the claim is to be given. If the claim had potentially more than one meaning the defendant may be successful in arguing that the narrowest meaning is the one that should be applied. This could result in the court finding that what the defendant has done does not fall within the scope of the narrower meaning of the claim.

Existing 49 Act patents must have claims which are sufficiently and clearly defined. In simple terms this is all about whether people can tell what the claims mean. If they cannot then the patent may be invalid. In one case it was said that:

It is the duty of the patentee to state clearly and distinctly . . . the nature and limits of what he claims. If he uses language which, when fairly read, is avoidably obscure or ambiguous, the patent is invalid, whether the defect be due to design, or to carelessness or to want of skill. Where the invention is difficult to explain, due allowance will, of course, be made for any resulting difficulty in the language. But nothing can excuse the use of ambiguous language when simple language can easily be employed, and the only safe way is for the patentee to do his best to be clear and intelligible. (*Natural Colour Kinematograph* v *Bioschemes* (1915) 32 RPC 256.)

The fundamental test for deciding whether the wording of the claims is sufficient and clear in defining the scope of the patent is

● whether the person skilled in the relevant field, on reading the description of the invention would be in doubt as to the scope of the monopoly claimed

If, after considering the claims in that light, their scope is still not clear, then the patent may be invalid.

Whether a patent claim of a 77 Act patent or a European Patent (UK) can be attacked in the UK Courts on the basis that it is too vague depends on whether it can be attacked on the ground that the complete specification does not

● disclose the invention in a manner which is clear enough and complete enough for the invention to be performed by a person skilled in the art

In the light of the 49 Act approach this seems to require an enquiry which might run as follows

● is the allegedly vague feature of the claim actually clear in itself. If it is there is no need to enquire further

● if the feature of the claim, taken on its own seems vague, does the description of the invention make clear what the claim means

● if the feature is still vague after considering the description of the invention then the claim is likely to be held to be invalid

If this chain of reasoning is followed then it seems the 49 Act approach to vague claims could be adopted in relation to 77 Act patent claims (i.e. the claim is not clear enough). The test of whether a claim is vague being judged through the eyes of the person skilled in the relevant field.

Whether this approach will also satisfy the requirement that a balance has to be struck between giving fair protection to the patentee at the same time as ensuring there is reasonable certainty about how far the claims of a patent go remains to be seen. However, it appears, at least in part, to be the approach adopted by the European Patent Office Technical Board of Appeal in opposition proceedings (*Re Naimer's Patent,* Decision T23/86 EPOJ 1987/7 316). The European Patent Office, in opposition proceedings consider the patent as a whole through the eyes of the person skilled in the art. It considers first whether the claim in itself is vague. If the claim is not the European Patent Office need go no further.

The third defect in patent claims

● an essential feature of a claim is missing

If a patent claim is not vague, then the next question to consider is whether the essential features of the 'invention' specified in it fairly reflect the kind of 'invention' disclosed in the description. If the claim is broader than the description justifies, then the patent or at least one or more of the claims could be invalid. The legal language used under the 49 Act for this situation was that the claims were said not to be 'fairly based' on the matter disclosed in description.

Each essential feature in a patent claim limits the scope of the patent. This is simply because the more characteristics something must have to fall within the scope of the patent claims, the narrower the range of things that can potentially come within the ambit of the patent claims.

Take the example of the case concerning the Epilady and Lady Remington Smooth and Silky hair removing devices mentioned above. If the claims of the patent in that case had simply left out any reference to an helical spring or any similar device then the claimed 'invention' could have covered hair removing devices which operated in many other ways. This would simply not have been justified on the basis of the verbal description and drawings of the invention in the patent.

Whether a patent claim of a 77 Act patent or a European Patent (UK) can be attacked in the UK Courts on the basis that it is too broad, again, depends on whether it can be attacked on the ground that the complete specification does not

● disclose the invention in a manner which is clear enough and complete enough for the invention to be performed by a person skilled in the art

In the light of the 49 Act approach this seems to require an enquiry which might run as follows

● look at the 'invention' disclosed in the description in the patent specification

● from that description, what seem to be the essential features of that 'invention'

● compare those essential features with the essential features of the 'invention 'specified in the patent claims

● does the 'invention' disclosed in the description seem to have more essential features than the claims

If not there is no need to go any further. If it has, then the claim, or even all the claims may prove to be invalid because it may not be clear from the description how the invention can be made to work with the fewer essential features specified in the claim. If that is the case then it may be that, under the 77 Act, the patent specification will be treated as not disclosing the invention clearly or completely enough. Thus, the entire patent, or those claims that are too broad, may be invalid.

In the European Patent Office it appears that the Technical Board of Appeal treats claims in patent applications as not being clear if any essential features of the invention, as disclosed in the description, are omitted from the claims (*Re Imperial Chemical Industries plc*, Decision T32/82, EPOJ 1984/8 354).

The description and drawings

Where there is nothing wrong with the patent claims then there is only one area in which the specification of the invention can basically be defective. This is that

- the description, although disclosing something that clearly appears to be a patentable invention simply does not give enough information or does not give it clearly enough so that people can make the invention work

For all 77 Act patents and European patents (UK) it is a requirement that the specification of the patent shall

- disclose the invention in a manner which is clear enough and complete enough for the invention to be performed by a person skilled in the art

Under the 49 Act the specification had to

- sufficiently and fairly describe the invention and the method by which it is to be performed
- to disclose the best method of performing the invention known to the applicant

For both 49 Act and 77 Act patents, failure to meet the requirements after the patent is granted can lead to it being challenged and revoked if the challenge is upheld.

The requirement of a sufficient and fair description comes into play when the essential nature of the invention is understood but there is some information missing from the description which is needed to enable people to make the invention work.

It appears from decided cases that, for 49 Act patents, this means

- the description of an invention in a patent must contain sufficient information so that someone skilled in the relevant field can put the invention into effect
- the description of the invention does not have to give every detail of how to make the invention work which would be obvious to a person skilled in the relevant field
- some aspects of an invention may require some experimentation by way of trial and error in order to find out which variations might be suitable to a particular application. Experimentation of this sort that requires no inventiveness in order to make the invention described in the specification work does not mean the description is not sufficient or fair

The requirement that the specification must disclose the best method of performing the invention known to the applicant must be satisfied at the date the patent application is made. It doe not matter if the applicant for the patent discovers a better way of doing things after the patent is applied for.

Under the 77 Act, unlike the 49 Act, there is no requirement that the description must describe the best method. This can be an advantage as there may be some things that the inventor has done which are best kept secret from the patentee's point of view. Provided the description is clear and complete so that others can make the invention work then the 77 Act's requirements have been met. The patentee can still retain any commercial advantage there may be in the 'know-how' involved in making the invention work to the very best possible effect.

There seems to be little difference if any from the first requirement under the 49 Act. Provided the description contains enough information to enable someone skilled in the relevant field to make the invention work and provided that person does not have to invent in order to do so then the disclosure should be clear enough and complete enough. The approach of the European Patent Office is similar as indicated in its guidelines for examination and as indicated by the Technical Board of Appeal in two cases (*Tokyo Shibaura Denki (Decision T73/82); Sumitomo Chemical Co. Ltd (Decision T14/83)* Official Journal EPO 1984, p. 105).

AMENDING PATENTS

If a patent specification is defective an alleged infringer may be able to attack the validity of the patent. This is quite common because once the patent is revoked or found to be only partially valid the attack on validity may get the alleged infringer 'off the hook'. However, sometimes it is possible to amend a patent thereby saving it from invalidity. Furthermore, if you have been examining someone else's patent and discover the specification is defective, do not assume that the patent is invalid or cannot have the potentially fatal defect removed by amendment. It is therefore important to know when it is likely that a patent can be amended and what sorts of things can be changed.

The scope for amendment of a 49 Act patent was quite narrow. Under s. 31 of the 49 Act the patent specification of a 49 Act patent can only be amended to correcting an obvious mistake, to reduce the scope of the patent by amending the claims or to clarify the existing verbal description of the invention.

The consequences for correcting the sorts of defects described on pages 66 to 73 are that

- it may be impossible to amend to remove inessential features from the claims because this may have the effect of broadening the claim

- it should be permissible to add an essential feature to a claim as this reduces the scope of the claimed invention

- it should also be possible to amend vague claims provided this cuts down their potential scope rather than increasing it

- it may be possible to expand on the explanation of an aspect of the invention already mentioned in the specification. This can only be done to correct obvious errors but not to add explanations of further aspects of the same invention

Amendment by exercise of discretion

Permission for amending a granted 49 Act patent is discretionary. One factor that is of considerable importance is the conduct of the patentee. If the patentee has simply been taking advantage of the legal rules in order to unjustifiably obtain broad protection for as long as possible then amendment is unlikely to be permitted. Factors that are relevant are

● how long the patentee had been aware of the defect in the patent

● had the patentee had previous opportunities to amend which were not taken advantage of (e.g. previous proceedings)

When allowing amendments various conditions can be imposed, such as not bringing proceedings for acts carried out before the amendment was allowed.

Scope for amendment under the 77 Act

Amendment before grant
No amendment is allowed to a patent application if it results in the application disclosing matter which was not contained in the original application when it was filed (77 Act, s. 76).

This basically means that

● when first making a patent application make sure the initial specification covers everything

For example, it may be realised after applying that the description of the invention is too narrow and as a consequence the claims are as well. An amendment to correct such a situation will not be allowed if its effect is to broaden the scope of the originally disclosed invention. (It may be possible to take out a further patent for the broader invention but only it if it comprises a further invention in itself — obviousness in the light of the earlier application will not count against the further application prior to official publication of the specification of the earlier application but it may be treated as not being new in the light of the earlier application.)

Thus, subject to the above proviso, the scope for amendment of a 77 Act patent before it is granted is broad.

For the claims

● it may be possible to amend to remove inessential features from the claims even though this may have the effect of broadening the claim

● it should be permissible to add an essential feature to a claim as this reduces the scope of the claimed invention

● it should also be possible to amend vague claims provided this cuts down their potential scope

For the description

● it may be possible to expand on the explanation of an aspect of the invention already mentioned in the specification but

- it will not be permitted to add explanations of further aspects of the same invention which might result in a broader patent than the initial filed specification would justify

Amendment after grant

No amendment can be made to a 77 Act patent after it is granted which

- results in the specification disclosing additional matter, or
- extends the scope of the protection conferred by the patent

This is similar to the 49 Act.

Amendments to a 77 Act patent application can be made by right. The Patent Office cannot refuse any lawful amendment, provided it is made within the time-limits allowed.

After grant, the patent cannot be amended by right. The main considerations are similar to the position under the 49 Act.

Amendment and European patent applications

Under the EPC the question of amendment is only relevant before the European Patents are granted. After grant, amendment is governed by the local law of the EPC country concerned. Thus, amendment of European patents (UK) is governed by the 77 Act rules set out above. The only exception is that amendment may be effected in the European Patent Office after the patent is granted but this only applies in the course of opposition proceedings. These can only be commenced in the nine months following official publication of the fact that the patent has been granted.

As far as amendment before the grant of the patent is concerned, Article 124 of the EPC provides that the applicant must have at least one opportunity to amend the patent specification. The only qualification on amendment is similar to that under the 77 Act. The patent specification filed with an application for a European patent cannot be amended in such a way that it contains matter which extends beyond the content of the application as filed (EPC Article 124(2)).

NOVELTY AND OBVIOUSNESS

Distinguishing what is 'new' from the 'obvious'

Sometimes inventions are only slightly different from what has been done before but might, because of the slight difference be 'new' in patent law terms. Thus, if the invention is 'new' in this sense, whether it is patentable turns on whether the slight difference is obvious. It is vital to grasp this distinction.

Additionally, sometimes inventions are described as being different from what has been done before whereas the differences specified in the patent specification are immaterial and there is no real difference. Hence, the invention is not really new.

Novelty

Whether an invention is new or not depends on whether or not anyone else knows about it. Thus, there are two basic ways in which an invention can fail to be new; the inventor has failed to keep the invention secret or others have either made the same invention or learnt of it in some way and made the details public.

In either case the invention could have been disclosed

— by word of mouth
— in a document
— by making an example of the invention freely available
— as a result of someone else doing the same thing

As the 49 Act and 77 Act requirements for novelty are different, the 49 Act requirements will be examined first.

What's new and the 49 Act

The most surprising aspect about disclosure under the 49 Act is that it only needed to be made to one person who was not bound to keep the details of the invention secret. Once this had happened the invention was, technically, no longer new.

Under the 49 Act the validity of a patent can be attacked on the basis that the invention was not new at the time the patent application was made. The grounds on which a granted 49 Act patent can be attacked are that

● the invention was already known or used in the UK
● the invention was claimed in an earlier patent
● the invention was secretly used in the United Kingdom before

The invention was already known and used in the UK

The case of *Molins* v *Industrial Machinery Co. Ltd* (1938) 55 RPC 31 concerned the invention of an improved cigarette making machine. It is a striking example of the way the law works.

Early cigarette making machines operated at speeds of about 250 cigarettes per minute. As machines were improved, the speeds increased to around 1,500 cigarettes per minute. However, one particular problem arose at the higher speeds with one particular kind of machine. The type of machine was known as a 'continuous rod type'. This was because the tobacco was formed into a continuous rod of tobacco.

The way the machine worked started with the tobacco being put into a hopper. The hopper had a series of rollers. The rollers were used to loosen up and separate the tobacco strands for the next stage of the process.

The separated tobacco was showered by the last of the rollers into a trough. At the bottom of the trough was a moving band. As the tobacco was showered into the trough it fell on to the moving band. In turn, as the band moved through the machine its edges were rolled over so that it temporarily formed a tube shape with the tobacco rolled up within it. This had the effect of forming the once loose tobacco into a continuous moving rod of tobacco.

The final stages, which are not important to cover in any detail, involved wrapping the continuous moving tube of tobacco in a continuous moving strip ('web') of cigarette paper. The cigarette paper, as it carried the rod of tobacco on it, had glue applied. The combination of the rod of tobacco and glued web of cigarette paper passed through another tube in order to form what can be thought of as a very long moving cigarette. The very long moving cigarette was then chopped up into the appropriate sized individual cigarettes.

Now, the problem with all of this was that for some reason the rod of tobacco was not uniform. In some parts of the rod there was more tobacco than at others. This meant that the quality of the finished cigarettes was not the same, some having more or less tobacco in than others.

The invention lay in the discovery or realisation that the problem lay in the stage where the tobacco fell on to the moving band. The tobacco fell straight down, but the band was moving at high speed. As a result, sometimes the tobacco would slip on the band or bounce when it fell with the result that there would be more tobacco on some parts of the moving band than on others.

The invention solved the problem in a simple, yet effective way. If the tobacco, instead of falling straight down, could be moving in the direction of the band as it fell then this reduced the tendency for it to slip or bounce. This, could be achieved in a number of ways. The route the inventor chose was to set the trough, into which the tobacco was showered, at an angle so that it operated like a chute. As the tobacco fell it would be given a horizontal motion in the direction the band was moving.

This problem did not arise with the older machines because they did not and, in their time, apparently could not, operate at the much higher speeds of the later machines.

Now comes the critical aspect. The essential features of the invention were specified in the claims as

A cigarette making machine of the continuous rod type wherein the tobacco showered into the trough of the machine *is given a movement in the direction of movement of the cigarette rod prior to the same engaging with the band or web* of cigarette paper

Unfortunately, a previous design of cigarette making machine of the older slower type had an inclined trough. No information was available during the case to explain why it had the inclined trough. However, what was plain was that having the inclined trough on the earlier machine meant the machine *had each of the essential features of the 'invention' claimed in the patent claims*.

Now note that

- the 'invention' for these purposes is that specified as having the essential features set out in the claims of the patent and

- if something else had those features before then the invention was not new

The patent was held to be invalid. However, it was clear to the court that the invention had merit. But note that the only way the court was able to ascertain this was from reading the description of the invention and thereby ascertaining that the claims were defective.

It was clear from the description that the invention was valuable for machines that worked at higher speeds than the earlier machines. The court therefore allowed the claims to be amended by the addition of a further essential feature of the invention, namely that it only covered continuous rod type cigarette making machines arranged to move at a high speed (i.e., equivalent to about 900 cigarettes per minute or more).

Note from this example that

- it was irrelevant that the earlier cigarette machines did not have an inclined trough *for the purpose of achieving the improvement described in the patent*
- all that mattered was that earlier machines had all of the features specified in the claims as being essential elements of the invention

There have been other cases concerning patents not being new as a result of matter disclosed in documents made available in libraries. There has been a case under the 49 Act of someone disclosing details of an invention in order to exploit it commercially before a patent has been applied for. Even though the disclosure was in confidence the court was obliged to decide the invention was not new because the law was directed to preventing people obtaining monopoly patent rights after they had already had commercial dealings with the invention (i.e., commercial dealing amounted to making 'use' of the invention). There has been a case concerning making just one or two examples of an invention available to others without restricting them to keeping the invention confidential. Although the particular people who received examples of the invention did not have the technical capability to discover how it worked, under the 49 Act, making an invention available to someone without restricting them to keep it confidential was sufficient disclosure to make the invention no longer new.

The rules on prior disclosures may seem harsh but that is the way the 49 Act works. In return for an absolute patent monopoly on an invention the inventor must make sure the details are kept secret before applying for a patent.

The invention was claimed in an earlier patent
In this instance the claims of the patent are compared only with the claims of a previous patent. It is not a question of whether the invention has been disclosed in some other way before that is in issue. The question is

- whether the essential features of the claims of a previous patent cover the essential features of the later invention specified in the claims of the later patent

There have been conflicting decisions on one aspect. The conflict is over whether it is necessary for the earlier patent claim to be exactly identical. It could, for example, happen that the earlier patent claim was not as broad in scope as the later one but all of the essential features of the earlier claim may be covered by a later patent claim. Indeed, the reverse could occur in that the essential features of the claim of the earlier patent were broader in scope but still covered all the essential features of the invention claimed in the later patent.

The conflict has not yet been finally resolved. However, fortunately, this ground of objection to a patent only applies to a 49 Act patent. It is not a specific objection under the 77 Act or EPC.

The invention was secretly used in the UK before

The third objection under the 49 Act to a patent not being new regards secret prior use of an invention. This objection is again one that is unique to the 49 Act; it does not apply to 77 Act patents.

Any secret use, whether by the inventor or anyone else could invalidate a patent. The only exceptions were use

- for the purpose of reasonable trial or experiment

- by a Government department or person authorised by a Government department in certain circumstances

- unauthorised secret use by someone obliged to the patent applicant to keep the invention secret

What's new and the 77 Act

The 77 Act specifies that an invention shall be taken to be new if it does not form part of the state of the art (77 Act, s. 2(1)).

The 'state of the art' is to be taken to comprise all matter (whether a product, a process, information about either, or anything else) which has at any time before the priority date of the invention been made available to the public (whether in the United Kingdom or elsewhere) by written or oral description, use or in any other way (77 Act, s. 2(1)).

The corresponding provision for patent applications made under the EPC is almost identical.

In essence, this means that it does not matter how or where the same thing has been done or devised before. If it has and details have been disclosed to the public then the invention is not new.

Thus,

- not only is the new law as tough as the old but it is tougher as it covers disclosures made anywhere at all and not just within the UK

Note, however, that there are no equivalent grounds under the 77 Act to those of secret prior use and prior claiming which apply under the 49 Act. Thus, there ought to be no problem under the 77 Act with disclosing the invention in confidence to others prior to filing an application for a patent. However, it is not a wise practice. As will be seen later in this section, there can be a problem if those others do not keep the invention secret.

Exceptions to the strict rules on prior disclosures

There are one or two important exceptions to the 77 Act rules on prior disclosures of inventions (contained in s. 2(4) of the 77 Act). However, the problem with the exceptions is that they only apply if the patent application is made no later than six months after the disclosure occurred. This can be a problem if the research into all aspects of the invention has not been completed.

There are similar exceptions for applications for European patents under the EPC.

The first and probably the most important exception to the 77 Act's strict rules on disclosure is that

- the disclosure was made unlawfully or in breach of confidence

Thus, this exception can help, for example, where employees go off to work for competitors or details of the invention are supplied to others in confidence so that they can evaluate the invention.

The second exception to the 77 Act's strict disclosure rules is rather limited and relates to disclosure of the invention at certain kinds of exhibitions. Special conditions have to be satisfied.

The third exception to the 77 Act's strict rules on disclosure is of great importance in the pharmaceutical industry. If a substance is known but a use is later discovered for it in surgery, therapy or diagnosis for humans or animals, the fact that the substance is known does not prevent the substance being new for the purpose of obtaining a patent for it.

Obviousness

The question of whether or not an invention is obvious is the most difficult to answer in patent law. The fundamental reason for this is that what is obvious to one person is not obvious to another. Thus, first

- it is necessary to decide through whose eyes obviousness is to be judged

It is then necessary to decide

- what knowledge such a person would have

In order to deal with the first question the courts have come up with the hypothetical 'person skilled in the art'. Such a person is assumed not to have any inventive ability at all. The courts have gone on to formulate tests or criteria to assess what such a hypothetical person would know and what skills such a person would have.

The law in this area has become quite sophisticated. Consequently, one of the difficulties with the question of what is inventive or obvious lies not so much in what tests and criteria to use but in applying them and coming to decisions of fact on the basis of the evidence presented to the court.

For example, if there are only a handful of people in the world who know anything about a particular subject, there could easily be conflict between them about whether a particular advance in the field was an obvious one to take.

Before examining the legal tests of obviousness and the approach to be adopted in assessing whether an invention is obvious, there are two points to understand

- what is the essence of invention in patent law?
- does it matter how someone comes by an invention?

The essence of invention
The essence of invention can be summed up very simply. Despite the simplicity, the broad concept is fundamental. Invention lies in

● finding out something new that is not obvious to find out

If the other requirements for inventions to be patentable are met then the invention may be a patentable one.

By way of illustration consider the example of the cigarette making machine given on pages 76–78.

The problem was that with high-speed cigarette making machines some cigarettes had more tobacco in them than others. The thing that was new was that the inventor found out *why this happened.* Having found out why, it was possible and in fact obvious to specify the essential features such machines needed to have to solve the problem.

The problem the invention was directed to solving was that when the tobacco fell on to the moving band it bounced and slipped causing it to bunch up at various points in the continuous rod of tobacco. The solution was to ensure the tobacco was moving horizontally in the direction of the moving band. This ensured that even if the tobacco did bounce it would not bunch up and because it was moving in the direction of the band it did not tend to slip either at all or as much as before.

Thus, note that what was new and not obvious was in

● finding out why the tobacco was unevenly distributed

There could have been several different ways of ensuring the tobacco was moving horizontally in the direction of the moving band. Just one of these was to use an inclined trough. However, having found out why the tobacco was unevenly distributed the inventor was therefore entitled to claim in the patent not just the one way of achieving the desired result as described in the patent but every way this could be achieved. It did not matter that, once the cause of the problem had been discovered, the solution was obvious. This is another absolutely fundamental aspect of patent law

● once the inventor discloses in the patent what he or she has found out that enables a particular result to be achieved then it does not matter how many different ways there are of applying what is discovered to achieve the desired result. A patent for the essential aspects of the invention can cover all applications embodying the essential features

Does it matter how the inventor came by the invention?
If what distinguishes invention from everything else is finding out something new that is not obvious to find out then it should not matter how it is found out (discovered).

The point to note is that

● as far as the validity of a patent is concerned, even if the invention is arrived at by plodding work, it ought not to matter how the inventor comes by the invention provided not all the steps taken were obvious ones to take and conversely

- even if the work and effort required is substantial and painstaking, if what is done is obvious to the ordinary people skilled in the field using their ordinary skills and techniques, then regardless of what is newly discovered, the invention based solely on that new information and nothing else that is new, will be uninventive

Under the 49 Act, a test applied by the UK courts was whether the research team would be directly led as a matter of course to try a particular route. This is different to applying a test of whether one route or another *might* be expected to lead to an invention.

Another point to note is that under the EPC, the approach adopted by the European Patent Office is not to treat an invention as obvious, even if the steps taken to arrive at it were obvious, if the invention has some unexpected useful result.

The requirement of inventiveness under the 49 Act and 77 Act
Under the 49 Act, s. 32(1)(f), a granted patent can be attacked on the basis that

the invention, so far as claimed in any claim of the complete specification, is obvious and does not involve any inventive step having regard to what was known or used, before the priority date of the claim, in the United Kingdom

Under the 77 Act, s. 3 a patent must satisfy the following requirement before it is granted and it can be validly attacked after it is granted where it is found later not to satisfy the requirement

An invention shall be taken to involve an inventive step if it is not obvious to a person skilled in the art, having regard to any matter which forms part of the state of the art

The requirement of inventiveness applied under the EPC is phrased in a similar way to the 77 Act and it is to be expected that the tests applied in the UK courts should be similar to those applied by the European Patent Office.

As the wording of the inventiveness requirement under the 49 Act is essentially little different to that under the 77 Act and EPC, the cases under the 49 Act are likely to apply equally to the new law under the 77 Act.

The chain of reasoning in making the assessment
Consider the chain of reasoning a court might have to go through in assessing whether the 'invention' specified as having the essential features set out in the claims of a patent is or is not obvious

- what type of person is to be considered to be the notional person skilled in the field (art)?
- what knowledge is such a person to be taken to have?

- what skills is such a person to be taken to have?
- what is it about the claimed invention that is new?
- looking at the invention as a whole, is what is new inventive in the eyes of the notional skilled person?

The links in the chain will be examined one by one.

Who is the notional skilled person?   It is not easy to lay down any hard-and-fast criteria to identify what sort of person is to be considered to be the ordinary person skilled in the art in question.

For any particular field, there may be a large number of people skilled in the art. For other fields there may be very few. Sometimes an invention will require knowledge of several different fields and may have involved a team of people skilled in the areas in question. In some areas, the level of skill and knowledge of those who normally practise the art concerned may be very low whereas in other fields, especially 'high technology', the level of skill and knowledge of the ordinary skilled person may be very high. Thus, the level of skill and knowledge of the ordinary skilled person will vary depending on the field concerned.

It appears from decided cases that the notional skilled person

- is not a person of exceptional skill and knowledge
- has a reasonable degree of skill and common knowledge of the art
- does not have the capacity to make elaborate additions to or modifications of what was disclosed and illustrated in a patent specification

Remember that, as far as proceedings in a court are concerned, all the court can go by in assessing who the notional skilled person is is the evidence presented to it by the various parties to the proceedings.

How can anyone skilled in some technical field be considered to be uninventive?   What might seem to be the most confusing aspect of the way obviousness is assessed under patent law is

- how the notional skilled person can sensibly be considered not to be inventive

Surely, everyone to some degree or another must have some degree of inspiration from time to time? Although it is contrary to the approach adopted by the courts, ignore the suggestion that the notional skilled person is wholly uninventive.

The approach is to ask

- whether the alleged invention is inventive in the light of what is already known when viewed through the eyes of the notional skilled person

Thus, the question is not whether the notionally skilled person is or is not inventive. That is distracting and misleading. The question is whether that person would have to do something that is not obvious or to find out new information that was not known before in order to solve the problem.

Ultimately the question is whether the skilled person has to be inventive to solve the problem. This may look like the whole question of whether an invention is inventive has come full circle. In fact that is correct. What is different is that the assessment is put on as rational a basis as is possible. The court, through the evidence presented to it, is basically saying it now believes it knows what the ordinary person skilled in the field in question knew just before the patent was applied for. In the light of that knowledge the court makes what is hopefully as informed an assessment as it can of whether the alleged invention can be considered obvious or inventive.

What does the notional skilled person know?   The notional skilled person is not taken to know everything. The notional skilled person is taken to possess the common general knowledge relevant to the field in question.

Thus, evidence will be required of what is common knowledge, such as what is found in textbooks, what is taught to students and the like. Information which can only be obtained after extensive research is not to be considered common general knowledge, nor are things like patent specifications unless it can be shown that a particular patent specification is one which is commonly referred to generally by those skilled in the relevant field. Even articles in widely read journals are not part of the common general knowledge unless it can be shown that the particular article concerned is commonly accepted. Additionally, evidence from people who are skilled in the field or fields in question may be relevant, particularly in relation to what is actually done and what technical skills and techniques are commonly used.

Thus,

- what comprises the common general knowledge of the person skilled in the art is taken from quite a narrow range

What skills is the notional skilled person to be taken to have?   The notional skilled person is not to be taken to be a person of exceptional skill and knowledge and is taken to have a reasonable degree of skill and common knowledge of the art. Again, this is very much a matter of evidence.

What is it about the claimed invention that is new?   Clearly, the court is going to have to assess the alleged invention through the eyes of the notionally skilled person. Now the first point is that there must be something new about the invention. The question of obviousness does not arise if the invention is not new. However, there are two steps to take in assessing whether an invention is obvious. First it is necessary to identify what it is about the invention that is different from what has been done before. Then the question arises whether what is new (in the context of the entire invention) is obvious. And

- in assessing what is new, it is the 'invention' specified as having the essential features set out in the claims of the patent which must be considered

It is not always easy to assess exactly what it is about a claimed invention that is the 'new' allegedly inventive part

- when assessing what is new about a claimed invention it is important to consider all of the essential features, both new and old, together in context rather than as separate constituent parts

Is what is new inventive in the eyes of the notional skilled person? The question is whether, in the light of what the skilled person knows and would do and in the light of the state of the art, is the invention obvious? This is where a considerable amount of confusion can arise if two things are not distinguished. It is essential to distinguish

- the common general skills, techniques and knowledge of those skilled in the art

from

- the state of the art itself

The state of the art includes all information about a field that has ever been made available to the public. The ordinary skilled person cannot possibly be expected to know all of that and is not expected to be able to.

There are two different situations. In the first, the question to be answered may be whether the invention was an obvious one for someone skilled in the field to make just on the basis of the common general knowledge and skills of such a person.

The second situation is where there may have been some relevant information made available before the patent was ever applied for which was not commonly known to those skilled in the field. The information may not cover exactly what is claimed as an invention but it is close or it suggests a line of work that might be undertaken which might end up leading to the invention. What the court has to do through the eyes of the notional skilled person, is to ask itself

- knowing what I know as a person skilled in this field
- having the common general knowledge and skills of the field
- would it be obvious to me, once I have been given this information, even though I do not normally have this information, to do what the inventor has done?

Thus, an invention can be obvious in two ways

- an invention can be obvious simply on the basis of what those skilled in the field commonly know and can do

or

- an invention can be obvious to someone skilled in the relevant field *from information made available to the public*

It is easy when you know how
Now, there is a problem with this approach to examining whether an alleged invention is inventive. The problem is a simple one. It is all too often too easy

for someone, such as an expert witness, to proclaim to the court that, having seen the invention, having been given some specific information about what was being done before the patent was applied for and in the light of what the expert knows as someone skilled in the field, the invention is an obvious solution to a problem.

The problem is that

● everything seems obvious once you have been shown how to do it

In relation to answering the question whether or not the invention is obvious two points arise

● what is meant by the state of the art?

● what criteria can be applied to tackle the problem of hindsight?

What is the state of the art?
The main difference between the state of the art for 49 Act patents, 77 Act patents and European patents (UK) is that the state of the art for 49 Act patents covers only what is made available to the public in the UK. For 77 Act patents and European patents (UK) it covers everything made available to the public anywhere in the world.

The state of the art under the 77 Act and EPC is the same as it is for assessing whether an invention is new. However, it does not include patent specifications of other patents which have been applied for before the priority date of the patent in question but which had not been published at the priority date of the patent in question. (If a patent specification has not been published then no one knows about it.)

When attacking the novelty of an invention it is simply not permitted to put together a selection of things that were previously known, used or published and say that, taken together these show that the invention is not new (making a 'mosaic' of prior knowledge, publication or disclosure). Whether or not an invention is new depends upon whether exactly the same thing was done, known or used before.

The position is quite different when attacking a patent on the basis that it is obvious. It is permitted to put together a selection of the prior art and then say that the skilled person, having the common general knowledge and skills, would consider the invention an obvious one.

A defendant in a patent infringement case, in attacking the validity of a patent, may carry out extensive research to find previous publications which, when read together, might indicate that the invention is obvious. This can be a wholly artificial way of approaching the question of obviousness and the courts are wise to the dangers.

Making a patchwork of what was known before
Just because a combination of matter in the prior art might show that an invention is obvious is not conclusive. The court may consider that the skilled person might not have come across the documents at the same time and not made the connection between them that would lead to the inventor's invention.

It may also be that the court will consider that the skilled person would not make the connection between the documents to lead to the inventor's invention. This could perhaps be because the documents deal with different fields of technology or alternatively that the documents would be one or two hidden in a vast amount of other literature and which would be unlikely to be associated with each other or read together in the same light.

Has the invention been a commercial success?
Another thing that might be indicative of whether the invention is inventive is whether it has proved to be a commercial success. The argument being that if the invention is obvious how is it that no one else has ever done the same thing before — how in such a circumstance can the invention be obvious if it has proved to be so successful?

The basic counter-argument to this is that no one may ever have wanted to do the same thing before. It may well be that the invention is directed to a wholly new problem.

Take the example of the cigarette making machine. The invention in that case was designed to overcome a new problem. The problem was new because previous cigarette making machines could not operate at sufficient speed for the problem of unevenly distributed tobacco in cigarettes to arise. Until the new problem had arisen no one would have been at all interested in trying to solve it.

Sometimes the manufacturers in a particular market have little incentive to innovate. It may well be that the market is well served by one or two suppliers and no one else is very interested in it because the profit margins are likely to be low. Thus, the existing manufacturers may have little or no competition and can keep on providing the same basic products year after year. Furthermore, some things are commercially successful because of sound marketing, a good sales team, a lower price than competing products and a host of other reasons which may have little to do with any inventive aspect of the product. Thus, evidence of commercial success of an invention may be useful but, if there is no evidence of what is called a 'long-felt want' for the solution to whatever problem the invention provides then evidence of commercial success in itself may prove to be insufficient.

Difficulties the inventor has overcome
Another useful indication of inventiveness is whether it was easy or difficult for the inventor to make the invention. If the inventor had to overcome considerable difficulties in arriving at the invention this can be indicative of the fact that the invention was not an obvious one to find out.

However, the reverse of the coin is that just because the invention is simple and easy to come by does not make it obvious. Take again the example of the cigarette making machine. It was the discovery of what caused the cigarettes to have an uneven distribution of tobacco in them that led to the obvious solution to the problem. However, the solution was not obvious until the inventor discovered what the cause of the problem was and that was not obvious.

INFRINGEMENT

Introduction

It should by now have become easy to guess that infringement of a patent must have something to do with

- reproducing something that has all of the essential features of the invention specified in one or more claims in the patent specification

However, infringement does not just encompass reproducing the invention in some form.

Remember also that, although a patent protects against copying, it is not necessary to copy to infringe. Even if the allegedly infringing product looks nothing like the example of the invention shown in drawings in the patent, it can still infringe if it exhibits the essential features claimed in the claims of a patent.

It is important to bear in mind that, in general, where the invention is for a product or where infringement consists of dealings with products produced by a patented process, innocence is no defence. The patent monopoly is absolute. The infringer may never have seen or heard of the invention but it is still infringement to make something which has the essential features set out in the claims. Where the invention is a process, innocence can sometimes be a defence to infringing use of the process, but once the infringer has notice of the fact that the process is covered by a patent, innocence is no defence to further use of the process.

The law governing infringement of 49 Act patents, 77 Act patents and European patents (UK) is the same. It is that set out in s. 60 of the 77 Act.

What amounts to infringement

Where an invention is a product, infringement consists of doing the following without the permission of the patentee

- making
- disposing of
- offering to dispose of
- using
- importing, and
- keeping (whether for disposal or otherwise)

products embodying the invention.

This is extremely broad. Notice that it even covers keeping a product embodying the invention.

One aspect of infringment which is not clear concerns offers to dispose of products embodying a patented invention, such as offering them for sale. If the offer is made in the UK, is it still infringement if the products never come into the UK, but perhaps are shipped from one foreign country for use in another?

The question has no answer at this stage. It is one that can be relevant when trade fairs and exhibitions are taking place in the UK.

Where an invention is a process, infringement consists of doing the following without permission

- using the process in the UK
- offering the process for use in the UK

knowing that such use without permission would infringe, or doing so where it is obvious that there would be an infringement.

In relation to products produced directly by a patented process, infringement consists of

- disposing of or offering to dispose of them
- using them
- importing, and
- keeping them (whether for disposal or otherwise)

Thus, the law even covers products produced abroad by a patented process where they are dealt with in the UK. Although this may, at first sight, seem odd, manufacture outside the UK can never infringe a UK patent. Thus, without this provision, a UK patent monopoly could be evaded by importing products produced abroad by a process covered by the patent.

Secondary patent infringement

It is also patent infringement to supply or offer to supply anything relating to an essential element of an invention to others. This kind of infringement can only be committed in certain circumstances.

What is supplied must be something for putting the invention into effect, such as a component for a product or materials or equipment for a patented process. The person supplying the thing is not liable unless he knows that it is suitable for putting the invention into effect and is intended for that purpose. Alternatively, if such is obvious to a reasonable person then there is infringement.

This kind of infringement is not committed by the supply of staple commercial products. Staple commercial products include things like petrol, cement, drawing-pins, nuts and bolts. There is one circumstance where the supply of staple commercial products could amount to infringement and that is when the supply or offer is made to induce someone else to infringe.

What is not infringement

Implied licence
When products covered by a patent are put on the market, either by the patentee or with the patentee's consent, often, no restrictions are placed on what can be done with the product. Clearly, it must be implicit that the purchaser can use, keep and dispose of the product.

The law recognises the concept of the implied licence but it is not settled quite how far an implied licence goes. The implied licence should permit the product to be dealt with as any other piece of physical property, such as to repair it or to replace parts which break or wear out. However, a distinction needs to be drawn between repairing an item when parts of it wear out and remaking a patented item.

Also note that the patentee can impose restrictions on what can be done with a product covered by a patent at the time it is first put on the market. Although it is extremely rare for mass-produced items, imposing restrictions on how an item can be dealt with, who can use it and the like has great potential for exploiting patent rights to the greatest effect.

There are limitations on the kinds of restrictions a patentee can impose. These will not be considered here in detail. Some restrictions are contained in the 77 Act, such as in relation to prohibitions on acquiring other unpatented items other than from particular sources. Others arise by virtue of UK and EEC competition law.

Exhaustion of rights
The concept of exhaustion of rights arises under EEC law and is dealt with in chapter 9. It is not limited to patent rights but applies to all intellectual property rights.

If a product covered by a patent is placed on the market anywhere in the EEC, the patentee's rights in the product become 'exhausted'. This applies where the product is first marketed by the patentee or with the patentee's permission. Provided no express restrictions are imposed on what can be done with the product, then the product can be imported into the UK or any other EEC country without this amounting to infringement.

Private and non-commercial purposes
Things done for private and non-commercial purposes do not infringe a patent. Thus, making working models of patented items as a hobby should not infringe, but activities like selling a model made for a hobby would infringe even though it is a private sale.

Experimental purposes
Things done for experimental purposes do not infringe a patent. However, do not confuse what is done for truly experimental purposes with what is done for commercial purposes. For example, experimenting to find out whether commercial manufacture would be possible is not covered by this exception.

Individual prescription
Where a pharmacist extemporaneously makes up a prescription for an individual and does something that would infringe, this is expressly not treated as infringement.

Ships and aircraft
The temporary importation of items which would otherwise infringe and which are needed for the operation of the ship or aircraft carrying them is not infringement.

Certain kinds of aircraft are exempted under the civil aviation legislation from seizure in respect of patent infringement.

Prior use

Under s. 64 of the 77 Act if, before a patent is ever applied for, someone in good faith

- does an act which would constitute an infringement of the patent if it were in force, or
- makes effective and serious preparation to do such an act

then that person has the right to continue to do the act or, as the case may be, to do the act notwithstanding the grant of the patent.

DURATION OF PATENT RIGHTS AND A FEW POSSIBILITIES FOR GETTING AROUND THEM

Introduction

All patents last for 20 years, whether existing 49 Act patents or 77 Act patents or European patents.

The basic rule is that the 20-year period starts to run from the date the patent was filed. No patent infringement proceedings can be commenced for infringement prior to the date the patent is granted and the date of grant can be sometimes several years after the application is filed. However, this does not mean the patent is ineffective for the period between application and grant. Infringement occurring between application and grant can still be the subject of proceedings. It is just that the infringement proceedings cannot be started until the patent is granted.

Renewal fees

From the end of the fourth year from the date of application, and provided the patent has been granted by that time, a patent must be renewed annually and an annual renewal fee paid. The current fees range (in various increasing increments) from just under £100 for the earliest years to nearly £350 for patents in their 20th year.

Failure to renew

A failure to renew a patent results in it automatically ceasing to have effect at the end of the period fixed for payment of the renewal fee. Note that it is possible to have searches of the register carried out to see whether a patent is still in effect and whether the renewal fees have been paid on time. This can be important if you are checking on the status of someone else's patents. You may be considering reverse engineering or simply checking on whether there are any patents which could affect development work on a new product. However, just because the renewal fee is not paid promptly, this does not mean the patent is automatically revoked. There is a six-month period of grace within which it is possible to restore the patent by paying the fee plus an additional fee.

Furthermore,

● for the six-month period of grace, any infringement committed still amounts to infringement if the patent is subsequently renewed

Even if the renewal fee is not paid within the period of grace it is still possible for an application to be made to have the patent restored to the register of patents. The details of how this can be done will not be dealt with here. However, if the patent is restored, there is a limited provision to exempt others from being treated as infringing.

The exemption applies to people who have in good faith embarked on potentially infringing activities after the six-month period of grace has expired and before the notice for restoration of the patent has been published. However, it may not be wise to try to rely too heavily on this provision because of its limitations. Thus,

● if it looks like a patent has lapsed and cannot be renewed, take advice before committing expenditure or other resources to a course that would have infringed had the patent not expired

Licences of right and compulsory licences

Despite the fact that a patent is still in existence, it may be possible to get around it in certain circumstances. There are provisions entitling others to what are called licences of right under an existing patent. Where a patent is subject to a licence of right anyone has the right to a licence under the patent. This means that it is possible to force the patentee to give permission for activities which would otherwise amount to patent infringement.

Additionally, there are provisions under which a patentee can be compelled to grant a licence. These provisions concern what are called compulsory licences. A patent subject to a compulsory licence does not mean anyone is entitled by right to a licence. Individual applications have to be made and a licence does not have to be granted unless certain conditions are satisfied.

Licences of right
The most important aspect of licences of right concerns existing 49 Act patents. 49 Act patents will still be around until 1 June 1998. This is because patents granted under the 49 Act used to last for 16 years but the period was extended to 20 years by the 77 Act.

However, to balance the windfall extension of the period of protection, the 77 Act provides that existing 49 Act patents are to be subject to licences of right for the last four years of their 20-year duration. For these patents a licence of right can be obtained either by negotiation with the patentee, or, failing this, by application to the Comptroller of Patents. The Comptroller has power to settle the terms of the licence, including how much the licensee is to pay in royalties. An application to the Comptroller can be made at any time after the start of the 16th year of the patent, i.e., five years before it terminates and 12 months before the licence can take effect.

Voluntary endorsement of licence of right

The patentee can apply to the Comptroller of Patents for the patent concerned to be 'endorsed licence of right' under s. 46 of the 77 Act. The effect of this is the same as for existing 49 Act patents which are automatically endorsed 'licence of right' in their last four years. However, it will also be clear for anyone carrying out patent searches anywhere in the world that they will be able to obtain a licence under the patent (whether a European patent (UK) or a patent applied for and granted under the 77 Act) from the patentee or by application to the Comptroller of Patents. The endorsement can be cancelled on the patentee's application if there are no existing licensees or all of them consent.

Compulsory licences

An application for a compulsory licence cannot be made earlier than three years from the date of grant of a patent. The compulsory licence provisions apply to 49 Act patents, 77 Act patents and to European patents (UK). The relevant legislation is in ss. 48–50 of the 77 Act.

The application can be

- for a licence,
- for the patent to be endorsed 'licence of right'
- for a licence to be granted to a specified person (this only applies to applications by a government department)

The grounds of an application are

- the invention is not being worked in the UK to the fullest extent that is reasonably practicable
- demand for products covered by the invention
  - is not being met on reasonable terms
  - is being met to a substantial extent by importation
- the invention is being prevented or hindered from being commercially worked in the UK by
  - importation of products embodying the invention
  - importation of products made by the patented process
- the patentee is refusing licences on reasonable terms resulting in
  - an export market not being supplied
  - the working of another invention is being hindered (this only applies to other inventions which 'make a substantial contribution to the art')
- by reason of conditions imposed in various ways by the proprietor this unfairly prejudices
  - the use or disposal of materials not protected by the patent
  - the establishment of commercial or industrial activities

The grant of a licence is in the Comptroller's discretion. However, the Comptroller must aim at achieving the following

- inventions which can be worked on a commercial scale in the UK and which in the public interest should be, are to be so worked without delay and to the fullest extent possible
- there should be adequate remuneration for the person beneficially entitled to the patent
- the interests of the patentee or anyone else exploiting or developing a patented invention should not be unfairly prejudiced

The Comptroller must consider

- the nature of the invention
- the time that has elapsed since the patent was granted
- the measures taken by the patentee or any existing licensee to exploit the invention fully
- the ability of the applicant to exploit the invention to public advantage
- the risks to be undertaken by the applicant in providing capital and exploiting the invention

Monopolies and licences of right
Where the Monopolies and Merger Commission has laid a report before Parliament concerning competitive aspects of mergers, monopolies, anti-competitive practices, or activities which operate against the public interest, the appropriate government minister can apply to the Comptroller of Patents to take action which can result in

- the cancellation or modification of conditions in patent licences by the Comptroller, and
- the endorsement of any relevant patents as 'licence of right'

6 Protection of Form and Appearance

COPYRIGHT WORKS, DESIGNS, SEMICONDUCTOR CHIPS AND PERFORMANCES

This chapter is concerned with how the law goes about protecting what things look like, such as in the case of products how they appear to the eye; the shape and appearance of the products; the design aspects.

In the case of some intellectual creations, like music and performances, what is protectable is how they appear both on paper (e.g., musical scores, plays and screenplays) and how they appear to the eye and ear, including how they are performed by a particular performer.

Copying

There are many different ways people create. People create things, physical articles, products and designs. They also devise theories, create ideas, music, works of literature, perhaps even fictional characters in books or ways of portraying characters in performances.

There are many ways in which people can copy. Most people, when they use the word 'copy' use it to cover all kinds of copying. The word is used without distinguishing the kind of copying whether it is other people's ideas, concepts, inventions, the way they walk, talk, sing, dance, dress, the things they do, how they run their businesses, what their products look like, themes they use in advertising campaigns.

Different kinds of protection are available against different kinds of copying. Not all copying is prohibited. The law has the task of identifying what can be protected and what people should be able to copy freely. As a consequence it has become finely tuned.

With regard to copying form and appearance, and because people create in many different ways, the law has identified many different kinds of creations which can be protected. The nature and scope of protection can seem complicated and daunting. As a consequence it is not easy to explain what is protectable and how it is protected in a very simple way without dangerously over-simplifying.

The law has broken down what can be protected into broad categories and applied different schemes of protection. The different schemes can and do overlap. In addition to general copyright, there are two schemes of protection for aspects of product design as well as special rights in performances and semiconductor chip designs.

Copyright is about protecting form

Copyright is intended to protect against others copying and exploiting the *form* in which a copyright work exists, namely, what it looks like. Although in some cases it can be difficult to distinguish the form from the idea, copyright is not intended to protect ideas. The same applies to the other rights protecting form and appearance.

If there is no copying there is no protection

If people independently use their own resources in creating and do not copy the form or appearance of things created by others then they are not infringing rights conferred by the law for the protection of form and appearance. This applies even though they may adopt or copy a similar general theme or idea created by someone else.

Protection is automatic

Another aspect of copyright protection is that it is automatic. The moment a copyright work is created it is normally protectable by copyright. There are no formalities, no registration procedures. Nothing needs to be done to 'copyright' something. This basic principle applies to all the rights protecting form and appearance except the law of registered designs.

People do not realise how far protection can extend

Copyright, like other intellectual property rights, covers a wide range of subject-matter and has significant commercial value. The most obvious examples of commercially valuable copyrights are those in films, videos, music records, pre-recorded tapes and compact discs. But like other industrial property rights copyright goes even further than might initially be expected.

Example
In the run-up to Christmas 1983, Wellingtons Ltd put a range of bubble-bath products on the market which were packaged in bottles which parodied famous drink brands. One example was a bottle in the distinctive square shape of the Johnny Walker Red Label whisky bottle. The labels were in the same style as the Johnny Walker label, using the same colours, shape and layout. The main Johnny Walker label was affixed diagonally on the bottle and Wellingtons did the same thing. The final touch was to call the product 'Jolly Waters'.

The product was eye-catching and could be mistaken in passing for the real thing until given a slightly closer examination. Another Wellingtons product was in the shape of the Schweppes tonic water bottle. Again, the same colours, shape and layout of label were used. The name for this product was 'SCHLURPPES'.

Schweppes Ltd was not amused. It sued for infringement of copyright *in its labels as artistic works,* nothing else. It succeeded. The court decided that Wellingtons had copied a substantial part of Schweppes's artistic works, the labels. The whole matter was over in no time at all (judgment was given on 29 November, 1983 — four weeks before Christmas).

The outcome must have been no laughing matter for Wellingtons. All the time and money spent in developing the product, putting it into production and marketing it would be wasted together with all the unsold stocks.

These are all property rights

All of the rights protecting form and appearance are property rights. The concept of property has been considered in Chapter 2. As a form of property, they can be owned and like other forms of property they can be bought and sold. So the rights can be commercially exploited.

Scope of this chapter

For simplicity, this chapter will deal with the principles of and rationale underlying copyright protection, performers' protection and protection for designs set out in the Copyright, Designs and Patents Act 1988 (the '88 Act'), of design protection set out in the Registered Designs Act 1949 as amended (the 'RDA 49') and the Design Right (Semiconductor Topographies) Regulations 1989 (the 'New Chip Regulations').

The 88 Act introduces some new law as well as restating the old law and substantially came into effect on 1 August 1989. Although some of the old law will still be of relevance in relation to pre August 1989 subject-matter, this chapter is concerned in the main with the operation of the new law. The old law will continue to be relevant for some time so each section will point out the differences between the old and new law and how these operate in combination.

This book will not be dealing with the position in relation to works created before 1 July 1957 when the 56 Act came into effect. This area could be of interest in advertising, broadcasting and the performing arts where it may be desirable to copy or make use of pre July 1957 works.

International aspects

Many other countries will have corresponding protection, operating on similar principles to some but not all aspects of the UK law. However, the methods and manner of implementation of law can vary widely in detail. Many countries which are signatories to international conventions (agreements between governments and countries) afford the same protection to other nationals as to their own nationals. It is beyond the scope of this book to attempt to describe the forms of protection afforded in other countries, but it is well worth being generally aware that it may be possible to obtain broadly similar kinds of protection in other countries.

RECOGNISING WHAT CAN BE PROTECTED

Most people when creating something do not whilst doing so think 'I am creating a copyright work/a design protected by design right/a registrable design'. For the most part, they just create it. The lawyers, on the other hand, need to be able to identify and define what is protectable. The result is a delightful *mélange* of schemes of protection for the different kinds of things people create

- the object of this section is to introduce all of the legally defined kinds of protectable subject matter in one go to assist in recognising what might be capable of protection
- unless what is capable of being protected is recognised whilst being created, it may be more difficult to protect later
- if something like a competitor's product is going to be copied, it is important to recognise whether the product might be protected and whether there could be problems with intellectual property rights
- if rights to manufacture a product are being acquired, there is no point paying for something that can be copied freely

Copyright works

Introduction
The new law is broader than the old, pre August 1989 law and changes the previous definitions of what can and cannot qualify as 'works' for copyright protection. The new definitions include more than the 56 Act definitions did. Thus, sometimes a distinction may need to be made depending upon whether a work was made before or on or after 1 August 1989.

The provisions dealing with the transition between the old and new law are complicated and, if in doubt, professional advice may be appropriate.

The works
The types of works covered by UK copyright law are listed in s. 1 of the 88 Act. These include the group of works which are covered by what are sometimes called the 'author's rights'

- literary,
- dramatic,
- musical and
- artistic works,

and, a sort of 'odd man out'

- the typographical arrangement of published editions

as well as what are sometimes called the 'mechanical rights', or 'neighbouring rights'

- sound recordings,

- films,
- broadcasts and cable programmes

Literary works
A literary work is defined in s. 3 of the 88 Act as:

> . . . any work, other than a dramatic or musical work, which is written, spoken or sung, and accordingly includes:
> (a) a table or compilation, and
> (b) a computer program.

Examples of matter that has in the past qualified as literary include listings of television programmes, lists of racehorses, football fixture lists and street directories. Mathematical tables and lists of telegraph codes qualify as literary works as does any other kind of compilation. Thus,

- literary works are not limited to what is expressed in words

- the 88 Act provides that a work, as an intellectual creation, can exist as a thing in itself, without ever having been written down or recorded in some other way

Thus it is clear that

- what is said in an extempore speech or an interview given to the press or a recitation or live performance qualifies as a literary work even though it has not been recorded in any way

Even speech generated and spoken by a machine may qualify as a literary work.
What appears to be at the heart of the approach of the 88 Act to literary, dramatic and musical works is

- the 88 Act attempts to distinguish the essence of what constitutes the 'work' from the medium in which it is recorded

This is a subtle distinction. It provokes deeper consideration of what constitutes any particular kind of work; what is its essence. The approach also will lead inevitably to the boundaries between different kinds of copyright works becoming less well defined.

A work must be recorded
Under the 88 Act, s. 1(2)

- a literary work will not qualify for protection until it has been recorded in writing or otherwise

Writing includes any form of notation, whether by hand *or otherwise* and regardless of the method by which, or medium in or on which, it is recorded (88 Act, s. 178)

- the words 'or otherwise' indicate that practically any means of recording a literary work should be sufficient

Literary matter stored in computer databases, on tape, disk or any other way will qualify as having been sufficiently recorded for copyright purposes.

- almost anything can qualify as 'literary' if it is capable of being recorded in some way in print regardless of how it is actually recorded

A tape recording of speech is sufficient means of recording spoken words for the spoken words to qualify as having been recorded for copyright purposes.

Single words and titles

There are problems with trying to obtain copyright protection for single words, titles for books, songs and the like.

In one case the Court of Appeal considered that a word alone and by itself cannot properly be considered as a 'literary work', the subject of copyright (*Exxon Corporation* v *Exxon Insurance Consultants International Ltd* [1982] Ch 119).

The word 'Kojak' from the 1970s television series was not protectable by copyright because 'so far as the law of England is concerned, we do not recognise any copyright . . . in any names or words, whether invented or not' (*Tavener Rutledge Ltd* v *Trexapalm Ltd* [1977] RPC 275).

The title of a song, 'The Man Who Broke The Bank At Monte Carlo', was considered not to be by itself a proper subject-matter of copyright although the court acknowledged that in some circumstances a title might conceivably be afforded the protection of copyright (*Francis, Day & Hunter Ltd* v *Twentieth Century Fox Corporation Ltd* [1940] AC 112).

It seems that words, the 'building blocks' of common everyday language, cannot be monopolised using copyright. This raises interesting issues for creators of new languages, such as creators of new computer programming languages.

Musical Works

There was no statutory definition of music under the 56 Act. Although the position is the same under the 88 Act, the Act makes express provision concerning certain aspects of what is and is not music

- music is to be distinguished from any accompanying words to be sung, spoken or performed or actions intended to be performed with the music (88 Act, s. 3(1)).

The lyric will be treated as a literary work and not as part of the music. Instructions for actions to accompany music may be treated as literary works or as dramatic works or both. Like a literary work, a tune which is hummed or sung will not qualify for protection until it has been recorded in some form. Even improvisation should qualify as music under the new law provided it has been recorded in some way.

Modern electronics technology has developed to the extent that it can be relatively inexpensive for the consumer to obtain equipment which can be used to digitally sample existing recorded music. Perhaps the way a particular musician plays particular notes can be captured digitally. The note sequences and durations, the 'wave packet' or 'envelope' may be altered and reproduced to make a recording of another totally different piece of music. Perhaps it may even be possible to capture the musical equivalent of a fingerprint for a particular musician so that music can be reproduced, say, on an electronic keyboard/synthesiser, which sounds as if that particular musician played the piece. Is there any copyright work being infringed? Like a single word can a single note be disqualified from protection? What about a sequence of single notes?

Dramatic works

The 56 Act defined a dramatic work as including 'a choreographic work or entertainment in dumb show if reduced to writing in the form in which the work or entertainment is to be presented, but does not include a cinematograph film, as distinct from a scenario or script for a cinematograph film' (56 Act, s. 48(1)).

There is no definition of what constitutes a dramatic work under the 88 Act save to the extent that the 88 Act specifies that works of dance or mime are included as dramatic works (88 Act, s. 3(1)). However, from the decided cases it seems

- a dramatic work does not necessarily have to be a play or screenplay
- the essence of a dramatic work under the old law seems to be in the instructions for action or the manner of presentation of some kind of performance

Under the 56 Act any form of notation depicting dance steps could qualify for protection as a dramatic work. A dramatic work also included the descriptions of scenes, the manner in which a character is to appear, deliver lines and such like. A dramatic work in the form of a play or screenplay could qualify both as a dramatic and as a literary work. However, unlike the 56 Act,

- under the 88 Act the instructions for the performance can be recorded in any form (88 Act, s. 3(2))

Although a dramatic work must have been recorded 'in writing or otherwise' before it can qualify for protection, this implies that a work which has not been recorded also qualifies as a work. It simply cannot be protected until recorded. Thus an ad lib performance could qualify as a dramatic work. If it is recorded, say on video or as a sound recording, then copyright protection may be afforded to it. It will be interesting to see whether sports which are rehearsed or choreographed like the prearranged and well rehearsed set piece displays in gymnastics will be treated as dramatic works. It certainly may prove difficult to distinguish them from dramatic works or performances.

Typographical arrangements of published editions of literary, dramatic and musical works

The layout, arrangement and appearance of the printed page in published editions of literary, dramatic and musical works qualifies as a work for copyright purposes (88 Act, s. 8 and 56 Act, s. 15). The copyright protection is available even if the literary, dramatic or musical work does not itself qualify for or is no longer in copyright.

Artistic works
The categories of 'artistic work' are defined in s. 4 of the 88 Act as including

- a graphic work,
- a photograph,
- a sculpture or
- a collage,

Section 4 also includes as artistic works

- a work of architecture being a building or a model for a building, and
- a work of artistic craftsmanship

Note that artistic quality is ignored for graphic works, photographs, sculptures and collages. In plain terms this means that no matter how unartistic something may seem, if it qualifies as one of the defined works it will be treated as an artistic work capable of protection by copyright. So, as in one case under the old law, design drawings for motor car exhaust systems qualified as artistic works (*British Leyland Motor Corporation Ltd* v *Armstrong Patents Co. Ltd* [1986] AC 577). As will be seen later in the section dealing with protecting designs of products, this had and will continue for 10 years to have considerable commercial importance.

Sound recordings
Under the 56 Act, s. 12(9), a sound recording was defined as the

- aggregate of the sounds
- embodied in, and capable of being reproduced by means of,
- a record of any description,
- other than a sound-track associated with a cinematograph film

A record was in turn defined as 'any disc, tape, perforated roll or other device in which sounds are embodied so as to be capable (with or without the aid of some other instrument) of being automatically reproduced therefrom' (56 Act, s. 48(1)).
Under the 88 Act (s. 5) a sound recording is defined as either

- a recording of sounds,
- from which sounds may be reproduced,

or, it can be

- a recording
- of the whole or any part of a literary, dramatic or musical work,
- from which sounds reproducing the work or part may be produced,

In either of the above two cases the recording will qualify as protectable regardless of

- the medium on which the recording is made or
- the method by which the sounds are reproduced or produced

Overlap with literary works

The second part of the 88 Act definition of sound recording provides that a recording of the whole or any part of a literary, dramatic or musical work can be a sound recording. The only requirement is that sounds reproducing the work or part of it can be produced from the recording. Again, this is 'regardless of the medium on which the recording is made or the method by which the sounds are reproduced or produced'.

A tape recording made by a journalist of an interview is (or embodies) a literary work. It is also a sound recording. A tape recording of an extempore dramatic performance is a sound recording and it is (or embodies) a dramatic performance.

Sound-tracks

The sound-track of a film will be treated as a sound recording. Under the 56 Act it was treated as part of a film.

- the new rule applies to all films and sound-tracks regardless of whether they were made before 1 August 1989

Film

Under the 56 Act a cinematograph film was defined in s. 13(10) as

- any sequence of visual images
- recorded on material of any description (whether translucent or not)
- so as to be capable, by use of that material,
- of being shown as a moving picture, or
- of being recorded on other material (whether translucent or not), by the use of which it can be so shown.

Under s. 5 of the 88 Act a film is defined as

- a recording on any medium from which a moving image may by any means be reproduced.

Both the 56 Act and 88 Act definitions quite happily encompass both photographic film as well as videotape and video disc. The storage medium in both cases is irrelevant. However, the 88 Act

- does not require the recording to be of images, and to the extent that images are recorded
- the recording does not have to be of visual images

All that seems to be required under the 88 Act is that there is some type of recording. The recorded information does not have to be a recording of an image. It would be bizarre if a recording of random signals used as the data to enable a machine to generate abstract pictures on a computer terminal screen could be a film under the 88 Act but that seems to be what the 88 Act means.

Cartoons, computer animation and interactive video
A cartoon made from sequences of hand-drawn pictures is a film. The individual images may also be artistic works. Similarly, computer animation data used to display animated images should be protectable as a film. The position is not clear with interactive video where the viewer can influence what happens such as in the case of an interactive computer game. What is displayed ceases, in part, to be a moving image produced from a recording.

To the extent that interactive video images are built up of 'still' images, the individual images may qualify as artistic works. However, as the 88 Act does not explicitly include artistic works created on a computer, it would be prudent to print out the individual images if they are created solely on a machine.

Broadcasts and cable programmes
If asked, most people would probably describe broadcasts as the programmes (images and sounds) that they see and hear on television or hear on the radio. This is roughly correct in copyright law also.

Basically the nature of a cable programme is the same as a broadcast, namely visual images, sounds and other information, but sent by cables instead of wireless telegraphy. In fact, the method of transmission is the fundamental difference between the two.

Some broadcasts are of matter that is protected by copyright already, such as films and sound recordings, live performances of copyright dramatic and musical works and recitations of poetry. However, other images and sounds which broadcast can be of matter which is not protectable by any type of copyright, for example, 'live' (i.e., no film or sound recording is made of the material being broadcast before it is transmitted) coverage of sports. Games, like a football match, are not a type of copyright work (although some 'sports', like the prearranged and well rehearsed set-piece displays in gymnastics, may prove difficult to distinguish from dramatic works or performances).

So if there is potential for copyright protection, why have a further category of protection for 'broadcasts'? Considerable time and resources can be taken up in preparing and making broadcasts of live events or of existing copyright works. Skill and judgment will have been employed in selecting and arranging the material to be transmitted, and effort and expenditure can be made in providing equipment and arranging for and directing the camera or radio crews to cover an event and in purchasing rights, say, to cover sports events or to broadcast existing copyright works.

Whether what is broadcast is protectable by copyright in its own right, like a play, or not, such as a football match, in either case the broadcaster may not actually own copyright in the material being broadcast. If no copyright in broadcasts existed it is possible the broadcaster would not be able to prevent others copying the content of and rebroadcasting the broadcast. Essentially,

- what the legislation seems designed to prevent, as with other kinds of copyright works, is others taking the benefit of the investment, skill, judgment and effort involved in making the broadcast

A cable programme is defined under s. 7 of the 88 Act as

- any item
- included in a cable programme service

This is similar to the 56 Act definition (56 Act, s. 14A).

Under the 56 Act any sequence of images capable of being viewed as a moving picture were sufficient to amount to a cable programme for infringement purposes (56 Act, s. 14A(7)). It did not matter under the 56 Act how few images made up the sequence. Making a photograph of a substantial part of any image forming part of a cable programme amounts to copying under s. 17(4) of the 88 Act so this is an indication of how much transmitted information might be considered to comprise an 'item' under the new law. Thus, under the 56 Act and the 88 Act,

- a cable programme could be just a few seconds of sounds, visual images and other information transmitted or even less

A cable programme service is defined by s. 7 of the 88 Act as a service which consists wholly or mainly in

- sending
- by means of a telecommunications system,
- otherwise than by wireless telegraphy
- visual images, sounds or other information

This is very similar to the 56 Act definition.

The definition requires that the visual images, sounds and other information must not be sent by wireless telegraphy

- this simply means wires and cables must be used and not radio and television transmissions sent through the air

A telecommunications system is defined as 'a system for conveying visual images, sounds or other information by electronic means' (88 Act, s. 178). Electronic is defined as meaning 'actuated by electric, magnetic, electromagnetic, electrochemical or electromechanical energy' (88 Act, s. 178).

- this definition covers all current modern forms of transmitting information along cables, including fibre optic cable systems

To qualify as a cable programme service under s. 7 of the 88 Act, the service must be one either

- used to present cable programmes to the public or
- simply one which can be received in more than one place

Thus, a cable programme service which can send cable programmes at different times to different places at the user's request is covered

● a cable programme service therefore can (subject to the exceptions in the 88 Act) include any type of computer network such as database and information services.

Exceptions include private (domestic or business) cable systems which do not qualify as cable programme systems under the 88 Act if they are not connected to any other telecommunications system and are not used to providing a service to others (88 Act, s. 7(2)).

Take the example of a car manufacturer providing parts information to distributors and dealers via a computer system linked to the telephone network. This could qualify as a cable programme service. Although this is a private system it is connected to a telecommunications system (i.e., the telephone network) and it is providing a service to others, namely the dealers and distributors. The position would be different if the dealerships and distributorships were all part of the car manufacturer's business as this would not be providing services to others. However, one of the 88 Act's exceptions causes a problem with these kinds of interactive information systems.

The 88 Act is not clear about whether or to what extent interactive cable systems like British Telecom's Prestel service or other online database and similar services are excluded (the definition concerned in s. 7(2)(a) seems confused and ambiguous). The 88 Act, however, thoughtfully contains a power for the appropriate Secretary of State to add to or remove the exceptions (88 Act, s. 7(3)) but unfortunately it does not allow any of the exceptions to be amended.

Performances

The 88 Act creates a new regime of protection for performers in relation to their performances.

● a performance is not a type of copyright work
● it is a new type of protectable subject-matter in which performers obtain rights

Under the old law, various criminal offences were committed by the recording or filming of performances without consent and by commercial dealings in such records or films. However, from the point of view of the performer and an authorised recording company or film company this was not adequate. The criminal penalties were inadequate in relation to the rewards to be gained by making recordings and films illicitly. Additionally, the authorised recording and film company had no rights recognised by the civil law to obtain compensation by way of damages from an infringer.

The 88 Act continues the criminal scheme of protection but also introduces specific civil law rights for performers concerning the right to make recordings and films of performances. It also introduces civil law rights for anyone having exclusive rights from the performer to record or film the performer's performances.

Although rights in performances did not exist under the pre August 1989 law,

- the new law will apply on and after 1 August 1989 to performances made before August 1989

This will not, however, affect acts done or agreements made before 1 August 1989 (88 Act. s. 180(3)).

Under the 88 Act (s. 180(2)) a performance means a live performance given by one or more individuals and means:

- a dramatic performance (including dance and mime);
- a musical performance;
- a reading or recitation of a literary work;
- a performance of a variety act or similar presentation.

Additionally, note that

- the performance must be a live performance

This requirement is simply to distinguish a live performance from a performance (replaying) of a film or sound recording. Do not, however, assume that the performance must be before an audience. The rights in performances can apply equally to performances made in studios for the purpose of recording them in sound recordings and films.

DESIGNS OF PRODUCTS

The new law adopts a subtle approach to designs. It treats a design as a thing in itself

- the design is treated as if it were wholly independent from whatever means is used to make a record of it

Consider a drawing of a simple bolt. The drawing in itself is an artistic work for copyright purposes regardless of what it represents as a picture. However, what the drawing depicts is an item. The drawing is the means used to record the 'design' of the bolt. To put this another way, the design is the means of describing the appearance of the bolt without anyone actually making the bolt. The drawing is simply one means of depicting or recording the design.

A drawing is not the only means that can be used to depict or describe the appearance of the bolt. It is possible to describe the design of the bolt in words rather than using the medium of a drawing. The length, diameter, pitch of thread, size of hexagonal head, other features of shape, the materials to be used in and methods of construction can all be described in words. Again, the words embody the design. They are a means of recording or describing the bolt without making one.

Another way of depicting or recording a design is to build a model or prototype. Indeed, it is possible to retain the details of how something is designed in one's mind and never record them in any other way. With the example of the bolt this is relatively easy to contemplate. Thus, the medium used as a record of a design must not be confused with the design itself.

Under the new law the medium recording a design, such as a drawing depicting a design of an article, is described as a 'design document' and a prototype or model is described as embodying a design (88 Act, ss. 51 and 263(1)).

There are four different mechanisms for protecting designs. Copyright, design right, design right in semiconductor chip designs and rights in registered designs. Each operates differently, covers different aspects of designs and gives to some extent overlapping protection.

Copyright protection for products

Where a design is recorded in a document or is embodied in a model (e.g., a prototype) the 88 Act, specifically states that copyright is not infringed by making an article to the design (88 Act, s. 51).

So it might seem as if copyright does not protect designs. However, there are exceptions.

The first exception concerns designs which do not fall within the definition of designs excluded from copyright protection. For example, if an artistic work embodies a design and the design is not covered by the 88 Act's definition of designs excluded from copyright protection then the design may be protected by copyright in the artistic work used to record the design. The definition of 'design' will be looked at later.

If the design is for something which in itself is an artistic work then copyright protection will still apply.

Thirdly, if the design is for a typeface then copyright protection will still apply.

The fourth and most important exception of all concerns designs recorded or embodied in design documents or models before 1 August 1989. If the form in which the design is recorded qualifies as an artistic work in its own right, like a drawing or work of artistic craftsmanship, then copyright protection still applies. The protection will apply for up to 10 years from 1 August 1989.

Designs excluded from copyright protection
Before examining each of these exceptions the definition of 'design' needs consideration.

Anything that is not a 'design' as defined in the 88 Act may still be protectable by artistic copyright.

A 'design' is defined for copyright purposes by s. 51(3) of the 88 Act as the design of

- any aspect
- of the *shape or configuration* (whether internal or external)
- of the *whole or part* of *an article*
- other than *surface decoration*

Shape and configuration are normally taken to refer to three and not two dimensions. However, the only two dimensional aspect of a design which is expressly excluded from falling within the definition of 'design' is surface decoration. This, by implication, suggests that other non-decorative two-dimensional aspects of designs might be treated as aspects of 'shape' or 'configuration'.

So, it seems that

- copyright protection for two-dimensional aspects of designs is still available

For example, designs for wallpaper patterns, fabric patterns, carpet patterns, motifs, engraving, decorative embossing and suchlike

- these kinds of designs must of course be recorded in an artistic work for copyright in the artistic work to be relied upon to protect against copying

The exceptions covered by copyright
Surface decoration included as part of a design is covered by copyright as it does not fall within the definition of 'design' excluded from copyright protection. In order to obtain the benefit of copyright protection the design must be recorded in a copyright work.

If a design is for something that is a three-dimensional artistic work or a work of artistic craftsmanship (say, wrought iron work or jewellery or engravings or possibly cut glass or even a work of architecture), provided the design is recorded in a form that qualifies as an artistic work itself, the 88 Act operates so that artistic copyright protects the design against copying.

An example of an artistic work is a sculpture. Design drawings, for example, could be made as an initial stage in producing a sculpture. The design drawings would be the design documents and what they depict could qualify as an artistic work, a sculpture. The design drawings would qualify as artistic works in themselves and what they depict would be a design of a three-dimensional artistic work. Hence the design should be protectable by copyright.

The design of a typeface can be protected by copyright provided it is recorded in an artistic work. The only definition in the 88 Act of 'typeface' is that a typeface includes an ornamental motif used in printing (88 Act, s. 178.

Under an international convention, the Vienna Agreement for the protection of typefaces, a typeface is defined as sets of designs of letters, alphabets, accents and punctuation marks. Also included are numerals, conventional signs, symbols and scientific signs. The definition also includes 'ornaments such as borders, fleurons and vignettes, which are intended to provide means for composing texts by any graphic technique'.

So it seems

- a typeface is the entire set of symbols used in printing and not just individual letters or characters

A design made before 1 August 1989
Copyright protection for designs made before 1 August 1989 will continue for up to 10 years from 1 August 1989.

This protection for designs is important because it means

- mundane things like exhaust pipe designs will continue to be protectable under the 88 Act for 10 years under the old copyright rules

Additionally,

- the old copyright rules give extremely broad protection and make it extremely difficult to manufacture things like spare parts which need to an extent to be copied so that they will work and fit

Design right protection for products

Design right protection only applies to designs made on or after 1 August 1989 (88 Act, s. 213(7)).

What is a design?   A 'design' for the purposes of design right protection is not a species of copyright work. It is a new species of subject-matter covered by the 88 Act which is protectable by a new right called 'design right'.
'Design' is defined by s. 213(2) of the 88 Act as

- the design
- of *any aspect*
- of the *shape or configuration* (whether internal or external)
- of the *whole or part* of an article

It seems that

- to protect two dimensional aspects of a product design it will probably be necessary to rely upon copyright protection for artistic works or registered design protection

However, the position is not absolutely clear. In addition, surface decoration is specifically excluded from design right protection (88 Act, s. 213(3)).

Design right and computer programs   Designs of things that do not have 'shape or configuration' will not be protectable by design right. For example, a computer program may be protectable as a literary work and the screen displays may be protectable as artistic works. However, what is called the 'look and feel', the program design, how it operates, how it is used, how it appears to the user, is not protectable by design right, nor by copyright or registered design rights. The basic point is that

- there is no design protection *per se* for products like computer programs

No protection for recipes and materials   The law covering form and appearance affords no protection against others copying the same ingredients, say, for new food products. Additionally, despite how important the choice of materials is in mechanical engineering, there is no protection to prevent anyone copying the kinds of materials used in the construction of a product (unless there is some form of patent protection, which is unusual).

How must a design be recorded?

- a design must be recorded in an article or a design document before design right will be afforded to the design (88 Act, s. 213(6)).

However, a design document includes any record of a design, whether in the form of a drawing, a written description, a photograph, data stored in a computer or otherwise (88 Act, s. 263(1)). Thus, unlike copyright protection for artistic works,

- it is clear that computer created designs stored in electronic form can qualify for protection

Functional features   Features of

- shape or configuration which
- enable an article to fit with another article
- so that either article can perform its function

are excluded from protection (88 Act, s. 213(3)).

Thus features of shape or configuration of, for example, the teeth of a cog which enable the cog to fit with another cog to perform their function are not protectable. (This exception will be referred to in this book as the 'functional features exception'.)

Integral features   Additionally, where one article is

- intended to form an integral part of another article,
- features of shape or configuration
- which are dependent upon the shape of the other article

are not protectable (88 Act, s. 213(3)).

Thus, where features of the design of items like pipe fittings or valve guides for engines are dependent upon the item they must fit with, then design right will not protect those features. (This exception will be referred to in this book as the 'integral features exception').

Purpose of the integral features and functional features exceptions   These exceptions were introduced to permit, for example, manufacturers of spare parts to manufacture competing items without infringing *to the extent that* those items had to be able to fit with other parts

- functional combinations or integral features of a design do not qualify for copyright or registered design protection, so it ought to be safe to copy such features for post 31 July 1989 designs

However, care needs to be taken in relation to the functional combination and integral features exceptions. If, say, the design of the teeth of a cog has a combination of some features which fall within the terms of the exception and some which do not, say features which enable less metal to be used in combination with others which provide greater strength, then, in theory, the features which do not fall within the exceptions might still be protectable. Thus,

- it may not prove to be safe to assume it is possible to copy *all* aspects of the design, like those of the cog's teeth

Remember also that copyright protection for pre 1 August 1989 designs continues for up to 10 years and the functional and integral features exceptions do not apply to designs protected by copyright.

Methods or principles of construction excluded Methods and principles of construction are also excluded from protection under the design right (88 Act, s. 213(3)). In other words, it will not be possible to obtain a broad design right protection where some aspects of the design depend on basic methods or principles involved in constructing something to the design.

Take, as an example, an article made from aluminium. Because of the nature of the material used, if a shape is to be fashioned by a process such as extrusion, there are limitations on aspects of shape. Because the material can be bent or distorted only so much, all corners or edges may have to be bends rather than right-angled edges. There may be also be a limit on how sharp a bend can be or how much curvature can be applied to a surface. These aspects of the design result by necessity from the nature of the material used and the methods and principles underlying how articles can be made using aluminium.

So,

- perhaps the effect of the exception will be to ensure that features in articles which result from the method or principle employed in construction will not be afforded design right protection

Possible design right protection for circuit diagrams It is possible that, for the first time, electronic circuit diagrams may be protectable. Electronic circuit designs have been difficult to protect despite the time the designs can take to develop. This is because they simply show schematically the relative arrangement and connections of electronic components making up the circuit. They do not show the exact layout and arrangement of components on a specific finished article such as a printed circuit board ('PCB') on which the electronic components are assembled.

It is possible that exactly the same electronic circuit can be implemented in many different ways on a PCB, each PCB design differing in the positions of the components and of the tracks printed on the board to connect the components. So, despite the circuit design being usually the principal aspect of the design of a PCB, unless patent protection had been obtained for the inventive aspects of the circuit design, others could copy the circuit by producing their own PCB layout without infringing any rights.

The PCB design itself was protectable under the old copyright law but not the underlying electronic circuit diagram.

A drawing of a PCB was protectable by copyright as an artistic work under the pre August 1989 law. It was an infringement to make a reproduction of the drawing in three or two dimensions.

However, a circuit diagram often looks quite unlike the finished assembled PCB. The circuit diagram does not show the positions of components on a PCB but only what the components are and their relative connections. The only similarity between the diagram and the PCB is often in the components used and their relative connections (i.e., the topological aspects).

Under the new law it is arguable whether a circuit diagram should be treated as part of the 'design' of the PCB for design right purposes. Design right protects designs but is limited to designs of *aspects* of shape or *configuration*.

If in the definition of 'design'

- the 'configuration' can mean the topological arrangement of components and
- 'aspect' is construed in the sense of being something that has a bearing on the configuration

then

- the aspect of design in the form of the circuit diagram showing the relative connections of components might be protectable

There could be arguments about whether the circuit diagram is the method or principle of construction and about whether each feature of the diagram is an integral feature of the whole design or even that every feature is wholly functional and therefore not protectable.

Summary of design right protection

- design right applies to designs of three-dimensional features of articles
- it seems two-dimensional features are not covered, but
  - surface decoration is expressly excluded
  - it may be possible that non-decorative two-dimensional aspects of designs may be covered by design right
- features of design which enable an article to fit with another article to perform a function are not covered
- nor are features which enable an article to fit with other articles as integral parts
- features consequent upon a principle or method of construction of an article may also not be covered

Additionally,

- two-dimensional decorative aspects can be protected by copyright or by registered design right
- the three-dimensional aspects of designs which are not protectable can be freely copied, but care should be taken when doing so

Registered designs protection for products

Most people can cope with the distinction between artistic works under copyright and designs protectable by design right. When the further concept of registered designs is introduced confusion can arise. Remember that

- registered design protection is only available for designs which are attractive; those which 'appeal to the eye'

Protection for registrable designs is, unlike the other rights protecting form and appearance, not automatic. The design must be registered at the Designs Registry. The legislation governing registered designs is the Registered Designs Act 1949 ('RDA 49') as amended by the 88 Act.

What designs are registrable? In respect of applications for registration made on and after 1 August 1989 a registrable design is defined by RDA 49, s. 1(1) as amended, as

- features
- of shape, configuration, pattern or ornament
- applied to an article
- by any industrial process,
- being features which in the finished article appeal to and are judged by the eye

Before 1 August 1989, the definition was expressed in a slightly different way but the changes should not make any practical difference to the way the law operates.

Designs of articles Note that what is registered is a design in relation to a *specified article or specified articles.* For example, the design of the shape of a motor car may be registered as a design for cars. If someone makes chocolates in the shape of the motor car, the registration of the design for motor cars will not operate to prevent this being done (but it may be an infringement of design right or copyright).

- in order to cover any kind of article to which the design might be applied, it should be registered for all of them
- if it is not, the rights will not be infringed by applying the design to an article not specified in the registration.

Spare parts A design for part of an article can be registrable because 'article' is defined as including any part of an article if the part is made and sold separately (RDA 49, s. 44). Thus, features of designs of spare parts can be registrable in their own right.

Sets of articles A design to be applied to a set of articles can also be registered (RDA 49, s. 1(2)). This covers designs of different items which are supplied in sets with substantially the same pattern applied to each of the articles. Tea services, sets of crockery and cutlery are covered by this. Another example is where the same design is applied to separate units of a hi-fi system, so that all the units have common features of design so that they are clearly part of a matching range.

Shape and configuration Registrable designs include two and three-dimensional aspects of design. However, some kinds of two-dimensional designs are not registrable. By r. 26 of the Registered Designs Rules 1989, copyright protection must be relied on for the following, no matter how attractive they may seem:

- wall plaques, medals and medallions;

- printed matter primarily of a literary or artistic character, including book jackets, calendars, certificates, coupons, dress making patterns, greetings cards, labels, leaflets, maps, plans, playing-cards, postcards, stamps, trade advertisements, trade forms and cards, transfers

- *and similar articles*

Design not registrable if appearance is not material For applications for registration made on and after 1 August 1989, if the appearance of an article is not 'material' its design is not registrable. All this means is that designs of kitchen utensils are always likely to be registrable whereas motor-car exhaust systems or oilfield valves are not. Appearance is normally irrelevant to the decision to use or buy exhaust systems and oilfield valves but relevant in relation to the kitchen utensils.

The rule was probably the same under the law before 1 August 1989.

Principles or methods of construction excluded Like a design for design right purposes, principles or methods of construction do not qualify for registered design protection.

Integral features are excluded The integral features exception (explained on page 000) applies to applications for registration made on and after 1 August 1989 but not to those made before that date (88 Act, s. 265(2)).

Features dictated by function excluded Unlike designs under the design right, there is no functional combination exception. Instead features which are solely dictated by the function an article has to perform are not protectable (RDA 49, s. 1(3), and RDA 49, s. 1(1)(b)(i) as amended by the 88 Act).

It seems that

- even if the designer tries to incorporate features of good design, if the features are intended solely to make the article work they are not registrable designs

Summary

● both two and three-dimensional aesthetic features of an article are registrable

● unless aesthetic features of the article as a whole are not normally taken into account by people who use or buy that kind of article

● features consequent upon a method or principle of construction are never protectable by registration,

● nor are features where the appearance is dictated solely by the function the article concerned has to perform,

● nor (for applications for registration on and after 1 August 1989) where the features depend upon the appearance of another article

Semiconductor chip design protection

The designs of semiconductor chips have their very own legal protection. Initially this protection was introduced under the Semiconductor Products (Protection of Topography) Regulations 1987 (the 'Old Chip Regulations'). These regulations applied to semiconductor chip designs created on and after 7 November 1987.

The Old Chip Regulations have now been superseded by the Design Right (Semiconductor Topographies) Regulations 1989 (the 'New Chip Regulations'). The New Chip Regulations protect the topography of semiconductor chip designs by including them in design right protection.

Form not function is protected   It is important to be clear from the outset that

● the Old and New Chip Regulations are not intended to prevent anyone making a chip which performs the same *function* as another chip

There is plenty of scope for patent law to give protection to inventions featured in the design of a chip, including chips which are functionally inventive.

● the New Chip Regulations and the Old Chip Regulations protect the design of the *topography* of the semiconductor chip against copying.

Again, this is another aspect of the protection of *form*.

When the design was made may affect its protection   The New Chip Regulations apply to all semiconductor chip designs created on or after 7 November 1987 and the Old Chip Regulations are revoked. Chip designs created on and after 7 November 1987 and before 1 August 1989 may be protectable by copyright but only in part. Chip designs created before 7 November 1987 (before the Old Chip Regulations took effect) may be protectable by copyright under the 56 Act.

What is protectable about semiconductor chip designs?   The New Chip Regulations protect the 'topography' of a 'semiconductor product'.
According to New Chip Regulations, reg. 2 a semiconductor product is:

- an article
- which performs an electronic function
- consisting of layers
- at least one layer must be a semiconducting material
- at least one of the layers must have a pattern
- the pattern must relate to the electronic function of the chip

What is a semiconductor topography? 'Semiconductor topography' means a design as defined under s. 213(2) of the 88 Act. However, the New Chip Regulations specify what aspects of design are covered. Each or any combination of three aspects of semiconductor chip design are protectable:

- the pattern of a layer of the end-product
- the pattern of a layer which is an intermediate pattern created during the course of manufacture — this includes the design of each of the photographic masks
- the arrangement of the layers in relation to each other

IS IT A COPY OF SOMETHING ELSE?

In recognising what can be protected there is one concept which must be firmly understood as it is of vital importance to the whole scheme and rationale of protection for form and appearance.

It is fundamental to the whole concept of copyright protection that a work which is a copy of another work is not protectable.

Copright works

Literary, dramatic, musical and artistic works   The 88 Act expressly requires literary, dramatic, musical and artistic works to be 'original' (88 Act, s. 1(1)(a). The position was the same under the 56 Act (ss. 2 and 3).

- originality does not mean the works have to be inventive

The classic statement of the law is by Petersen J in the *University of London Press Ltd* v *University Tutorial Press Ltd* [1916] 2 Ch 601 (emphasis added)

The word 'original' does not . . . mean that the work must be the expression of original or inventive thought. Copyright Acts are not concerned with the originality of *ideas,* but with the *expression of thought* . . . in print or writing. . . . But *the Act does not require that the expression must be in an original or novel form,* but that *the work must* . . . *originate from the author.*

Thus, two people can create very similar works. Provided they have not copied from each other or from a third party, each may have produced original works for copyright purposes. In essence,

- what is being protected is the skill, effort and judgment expended by the author in creating a work

Not all works are totally original. Many are not. However,

- to the extent they are not copied they may qualify as original

Example A telephone directory is a compilation of names, addresses and telephone numbers. The telephone company did not devise all the names and addresses. Each one was copied from the name and address given orally or in writing by the subscriber. However, the telephone company expended effort, skill (albeit not a high level of skill in that many people have the skill of being literate) and judgment in compiling the list in alphabetical order. The telephone company has added something that makes what it has produced the result of its efforts. Thus, to the extent that the directory is not copied it may be protected as an original work.

A photograph of a photograph A photograph of a photograph is a good example of a potentially original copyright work.

- to the extent that one photograph is a copy of another it is not original

Consider the position where skill, effort and judgment have been employed so that the second photograph is not an exact copy. The second photographer may have selected various photographic filters and lighting to produce effects in the second photograph that did not exist in the first photograph. A particular kind of photographic film may also have been selected and the aperture and period of exposure selected. As a result

- the second photograph may have features which give it its specific individuality over and above the features of the first photograph from which it has been copied

The extent to which a work is original is relative. The measure of originality can be thought of as

- the extent to which the author has expended skill, judgment and effort in producing it

Originality and substantiality The question of infringement is judged in relation to whether a substantial part of a work has been copied. Substantiality is judged in terms of quantity and quality. If very little in terms of quantity has been copied there can still be infringement if what has been copied is of high quality and

- this can be judged in terms of the amount of skill judgement and effort expended in creating what has been copied

In one case an outline picture of a hand holding a pencil in the act of marking a ballot paper was considered of low originality so that only making an exact copy would have been considered infringement.

Showing something is original   The need to prove a work is original can apply both to someone who wishes to prove a work is protected by copyright and to someone who is accused of infringement. If it is possible to show the alleged infringing work is wholly original in itself then there can be no prospect of an infringement action succeeding.

To an extent everything people create is copied in one way or another from the stock of knowledge and skill each person has built up over his or her lifetime. Take a mundane example. A design draftsman may choose to fix two pieces of metal together using a drilled hole and bolt. This is a common method of fixing things which has been used for many years. The designer may carry out calculations to assess a suitable bolt diameter, thread size and length as well as calculating the depth of hole and length of thread required. The bolt eventually selected will usually be selected from standard bolt sizes with standard threads.

Certainly, some aspects of the design can hardly be considered original. So what has the designer done that could be original from the copyright perspective?

First, the metal pieces could have been joined in other ways. They could have been welded, riveted, clamped or held together with a nut and bolt instead of a bolt and tapped hole. The position of the bolt could possibly have been placed elsewhere or several bolts of lesser strength could have been used. Perhaps there was a choice over thread sizes and there could be other aspects where choices were available.

- the designer has exercised judgment and skill in making the choices

Thus, in part what has been designed is

- copied from prior knowledge and
- to an extent skill, judgment and effort have been expended in selecting the final design

Originality, subconscious copying and reverse engineering   Associated with the concept of originality is the concept of subconscious copying. This more often arises in relation to infringement, especially in relation to music copyright infringement cases. In music cases, where there are significant similarities between two pieces of music, it is sometimes alleged that the composer must at some time during his or her lifetime have heard an earlier piece and inadvertently copied it in producing a later composition.

- the concept of subconscious copying is a dangerous one in the realms of reverse engineering.

When a manufacturer produces a new product it is the natural thing for a competitor to obtain an example. The competitor may 'reverse engineer' by taking the product apart and examining it in detail to see what is new and whether any of the features need to be incorporated into its own competing product.

If the competitor's design team have seen the product that has been taken apart (and usually the design team will have had a hand in taking it apart) then it may prove extremely difficult for them to forget the form of what they have seen when designing or redesigning their competing product. There is a risk that they may inadvertently have their own design choices influenced by what they have seen. This may raise the inference of copying. Additionally, the ordinary designer probably does not realise that what he or she is doing amounts to unlawful copying.

It is possible to 'reverse engineer' and be able to show that the competing design has been produced without copying. However, because of the dangers of having an immediate injunction granted to prevent manufacture and sale, when the new product is launched this is not a course that should be embarked upon without taking and following expert legal advice during all stages of design and development and carefully documenting the design and development process.

Important aspects of proving originality

- proof of originality can be by oral evidence of those involved

- it is far safer to document the creation of a work

- the documentation may be evidence of originality but if there are legal proceedings and originality is in dispute, oral evidence of witnesses will usually be essential

- the records of the design process are frequently vital in assisting the authors in giving evidence to recall what was done in creating a work

Typographical arrangements of published editions   The 88 Act expressly provides that the typographical arrangement of a published edition is not protected by copyright *to the extent that* it reproduces the typographical arrangement of a previous edition.

The literary work itself does not have to be original, merely the typographical arrangement.

Sound recordings and films   The 88 Act expressly provides that to the extent that a sound recording or film is a copy taken from a previous sound recording or film respectively neither will be protected by copyright (88 Act, s. 5(2)). It will be interesting to see what attitude the courts may take to digital remastering of old sound recordings which are out of copyright and also to 'colourised' black and white films which are out of copyright. There may be a reluctance to treat the remastered recording or colourised film as a separate new work with copyright protection.

Broadcasts and cable programmes   The 88 Act, specifically provides that *to the extent that* broadcasts and cable programmes infringe copyright in another broadcast or cable programme the broadcasts and cable programmes are not protected by copyright (88 Act, s. 6(6) and 7(6)(a)). This is different to the position for sound recordings and films.

A cable programme or a broadcast which is a *reproduction* (e.g., a repeat broadcast or transmission) of a previous cable programme or broadcast can be protected by copyright. It only fails to obtain protection if it *infringes* copyright. This ensures that repeat broadcasts and cable programmes are still protected by copyright in their own right even if they are exactly the same as a previous broadcast.

Performances

As a performance may, by its very nature, be repeated by the performer, a repeat performance is protected no matter how many times it is repeated.

Designs of products

Copyright   The same requirement of originality applies to designs protected by copyright as discussed on page 117. If an artistic work like a design drawing is not original then copies of it are not protected.

Design right   Only original designs can be protected by design right (88 Act, s. 213(1)). The term 'original' is likely to have the same meaning as for copyright works. However, the 88 Act, s. 213(4), specifies that a design is not original

- if it is commonplace in the design field in question

In other words, designers in any field of design may use, as standard practice, certain features of design, i.e., they all 'copy' from a common stock of design knowledge, but to the extent they exercise skill, judgment and effort their designs may still be protected. However, the courts may make a broader use of the express exclusion of 'commonplace' features to reduce the scope of design right protection.

The term 'design' does not necessarily refer to a design for an entire object. 'Design' is defined as

- *any aspect*
- of shape or configuration of. . . . an article

This means that

- only the parts of an article which have a commonplace design are not protected.

The rest of the article will be protected to the extent that the design of the shape or configuration is not commonplace.

Registered designs   For a design to be registrable it must be new. This is different both from copyright protection and design right protection.

The concept of 'new' does not mean a design must be novel or inventive. It simply means that

- the features claimed to be new when taken together have never before been the subject of a previous application for registration or previously published in the United Kingdom

To publish a design does not mean making an example embodying the design available to the public

● it is enough to describe the design in any way in a document

Even if

● only one copy of a description of the design is put somewhere in the United Kingdom

● where even only one member of the public might freely obtain access to it

that can be sufficient publication to make the design not 'new'.

● it is important therefore to keep anything which might be the subject of a registered design application absolutely secret

Only publication in the United Kingdom will affect whether a design can be registered. Foreign publication is irrelevant.

A 'design' can have existed for many years and still be 'new' (RDA 49, s. 6(4)). An example from one case is a representation of Westminster Abbey applied to a spoon which had been copied from a photograph (*Saunders* v *Wiel* (1893) 10 RPC 29). The trigger which makes a design not new for the purposes of registration is that

● the idea of applying it to an article is published

Prior publication of the photograph of Westminster Abbey would not affect the application for registration of the design applied to the spoon if there was no suggestion that it should be applied to any article.

Semiconductor chip designs

The same requirement as to originality applies to semiconductor chips as to design right.

THE RIGHTS PROTECTING FORM AND APPEARANCE

Introduction

This section will be looking at the legal rights available for protecting form and appearance and what they cover. Four main areas will be considered, for each area of law

● what the rights are
● what is infringement
● what is not infringement
● what criminal law offences apply

The rights protect more than straight copying
The rights protecting form and appearance go much further than controlling copying. The general approach of the law running through all of the intellectual property rights protecting form and appearance is that

- there are the basic acts which are the exclusive right of the rights owner and amount to primary infringement

Then there is what is called secondary infringement. In simple terms

- secondary infringement covers things done with infringing copies like commercially dealing in infringing copies, i.e., the primary infringement has been committed and hence the infringing copies already exist

For copyright there is a new and perhaps unexpected concept of tertiary infringement

- tertiary infringement covers things done which are not primary or secondary infringement but which help someone else commit the primary or secondary infringement.

There are also rights called moral rights

- moral rights give the author of a copyright work and, in a few instances, other people, control over what is done with a copyright work

The rights apply even though those people do not own any copyrights in the work concerned. The moral rights can be important for anyone purchasing a copyright or buying a permission (a licence) under copyright. This is because the moral rights can limit or affect what can lawfully be done with the copyright work.

Knowledge and liability
For secondary and tertiary infringements and also for the criminal provisions it is usually a precondition of liability that

- the infringer or offender must have had knowledge or a reasonable belief that what was done related to infringement

This is not a requirement for primary infringement.

Although the question of knowledge or reasonable belief will not be dealt with in detail, it should be remembered that marking products and other protected material with notices warning that they are protected may be sufficient.

Additionally, a warning letter sent by a rights owner to an alleged infringer might be sufficient to give the infringer the requisite knowledge or belief. This can be so even if the infringer claims later that he or she did not believe the person concerned was entitled to the rights or that the material concerned was protected or protectable.

The concept of substantial reproduction
It will be seen that there is a common concept of substantiality running through all of the rights protecting form and appearance. This is a fundamental concept which needs to be understood.

The rights and what amounts to infringement apply not just to the entire work or other matter covered by the rights but also to a 'substantial part' of it. The concept of substantiality covers both quantity and quality. If, say, a copyright work is extremely simple or not of particularly high quality, then a substantial part might be nothing less than the whole work. However, for a work of high quality, committing a potential infringement in relation to just a small part of the work might still be infringement because the part concerned was substantial in terms of quality.

Regulation of general licensing schemes
There are provisions concerning general licensing schemes run by private organisations like the Performing Rights Society ('PRS'), Phonographic Performance Ltd ('PPL') and the Copyright Licensing Agency Ltd ('CLA'). These organisations represent various categories of authors who are their members and administer certain aspects of intellectual property rights protecting form and appearance in order to ensure their members obtain remuneration under the rights. The organisations give permission (grant licences) to anyone who wants it, subject to a fee, to do some things that would otherwise be infringement.

- the PRS regulates rights in music to perform the music in public places like night-clubs, public houses and theatres
- PPL regulates rights in recordings to perform the recordings in public places
- CLA regulates rights in published literary works like books for purposes like photocopying

There are other similar organisations and there could be new schemes set up in future.

Under the 88 Act, a statutory body called the Copyright Tribunal can review the operation of general licensing schemes. The powers and terms of reference are broad and cover a wide variety of things like the terms on which licences are granted, the amounts to be paid for the licences and whether someone has wrongfully been refused a licence.

Trading standards and other laws   There may be other laws which can be equally or more effective in dealing with infringements in the form of counterfeit products. A counterfeit product is usually an exact copy right down to the packaging and product name and manufacturer's name.

Laws concerning things like applying a false or misleading trade decription might be used where such a copy of a product is put on the market by an infringer. Additionally, trading standards departments of local authorities have a good record in dealing with this area of the law and can be effective and efficient in prosecuting. Where a case is taken up by a trading standards department this can take a great deal of the burden of pursuing infringement from the injured party.

The copyrights

The basic copyrights
There are several basic activities that copyright gives the copyright owner the exclusive right to do in relation to a copyright work. It is at this stage that the

distinctions between the different activities that the non-lawyer might generally describe as copying start to appear.

First,

- copyright covers copying.

But it also includes

- the exclusive right to put copies of a copyright work into circulation for the first time
- performing or showing or playing a copyright work in public
- broadcasting a copyright work or including it in a cable programme service
- renting films, sound recordings and computer programs to the public
- adapting a copyright work
- doing any of the above in relation to an adaptation

Each of these copyrights is separate from and independent of the others. Any one of the copyrights can be bought and sold independently of the others. Additionally, if a copyright licence under one of the copyrights is obtained but what is done infringes another copyright then this is still infringement despite the existence of the licence.

What is 'copying'? In copyright law the concept of copying is narrower than 'copying' in everyday speech. In simple terms

- copying means copying the form or appearance of a copyright work

It has little to do with copying general ideas, themes or concepts. For example, the sparkling French spring water, Perrier has had a long-running advertising campaign centred around the French word for water, '*eau*'. The word 'eau' sounds like 'oh' in English and the advertising campaign has used this phonetic equivalence in a variety of ways. For example, one slogan was 'the mineral water greaus up'.

A cheeky competitor took advantage of the association that had been developed between the Perrier drink and the French word '*eau*' and advertised their mineral water based drink, Piermont, with the slogan 'Anything else is just seau, seau'. As far as copyright law is concerned this type of thing is not copying.

But I only copied a little bit Another aspect of copying which people often do not understand is that it can still be copying even if only part of a copyright work is copied. It also does not matter if the copying is not exact. It is enough if a *substantial part* of a copyright work is copied. One person may copy a painting and try to make the copy look different. If there is sufficient *objective similarity* between the two pictures copying may be considered to have occurred in the copyright sense.

Thus, there are two concepts to grapple with in relation to what copying is

- what is 'objective similarity' and

● how to assess what a 'substantial part' of a copyright work is

Copying and objective similarity Where a copyright work and something alleged to be a copy are identical in every respect the question of whether one is objectively similar to the other can be quite simple where a visual comparison is possible. Where the copyright work and the alleged copy are not identical the question of the extent to which the copyright work and the alleged copy are similar arises.

It may prove necessary to make a list of similarities and differences. This can be particularly necessary where a straight visual comparison is not that easy as in the case of a computer program.

However,

● just because there are objective similarities does not necessarily mean there has been copying

Some similarities may have more to do with ideas than with form and appearance. For example, if one painter includes a cottage as a feature in a picture, there can be no complaint if someone else uses the idea by including a quite different looking cottage in another picture. Even if the cottages look identical, this may not be the result of copying. It may be that the two artists just happened to paint the same scene from the same spot on similar sunny days. Even if they do this shoulder to shoulder on the same day, provided they do not copy each other's painting, there is no copying in the copyright sense. Indeed

● too often people infer copying has taken place where there are objective similarities without considering reasonable explanations about why the similarities exist

However, things start to get suspicious when the explanations for the similarities are a little thin. It is highly unlikely that two artists painting the same scene on different days would paint the same numbers of clouds in the substantially the same positions having substantially the same shape for example.

The question of whether copying has taken place is a matter for the court to decide on the basis of the evidence presented. If the explanation of a witness about why there are particular objective similarities sounds implausible then the judge may not accept the witness's evidence as being accurate. It may be the judge will decide all or many of the objective similarities arose from copying.

A substantial part Despite what some people may tell you about it being legitimate to photocopy 5, 10 or 15 per cent of something like a book

● there are no fixed legal rules that say how much of something like a book or an article can be copied without infringing copyright
● the question of substantiality is a question both of quality and amount

If a great deal of skill, judgment and effort has been invested in creating a copyright work it may be considered a work of high quality in which case copying just a little of it might still amount to infringement because the quality of what is taken is high.

On the other hand it may be that only a copy of the whole work is a copy of a substantial part and possibly the copy may have to be almost exact. This may be the case where the work is considered to be very simple or of low quality.

Transient or incidental copies Copying includes making copies which are transient or incidental to some other use of a copyright work (88 Act, s. 17(6)). This can mean that

- using a computer program can infringe copyright

This is because parts or even all of the program are temporarily copied into the computer's electronic memory when the program is used on the computer.

In the realm of electronic publishing, if information is made available in electronic form then

- even displaying words on a computer terminal screen can be copying

This is because the words on the screen are a transient copy of the information stored on the magnetic disk, tape, optical disc or whatever other means of storage is used.

Issuing copies of a work to the public

- only the copyright owner or someone with the copyright owner's permission has the right to issue copies of a copyright work to the public
- once the copies have been put into circulation by the copyright owner or with permission then anyone can buy and sell the copies, and deal with them in any way

There are two exceptions to this

- importation
- rental

Rental right — sound recordings, films and computer programs

- sound recordings, films, and computer programs cannot be rented to the public without the copyright owner's permission

This applies even if the copies have previously been put into circulation by or with the copyright owner's permission. However,

- the new rental right does not apply to copies of films, sound recordings and computer programs acquired before 1 August 1989

This is provided they were acquired for the purpose of renting them to the public (88 Act, sch. 1, para 14(2)). This means that existing rental businesses will not be committing copyright infringement in relation to their stocks acquired prior to 1 August 1989.

ce in public   Performance is an area where the potential complexity
raction of different copyrights starts to become apparent.
yright owner has the exclusive right under s. 19(1) of the 88 Act

- to perform or
- permit others to perform a copyright work
- in public

The corresponding right for copyright works like a sound recording, film,
broadcast or cable programme is the exclusive right under s. 19(3)

- to play or show the work in public

Do not confuse the copyright owner's rights relating to

- the right to *perform* a literary, dramatic or musical work in public

with

- the *personal* rights given to *performers in their performances*

These rights are totally independent of each other. For example, a performer
could recite a poem. The performer needs permission from the owner of the
copyright in the poem to recite (perform) the copyright work (poem) in public.
The performer's rights to control the making of a recording of the performance
are totally separate. The performer could give someone permission to record
the recitation. That person would not be infringing the *performer's rights*.
However, if the permission of the owner of the literary *copyright in the poem*
has not also been obtained, the making of a sound recording could infringe the
literary copyright even though the performer's permission to record has been
obtained.

A performance in this context includes

- lectures, addresses, speeches and sermons

It also includes

- any visual or acoustic means of presenting literary, dramatic and musical
  works

This means that putting a television set in a public place so that the public
can watch a performance of a musical work can be infringement of the
performing copyright in the *musical work*. The same applies to recitations or
performances of literary, dramatic and musical works recorded in sound
recordings and films. Showing the film or playing the sound recording in public
could infringe performing copyright in the literary, dramatic or musical work.

Broadcasting and inclusion of copyright works in cable programmes   The owner
of copyright in some kinds of works has the exclusive right to broadcast or
include the works in cable programmes. The right also includes the exclusive
right to give others permission to do so, (88 Act, s. 20). The copyright works
covered by this right are

- literary, dramatic, musical and artistic works,

- sound recordings, films and even other broadcasts and cable programmes

Take the example of a photograph or sculpture. Either of these can qualify as artistic works. Hence, if the photograph or sculpture is broadcast on television this could be an infringement of copyright if done without the copyright owner's consent (subject to exceptions – see p. 135).

Making adaptations of copyright works   The copyright owner has the exclusive right under s. 21 of the 88 Act

- to make and permit others to make adaptations of literary, dramatic and musical works

Just because the adaptation copyright is limited to literary, dramatic and musical works do not think it is permissible to tinker with other kinds of copyright works. Remember that it can still be infringement to copy a substantial part of other copyright works so if an adaptation of a sculpture, film, sound recording or broadcast, for example, reproduces a substantial part of a copyright work there can still be infringement by copying regardless of whether there can be infringement by adapation.

It is also the copyright owner's exclusive right under s. 21(2)

- to control what is done to an adaptation of a copyright work

This means that

- if permission is given to adapt a copyright work once, further permission is required to make an adaptation of the first adaptation and so on

The right to control what is done to an adaptation of a literary, dramatic or musical work applies to all of the basic copyrights such as

- copying an adaptation,
- issuing copies of an adaptation to the public,
- performing an adaptation in public,
- playing or showing an adaptation in public and
- broadcasting or including the adaptation in a cable programme service

An adaptation is made when it is recorded in writing or otherwise (88 Act, s. 21(1)). An adaptation could be made, for example, simply by making an ad lib parody of the lyrics of a song (a literary work) and recording the parody on film or in a sound recording.

However, it is immaterial whether an adaptation has been recorded in writing or otherwise when it is copied, or copies of the adaptation issued to the public, or it is performed or played or shown in public or broadcast or included in a cable programme service. Although perhaps circumstances may arise in future where this rule might have unexpected results, it is not as complicated as it first seems. For example, an adaptation of a literary, dramatic or musical work could be made by a performer perhaps by improvising on a piano, or by singing or by reciting a literary work. This kind of adaptation may not be recorded when it is made but it could still amount to an infringement because it could be a *performance in public* of *an adaptation* of a copyright work. Thus, the performer, even if he or she has the right to perform the unadapted work, can infringe copyright by creating an unauthorised adaptation by improvisation. If the performance is recorded then there is a further infringement by copying a substantial part of an adaptation.

Types of adaptations   By s. 21(3)(a)(i) of the 88 Act

● translation of a literary or dramatic work is an adaptation

So if the script of a play (dramatic work and literary work) written in the Hindi language is translated into Urdu that is a translation and therefore an adaptation. If the Hindi version is translated into English then that is an adaptation of an adaptation.

The translator of the play is the author of the translation as an original copyright work. This is because although to a certain extent the translation is copied from the first version of the play, skill, judgment and effort have been expended in creating the translation. The translator has added something which is original in copyright terms.

It is also an adaptation to make a dramatic work into a non-dramatic work and vice versa (88 Act, s. 21(3)(a)(ii)). This means that if the Hindi play is converted into a novel this is an adaptation. Likewise if the Hindi play was based on a novel then the play is an adaptation of the novel.

It can also be an adaptation of a literary or dramatic work to convert the work into a version in which the story or action is conveyed wholly or mainly in pictures. This is provided the pictorial version is suitable for reproduction in a book, newspaper, magazine or similar periodical (88 Act, s. 21(3)(a)(iii)). So, converting plays and novels or any other kind of literary or dramatic work into a kind of 'comic strip' presentation can amount to adaptation.

An arrangement or transcription of a musical work is an adaptation (88 Act, s. 21(3)(b)). For traditional musical scores this is quite straightforward. For some of the things done with modern electronic technology, such as synthesisers and digital sampling equipment, the implications are interesting.

For a computer program, a 'translation' includes a version of the program which is converted into or out of a computer language or code or into a different computer language or code (88 Act, s. 21(4)). This means that converting a computer program from the FORTRAN programming language into BASIC is an adaptation. It can also be an adaptation to compile or decompile or assemble or disassemble a computer program.

The only time converting a computer program does not amount to adaptation is when this happens incidentally whilst running the program itself. This is only fair as it could otherwise mean that using a program for its intended purpose could amount infringement by adaptation.

Copy-protection   There is a special right newly created for works supplied in electronic form like computer programs (88 Act, s. 296). The right applies where the copyright work in question is supplied in a form in which it is 'copy-protected'

- copy-protection does not only mean a form of protection which makes copying difficult or impossible without special equipment

It includes

- protection under which copies can be made but the copy is not useable or it is impaired or its quality is affected (88 Act, s. 296(4))
- the right is not limited to computer programs but can also apply to things like compact discs and pre-recorded tapes which are designed not to be copied

In the computer industry it has been common in the past for programs supplied for personal computers to have various methods of preventing the user from making extra copies. Sometimes, using special software like bit copying programs or other devices, people make extra copies of a program to supply to friends or colleagues at work or to use on more than one machine instead of buying extra copies

- the new special right is given to the person who issues the copies of a copy-protected work to the public
- the right is not given to the copyright owner (unless the copyright owner is the same person of course)

Thus, the proprietors of ordinary high street retail outlets, for example, might be able to use the right. They issue copies of the work to the public. However, in practice the cooperation of the copyright owner may be required in order to prove the existence of copyright.

The supplier of the copy-protected work is given the same rights as the copyright owner. However,

- these rights only apply against someone who supplies any device designed or adapted to circumvent the form of copy-protection used to protect the work

More specifically the rights apply against

- anyone who makes, imports, sells, hires or offers or exposes for sale or hire any such device

This might operate to outlaw hi-fi systems which have a compact disc player and the more conventional tape-recording facilities which can be used to record from compact discs. It may depend upon how broadly the courts interpret the words '*specifically designed or adapted* to circumvent the form of copy-protection employed'.

- the right also applies against anyone who publishes information intended to enable or assist people to circumvent the form of copy-protection employed

In other words one example of someone who can be liable is any person who advertises special software or hardware in personal computer magazines for copying copy-protected software. Someone who publishes articles explaining how to circumvent copy-protection can also be liable.

There is a similar kind of right given to someone who charges for the reception of programmes included in broadcasts or cable programme services and also there is a right given to someone who makes encrypted transmissions of any kind (88 Act, s. 298).

Secondary infringement
Once the basic copyrights and infringements are identified there are a host of acts which, if done in relation to an infringing copy, amount to secondary infringement. For the secondary infringer to be liable for secondary infringement

● some form of knowledge or reasonable belief on the infringer's part that infringement is likely to be committed is required

The following is a rundown of secondary infringements.

(a) Importation into the UK of infringing copies of a work can be infringement if it is otherwise than for private and domestic use (88 Act, s. 22).

An article made abroad can be an infringing article even if it was made with the permission of the owner of copyright (88 Act, s. 27(3)). This may seem peculiar but it is quite logical. The copyright owner may give someone permission under copyright to make copies of a copyright work but the permission is limited to a particular country. Making copies of the work in the country concerned will not infringe copyright. However, it would make nonsense of the limited permission if copies could be made in the country concerned and then imported into the UK.

Thus, an article can be an infringing copy if it has been or is proposed to be imported into the UK.

(b) Possessing and commercially dealing in infringing copies of a copyright work can be infringement of copyright (88 Act, s. 23).
(c) Making or importing or possessing in business anything designed or adapted for making copies of a copyright work can be infringement (88 Act, s. 24). This also applies to selling or hiring such a thing or offering such a thing for sale or hire.
(d) Transmitting a copyright work on a telecommunications system can in certain circumstances amount to infringement (88 Act, s. 24).

Tertiary infringement
There are several ways people who do not commit a primary or secondary infringement can be liable for infringement committed by someone else (88 Act s. 26). This applies where infringement is committed

● by public performance or
● by playing or showing a work in public

The main act of infringement must be committed by someone who *uses* apparatus

- for playing sound recordings or
- for showing films or
- for receiving broadcasts, or cable programmes or

where the main infringer uses some other apparatus

- for receiving visual images or sounds by electronic means

Once the main act of infringement has been committed

- the 88 Act also makes others liable for the main act of infringement even though they did not actually commit it

For example,

- the *supplier* of apparatus for playing or showing a work in public can be liable for the infringement committed by the person who actually plays or shows the work in public

Similarly,

- allowing the apparatus to be brought on to premises can make the occupier of the premises liable for the other person's infringement

Additionally,

- the supplier of a copy of a work used to infringe can make the person concerned liable for the infringement

In each case for the supplier or occupier to be liable he or she must have known or had reason to believe there was a likelihood of infringement (88 Act, s. 26).

What is not copyright infringement

There are lengthy and detailed provisions concerning what kinds of copying and other acts done in relation to copyright works are permissible for various activities such as for

- educational purposes
- libraries and archives
- various things done for public administration like copying for the purposes of judicial proceedings

These provisions will not be dealt with in this book. There are also what are known as the 'fair dealing' provisions concerning

- research and private study,
- criticism and review
- news reporting,

There are also special provisions concerning

- the incidental inclusion of copyright works in artistic works, sound recordings, broadcasts and cable programmes
- recordings and records of comments, quotes and the spoken word generally for the purposes of journalism
- the use of typefaces

There are provisions concerning

- the transfer of copies of works in electronic form,
- rebuilding buildings,
- advertisements of artistic works for sale,
- home copying of broadcasts and cable programmes

Fair dealing   'Fair dealing' is not an infringement of copyright in literary, dramatic, musical and artistic works if the fair dealing is done

- for the purposes of research or private study (88 Act, s. 29(1))

The private study aspect of this provision is probably of no great importance. However, the research aspect is.

For example, a computer program is a literary work. The fair dealing provision could allow computer programs to be copied and adapted for the purposes of commercial or academic research. It is an area to take careful note of. If reverse engineering is dressed up to look like genuine research the courts are not likely to be impressed. At the same time, genuine research activities involving, in part, competitor's products and the results of the research might be lawfully used for the purposes of making competitive products. The dividing line can be a fine one.

Fair dealing with any copyright work for the purposes of criticism or review is not infringement

- provided it is accompanied by a sufficient acknowledgment (88 Act, s. 30)

An acknowledgment is not sufficient unless the copyright work is

- identified by its title or other description and
- the author is identified (88 Act, s. 178)

The author does not have to be identified if the work was published anonymously. Alternatively, if the work is unpublished and it is not possible to ascertain the identity of the author by reasonable enquiry then the author does not have to be identified either.

Fair dealing for the purpose of reporting current events does not infringe copyright (88 Act, s. 30(2)). If the reporting is by means of sound recordings, films, broadcasts or cable programmes then no acknowledgment is required. In any other case a sufficient acknowledgment is required.

The concept of fair dealing is somewhat difficult to pin down. It seems from what was said by Lord Denning MR in *Hubbard* v *Vosper* [1972] 2 QB 84 that fair dealing is a matter of fact and impression, to which factors that are relevant include the extent of the quotation and its proportion to comment (which may be justifiable although the quotation is of the whole work); whether the work is unpublished; and the extent to which the work has been circularised, although not published to the public.

It was not fair dealing for the purposes of research and private study to publish three different study texts with annotations for students. The texts reproduced quotations and extracts totalling respectively around 10 per cent of *The Loneliness of the Long-distance Runner* by Alan Sillitoe, 10 per cent of *Cider with Rosie* by Laurie Lee and 5 per cent of *St Joan* by George Bernard Shaw. The reason why this was not considered to be for the purposes of research or private study was that the authors of the annotated texts when creating them were not engaged in research or private study (*Sillitoe* v *McGraw-Hill Book Co. (UK) Ltd* [1983] FSR 545.

Other factors which have been considered by the courts are

● whether the potentially infringing work is competitive with the copied work and
● the quantity or value of what has been used

Incidental inclusion in films, broadcasts etc. By s. 31 of the 88 Act, the incidental inclusion of any copyright work in

● an artistic work (e.g., a photograph),
● sound recording, film, broadcast or cable programme

is not infringement.

If a camera crew goes to a private house to record an interview and just happens to film some works of art in the house incidentally during the interview then this is not infringement. Similarly if a photographer takes a photograph of an event and just happens to catch some copyright works in the picture this is not infringement.

If the filming of the interview or the taking of the photograph is not infringement then it is not an infringement

● to broadcast the interview or the photograph or
● to play or show it in public or
● include it in a cable programme service or
● to give or sell copies of the film or the photograph to the public

The same applies to any other artistic work, sound recording, film, broadcast or cable programme that incidentally includes a copyright work.

If the inclusion of the copyright work is not incidental but deliberate then the position would be different and there could be infringement. So do not think that this exception is a *carte blanche* to paint, photograph or film things 'incidentally on purpose'.

Additionally, the 88 Act makes clear that deliberately including certain kinds of copyright works 'incidentally' is not the sort of 'incidental' inclusion that is permissible. For example, if certain kinds of copyright works are included deliberately, like background music in a drama scene, then this is not incidental inclusion. The copyright works concerned are musical works and lyrics as well as sound recordings, broadcasts and cable programmes which include musical works and lyrics.

Home recording and time-shifting It is quite common for people who possess video recorders to record television programmes. The 88 Act recognises this as a fact of life and permits this type of recording in certain circumstances (88 Act, s. 70).

The recording can be of a

● broadcast or cable programme and

● must be made for private and domestic use

It must also be made for the purposes of viewing or listening at a more convenient time. Provided these conditions are met then no copyright infringement is committed by making the recording. It is interesting that, if a home-made copy is not an infringing copy then none of the 88 Act's provisions concerning dealing in infringing copies apply.

Typefaces It is not infringement of copyright in a typeface to use the typeface in the ordinary course of typing, composing text, typesetting or printing, even if whatever is used is an infringing copy. It is also not infringement to possess anything for such use or to do anything with material produced by such use (88 Act, s. 54.

Infringement in relation to typefaces is committed by making, importing or dealing in articles specifically designed or adapted for producing material in a particular typeface (88 Act, s. 54).

This means that making, importing or dealing in things like typewriters, any kind of computer printer or conventional type can be infringement if the typeface is infringing. However, the period of protection is limited to 25 years from the end of the calendar year of first marketing anywhere in the world by or with permission of the copyright owner. If the marketing occurred before 1 August 1989 then the period runs for 25 years from 1 August (88 Act, sch. 1, para. 14(5)).

Works in electronic form — computer programs and electronic publishing There is a special provision concerning second-hand copyright works sold in electronic form (88 Act, s. 56). The provision does not apply to works purchased before 1 August 1989 (88 Act, sch. 1, para. 14(6)).

The provision is meant to entitle the purchaser of the second-hand copy to copy and adapt the copyright work if the first purchaser was entitled to do so. In other words, if a work in electronic form like a computer program was bought by one person and then sold to someone else, the second purchaser might be entitled to copy and adapt the program if the first purchaser was entitled to do so.

The problem with this special provision is that it does not apply to computer programs which are licensed for use, i.e., where nothing is actually sold to the user. This is what normally happens in many large computer installations. The consequence is that

- when the computer is due to be sold it may not necessarily be permissible to transfer either the computer program or the licence governing its use

Additionally, the qualifications to the right can negate its effect. This can be the case where the copyright owner has imposed conditions on the transfer of the copy of the computer program or other work supplied in electronic form. Thus, from the copyright owner's point of view

- the informed copyright owner should ensure sufficient restrictions are imposed on the first purchaser to negate the effect of the new provision

Quotations of spoken words for reporting, broadcasting and cable programmes There is a special provision which permits what people say, for example, in interviews or indeed on any occasion, to be recorded, copied and reported, whether in the press or on television or similar services (88 Act, s. 58).

- this provision is highly important for journalists

There are conditions to be met for this provision to apply. The first is that

- the record must be a direct record of what was said

It must not be copied from another record or taken from a broadcast or cable programme.

- the person speaking must not have prohibited the making of a record of what was said

This means that, for example,

- recording comments given to the press 'off the record' can infringe copyright

Additionally, if the speaker gave permission for the record to be made but prohibited its use for reporting whether in the press or on television or in a cable programme, then it can be copyright infringement to do so. The record must also not infringe copyright in an existing copyright work. This could occur where a document is quoted by the speaker.

Buildings and public exhibitions By s. 62 of the 88 Act, it is not infringement of copyright to

- photograph,
- film,
- include in a broadcast or cable programme,
- paint or make some other kind of graphic work of
- certain kinds of artistic works

It is also not an infringement to issue copies of any such films, photographs or graphic works to the public. It is also not infringement to broadcast or include in a cable programme any such films, photographs or graphic works.

The copyright works covered by this exception are

- buildings
- sculptures,
- models for buildings and
- works of artistic craftsmanship

The provision only applies to the three latter kinds of copyright work where these are permanently situated in a public place or in premises open to the public.

- the provision does not cover other works of art like paintings and drawings or even murals.

It is therefore open to anyone to photograph buildings like the National Westminster Tower or the Lloyd's building in the City of London. The photographs can be sold. The same applies to *permanent* displays in museums and even the Henry Moore sculptures permanently situated in London's Hyde Park.

Note that

- this provision does not cover anything which is on temporary display

Public reading or recitation   By s. 59 of the 88 Act, it is not infringement of copyright in

- a *published* literary or dramatic work

for

- *one person*
- to read or recite a reasonable extract in public

Nor is it infringement

- to make a sound recording of the reading or recitation
- or to broadcast it
- or to include it in a cable programme service

This is all provided that

- the sound recording, broadcast or cable programme consists mainly of other material in relation to which it is not necessary to rely on this exception to avoid infringement

Moral rights

The 88 Act introduces some new rights which are called moral rights. Authors of literary, dramatic, musical and artistic works and directors of films obtain the moral rights

- to be identified as such and
- to object to derogatory treatment of the work

The rights also include a right, which existed under the 56 Act, for anyone

- to prevent any false assertion that he or she is the author of a literary, dramatic, musical or artistic work or director of a film

The above rights only apply

- to literary, dramatic, musical and artistic works and films
- where the work concerned is actually protected by copyright and

There is also

- a right to privacy for photographs or films
- made for private and domestic purposes

The right can operate to prevent publication, exhibition to the public and broadcast or inclusion in a cable programme service.

Right to be identified as author or director   Without going into the detail of the 88 Act, the times when the right to be identified as author or director apply are when the work or film or copies are

- commercially published
- performed, shown or exhibited in public
- broadcast or included in cable programme services
- issued to the public

In the case of buildings this can mean the inclusion of a plaque on it in a prominent place. In the case of other kinds of works the author or director must be identified in such a way that people are likely to notice it.

Derogatory treatment   By s. 80(2) of the 1988 Act, 'treatment' means any addition to or deletion from a work. However, it does not include

- translating a literary or dramatic work
- arranging or transcribing a musical work which only involves a change of key or register

'Derogatory treatment' means distorting or mutilating it or treating it in a way which is prejudicial to the honour or reputation of the author or director.

Moral rights cannot be bought and sold   The moral rights are personal to the person concerned. This means they cannot be bought and sold. Only the person concerned or the executors or personal representatives (in the event of death of the person concerned) can exercise and enforce the rights.

Although the rights cannot be bought and sold, the author, director or other person having moral rights can waive the rights.

The moral rights are wholly separate from all the other copyrights. This means that anyone who is not the author or a director or other person having moral rights and is the copyright owner or is licensed under copyright could be affected by the exercise of the moral rights. This means the moral rights cannot be ignored.

Computer programs and typefaces   The rights to be identified as author and to object to derogatory treatment do not apply to computer programs and computer-generated works (88 Act, ss. 79 and 81). As computer programs can have many authors during the course of development and are often adapted, improved and altered it would be somewhat inconvenient for any of the authors to be able to assert such rights.

The right to be identified as author does not apply to typefaces (88 Act, s. 79). Again, it would be somewhat inconvenient if, every time a newspaper is printed, the author of every typeface had to be identified.

Fair dealing   The rights to be identified as author and to object to derogatory treatment do not apply to some of the acts which the 88 Act, specifies do not amount to copyright infringement (88 Act, ss. 79 and 81). For example, some acts which amount to fair dealing will therefore also not be infringement of any moral rights.

The right to be identified as author must be asserted   From the author and director's point of view it is important to note that the right to be identified as author must be asserted. This can be achieved in several ways which will be outlined here.

One way to assert the moral rights is to do so in the document (an assignment) which is required to effect a sale of some or all copyrights (88 Act, s. 78).

This method of asserting the rights is effective only against

- the person buying the copyright,
- any subsequent purchaser and
- any licensee of any purchaser (even if the licensee does not know about the assertion of the right).

This method does not affect anyone else so, unlike the other copyrights,

- the moral rights may not apply against everyone.

In other words this method of assertion does not give the person having moral rights exclusivity against everyone in the UK.

Another way to assert the right is to

- give notice in writing under s. 78 of the 88 Act

This is effective against anyone who finds out about the assertion.

In relation to artistic works exhibited in public the right can be asserted under s. 78 of the 88 Act

- by ensuring a notice is put on the work before the author (or the first owner of copyright) hands it over to whoever is going to exhibit the work

If a copy of the work is to be exhibited then the same can be done with the copy which is to be exhibited.

- this method is effective against anyone who obtains the exhibited original or the exhibited copy
- even if the notice later falls off, wears off or becomes no longer visible

The right to be identified as author at a public exhibition of an artistic work can be asserted in another way. This method relates to a situation where the author or first owner of copyright gives permission for copies of the work to be made.

- if it is ensured that whoever gives the permission to exhibit a copy of the work includes a notice in the permission that the author asserts the moral right to be identified as author then this is sufficient
- this method is effective against anyone who obtains one of the authorised copies

The position before and after 1 August 1989   None of the 88 Act rules about moral rights apply to anything done before 1 August 1989.

Instead, only the previous 56 Act rules about falsely attributing authorship will apply (88 Act, sch. 1, para. 22). The rights also do not apply to certain copyright works made before 1 August 1989 or where the author of certain works died before that date. They also may not apply where copyright has been sold or licensed prior to 1 August 1989. The privacy right for photographs and films does not apply to those made before 1 August 1989.

Summary

- for anyone who obtains a copy of a copyright work or becomes the owner of copyright or obtains a copyright licensee should take note of the potential effects of the moral rights
- if there is any doubt about whether a right has been asserted or waived, ensure the author is always identified
  - this can be inconvenient for things like radio and television advertisements
- if the identity of the author (or director) is not known then this is a problem
- if there is going to be any prospect of needing to adapt or change a copyright work then it is important to ensure the author or director has not and will not assert the rights
- this could mean obtaining a signed waiver of the rights from the author or director

It would also be prudent

- to obtain contractually binding warranties, representations and guarantees from whoever is selling the copyright or a licence under copyright that the moral rights have been waived and
- to obtain the original written waiver

Criminal offences and copyright

There are several kinds of criminal offences associated with infringement of copyright. The penalties for committing a criminal offence can be steep

- the penalties include fines and imprisonment for up to two years

A criminal court is also given by ss. 108 and 114 of the 88 Act the useful power

- to order the offender to give any infringing copies to the copyright owner or
- to have them forfeited or destroyed

It will also be possible under s. 109 of the 88 Act for the police to obtain search warrants

- if there are reasonable grounds to believe that certain of the criminal offences relating to copyright have been or are about to be committed in premises or
- that evidence of offences can be found in the premises concerned

However, note that

- just because something is copyright infringement does not make it a criminal offence as well

The offences Certain acts, if done for business purposes in relation to infringing copies with knowledge that the copies are infringing, can be offences (88 Act, s. 107). These include

- making,
- importing,
- possessing and
- dealing in infringing copies.

Dealing in infringing copies includes

- selling or letting for hire,
- offering or exposing for sale or hire,
- exhibiting in public and
- distributing

It can also be a criminal offence to widely distribute infringing copies

- even if this is not done commercially

Where something is designed or adapted to make infringing copies of a particular copyright work,

- knowingly making or having that thing can be a criminal offence

Where public performance and the playing and showing of certain works in public amounts to copyright infringement these acts can also be criminal offences if done knowingly (88 Act, s. 107).

Rights in performances

The owners of the rights
There are two sets of people who can have rights in a performance

- the first is the performer
- the second is somone who has the benefit of an exclusive recording contract with the performer
  - (i.e., someone who might qualify as the owner of the recording rights conferred by the 88 Act)

There are correspondingly two sets of rights

- the performer's rights and
- the recording rights

The performer's rights
The performer's rights control

- recording (sound recording),
- filming,
- broadcasting or including in cable programme services the performer's performances.

The rights also include the rights

- to control public showings,
- broadcasts or inclusion in cable programme services
- of recordings and films of the performances

The recording rights
The recording rights are rights to

- record and film performances and
- to exploit those recordings and films

The way others can become entitled to recording rights is complex. It does not just depend upon who has the benefit of an exclusive recording contract. Rights in performances are unique amongst intellectual property rights in the way ownership of the rights depends on the nationality requirements (see p. 166).

Primary infringement
The rights of the performer and of someone with recording rights are infringed if anyone without consent

- makes a film or sound recording
- of any substantial part of a performance (88 Act, ss. 182 and 186)

The only exception is if this is done for private and domestic use. Thus anyone who tapes, say, a rock concert or a play or makes a video of an open-air concert can do so for private and domestic use but not for any other purpose.

It can also be an infringement of a performer's rights (but not of the recording rights)

- to broadcast any substantial part of a performance live

The same applies to a performance included live in a cable programme service (88 Act, s. 182).

Secondary infringement
The performer's rights and the recording rights are also infringed by certain things done with an illicit recording (88 Act, ss. 183 and 187). Like copyright,

- secondary infringement requires knowledge or a reasonable belief that the recording was made without consent

Using an illicit recording

- to show or play the whole or a substantial part of a recorded performance in public

infringes the performer's rights and the recording rights (88 Act, ss. 183 and 187).

The performer's rights and the recording rights are also infringed

- by use of an illicit recording to broadcast any substantial part of a performance

The same applies to including any substantial part of a performance in a cable programme service by this means (88 Act, ss. 183 and 187).

Importation of an illicit recording other than for private and domestic use infringes the performer's rights and the recording rights. This also applies to commercial dealings in illicit recordings. The commercial dealings relate to doing certain things in the course of business, namely

- possessing,
- selling,
- letting for hire,
- offering or exposing for sale or hire
- distributing

illicit recordings (88 Act, ss. 184 and 188).

Exceptions to infringement
Certain activities do not infringe performers rights or recording rights. The list is long and detailed (see sch. 2 to the 88 Act). In very broad terms the list of non-infringing activities is similar to but not the same as the corresponding list applicable to copyright works.

Criminal offences
There are several kinds of criminal offences associated with infringement of performer's rights and recording rights. The penalties include

- fines and
- imprisonment of up to two years (88 Act, s. 198)

As with copyright, a criminal court is also given the useful power to

- order the offender to give any infringing copies to the copyright owner or
- to have them forfeited or destroyed (88 Act, ss. 199 and 204)

It will also be possible for the police to obtain search warrants

- if there are reasonable grounds to believe that certain of the criminal offences concerning illicit recordings have been or about to be committed in premises or
- that evidence of offences can be found in the premises concerned (88 Act, s. 109)

Certain acts are offences if done for business purposes in relation to illicit recordings

- with knowledge that the copies are illicit

These include

- making,
- importing, and
- possessing illicit recordings
- for the purposes of infringement
- and dealing in illicit recordings

Dealing in illicit recordings includes

- selling or letting for hire,
- offering or exposing for sale or hire, and
- distributing (88 Act, s. 198)

Where infringement consists of showing or playing a recording in public or of broadcasting or including a recording of a performance in a cable programme service a criminal offence can be committed (88 Act, s. 198). This applies where the recording was made without consent and the person who causes the infringement knows or has reason to believe the performer's rights or recording rights are infringed by the acts of infringement.

It is also an offence for someone to falsely represent he or she is authorised to give consent to something that amounts to infringement of performer's rights and recording rights (88 Act, s. 201).

Where a corporate body like a limited company commits an offence the directors, secretary or other officers, the manager and anyone who represents themself as such can be liable for the same offence (88 Act, s. 202). This applies where the offence is committed with the consent or connivance of any of these people.

RIGHTS IN PRODUCT DESIGNS

Copyright in designs

The rights and what amounts to infringement in relation to two and three-dimensional designs protectable by copyright are no different to those set out on pages 122–38 concerning copyright in designs which qualify as works such as artistic works. Remember that after 1 August 1989 copyright is really only applicable to

- designs of things that will be artistic works when they are made to the design (e.g., sculptures and typefaces)
- attractive two-dimensional designs like wallpaper patterns, logos and the like

For designs made before 1 August 1989, copyright will still apply for up to 10 years and none of the following exceptions will apply to permit copying

the design right exceptions

- functional features
- integral features
- methods or principles of construction
- surface decoration
- commonplace features

the registered design right exceptions

- functional features
- integral features
- methods or principles of construction
- where the appearance is not material to the decision to buy

nor (by virtue of the New Chip Regulations, reg. 8) will the additional exceptions for semiconductor chip designs apply, e.g., reproducing the design

- privately for non-commercial aims
- for the purpose of analysing or evaluating the design or
- for analysing, evaluating or teaching the concepts, processes, systems or techniques embodied in it

nor will it necessarily be lawful

- to create another original semiconductor topography as a result of an analysis or evaluation of a topography or of the concepts, processes, systems or techniques embodied in it

Spare parts

In *British Leyland Motor Corporation Ltd* v *Armstrong Patents Co. Ltd* [1989] AC 577, the House of Lords introduced a new rule under the old copyright regime of protection in relation to the manufacture of spare parts. Whenever someone purchases an article they have an implied right to repair and maintain it. What the House of Lords in effect decided was that the right to repair should not be so limited as to prevent people obtaining spare parts from independent manufacturers. The problem is that it is not absolutely clear how this rule should be applied not whether it applies to any kind of spare part.

Design right

Primary infringement

Under s. 226 of the 88 Act, the owner of design right has

- the exclusive right
- to reproduce the design
- for commercial purposes

Reproduction in this context means two different things. It means

- making articles to the design or
- recording the design in a design document for the purpose of making articles to the design

Reproducing articles to a design includes

- making articles substantially to the design

Remember that some aspects of designs can lawfully be copied

- functional features
- integral features
- methods or principles of construction
- surface decoration
- commonplace features

The reproduction must be for 'commercial purposes' to infringe. Commercial purposes in relation to an article covers

- anything done with a view to selling or hiring the article in the course of business (88 Act, s. 263(3))

If something is done which is not for 'commercial purposes' then there is no infringement.

There is no exception, as there is in copyright, concerning research not amounting to infringement. Thus great care may need to be taken in relation to reverse engineering

- it can be infringement of design right to make drawings of a competitor's product even though this is quite common in reverse engineering

In the light of the extent of design right primary infringement covers

- making articles to the design or
- recording the design in a design document without consent

However, primary infringement also includes authorising anyone

- to make articles to the design or
- to record the design in a design document if the authorisation is given without consent

Secondary infringement
Design right can be infringed under s. 227 of the 88 Act by certain things done in relation to infringing copies of a design. These are

- importing,
- possessing, and
- dealing

in infringing articles for commercial purposes.
Dealing in infringing articles means

- selling,
- letting for hire,
- offering or exposing for sale or hire.

Secondary infringement of design right requires knowledge or a reasonable belief that the articles concerned are infringing articles.

As with copyright, an article made abroad can be an infringing article even if it was made with the permission of the owner of design right (88 Act, s. 226).

Additionally, if the owner of design right gave someone an exclusive licence under the design right covering the UK, then articles made abroad, even if made by the design right owner can be infringing if imported into the UK.

However, under design right, an article can even be an infringing copy if it is *proposed to be imported* into the UK.

Criminal offences
There are no criminal offences specifically created under the 88 Act in relation to infringements of design rights.

Registered rights

The fundamental point about registered designs which makes them different from the other rights protecting form and appearance is that the right can be infringed without copying. In this respect registered designs are like patents. If anyone produces an article covered by the registration which is substantially similar to the registered design then this amounts to infringement.

Primary and secondary infringement

The effect of obtaining a registration for a design gives the registered proprietor of the design certain exclusive rights (RDA 49, s. 7). The proprietor of the registered design has the exclusive right

- to make and
- to import

articles to which the design has been applied.

This right is limited to certain specified purposes. The purposes covered by the right to make and import are

- selling,
- hiring or
- using for the purposes of any trade or business

So, it is not an infringement

- to make or import for private and domestic purposes or
- for any other purpose which is not for the purposes of a trade or business

The proprietor also has the exclusive right to deal in articles to which the design has been applied. So even if making or importing for private and domestic purposes does not infringe

- it could still be an infringement to deal in an article made for private and domestic or other non-infringing purposes

In this context dealing means to

- sell,
- hire or
- offer or expose for sale or hire

It can also be an infringement of registered design rights to make anything for use in the manufacture of infringing articles (RDA 49, s. 7(3)). This could cover practically anything which enables infringing articles to be made, including drawings, tools, moulds and dies.

Remember that some aspects of registered designs can lawfully be copied or reproduced

- functional features
- integral features
- methods or principles of construction
- where the appearance is not material to the decision to buy

When proceedings can be commenced

Until the application for registration is granted by the issue of the certificate of registration no proceedings for infringement can be commenced (RDA 49, s. 7(5)). However, once registration is granted it takes effect from the date of the original application (or the date which is treated as the date of application in relation to a foreign design given priority as a consequence of reciprocal protection provisions) (RDA 49, s. 3(5)).

Ignorance of the existence of the registration

Absence of knowledge of the registration of a design or absence of a reasonable belief that the design is registered might help the infringer avoid having to pay damages (RDA 49, s. 9). This applies up to the point at which the infringer had knowledge.

If the product itself has only been marked with the word 'registered' or some abbreviation of that word, this is not sufficient in itself to give the infringer the requisite knowledge but

- if the registered number is included as well this could be enough

Criminal offences

There are no criminal offences specifically created in relation to infringements of registered design rights.

Semiconductor chip design rights

The rights of the owner of semiconductor chip designs are a little different to those of the owner of design rights. The general scheme of the rights is on broadly similar lines. In this section only the differences from ordinary design right will be examined.

Primary infringement

The owner of rights in a semiconductor chip design has the same exclusive rights as the owner of design rights but there are exceptions. Under reg. 8 of the New Chip Regulations, the exclusive rights do not prevent reproducing the design

- for private non-commercial aims
- for the purpose of analysing or evaluating the design or analysing or
- for evaluating the concepts, processes, systems or techniques embodied in it.
- for the purpose of teaching the concepts, processes, systems or techniques embodied in it

It is also not an infringement of design rights in a semiconductor topography to create another original semiconductor topography as a result of an analysis or evaluation of a topography or of the concepts, processes, systems or techniques embodied in it (New Chip Regulations, reg. 8). Thus, the path is open for reverse engineering. However, it is still important to ensure that any design derived from analysing a competitor's design is truly independent.

Remember that unlike copyright there are special exclusions permitting copying in relation to certain aspects of semiconductor chip designs

- functional features
- integral features
- methods or principles of construction
- surface decoration
- commonplace features

Secondary infringement

All of the secondary infringement aspects of design right apply to semiconductor chip designs but with some slight differences. If an article (a semiconductor chip) made to the design has been sold or hired in certain countries the secondary infringement provisions do not apply to

- *that particular example of the design*

if certain conditions are satisfied (New Chip Regulations, reg. 8). The conditions are

- if the article has been sold or hired in the UK by or with the permission of the owner of the design rights in the topography

or, alternatively,

- if the article has been sold or hired in any EEC member State or Gibraltar

The second condition is satisfied provided the selling or hiring was carried out by or with the permission of

- the person entitled to import it into, or to sell or hire it

in the EEC member State concerned or into Gibraltar.

This does not mean the secondary infringement provisions cease to apply to all other examples of the same article. They still apply to other examples of the same kind of article if the conditions are not satisfied.

Criminal offences

There are no criminal offences specifically created in relation to infringements of semiconductor topography design rights.

SO YOU THINK YOU HAVE SOMETHING THAT MIGHT BE PROTECTED

If you believe someone has infringed your rights and are just about to send a letter telling them so or if you are about to consult a lawyer about a suspected infringement, unless you have to move quickly because you want to try to obtain an immmediate interim court order to stop the infringer, stop and think. You have time. There are other issues. Do not send a threatening letter merely assuming you can prove everything necessary to establish your rights. You can look pretty stupid if it turns out there is nothing you can do to stop the infringer because you had not taken the appropriate steps to ensure protection is available.

If you receive a threatening letter accusing you of infringement do not take it for granted that the person who sent the letter is in a position to stop you doing whatever they complain about. They may have no right to stop you or even complain.

Identifying what can be protected and what rights are available is an important start in both obtaining and making use of protection and in avoiding infringement. However, where protection is automatic with the unregistered intellectual property rights like design right and copyright, it may be necessary to prove that the material concerned actually does qualify for protection and that the alleged owner can prove ownership of the relevant rights. This is one area in which the non-lawyer can fall foul of the legal rules, but with care the problems are avoidable.

These issues can arise with registered designs both in relation to obtaining a registration and, if the validity of the registration is challenged in legal proceedings, in proving the design was validly registered.

The remainder of this chapter will examine these issues. The following is a summary of points to be considered after identifying what can be protected and when addressing any copyright, design, registered design, performer's rights or semiconductor design issue:

- the identity and status of the author is of fundamental importance to various issues
   - proving a work qualifies for protection can depend upon the nationality of the author, ownership of or entitlement to rights can depend on who the author is and the author's status (e.g., employee or independent contractor) and the duration of copyright can depend on when the author died
- is the work of UK authorship?
   - if the work is a foreign work it has to qualify for reciprocal protection under UK law. Otherwise there is no protection.
   - if it is a work of UK authorship this may need to be proved to obtain protection
- does the person claiming to own the rights actually own them?
   - if not either there is no one who can prevent infringement or at least the alleged owner cannot prevent infringement;
- has the period of protection expired?
   - if so, then again no protection can be afforded
- what remedies are available?
   - there is little point enforcing a right if the benefit is minimal. Correspondingly, if there is a risk of infringing the rights of others, the extent of the risk should be assessed

Bear in mind that each of the above points can be relevant whether

- you have something you wish to protect; or,
- you want to copy a competitor's product; or,

- you are buying or selling intellectual property rights

Additionally, in order to obtain protection for works in some foreign countries there may be local registration requirements or marking requirements. For example, the symbol of a letter 'c' enclosed in a circle followed by the author's name and year of first publication may be essential for obtaining protection.

The remedies for copyright infringement are dealt with in chapter 7. This is for two reasons. Firstly some of the remedies are common to all intellectual property rights. Secondly, if copyright has been infringed, other intellectual property rights may have been as well, so it can be worth considering the remedies together and comparing them.

WHO IS THE AUTHOR?

At first sight it seems silly to ask who the author of something is. Those uninitiated into the world of intellectual property rights might say the author is the person who creates something. That is not a bad first attempt. But who is the person who creates a sound recording? Is it the person making the sounds or is it the person who operates the tape machine? What about a film or a broadcast? What about output produced by a computer? What about the position where several different people work together to produce something? Why not treat all of them as the author? If copyright protection and some of the other forms of protection are automatic why worry about who the author is?

There are two special issues with authorship which need separate treatment

- computer-generated works
- works of joint authorship

Computer-generated works need to be dealt with at an early stage because the question of whether a work is computer generated concerns all of the rights protecting form and appearance. Joint authorship can be dealt with at the end of this section. It is a relatively straightforward topic but it is important in relation to ownership of rights (particularly where the authors are a mixture of employees and independent contractors), to whether the rights can only be exercised by the authors where they all agree and to meeting the nationality requirements.

Computer-generated works

A computer is not an entity recognised by law as a kind of legal person. A computer cannot therefore own or dispose of property. It has no nationality. Consider the situation where a work is created on a computer and the computer is the only likely candidate to be considered the author. Unless some special provision covers the situation, a computer could never satisfy the nationality requirements in order for what is created to be given protection under UK law. If a computer is the 'author' or 'creator' of a work then there can be no legal owner of the copyright, unless the law deals expressly with the question.

What is a computer-generated work?
In practice, there seem to be three general categories of works which can be created using a computer. First, a document could be created on a computer, such as on a word processor. The author determines substantially the form and content of the document

- the final document is substantially the result of the exercise of skill, judgment and effort on the part of the author

The machine can be treated as a mere tool in a similar way to a typewriter. There should be no problem identifying the author.

Secondly, a document could also be created on a computer which is the result of both human and machine effort. A mailing list can be compiled by individuals typing names and addresses into a computer database. The order of names and addresses initially is unimportant. The computer can be used to reorganise the original information and to produce many kinds of lists, in different orders

- the final form of list is a combination of a translation of the original name and address information compiled by human beings and the 'skill, judgment and effort' of the computer in rearranging the original order into a new order

So, in the second example, the machine could conceivably be treated as creating a copyright work, perhaps jointly with the human authors or as creating a work itself by translating the original list compiled by the human authors. The end-result will have a relation to the original data which can be verified by comparing the lists with the original data.

A different situation arises with the third kind of computer-generated work where

- the computer produces a work where no direct visual comparison can be carried out between the initial data compiled or created by human beings and the final result created by the machine

Business accounts rely upon data concerning financial transactions of the business being supplied to the computer. The computer performs calculations on the data. For example, an initial trial balance could be created. The account balances shown will have been calculated solely by the computer by totalling and balancing the individual financial entries for each account. The individual financial entries do not appear on the trial balance. The document produced by the computer is one which is the result of the 'skill, judgment and effort' of the machine. Is the machine to be treated as the author in the third example and if not, who is to be treated as the author?

What did the old law say about computer-generated works?
Under the pre August 1989 law no provision had been made whether under copyright or registered designs law to deal with the question of computer-generated works. In one case under the old law, *Express Newspapers plc v Liverpool Daily Post & Echo plc* [1985] 1 WLR 1089 a program had been

written to calculate sequences of numbers to be used and published daily as a bingo game in newspapers of the Express Newspapers group. The judge decided that the programmer was the author and that the computer was merely a tool just as if the programmer had used a pen to work out the results himself.

What is a computer-generated work under the new law?
Under the new law (88 Act, s. 178), a work is computer generated if

- the work is generated by a computer in circumstances such that there is no human author

This is not very helpful in the light of the analysis (albeit elementary) set out above of the three general categories of computer-generated works. Essentially, Parliament has left the question to the courts to resolve. The position is much the same for design right and registered design right.

- a computer-generated design for design right purposes is one which is generated by computer in circumstances such that there is no human author (88 Act, s. 263(1)).

For registered designs there is no definition of 'computer-generated work'. The RDA 49 as amended refers to

- designs generated where there is no human author

Who is the author under the new law?
Under the 88 Act the author of copyright in computer-generated literary, dramatic, musical and artistic works is

- the person by whom the arrangements necessary for the creation of the work are undertaken (88 Act, s. 9(4))

This is a vague definition and could lead to confusion where more than one person is involved in the creation of a work. The position is much the same for design right and registered designs. Section 214(2) of the 88 Act provides that

- the designer of a computer-generated design is the person by whom the arrangements necessary for the creation of the design are undertaken

For registered design purposes where a design is generated in circumstances where there is no human author s. 2(4) of the RDA 49 provides that the author is

- the person by whom the arrangements necessary for the creation of the design were made

When is a work computer generated?
It may not always be clear who the author of the output from a computer is. In order to try to avoid uncertainty about who the author of computer generated works is, it seems that

- a clear management structure and division of responsibilities is required in order to ensure the person or persons responsible for making the 'arrangements' are clearly identifiable and that they are actually the ones who do make the 'arrangements' and

- have, whenever possible, express written agreements with all the potential authors, whether employees or independent contractors, about who is to own copyright in copyright works or designs created with the aid of a computer

IDENTIFYING THE AUTHOR

This section will look at the statutory provisions dealing with authorship of the various kinds of copyright works. There are special provisions concerning works published anonymously and under pseudonyms which it is not necessary to cover in this book.

Literary, musical, dramatic and artistic works

Under the pre August 1989 law

- 'author' was not defined in relation to literary, dramatic, musical and artistic works

There has been uncertainty, for example, about who would own copyright in a work produced where the originator dictates to a stenographer and the stenographer is the only person who commits the words to paper.
Under the new law

- the author of literary, dramatic, musical and artistic works is the creator (88 Act, s. 9)

This, taken with the fact that the new law explicitly recognises that a work which is spoken is protectable, indicates that

- the author of a dictated work is the person giving the dictation and not the person who takes the dictation down

- the creator is likely to be the person who expends skill, judgement and effort in making the work.

Photographs

There was a special provision concerning authorship of a photograph (an artistic work) under the 56 Act. Under the pre August 1989 law

- the author of a photograph was not the person who took it but, unusually,

- the person 'who, at the time the photograph is taken, is the owner of the material on which it is taken' (56 Act, s. 48(1))

This is changed under the 88 Act

programme included in the service (56 Act, s. 14A(1)). The new law is not, in effect, different the creator of a cable programme is the person providing the cable programme service in which the cable programme is included (88 Act, s. 9).

Authorship of performances

There is no definition of who the author of a performance is. This may seem confusing particulary where more than one performer takes part in a perform-ance. However, there is no concept of joint authorship or joint ownership of rights in a performance. Each performer is treated individually and hence is the author or creator of the particular part or role in the overall performance. This has interesting implications, particularly for the television and broadcasting industry as it makes the contractual arrangements concerning rights in performances highly complex.

Authorship of product designs

Copyright in designs
Authorship of designs protected by copyright is governed by the ordinary copyright rules dealt with previously.

Design right protection

The designer is the person who creates a design (88 Act, s. 214(1)). Where a design is computer-generated the designer is the person by whom the arrange-ments necessary for the creation of the design are made (88 Act, s. 214(2)). The problems with this kind of provision have already been noted in the section dealing with authorship of computer-generated works p. 153.

Authorship of registered designs

Under the new law

- the author of a registrable design is the person who creates it (RDA 49, s. 2(3))

This provision applies to all applications for registration made on or after 1 August 1989. Under the pre August 1989 law the 'author' was not defined in the legislation. In *Lazarus* v *Charles* (1873) LR 16 Eq 117, the author was held to be the designer. The designer must not only have the idea underlying the design but must also take some substantial part in actually creating it (*Kenrick & Co* v *Lawrence & Co.* (1890) 25 QBD 99).

The practical advice is to ensure that

- whenever there is any matter in law to be dealt with concerning the rights to a design, ensure that all potential designers are included
- even if there is doubt about whether the potential designers are 'authors' under law

- have express contractually binding agreements concerning ownership of rights with anyone who could conceivably be considered to be a designer

The RDA 49 provides that the author of a computer-generated design (i.e., where there is no human author) is the person by whom the arrangements necessary for the creation of the design are made. This provision applies to applications for registration made on and after 1 August 1989.

Authorship of semiconductor chip designs

In order to determine authorship the rules to be applied are identical to those applied to determine authorship of designs for the purposes of Design Right.

Joint authorship — special topic

Copyright works
Under the pre August 1989 law

- where two or more people collaborate and
- their contributions are not *separate*

then the work is one of joint authorship (56 Act, s. 11(3)).

Under the new law

- the work is joint if the contributions are not *distinct* (88 Act, s. 10).

The position under the old and new law seems to be that, say, where several people write one chapter each for a book, the book is not a work of joint authorship. If the authors each write and amend each chapter so that it is not a simple matter or not possible to identify who wrote which parts, then the book will be a work of joint authorship.

There is no concept of joint authorship for moral rights or rights in performances. Each author and performer is treated individually.

For designs protected by copyright the position in relation to joint authorship in copyright works has already been outlined above. For rights in designs protected by design right and semiconductor chip designs, a joint design means a design produced by two or more designers in which the contribution of each designer is not distinct from the contributions of the others (88 Act, s. 259). The effect of this provision will be likely to be the same as for copyright works. With regard to aspects of product designs protected by registered design rights the RDA 49 unusually makes no express provision concerning joint authorship. Thus, it would seem that when it comes to any question of entitlement to apply to register a design

- have express contractual agreement between all of the designers about who is to have the right to apply

CAN IT QUALIFY FOR PROTECTION? IS IT A FOREIGN WORK?

In broad terms, for the unregistered rights (copyright, design right, rights in performances and in semiconductor chip designs) protection can be obtained in two ways. The first is

- for the author, or designer or performer to meet certain requirements ('the nationality requirements')

The second is

- for first publication or marketing to take place in the UK or a country to which reciprocal protection is afforded

For copyright and registered design rights the rules are complex. The rules are also complex for rights in performances.
For design right and design right in semiconductor chip designs,

- not only are the reciprocal protection provisions complicated but also
- the range of foreign countries and therefore foreign designs which obtain protection are extremely limited

Additionally,

- for design right the reciprocal protection provisions are heavily stacked against the prospective owner of rights in a design which is not a UK or EEC design
- for prospective owners of design rights in non-UK and non-EEC designs, all prospect of protection can be lost very easily

There is even scope for 'ambushing' the prospective owner of rights in a design to ensure protection is lost. The position for the prospective owner of design right in foreign semiconductor chip designs is even more difficult. Although for UK competitors this may be good news, it is not such a good thing for UK importers and distributors of foreign goods.

The detailed reciprocal protection rules are set out in appendix 2. The following is a broad summary of how the rules operate in order to give a general working understanding of how they work.

Qualifying for protection

Where rights are unregistered, if it becomes necessary at any time to prove a work, performance or design qualifies for protection it will be necessary to show that the relevant criteria are met

- in the case of a UK national do not assume there can be no problems

It can still be necessary to produce proof that a UK national person meets the nationality requirements for a UK national. Problems can sometimes arise in obtaining the proof but if elementary precautions are taken at the appropriate time the problems are avoidable.

'Nationals'

The term 'nationals' is used here for brevity. The protection is not strictly limited to 'nationals'. However, the rule of thumb is that the protection is afforded to

- citizens,
- corporations incorporated under the relevant national law and to
- 'non-nationals' resident in a country which is afforded reciprocal protection

Bypassing the nationality requirements by first publication or marketing

If for any reason the nationality requirements are not met it is possible in some cases to bypass the problem because

- protection may also be afforded if *first* publication or first marketing takes place in a country afforded reciprocal protection

Some practical advice about keeping records

As a model for perfection for the prospective rights owner

- business records should be kept of the names, place or places of residence, and nationality of the relevant authors, designers and performers

Additionally,

- business records should ideally also be kept of all occasions on which examples of a work are supplied to third parties,
- who the third parties are and
- the countries to which the supplies were made.

The latter steps should be taken in the period up to and including the general launch of examples of the design or copyright work on the open market. In the case of performances records should be kept of where the performances took place.

Some practical advice about buying and selling rights

Where rights in UK or foreign works are being acquired, from the point of view of the prospective purchaser or licensee

- it would be prudent to obtain appropriate details of the authors
- as well as obtaining a contractually binding obligation from the person selling the rights to provide whatever assistance may be required later in proving the nationality requirements are met.

— the prospective purchaser or licensee might also consider it prudent to check whether the person selling the rights is in a position to provide the appropriate level of assistance

From the point of view of the seller of the rights

- try to avoid having to give any details of whether the nationality requirements have been met
  — this cuts down the amount of time required to do a deal and

— there may be difficulty providing documentation that satisfies the purchaser or licensee. This could result in the price being re-negotiated.

● avoid giving any guarantees, contractually binding representations or warranties, such as that the rights are valid and enforceable

— you can never be sure of this until the day comes to try to enforce them
— if it is commercially expedient to give them, cut down their scope and qualify them as far as you can to limit any potential exposure should anything go horribly wrong in the future

DOES ANYONE OWN THE RIGHTS?

To be able to enforce legal rights, naturally, one must prove ownership or some kind of entitlement to sue. This can be, unfortunately, another of those awkward problem areas where, if the right steps are not taken at the appropriate time, difficulties can arise. If the right steps are taken there should be little difficulty proving ownership. If you receive a letter from someone who alleges he is the owner of one of the unregistered rights do not assume he is in a position to prove his entitlement.

If rights are being bought and sold it may be important to be able to prove the alleged owner actually does own and can sell the rights. Often when rights are sold the seller gives warranties (legally binding promises) about ownership. If because of some technical legal defect the seller is not the owner then the seller may be liable to pay compensation in damages for breach of warranty.

Whether a work was created before or on or after 1 August 1989 can be relevant to which legal rules are applied in deciding who is the owner of copyright.

Ownership of copyrights

Literary, musical, dramatic and artistic works

The basic rule   The basic rule both under the 56 Act and the 88 Act is that *the author* of a literary, dramatic, musical or artistic work is the owner of copyright in it (56 Act, s. 4(1), and 88 Act, s. 11(1)).

Employees   The first exception to the basic rule concerns literary, dramatic, musical and artistic works created by employees. The exception is common to the 56 and 88 Acts. Copyright in a literary, dramatic, musical or artistic work created by an *employee* author *in the course of employment* belongs to the employer. This applies subject to contrary agreement between the employee and employer.

Often the question of ownership of intellectual property rights is not dealt with in a contract of employment at all or is not dealt with adequately. This means that the statutory rules set out in the 56 and 88 Acts are usually of considerable importance.

Work done in an employee's own time There are several misconceptions about ownership of rights created by employees. One is that if the employee creates the work outside of work hours it cannot belong to the employer. Another is that anything an employee creates during work hours belongs to the employer. Additionally, the rules relating to employees are often confused with those relating to ownership of rights in what an independent contractor produces.

Who is an employee? In the majority of cases there is often no difficulty identifying who is an employee and who is an outside (independent) contractor. Sometimes grey areas can arise, such as whether a director of a company is an employee and whether an outside contractor is really an employee in disguise. Avoid grey areas. Both the old and new copyright law leaves it open to have express contractually binding agreement on who is to own the rights in a work created by an employee or an independent contractor. If the provision is there use it.

When is an employee acting in the course of employment? 'Acting in the course of employment' is taken to mean acting within the scope of the employee's normal duties under the employment contract. So if the tea boy writes a report for the board of directors, then he will own the copyright in it as writing reports for the board is unlikely to be within the scope of his normal duties.

This, however, is still subject to the express terms of the tea boy's employment contract which can make express provision about ownership of copyright. Alternatively, express agreement can be made concerning ownership of any particular copyright.

The special rules under the 56 Act Under the 56 Act there were some curious rules about copyright for literary, dramatic, musical and artistic works which were commissioned or which were created by employees in certain circumstances. For example, the person who commissioned the taking of a photograph, or the painting or drawing of a portrait, or the making of an engraving owns copyright in it (56 Act, s. 4(3)). This was provided the person giving the commission agreed to pay for it or did pay for it in money or 'money's worth'. This rule still applies to works made before 1 August 1989 and also applies to works made on or after 1 August 1989 provided the commission was given before then (88 Act, sch. 1, para. 11(2)).

There was also a special rule about employees of proprietors of newspapers, magazines and similar periodicals. The rule applies only to works made before 1 August 1989. Under this rule the employer owns copyright if a literary, dramatic or artistic work was made in the course of the employee's employment. However, the employer only owns copyright to the extent that the work is to be published in a newspaper, magazine or similar periodical. The employee owns the copyright for all other purposes, (56 Act, s. 4(2)).

Typographical arrangements of published editions
Under both the 56 Act and the 88 Act the publisher is entitled to the copyright in the typographical arrangement of a published edition.

Sound recordings
Under the 56 Act the owner of copyright in a sound recording was the maker
(56 Act, s. 12(4)); see page 157. However, if a sound recording was commissioned for 'money or monies worth' (i.e. payment in cash or in kind), the person
who commissioned it was the owner of the copyright (56 Act, s. 12(4)) subject
to any contrary agreement having been made about ownership of copyright.

If the commission was made before 1 August 1989 then the 56 Act rules
apply even if the recording was made on or after 1 August 1989 (88 Act, sch. 1,
para. 11(2)).

Under the 88 Act the position is simpler. The author (see page 157) is the
owner of copyright (88 Act, s. 11).

Films
Under the 56 Act the owner of copyright in a film was the maker (56 Act, s.
13(4)). Under the 88 Act the owner of copyright is the author (88 Act, s. 11).
There is no material difference between the 56 Act and 88 Act definitions of
maker and author.

Broadcasts
Under the 56 Act only the BBC or ITA were the owners of copyright in
broadcasts (56 Act, s. 14(2)). Under the 88 Act, s. 11, the owner of copyright is
the author (see page 157).

Cable programmes
Under the 56 Act the owner of copyright in a cable programme was the person
providing the cable programme service (56 Act, s. 14A(3)). Under the 88 Act
the owner of copyright in a cable programme is the author. Essentially, the
position under the 88 Act is the same as under the 56 Act.

Moral rights

Moral rights are personal to the author or director. They cannot be bought or
sold but, with the exception of the right to object to false attribution of
authorship, the rights can be passed on by will when the author dies. If no
express provision is made in a will, the rights follow the ownership of copyright
or become exercisable by the deceased's personal representatives.

Joint ownership

Where copyright or any of the rights covered by copyright is owned jointly, it
seems that the joint owners can only exercise the rights jointly. They cannot
individually grant rights to their copyright or sue individually. The 88 Act
specifically states that references to the copyright owner are to all of the joint
owners and that where a licence (permission) is required the licence must be
given by all the copyright owners (88 Act, s. 173). Thus, for someone to obtain
permission from the copyright owner, all the joint owners must act together in
giving the permission.

Different rights owned by different people

Where different people own different aspects of the copyrights in a copyright work then they can deal freely in and exercise their rights under the part of the copyright owned by them. They do not need to consult or refer to the owners of any other aspect of the copyright (88 Act, s. 173). This is how the licensing organisations like the PRS, the CLA and the PPL operate. None of them need to own all of the aspects of the copyright which they administer, just the aspects relevant to what it is they do.

Joint authors and moral rights

Where a copyright work is of joint authorship the moral rights of the authors are exercisable by them individually. They do not need to refer to the other authors in order to assert or exercise their rights (88 Act, s. 88). However, what one joint author does in relation to his or her moral rights does not affect the other joint authors' moral rights in any way (88 Act, s. 88).

Copyright ownership in future copyright works

Where there is a commission, the copyright work does not exist at the time the commission is given so the copyright does not exist either. The way law deals with ownership of future copyright is quite simple. The starting-point is

● who the owner of copyright would be if there were no agreement about who is to own the future copyright

This person could be, for example, the author and will be referred to here as the prospective owner. If the prospective owner enters into an agreement, say, with a customer and the agreement provides that the customer is to own copyright, then,

● in all cases, the customer will own the copyright (56 Act, s. 37(1) and 88 Act, s. 91)

This applies provided the agreement is

● in writing and
● signed by or on behalf of the prospective owner

Additionally, to avoid doubt, the agreement should be worded so that the prospective owner states it is by way of assignment.

One problem with future copyright is that

● the person who contracts with the customer to transfer the copyright must actually be the prospective owner

Sometimes this does not happen, for example, where a subcontractor is engaged to produce the work. Another problem which can arise is that what is eventually produced is not what the original contract specified to be produced. Both of these problems are avoidable and easy to deal with by ensuring express agreement is reached at the outset of the commission with all concerned.

Performances

Performer's rights
The rights in a performance are personal to the performer. They cannot be bought and sold (88 Act, s. 192)

- the performer is therefore the first and only 'owner' of rights in a performance (88 Act, s. 180)

The only exception concerns death of the performer. The rights and their control pass on death by will. If there is no will or no provision in the will the rights are exercisable by the deceased's personal representatives.

Recording rights
Different people can be entitled to recording rights in a performance. In the first instance,

- the person who has an exclusive recording contract with a performer is entitled to the recording rights conferred by the 88 Act (88 Act, ss. 180 and 185)

This is subject to the person concerned satisfying the nationality requirements in order to qualify for entitlement to the recording rights under UK law.
Alternatively, if the benefit of the exclusive recording contract is sold,

- the person who has has bought the benefit of the exclusive recording contract is entitled to the recording rights conferred by the 88 Act

Again, this is subject to the person concerned satisfying the nationality requirements.

The licensee can be entitled to the recording rights
If neither of the people mentioned in the above section satisfy the nationality requirements the provisions of the new law dealing with this situation have some unusual and, in some instances, bizarre results. The 88 Act provides that, subject to certain conditions being met, someone else can be entitled to the recording rights conferred by the 88 Act instead. In essence, this applies if someone (the licensee) has obtained a licence (permission) to record performances with a view to their commercial exploitation. *The licensee may be entitled to the recording rights* conferred by the 88 Act if he or she satisfies the nationality requirements. This is provided

- the licence is one given by the person who has the benefit of the exclusive recording contract
- it must also be a licence to make recordings of performances
  - covered by the exclusive recording contract
  - with a view to their commercial exploitation (commercial exploitation means 'with a view to the recordings being sold or let for hire, or shown or played in public — 88 Act, s. 185(4))

Provided these conditions are met it does not matter if the benefit of the licence has been bought and sold ('assigned') a few times. Provided the current licensee meets the nationality requirements, then that person will be entitled to the recording rights conferred by the 88 Act.

The identity of the person entitled to the recording rights can keep changing
As can be seen from the above, the person who is entitled to recording rights depends upon

- who has the benefit of an exclusive recording contract,

or

- a licence under it

in either case, the person entitled to the rights depends on

- whether the person concerned meets the nationality requirements

Thus, on one day it is possible that the person with the benefit of the exclusive recording contract may not satisfy the nationality requirements and on another he or she may (and vice versa). This could happen in one of two ways

- the benefit of the exclusive recording contract can be sold to someone who does meet the nationality requirements, or
- as a result of a change of country of residence, the person concerned meets the nationality requirements

Additionally, if the person with the benefit of the exclusive recording contract ceases to satisfy the nationality requirements this means that one day the licensee may not be the person entitled to the recording rights conferred by the 88 Act and the next day he or she is (the reverse can also occur). This is because either

- the person with the benefit of the exclusive recording contract is entitled to the recording rights or
- the person with the benefit of the licence is instead

Relevance of the identity of the person with recording rights
The fact that the identity of the person with the recording rights can change must be borne in mind on various occasions. The reason for this is because only the person with the benefit of the recording rights can enforce them so it is important to consider this aspect, for example,

- whenever exclusive recording contracts and licences under them change hands
- whenever deciding who is entitled to commence proceedings for infringement
- in drawing up contracts (whether exclusive recording contracts or licences) where the entitlement to recording rights has a bearing on the terms of the contract

It should also be noted that the statutory recording rights apply only to the performances covered by the exclusive recording contract and not to all the performer's performances (unless of course the contract applies to them all). Thus, an exclusive recording contract could cover all of a performer's performances but it does not have to. It might cover just one or more specific performances or perhaps all performances given during a particular period. This means that there is scope for more than one exclusive recording contract. Thus,

- different people can be simultaneously entitled to recording rights but in relation to different performances

Additionally, the same applies to licences granted under an exclusive recording contract but there is no requirement that a licence under an exclusive recording contract must be an exclusive licence

- it is therefore not beyond the bounds of possibility for several people to have the right to record and exploit recordings of the same performance

Probably, such a situation is unlikely to arise in normal commercial dealings but it is possible so it should be noted when drawing up contracts like licences.

OWNERSHIP OF PRODUCT DESIGNS

Ownership of copyright in product designs

The ownership of copyright in a design protected by copyright is governed by the rules set out above governing the type of copyright work concerned.

Ownership of designs protected by design right

The overriding rule about entitlement to design right
Entitlement to design rights is mixed up with satisfying the nationality requirements. In relation to the question of entitlement to design right, there is one overriding rule

- if the only way a design can qualify for design right protection is by meeting the first marketing requirements then
- the owner of design right is the person who first markets articles made to the design (88 Act, s. 215(4))

This means that if the articles made to the design are not first marketed by the design right owner, then the exclusive licensee or even the exclusive distributor can become entitled to the design right. This can be a great bonus for a distibutor or exclusive licensee because they can copy the design without infringing design right in the UK and at the same time can sue anyone else under the design rights (even the foreign manufacturer who originated the design).

The rule applies if the only way a design can qualify for design right protection is by satisfying the first marketing requirements. In other words,

- the rule applies where neither
  - the designer,
  - commissioner, or
  - designer's employer

is a 'qualifying person' or 'qualifying individual'.

In any other case the following rules apply.
The first/prospective owner of design right

- is the designer if
  - the design is not created in pursuance of a commission
  - nor in the course of the designer's employment (88 Act, s. 215(1))
- is the commissioner
  - if the design is commissioned (88 Act, s. 215(2))
- is the designer's employer
  - if the design is created by an employee in the course of employment and
  - provided neither the employer nor the employee has been commissioned to produce the design for a third party, (88 Act, s. 215(3))

Like copyright, the basic rules on first ownership can be used to identify the prospective owner of design right in a future design. This is necessary, like the position with copyright, in order to track what happens to ownership where the prospective owner agrees to transfer the design right before the design is created.

- where there is an agreement between the prospective owner of design right to transfer a future design right, the customer will become the owner of design right automatically on creation of the design provided certain rules are followed (88 Act, s. 223(1))

Like the position with copyright, the agreement must be in writing signed by or on behalf of the prospective owner of design right. The agreement should, like copyright, be expressed as an assignment to avoid any uncertainty. Like copyright, if the person attempting to transfer the design right does not actually turn out to be the prospective owner of design right the customer does not get ownership of the design right.

Ownership of rights in registrable designs

Unlike the unregistrable rights,

- no one can be the owner of a registered design unless an application for registration has been made and the registration granted

However, there are rules about who is the 'proprietor' of the design

- the proprietor is the person entitled to apply for registration and is therefore the person entitled to be the 'registered proprietor' of a design

The 'original' proprietor is the first person to become entitled to apply to register.

Subject to exceptions, the original proprietor of a design (i.e., the first person to become entitled to apply for registration of a registrable design) is the author (RDA 49, s. 2(1)). For applications for registration made before 1 August 1989 if the designer produced the design for someone else for payment of some kind

- the person for whom the design was created is the proprietor (RDA 49, s. 2)

Where a design has been commissioned for payment of some kind ('money or money's worth') and the application for registration is made on or after 1 August 1989,

- the commissioner is the proprietor (RDA 49, s. 2(1A))

If a design is created by an employee in the course of employment and the application for registration is made on or after 1 August 1989 then the employer will be the proprietor (RDA 49, s. 2(1B)) unless the design was commissioned (in which case the commissioner and not the employer will be the proprietor).

The above rules about entitlement to apply for registration do not mean that the original proprietor must apply for a registration before rights in a registrable design can be transferred. It is possible to sell the rights in a design or to grant a licence (permission) to apply a design to articles.

Additionally, there is an important rule which can entitle many different people to apply to register a design

- where someone obtains an interest in a design, perhaps by buying the rights in the design or even obtaining a licence, that person may be treated as the 'proprietor' and thereby entitled to apply for registration (RDA 49, s. 2(1) and 2(2))

Ownership of rights in semiconductor chip designs

The overriding rule about ownership is that if a semiconductor chip design can only qualify for design right protection by meeting the first marketing nationality requirements then

- the owner of design right is the person who first markets articles made to the design (88 Act, s. 215(4))

This means that if the articles made to the design are not first marketed by the design right owner, then the exclusive licensee or even the exclusive distributor can become entitled to the design right. This can be a great bonus for a distributor or exclusive licensee because they can copy the design without infringing and at the same time can sue anyone else under the design rights (even the foreign manufacturer who originated the design). Remember also that the first marketing requirements for semiconductor chip designs are different to those for ordinary design right.

In any other case the following rules apply to determine ownership of design right.

The first/prospective owner of design right is the designer if the design is not created in pursuance of a commission or in the course of employment (New Chip Regulation 5). If the design is commissioned the commissioner is the first/ prospective owner of copyright (New Chip Regulation 5). However, unlike ordinary design right, the New Chip Regulations allow for express agreement about ownership of the design right which can contradict the statutory rules. This can be significant for the purposes of obtaining protection for a semiconductor chip design.

For example, if a foreign manufacturer does not meet the nationality requirements but commissions a designer who does meet the requirements, provided there is express agreement that the designer is to be the owner of the design right then the nationality requirements can be met. If, in such a situation, it is also expressly agreed that the foreign manufacturer is to be the exclusive licensee under the design right then, in commercial reality, the foreign manufacturer's position will be little different to that of the owner of design right.

Chip designs created by employees
If the design is created by an employee in the course of employment and provided neither the employer nor the employee has been commissioned to produce the design for a third party, the employer owns the design right (New Chip Regulation 5). What an employee is and what the 'course of employment' amounts to have been discussed in relation to the rules for copyright in literary, dramatic, musical and artistic works and the position is likely to be the same for design right in semiconductor chip designs.

Prospective ownership of future chip design rights
Where there is an agreement between the prospective owner of design right to transfer a future design right, the customer will become the owner of design right automatically on creation of the design provided certain rules are followed (88 Act, s. 223(1). Like the position with copyright and ordinary design right, the agreement must be in writing signed by or on behalf of the prospective owner of design right. The agreement should, like copyright, be expressed as an assignment to avoid any uncertainty. Like copyright, if the person attempting to transfer the design right does not actually turn out to be the prospective owner of design right the customer does not get ownership of the design right.

HAS THE PERIOD OF PROTECTION EXPIRED?

Once the period of protection has expired the subject-matter of the rights becomes freely copiable.

Additional significance of the end of protection

For the owner of rights it is important to be aware of the limited period of protection. If the rights owner is aware, steps can be taken at an appropriate time to produce, for example, a new product or to change a design, either completely or sufficiently to 'rejuvenate' it so that there is a prospect of having new protection in the revised design. For the purchaser or acquirer of rights, clearly, the closer the rights come to expiry the less they may be worth.

For the competitor there are various reasons why the period of protection is relevant. For example, it could be valuable to discover when a right is due to expire so that plans can be made in advance to bring out a competing product which is a copy. Additionally, for design right and registered design rights it may be possible to force the rights owner to give permission (a licence) to the competitor to exploit the design and thereby to produce a copy of the protected product. These licences are called licences of right and are available in the later years of the period of protection. They are not free. There will be payments to be made on a royalty basis (i.e., usually a percentage of the selling price will have to be paid to the rights owner).

Do not forget the effect of other intellectual property rights

Always remember that although intellectual property rights work in combination some expire at different times to others. Just because one right has expired or a licence of right has been obtained for one right it does not mean it is permissible to infringe other rights. There may be patent protection for ideas underlying a product. So care may need to be taken to avoid infringing patent rights. It also may not be permissible to copy the trade or service marks used by another on a product or the distinctive appearance or 'get-up' of a product or a business.

Copyright — periods of protection

As a general rule

- copyright protection can last for as long as the life of the author plus 50 years
- unless around 50 years have passed since the work was first published, in general, copyright will not have expired

The main exception is that

- copyright in typographical arrangements of published editions lasts for only 25 years from the end of the calendar year of first publication

There is also an interim period of 10 years from 1 August 1989 for copyright in designs created before 1 August 1989

- where a design is recorded in an artistic work before 1 August 1989 it will continue to be protected by copyright rather than design right for 10 years from 1 August 1989

For photographs, sound recordings, films and engravings, in certain circumstances copyright lasts only 50 years.

The detailed rules governing duration of copyright are set out in appendix 3. Please note, however, that this book does not deal with the rules relating to copyright works created before 1 July 1957 when the 56 Act came into effect.

Moral rights

The moral rights of authors and directors continue for as long as the copyright in the work concerned. However, the right to object to being falsely represented as the author of a work lasts until 20 years after the death of the person concerned (88 Act, s. 86).

Performances

Rights in a performance and recording rights last for 50 years from the end of the calendar year in which the performance takes place (88 Act, s. 191).

Copyright protection for products

Under the 88 Act the general rule will be that copyright protection for designs is abolished and replaced by design right protection. However,

- there are two main exceptions to the rule that copyright protection for designs has been abolished

The first of the two exceptions concerns designs made before 1 August 1989

- provided the copyright work recording the design qualifies for copyright protection, the design will continue to obtain copyright protection for up to 10 years from 1 August 1989

If the normal period of copyright protection would have continued after the end of the 10-year period the new rule ensures the protection will cease at the end of the 10-year period. If copyright expires during the 10 years then copyright ceases just as it would for any other copyright work (88 Act, sch. 1, para. 19).

The second exception to the general rule that copyright protection for designs of products is abolished is that copyright still applies to protect

- design documents or models recording or embodying designs for artistic works,
- to artistic works in their own right and
- to typefaces (88 Act, ss. 51 and 52)

The way the second exception to the general rule works is that

- once copies of the artistic work (including a typeface) are made by an industrial process, copyright protection is limited to 25 years

The 25-year period runs from the end of the calendar year in which the copied articles are first marketed. This rule makes a significant change to the law under the 56 Act

- under the old law if a design recorded in an artistic work (including a typeface) was capable of being protected as a registered design the period of protection was only 15 years

If the artistic work was made before 1 August 1989 it gets protection for up to 10 years (88 Act, sch. 1, para. 19) if it was recorded in a design document or model. If the artistic work is recorded in some way that does not qualify as a design document or model it does not matter when the work was made, whether before or after 1 August 1989. Provided

- it is an artistic work (including a typeface) in its own right or
- is a design for something that is an artistic work in its own right

the work gets protection for up to 25 years from

- first marketing of copies made by an industrial process

The Secretary of State can specify what constitutes making something by an 'industrial process'. Under the Copyright (Industrial Process and Excluded Articles) (No. 2) Order 1989, an article is to be treated as made by an industrial process if at least 50 are made and the article is a copy of an artistic work but it is not part of a set of articles for registered design purposes

or

- it consists of goods manufactured in lengths or pieces which are not hand-made

The order also specifies what types of things of a literary or artistic character will still be covered by the ordinary rules about copyright duration. These are as follows

- works of sculpture
  - other than casts or models used or intended to be used as models or patterns to be multiplied by any industrial process
- wall plaques, medals and medallions
- printed matter, primarily of a literary or artistic character, including: book jackets, calendars, certificates, coupons, dressmaking patterns, greetings cards, labels, leaflets, maps, plans, playing-cards, postcards, stamps, trade advertisements, trade forms and cards, transfers
- and similar articles

Design right

Design right lasts for a period of no more than 15 years. In some circumstances the period of protection can be less than 15 years but it will never be less than 10 years. The 15-year period runs from the end of the calendar year in which the design is created (88 Act, s. 216(1)). To be more accurate, the period runs from when the design was first recorded in a 'design document' or an article is first made to the design.

However,

- if the design is exploited anywhere in the world the period of protection can be up to five years less

The shorter period applies where articles are made to the design and are made available for sale or hire within five years from the end of the calendar year in which the design was created (88 Act, s. 216). Once articles made to the design are made available for sale or hire within the five-year period the period of protection is limited to 10 years from when this first happens.

Example
For example, if a design for a ladder is created in a drawing or by the construction of a prototype on 1 September 1989 the design is protected for 15 years from 31 December 1989 i.e., protection will expire on 31 December 2004. However, if ladders made to the design are sold or hired during 1990 then protection will be limited to 10 years from 31 December 1990 i.e., protection will expire on 31 December 2000.

Licences of right
Licences of right are available or can become available in two situations. First,

- licences of right are available in the last five years of the period of design right protection

Secondly,

- licences of right can become available where the Monopolies and Mergers Commission reports that a refusal to grant licences on reasonable terms or the conditions attached to licences operates or may be expected to operate against the public interest (88 Act, s. 144)

Registered designs

The maximum period of protection available for a registered design is 25 years.

- where an application for registration of a design was made before 1 August 1989 the period of protection is a maximum of 15 years

The rights last initially for a period of five years. The registration can be renewed for up to a maximum of two further periods of five years. Renewal is by application and payment of the appropriate fee to the Designs Registry.

- where the application for registration is made on or after 1 August 1989 the rights in a registered design can last up to 25 years from the date of registration.

The 25-year period is not automatic. Whenever the application was made, once a design is registered it is protected by registered design rights for an initial period of five years from the date of registration (RDA 49, s. 8). The registration can be extended for up to four additional periods of five years each. This is on application and payment of the appropriate fee to the Designs Registry.

Although the registration lapses if the renewal is not made on time there is a six-month period of grace. This applies whenever the application for registration was made. If the renewal application is made within six months of the expiry of the end of a renewal period (except the last) then renewal is permissible provided an additional fee is paid (RDA 49, s. 8).

There is a special period of protection for some but not all designs where the application for registration was made after 12 January 1988 but before 1 August 1989. The period of protection is limited to 10 years from 1 August 1989. Additionally, on and from 1 August 1989 anyone is entitled to a licence of right in relation to such registered designs.

Licences of right
The appropriate government minister can initiate a process under which licences of right become available in certain circumstances. The situations in which the procedure can be initiated include

- where the Monopolies and Mergers Commission finds that a monopoly situation exists, or
- in certain circumstances where a there is a merger, or
- where someone has been operating an anti-competitive practice or
- where a course of conduct has been pursued which operates against the public interest

Semiconductor chip design

The period of protection for semiconductor chip designs is slightly different to that for designs under design right.

- the basic period of protection is 15 years

However,

- the 15-year period runs from
    — the time the semiconductor topography is created or
    — an article (e.g., a chip) is first made to the topography (New Chip Regulations reg. 6)

Under design right the 15-year period is a little longer as it runs from the end of the calendar year of creation

- once the topography is exploited then the period of protection is reduced to 10 years

More exactly, the 10-year period runs from the time either the topography is first made available to the public for sale or hire or articles made to the topography are first made available for sale or hire (New Chip Regulations, reg. 6).

Licences of right
Unlike ordinary design right,

- there are no licences of right generally available for design right in semiconductor chip designs

- the only way licences of right can become available is on the intervention of a government minister following a report by the Monopolies and Mergers Commission

7   Protecting Image and Reputation

PASSING-OFF, TRADE MARKS AND SERVICE MARKS

Copying business image and reputation

This chapter is about the way people copy in order to benefit from the image and reputation of others and whether this kind of copying can be prevented or restricted by law.

People use labels as a means of identification

The image and reputation of a business, a product or a service lies in what people have come to know of it and their experience of it, whether through advertising, direct experience or in other ways.

Athough there may be many different ways in which people may benefit from copying the image, style and presentation of others, the law is concerned with certain particular ways in which this can be done and with preventing damage to trading image and reputation which might result. This chapter is concerned with image and reputation associated with company, business and trading names and logos, as well as with names and logos used to identify products and services. For brevity the word 'marks' will be used in this chapter to mean all of these identifying labels.

Marks are not the only kinds of labels that people use to identify businesses, products and services. Presentation and appearance, or what is called 'get-up' in this area of law, can also be protected. Get-up is used to perform exactly the same role as marks and hence, the law protects get-up in a similar way to the way marks are protected.

The law does not protect image and reputation directly

The law of registered marks and passing-off does not operate to stop others trying to promote a similar image to that someone else has created

- the concept or theme underlying a mark or get-up is not protectable

Just copying the image, style or presentation of another is not sufficient in itself to amount to an infringement in this area of law. There is no prohibition under this branch of law on adopting a similar image, style or presentation to that enjoyed by others

- provided the copier does not allow the public to be confused about the identity of the business, products or services concerned

Innocence may be no defence

- the law of trade marks, service marks and passing-off is not concerned with distinguishing whether anyone has deliberately set out to imitate

If someone has innocently adopted a business name, brand name, mark or logo that is confusingly or deceptively similar to that used by another business this may not save the innocent infringer from attack. The point is that innocent infringement is just as commercially damaging to the injured party as deliberate infringement.

Overlap with other branches of intellectual property law

If a product is copied in its entirety there may be infringement of copyright, design right, registered design right and any patents that might cover the product. If the copier goes one step further and confuses others about the identity of the supplier or the identity of the goods or services then there may be a mark infringement or passing-off.

An example of when this area of the law needs to be considered

When approaching the stage of launching a product or service or new business the question of what name to choose becomes a priority. How a product is to be packaged or whether a logo is to be used for the business and what kind of overall image is desired also needs to be finalised.

Current UK law

The law applicable to protecting commercial and trading image from unacceptable copying lies in two basic areas. The first is what is called the law of passing-off and the second lies in the UK legislation concerning registered marks.

Usually, in books on passing-off and registered marks, these two areas of law are considered separately. However, in the real world, when someone copies the image, style and reputation of another organisation, what is important is how the copier is stopped and not the means for doing so. Additionally, passing-off and registered mark infringement are broadly about the same thing but there are differences. It is much easier to see where the differences lie when each aspect of these areas is considered side by side and that is what will be done here.

HOW MARKS AND GET-UP WORK

Identity, image and reputation

The identity of anything is

- everything that can possibly be known about something so that it can be distinguished from everything else and identified individually

People carry around a mental 'picture' of the things they have learnt about and gained experience of. The mental picture may not cover every single thing that is known about something but it is usually sufficient for the thing to be identified and distinguished from everything else for any one person's purposes.
The mental picture is the image.

- a wide variety of factors come together in the mind, many unconsciously, as together representing the identity of one particular business, or a product or a service

For most people image and identity are synonymous. The fact that image and identity are synonymous enables a common identity or image to be created for a business, product or service.
When the term 'reputation' is used in this book it means

- the common image of the business, product or service concerned shared by people

Names, marks, logos and get-up

Names, marks, logos and get-up are a shorthand way of identifying something.
A name, for example, is a label to

- identify and
- distinguish

something from everything else. At the same time the name becomes part of the identity of the thing.
Thus,

- names, logos, marks and get-up come to 'mean' everything that people associate with a business, product or service and
- they are used by people to distinguish it from all generically similar businesses, products or services

Therein lies their commercial value and importance.
Names, marks, logos and get-up are used

- to represent the image and reputation of a company or business
- as a 'brand' to give a common identity and image to ranges of different kinds of goods and services
- as a mark to give an identity to particular products and services

People respond well to pictures and logos. Pictures and logos can play exactly the same role as words, letters and numbers do. Logos and pictures are used extensively whether with or without words to distinguish companies, as brands for goods or as marks for particular products.   Packaging and product appearance can also operate in a similar way to logos and other pictures. The image, style and presentation of a product or service can reflect on and represent the company that supplies it.

Take cars as an example. Companies like Rolls-Royce and BMW have for many years maintained a particular kind of styling for their cars. The consequence of this is that it has always been possible to identify a BMW or Rolls-Royce car by virtue of the styling and appearance. Additionally, the reputation and image of the companies are reflected in the kind of products they produce. This is true in fact of any company.

The point to note is that

● logos and get-up can fulfil the same three roles as names

   — identifying the company or trading entity

   — operating as a brand

   — operating as a mark

and can also be chosen to reinforce an image conveyed by names and advertising.

Image and reputation in context

● just because the same identifiers are used to identify different things does not necessarily mean that confusion is going to result

People can quite happily cope with a word or a name or some other kind of identifier being used to mean different things in different contexts without confusing the identities of the various things the word can be used to mean.

● new images can be created for existing marks and get-up without confusion arising

● others can use the same or similar marks in different contexts without confusion occurring

Some examples

Pop stars can have difficulty stopping others selling 'T'-shirts and the like with their names on. In one case the pop group Abba failed to obtain an interlocutory injunction against someone selling 'T'-shirts, pillow-cases, badges, and other items bearing the Abba name and a photograph of the group (*Lyngstad* v *Anabas Products Ltd* [1977] FSR 62).

If performers do not actually trade in 'T'-shirts then they have no business or trading reputation to protect in that area of activity. If no one is likely to associate the goods with the performers then the performers are unlikely to suffer any damage to their trading reputation as a pop group.

In the music and entertainment world often great effort is put into creating and promoting images for performers which are out of the ordinary. As a result the public are less likely to associate the image of a performer with a mundane business, such as, say, a hypothetical Rolling Stones chip shop or heel bar or 'T'-shirt vendor.

The position of performers and famous personalities is not a special case. It may come as a surprise to many people to discover that there is no general legal protection preventing the images or names of famous (or completely unknown) personalities being used as marks or get-up on products or services. If the identifiers are taken out of their normal context then they can be used to create a wholly different image or meaning without anyone being confused about the different identities of the things they are used to describe.

If there is no valid trade mark registration and if no one else has already created the trading goodwill then there is nothing in registered mark law or passing-off to prevent anyone selling Margaret Thatcher chewing-gum or Neil Kinnock chocolate together with photographs of the individuals concerned on the wrappers.

In some circumstances use of another's name or picture might prove to be defamatory such as in the case of *Tolley* v *J. S. Fry & Sons Ltd* [1931] AC 333. In that case a caricature of an amateur golfer was used to advertise chocolate. At the time this implied that the golfer had compromised his amateur status by accepting payment for what appeared to be an endorsement. The golfer sued for libel and succeeded.

This does not mean that it is possible to represent that a product is endorsed by a personality when it is not. Such a representation might amount to a misleading trade description under consumer protection and trading standards legislation.

Alternatively if the representation that a product is endorsed by a personality could damage that person's business goodwill, say, as a performer, as a result of confusion then it might be actionable passing-off.

RECOGNISING WHAT CAN BE PROTECTED

Passing-off

The law of passing-off applies whenever there is the prospect of confusion between marks or get-up or where there is the prospect of confusion of identity through the unauthorised use of similar marks or get-up. As a consequence of this, the extent of protection available under the law of passing-off is much broader than under the law of registered marks.

Because the main consideration in passing-off is whether deception or confusion is likely to arise, passing-off can be used to protect pretty much any kind of distinctive name, mark, logo or get-up used to identify a company or business as such as well as products and services.

Sometimes the identity of a product can become so uniquely associated with its appearance that it comes to be identified by and distinguished from all other products by that appearance. Thus, anyone else who adopts an appearance for his product which could confuse the public about its identity could be committing passing-off.

There have been many cases in which the get-up of a product has been sufficiently distinctive that the court has considered the public were likely to be confused into buying the similar looking product, thinking it was the original manufacturer's product. Copying of the get-up of packaging, business premises, the colour, shape and size of products such as bottles and other containers, pharmaceutical capsules and tablets have all at one time or another come under scrutiny in this branch of the law. A recent case which went to the House of Lords confirmed that the law of passing-off can even be used to protect the yellow plastic lemons used by Reckitt & Colman as containers for Jif lemon juice (*Reckitt & Colman Products Ltd* v *Borden Inc.* [1990] 1 WLR 491).

The concept of get-up even applies to get-up associated with services, such as the colour schemes for taxis, shop-fronts and the like.

Registered marks

There are two kinds of registrable marks: trade marks and service marks. Trade marks are marks used in relation to goods and service marks are marks used in relation to services. What can qualify as a trade or service mark will be examined here. The rules are the same for both kinds of marks.

Definition of a trade mark
A trade mark is defined in s. 68 of the TMA 38 as including

> any device, brand, heading, label, ticket, name, signature, word, letter, numeral, or any combination thereof

The definition of what a trade mark includes is broad. It covers a wide variety of things which can be used as labels for identifying and distinguishing goods from other similar goods.

Definition of a service mark
The definition of what a service mark includes is

> any device, name, signature, word, letter, numeral, or any combination thereof

This is similar to the definition of a trade mark and is equally broad.

Use of a mark
For trade marks, use of the mark must be on or 'in physical or other relation to the goods' concerned. The meaning of the quoted words is not readily apparent. They suggest that a mark cannot be registered if it is in fact an integral part of the goods. Thus, where the physical appearance (get-up) of the goods becomes distinctive of them, that appearance may not be capable of being registered as a trade mark.

For service marks, use is taken to mean use of the mark as part of any statement about the availability or performance of services or use which is otherwise in relation to services.

Thus,

- registrable marks do not have to be words and can include pictures, logos and even aspects of appearance
- sounds alone can never be registered as marks
- protection for get-up is more limited than under the law of passing-off

Identity of companies and businesses
Companies and businesses want to stop others adopting similar names, marks logos and get-up in order to avoid the identity of the company or business being confused with another.

The law of registered marks is simply of no assistance here

- marks are registrable only to the extent that they are used to identify goods and services, not companies and businesses

Registered marks as brands
The law of registered marks does extend to marks used as brands but the protection is limited in a particular way

- a registration only affords protection for a mark when the mark is used in relation to the classes of goods or services for which it is registered

Thus, if anyone else uses a registered mark without permission for classes of goods or services not covered by the registration then they do not infringe the rights given by the registrations.

There is a standard classification of goods and services. There are 34 classes for goods and eight classes of services. The classes are set out in appendix 4. It is not generally possible to register a mark in every class because the registration of a mark in a particular class is not valid if there was no bona fide intention to use the mark for goods or services in that class when the application for registration was made or if no such use has taken place within five years from the date of registration.

Get-up and registered marks
Whether the get-up of a product can be registrable as a mark has been considered in some cases.

The coloured drug capsules Re Smith Kline & French Laboratories Ltd's Applications [1975] 1 WLR 914 concerned pharmaceuticals supplied in capsules which consisted of two basic components: tiny spherical pellets containing the drug and cylindrical capsules. The spherical pellets were contained in the cylindrical capsule. Unless colouring was added, the tiny pellets were white and the capsule was transparent.

Smith Kline & French ('SKF') adopted the practice of applying different colours to the tiny spherical pellets and colouring one half of the capsule, leaving the other half clear so that the coloured pellets could still be seen. The company applied to register 10 different colour combinations of pellet and capsule colours as trade marks.

The problem with this type of mark is that it is getting close to the goods themselves. However, the House of Lords in the SKF case did not think that that was, in itself, an objection to registration.

The distinction the court seemed to draw was that the colours as applied to the pellets and capsule constituted the 'mark' rather than the thing itself which was marked, namely the pellets and capsule.

The court considered a previous decision which concerned coloured threads woven into stockings (*Re F. Reddaway & Co. Ltd's Application* [1914] 1 Ch 856). In that case the coloured threads were considered to be capable of acting as a trade mark. When deciding the coloured capsules case the House of Lords did not consider the previous case to have been wrongly decided.

The end-result was that the SKF trade mark applications were permitted to go ahead. The court considered that there was nothing in the legislation to prevent a mark from covering the whole of the surface of an article or requiring marks to be limited to some two-dimensional pattern to be applied to the surface of an article.

The SKF coloured capsule case needs to be contrasted with the Coca-Cola bottle case.

The Coca-Cola Bottle Case   *Re Coca-Cola Co.* [1986] 1 WLR 695 concerned applications by the Coca-Cola Company to register the well-known shape of the Coca-Cola drink bottle as a trade mark.

The House of Lords considered that the function of trade mark legislation was to protect the mark rather than the article to which it was applied and that a mark was apt only to describe something which distinguished goods rather than the goods themselves. A bottle was a container and not a mark.

Why bother to register any marks?
At this point you may be asking why anyone bothers to register a trade or service mark if passing-off affords a much broader protection. The simple answer is that it makes life much easier to have a registration.

With passing-off it is necessary to establish a right to prevent someone else using a confusingly or deceptively similar mark or get-up. The right is established partly by showing that the public actually does associate the mark or get-up with the particular business, product or service concerned. This is an expensive, time consuming and uncertain process involving many witnesses and can involve expensive market survey evidence.

With a registration on the other hand all that is required to establish the right to the monopoly is the certificate of registration. Thus,

- proving a right to a monopoly with registered marks is much simpler and cheaper than under the law of passing-off

DISTINCTIVENESS

What underpins the success of a mark or get-up in commercial terms and also whether it is protectable in law lies in two areas

- its inherent distinctiveness

● the extent to which it has become associated through use with the image or identity it represents (its 'distinctiveness through use')

These two concepts are easily confused. This is compounded by the fact that the law uses one word, 'distinctiveness', to refer to both of them. Not only does the law use the same word to describe both but it is not always clear from the context which of the two concepts is being referred to.

Although this sounds inept it is a natural consequence of the fact that a mark can be and normally is both distinctive in itself and distinctive because it has become strongly associated with some image. In other words, the two concepts are almost inextricably intertwined. Additionally, because all that people care about on the practical level is whether a mark or get-up is distinctive, they do not bother to separate the two concepts out in their own minds.

What is 'distinctiveness'?

'Distinctiveness' is actually used to mean 'overall distinctiveness'. In qualitative terms

OVERALL	=	INHERENT	+	DISTINCTIVENESS
Distinctiveness		Distinctiveness		Through Use

It is important therefore to be clear about what is meant by the terms 'inherent distinctiveness' and 'distinctiveness through use'. Please note that the terminology used here is not standard legal jargon nor is it in common use so if you use it do not expect people to immediately recognise these terms.

Inherent distinctiveness means

● the mark or get-up is distinct in itself from everything else, and

● no one can justifiably claim the right to want to use it

Take a trade mark like Kodak. The word is an invented word. The sequence of letters making up the word are unique. As far as most people are concerned there is no other word like it. It does not look like any other word nor sound like any other word (or at least this was so for all practical purposes when it was invented). Thus, in the first sense of the word 'distinctive', 'Kodak' is inherently distinctive in itself.

A word like 'the' is not inherently distinctive. It is not different from a word that everyone else might want to use in any context. If it were ever to be used as a mark it would be practically indistinguishable both visually and in what it sounds like from what anyone else might use in any normal context.

Thus, there is a notional scale of inherent distinctiveness running from zero to high. A word like Kodak originally had high inherent distinctiveness and a word like 'the' has zero inherent distinctiveness.

Very few marks are actually totally new. People create marks and get-up by using or adapting ordinary words, or using or adapting common pictures, designs or logos. Thus,

● one end of the scale of inherent distinctiveness is a mark or get-up which is totally unique and quite unlike anything else and

- the other end is a mark or get-up which is indistinguishable from what everyone else uses

The point is that

- inherent distinctiveness can be a question of the degree to which a mark or get-up is different from everything else

Distinctiveness through use

The concept of distinctiveness through use can be easily confused with inherent distinctiveness simply because of what happens in practice. Consider the mark 'Kodak' again.

As far as most people were concerned, before it was used as a trade mark for photographic film and cameras, 'Kodak' had no other meaning or significance. It could not therefore be confused with the identity of anything else because

- it had no image associated with it

Thus, once it was used as a mark only the image of the things it was used to identify became associated with it. In other words its inherent distinctiveness enabled it to easily become distinctive of the image it was to be associated with through use.

The concept of a mark or get-up being *completely* distinctive through use is therefore that

- as the mark or get-up has no association with any other image (i.e. it does not mean anything else) it can only come to mean the thing it is used to identify and nothing else

This means that once an inherently distinctive mark has acquired distinctiveness through use it should never be possible to confuse such a mark with anything else.

'Kodak' as a mark had a high overall distinctiveness because it had high inherent distinctiveness before it was ever used and once it was used it quickly acquired high distinctiveness through use. This combination made the mark 'Kodak' a powerful identifying label.

Strength and breadth of image weaken inherent distinctiveness

Inherent distinctiveness is a quality a mark or get-up can only have before it is used. Once it is used for one purpose and is then intended to be used for another, it will no longer be inherently distinctive for use for that other purpose or indeed any other purpose because it has acquired a meaning.

Two things can affect the extent to which inherent distinctiveness of a mark is weakened if it is to be used to identify other things. The first is the strength of image

- if a mark or get-up becomes strongly associated by people with one image and only one image then it is more difficult to give the mark another meaning by associating it with something else. People have to be taught the new association

The second thing that can weaken inherent distinctiveness of a mark to be used to identify more than one kind of thing is the breadth of image associated with the mark. If a mark is associated with broad general characteristics like high quality, fast service, low cost rather than with one particular kind of product like a motor vehicle then it is less capable of taking on a wholly new meaning. The old meaning or significance of the mark may be so broad that it overlaps with the proposed new meaning.

If an organisation proposes to use one of its existing marks to identify a new product or service, the breadth of image already associated with the mark may mean that the mark is only suitable for products or services which fit in with the original general image associated with the mark.

Conversely, if the image is particularly strong but narrowly associated with very specific qualities and characteristics, then, despite the mark or get-up being inherently distinctive, its use in other circumstances may not lead to confusion.

Thus, if someone opens up a legal practice called Kodak and Partners, the likelihood of confusion might be slight because the narrowness of the image would mean that very few people if any would be likely to confuse camera and film products with legal services.

Problems with descriptive marks

The problem with trying to rely on a mark which is descriptive is that success in court requires strong evidence. The court has to be convinced that you should be entitled to a monopoly in the use of an everyday word, mark or get-up in what is almost an everyday sense.

Consider the commercial consequences. To get protection under the law takes either

● a great deal of time and effort

or

● a great deal of money and effort

In order to create a second meaning for a descriptive mark or get-up which is stronger than its ordinary meaning requires everyone to learn the new meaning. It also means they must learn only to use the mark or get-up to identify the business, products or services concerned and not use it to describe them in the ordinary way. This can take a long time and considerable effort.

The alternative, if time is to be saved, is to teach people the new second meaning for the descriptive mark or get-up by using advertising and promotions of various kinds. This can take less time but considerable effort and money.

An example of a descriptive mark is the JIF lemon. Most people who buy lemon juice know that it comes from lemons. The courts decided that despite the container being descriptive of its contents, the shape and colour were capable in law of becoming so associated with the products of Reckitt & Colman *by use over a long period of time* that they indicated the products of Reckitt & Colman and no one else.

The point is that

- even a descriptive mark or get-up can come to identify and distinguish a particular business, product or service from all others through use

The mark is not distinctive at all in itself nor can it properly be described as being capable of taking on a new meaning in addition to its ordinary meaning. However, through use the strength of image associated with the mark can, in a particular context, become greater than the ordinary meaning of the word.

Strengthening distinctiveness

It is possible to strengthen the inherent distinctiveness of a mark or get-up as well as its distinctiveness through use.

Strengthening distinctiveness through use
The distinctiveness of a mark or get-up can be strengthened through use in two ways

- by the use of advertising, promotion or in other ways a mark or get-up can become more strongly associated by the public with what it is used to identify
- broadening the association to cover general rather than specific characteristics or general business activities or general ranges of product or services rather than specific ones

Strengthening inherent distinctiveness
It is difficult to make ordinary words which have an ordinary meaning inherently distinctive. There are basically only two things that can be done with them

- use them in a totally different context to their normal use
- change their appearance by adding distinctive features

The latter approach was used for the name 'Robin Hood' where the 'R' was represented as an archer holding a bow facing the 'D' at the other end of the word 'Hood'. The 'D' was represented as a bulls-eye style archery ring target (*Re Standard Cameras Ltd's Application* (1952) 69 RPC 125).

The Robin Hood kind of distinctiveness is, however, not very helpful if the sound of a word is going to be more important than the appearance. It is sometimes possible to devise a word which is at once invented but at the same time has a trace of a connection generically with what it is to be used to identify.

However, this is not as easy to achieve as it seems. This is partly because people simply want to slightly rearrange the spelling so that the words look or sound similar to their normal sound or appearance.

'Orlwoola', which was the subject of a trade mark application for garments, was not a good mark because it sounds like the ordinary phrase 'all wool' and others might justifiably want to describe their garments as 'all wool' (*Re Joseph Crosfield & Sons Ltd's Application* (1909) 26 RPC 837).

Another mark was 'Electrix' which was simply a phonetic equivalent of 'electrics' and hence failed to be treated as distinctive (*Electrix Ltd* v *Electrolux Ltd* [1960] AC 722).

An example of a word which was treated by the Trade Marks Registry as distinctive is 'Solio'. The mark was intended for use in identifying and for distinguishing photographic paper. Despite its significance in Latin as meaning 'sun' and despite 'sol' meaning sun in other languages the word was considered inherently distinctive because the association with the sun was considered to be too slight to affect its inherent distinctiveness (*Re Eastman Photographic Materials Co. Ltd's Applications* (1898) RPC 476).

Distinctiveness and others' marks

A mark or get-up needs to be distinctive in the sense that it needs to be sufficiently different from what others use. If the mark or get-up is already used by someone else to identify a business, goods or services then it is not inherently distinctive for all purposes but it can be inherently distinctive in context.

An example is the name 'Apple'. As long as it is not being used to describe anything to do with fruit or trees and the like then Apple is distinctive both on the inherent distinctiveness and distinctiveness through use scales. When 'Apple' is used in relation to computers and information technology it means both the Apple group of companies and the range of computers and software designed, manufactured and supplied by that group. A particular kind of image is associated with the name 'Apple' in this context.

However, when the name 'Apple' is used in relation to electronic and electromechanically recorded music and the 60s pop group the Beatles, it means the Apple recording studios and music publishing business. Even though two companies have the same or a similar name does not necessarily mean the public will become confused about which is which.

The first point to be made is that the same mark can be used by different organisations without there being any serious risk of confusion of identity.

However, if Apple the music recording and publishing business moves into electronically produced music, like synthesised music and computer-generated music, or if Apple the computer company did so then is there a possibility of confusion arising because the image of the 'Apple' name would then become less distinct having more than one image related to the name? A dispute between the two companies on this very aspect was settled by agreement between them (as reported in *Intellectual Property Newsletter,* vol. 12, issue 4).

Thus, the point is that

● exactly the same name can be used on goods or in relation to services without there being any risk of confusion arising

This is provided there is nothing which, in addition to the name, is likely to cause the identity or image to be confused.

Loss of distinctiveness

There is yet another aspect of distinctiveness which can be absolutely fatal but usually only for word marks. Sometimes the mark and what it is used to identify become so closely associated that the mark becomes generic. Names which were once distinctive have become descriptive generically, like gramophone, escalator, perspex and zipper. The names are now synonymous with the item and have become incapable of conveying any relationship with a person, quality of manufacture or original source of the items concerned. The words have simply become the names of the particular items.

In fact, in the cases of words like gramophone and perspex, only one source initially produced these products so everyone came to describe them generically by their trade mark. This was not surprising because there was no other name to use to describe the kind of goods concerned.

It is important to guard against the loss of distinctiveness. Once you allow people to start using marks generically they can fall into common use. 'Xerox' was at one stage in danger of becoming generic in relation to photocopiers. Xerox was the dominant force in photocopier technology and supply. People used to refer to 'Xerox copies' rather than 'photocopies' and to 'running off a xerox' and similar phrases. The mark was in danger of going the same route that 'zip' went. However, Xerox has taken measures, through various means including advertising, to teach its employees, customers and the public to use 'Xerox' as a mark and not generically.

It is an extremely dangerous practice to allow a mark or get-up to be used in a generically descriptive sense. It can often happen where a product or service is the only one in the market and there is no other name to describe the product or service. Words like linoleum and perspex were marks but came to describe the generic type of product because no other word was available.

Thus,

- if there is no generic name or identifier for a product other than its mark or get-up, then invent one

- make sure everyone uses the descriptive generic name to describe the general kind of business, product or service but uses your mark or get-up to identify and distinguish your business, products and services from everyone else's

PICKING A REGISTRABLE MARK

Distinctive marks and the law

Under the law of passing-off, despite a mark or get-up being descriptive, it may still be protectable provided there is sufficiently strong evidence of distinctiveness through use. The point being that the law of passing-off will afford protection if the mark is so distinctive through use that the public are likely to be confused if someone else uses a similar mark or get-up.

With registered marks the position is different but not completely so. There are in broad concept three categories of marks, only two of which are registrable

- marks which are distinctive in themselves
  - — i.e., marks which are inherently distinctive or inherently distinctive in context
- marks which are either not or are only partially distinctive in themselves and are permitted to be registered because there is evidence of distinctiveness through use
- marks which are treated by the courts as not being capable of being or becoming distinctive and are never registrable

Registrable marks

There are two sets of rules governing what kinds of marks are registrable. The first set are for marks registrable in Part A of the register and the second set are for marks registrable in Part B. The most important practical difference between a Part A registration and a Part B registration lies in the rights associated with the registration.

As far as obtaining a registration is concerned, the basic difference is that Part A marks are marks which are inherently distinctive either in themselves or in the context of the goods or services to be covered by the registration. Part B marks are marks which are in some way descriptive but which have become distinctive through use. Although it is an easy distinction to make, it is not wholly accurate for two reasons.

Some marks are permitted to be registered in Part A of the register which have low inherent distinctiveness but which have been shown to have become distinctive through use. Additionally, some marks which are registered in Part B of the register can be moved from Part B to Part A eventually on evidence of distinctiveness through use. This makes matters confusing and is a consequence of the muddled state of the law in in this area.

The technical legal difference between Part A and Part B marks is set out in s. 10 of the TMA 38. The difference is that for registration in Part A the mark must be *adapted to distinguish* and for Part B it must be *capable of distinguishing* the goods and services of the proprietor from those of anyone else. If it is not immediately clear what the distinction is do not be concerned because this provision has confused trade mark agents, patent agents, lawyers and everyone else for many years.

Inherently distinctive marks

There is one general category of registrable mark and it is simply

- any distinctive mark

There are also four specific categories of marks which are considered to be distinctive in themselves

- names represented as logos
- signatures
- invented words

- words having no direct connection with the characteristics or qualities of the goods or services concerned

The four specific categories are concerned with marks which are inherently distinctive in some way. The general category is concerned with marks which are inherently distinctive but it also can cover marks which have become sufficiently distinctive through use.

The four specific categories of registrable marks will be looked at first as they give an indication of what kinds of marks are considered *not* to be inherently distinctive.

Names represented as logos

The exact wording of the legislation for this category is

- the name of a company, individual or firm, represented in a special or particular manner

The basic reason for the existence of this category is that ordinary names are not in themselves capable of being inherently distinctive at all. However, a representation of a name in a particular manner adding features to a mark can give it some inherent distinctiveness.

As was seen above, the name Robin Hood was registrable where the letter 'R' in the name was represented as an archer and the letter 'D' was represented as a target (*Re Standard Cameras Ltd's Application* (1952) 69 RPC 125).

It is important to note that

- the registration of a name represented in some special or particular manner does not give a monopoly in the exclusive use of the name

- it gives a monopoly in the exclusive use of the name *as represented in that way*

Thus, getting a registration of a name represented in a special way does not prevent others using the same name for the same goods or services. Others are only prevented from using a similar *presentation* of the name.

Signatures as marks

The exact wording of the legislation for this category of registrable mark is

- the signature of the applicant for registration or some predecessor in his business

An example of a signature which is capable of registration under this head is the signature of Arthur Guinness which appears on the labels of bottles of Guinness stout and on the outside of cans of Guinness stout.

Signatures are not always very good marks. They may have high inherent distinctiveness but often they are not easy to read.

Again, the same comments about the extent of the monopoly apply here as to names presented in a special way

● the registration does not give exclusive rights to the name, only the name in the form of the signature

Invented words

Invented words are the best kind of word marks to have a registration for. Invented words such as Kodak have high inherent distinctiveness.

Invented words which are gross misspellings of ordinary words do not qualify as invented words capable of registration under this head. These include words like Orlwoola, Trakgrip and Litetrac.

The word 'Whiskeur' for whisky-based liqueurs was allowed to be registered as an invented word. Although this seems strange, there comes a point at which a decision has to be made about whether the word has or has not become sufficiently different from any other word or from any word anyone may justifiably want to use. Some invented words will fall just on one side of the line and others will fall just on the other side. Whisquer seems to have made it to the right side for the registered proprietor.

As a guide to what kinds of words may make it to registration as invented words, in *Re S. F. & O. Hallgarten's Application* (1949) 66 RPC 105, the Assistant Comptroller-General of Patents, Designs and Trade Marks gave examples of invented words which were considered to be sufficiently distinctive to be capable of registration. Some were registered in Part A and others were registered in Part B. The Part A marks were as follows:

Word	*A combination of*
Coffusa	Coffee and infuser
Bitumetal	Bitumen and metal
Frumato	Fruit and tomato
Aluminoy	Aluminium and alloy
Flavotainer	Flavour and container/retainer
Rumaica	Rum and Jamaica
Scrapaptiser	Scrap and appetiser
Glucoda	Glucose and soda

The Part B marks were as follows:

Word	*A combination of*
Liviar	Liver and caviar
Sweephat	Sweet and fat
Solupyridine	Soluble and pyridine

Quite how it is that of these marks came to be registered in Part A and how the decision was made about which were suitable for Part A or Part B is not easy to see.

Defensive registration

What may appear to be another potential advantage of invented words is that it may be possible to obtain what is called a 'defensive registration'. Defensive registrations are only available for invented word marks.

The advantage of a defensive registration is that it covers all classes and so prevents anyone else registering any mark which is confusingly or deceptively similar. Thus, defensive registration has the potential to pave the way for the registration of marks generally for use as brands. Defensive registrations are not common. They are not easy to obtain.

Defensive registration was originally available for trade marks but the new law extending the TMA 38 to cover service marks did not also extend the defensive registration provisions to cover service marks. Thus, it is only possible to obtain a defensive registration for a trade mark.

There are two basic conditions to be met by a trade mark before it can be defensively registered

- the mark must be an invented word
- the mark must be well-known

The problem with whether a mark is well-known is tricky. The mark must be so well-known that its use by others in relation to any goods would lead people to believe that there was a trading connection between the person who has made the mark famous and anyone else who uses it.

Thus, just because a mark is famous is not sufficient

- the association the public has with the mark must effectively be so strong that regardless of who else uses the mark and regardless of the kind of goods, confusion or deception must be likely to arise.

This is an almost impossibly difficult thing to show.

The other main problem with defensive registration is that it only covers words, and even more limited in that the words have to be invented.

Words having no direct connection with the characteristics or qualities of the goods or services concerned

The exact wording of the legislation with regard to this category of registrable mark is

- a word or words having no direct reference to the character or quality of the goods not being according to its ordinary signification a geographical name or a surname

The same rules apply to service marks. The main feature of this category is that it excludes from registrability marks which are descriptive in specific ways, namely, in relation to the character and qualities of goods.

Again, names are not treated as being inherently distinctive. In this case it is surnames that are treated as not being inherently distinctive rather than any name. An example of a word which was not permitted to be registered under this category is 'Cannon'. This was, by its ordinary signification a surname (*Cannon Trade Mark* [1980] RPC 519).

The reasons why geographical names are not inherently distinctive are similar to the reasons for names. First, the name is not inherently distinctive because it already identifies something (it has a meaning). Also, allowing someone to register a geographical place name could prevent others from justifiably describing their goods by reference to their geographical source.

For example, 'Livron' was not permitted to be registered for a liver tonic contain liver and iron. Livron was the name of a town in France. What was worse for the applicant for registration was that medicines were made there. Thus it failed the test of being inherently distinctive on both counts (*Re Boots Pure Drug Co. Ltd's Trade Mark 'Livron'* (1937) 54 RPC 327).

Thus, if the word is not by its ordinary signification a name or geographical name it can be registered provided it does not describe the characteristics or qualities of the class of goods or services in respect of which it is intended to be used and registered.

This is a test of whether the mark is inherently distinctive in context. 'Weldmesh' was not registrable under this category for use as a mark to identify steel wire mesh products (but it obtained a registration in Part B on evidence of distinctiveness through use).

This does not mean that the word has to be used in a way that is totally divorced from any ordinary meaning or association it may already have nor that it must not carry with it some built-in reference to the kind of goods or services it is to be used to identify as a mark. 'Kynite' was, for example, permitted for registration in relation to explosives.

Any other distinctive mark

For this category, there are two different tests of whether a mark is registrable. The first test is whether the mark is inherently distinctive in the context in which it is intended to be used. An example of such a mark is Apple for computers. In such a context 'Apple' is inherently distinctive. The second test applies if the mark is not sufficiently inherently distinctive and is whether the mark has become distinctive through use. The second test will be considered later in relation to marks which have become distinctive through use.

Note that, as an example of what may not be sufficiently inherently distinctive under this category, marks made up of three or fewer letters of the alphabet, like initials, can be difficult to register. The same applies to number and letter combinations. Their inherent distinctiveness is low as others may want to use them in many different contexts. Thus, these kinds of marks are best avoided.

Logos, pictures and the like can be distinctive

The 'any other distinctive mark' category can be applied equally to marks which rely for their distinctiveness wholly on visual aspects or which are combinations of words and logos, pictures and the like. These kinds of marks are usually referred to as 'device' marks or combinations of device and word marks.

Although the inherent distinctiveness and distinctiveness through use of these marks can be more difficult to assess, the basic concepts underlying what is distinctive are the same as those applied to word marks.

The difficulties in assessing distinctiveness lie in deciding

● what visual aspects of the marks give them their inherent distinctiveness

- what aspects of the marks stick in the mind so that people take notice and remember them above all others (i.e., what aspects give the marks their distinctiveness of Image)

Colours or colour combinations can be registered as distinctive marks. However, it may be difficult to obtain registrations for single colours on their own for broad classes of goods or services. Anyone may want to be able to use colours in any way for goods or services, even if just in a decorative way. Thus, colours do not on their own have a high inherent distinctiveness. However, if the context in which a colour is intended to be used is narrowed and a particular colour combination is selected then the inherent distinctiveness of the combination is increased and makes the combination more likely to be registrable because others will be less likely to want to use that particular combination in that particular context. An example is colour combinations used as get-up on pharmaceutical preparations like tablets.

Marks which have become distinctive

It is possible to register, in Part A and in Part B, marks which have become distinctive through use.

Section 9(2) of the TMA 38 provides that a distinctive mark is one that is adapted to distinguish the goods or services of the proprietor from those of anyone else. In considering distinctiveness it is permitted to take account of whether

- the mark is inherently adapted to distinguish

or

- the mark is adapted to distinguish through use or any other circumstance (TMA 38, s. 9(3))

In other words, if a mark word has become distinctive through use it may be registrable even though its inherent distinctiveness is low. However, if the inherent distinctiveness is low, the evidence of use and of association of the mark by the public with the goods and services concerned needs to be very strong in order to obtain a registration in Part A. Even if it is strong, there is no guarantee of obtaining a registration.

The mark Weldmesh was refused registration in Part A for use as a mark for steel wire mesh. It obtained a registration in Part B upon evidence of distinctiveness through use.

Part B marks and distinctiveness

The difference between Part A and Part B marks is that for registration in Part A the mark must be *adapted to distinguish* and for Part B it must be *capable of distinguishing* the goods and services of the proprietor from those of anyone else.

Basically, what happens in practice is that marks which are not considered by the Trade Marks Registry to have sufficient overall distinctiveness for Part A sometimes make it to Part B.

Because the law is confused in this area there is very little point going through any detailed discussion of the issues concerning what kinds of marks are registrable in Part B. Even if you think a mark is not likely to be registrable, it may still be registered. However, do not forget that the mark can be challenged later, on the basis that it should not have been registered.

Basically, as a rule of thumb, any mark may be registrable in Part B provided

- it has some, albeit slight inherent distinctiveness
- it can be shown that it has distinctiveness through use

The distinctiveness through use needs to be much higher to obtain a registration in Part A than for Part B.

Marks which are never registrable

The courts will not allow a mark to be registered if its inherent distinctiveness is too low even if on the scale of distinctiveness through use it scores 100%.

This happened in a case where the applicant sought to register Yorkshire for 'solid drawn tubes and capillary fittings, all being made of copper or non-ferrous copper alloys'. It was accepted that the word 'Yorkshire' had become 100% distinctive through use.

Thus, there is a direct contrast with the law of passing-off. In passing-off it seems that a mark or get-up can be protectable if it has high distinctiveness through use even though, on the scale of inherent distinctiveness it scores zero (e.g., Jif plastic lemons used as containers for lemon juice).

Under this category, and by the same kind of reasoning, laudatory terms like, 'best', 'greatest', 'perfect' and the like can never be registered because others may want to use them to describe any goods or services in any context. Thus, words of this kind can never be registered even if they have 100% distinctiveness through use.

RIGHTS AND INFRINGEMENT

Rights conferred by registration

The basic right the registered proprietor of a trade mark obtains is the exclusive right to use the mark. 'Exclusive' means exactly that,

- no one else is allowed to use the mark in relation to the goods or services in respect of which it is registered

Thus, registering a trade mark for footwear will not prevent someone else registering the same mark for animal feed.

- it is crucial to register a mark to cover all of the goods or services in respect of which it is going to be used
- this means
  - choosing the right classes in which to register the mark
  - and, if necessary, amending the wording of the standard classification in order to match the goods or services concerned

Additionally,

● the only way anyone else can be stopped from using the mark for *any description of goods or services not covered by the registration* is if a passing-off action can be sustained. If it cannot, regardless of what confusion may arise in the future, such use cannot be prevented

Non-business use is not infringement

The exclusive right only prevents others using the mark in the way of business as a trade or service mark.

Others are not prevented from using the mark simply to describe the goods or services if they do not do so in the way of trade or business. You will no doubt be immensely relieved to know that when writing out your grocery list, putting the names of branded goods like Kelloggs Cornflakes on it is not trade mark infringement and neither is handing the list to the shop assistant.

Limited business use is allowed

It is permissible for others to use a registered mark in a limited way in trade or business

● the extent of use other traders can make of registered marks can be very restricted and this is not something many people realise

Goods as marked by a manufacturer are often sold to wholesalers and distributors to be resold to retailers and eventually down the chain of suppliers to the consumer. It would be somewhat strange if the wholesalers, retailers and others in the chain were to be treated as committing trade mark infringement just by selling original goods, as manufactured, packaged and marked by the original manufacturer, and not altered or adapted in any way.

Where the goods are put on the market, it is recognised by the law that this can amount to implied permission to deal in the goods in the way they were originally marked. The law provides generally for this type of thing in that

● others can use registered trade or service marks in ways which are expressly or impliedly authorised by the proprietor

Use of a trade or service mark can be implicitly authorised in a wide variety of ways. Whether or not any particular use is implicitly authorised can depend on the circumstances. Thus, it is not safe just to assume that using a mark, even to describe the original supplier's goods or services, such as in an advertisement, is always going to be permitted.

With services, the law expressly permits use of a service mark to indicate that the services have been carried out. For example, a service mark may be used to describe a specialist service like woodworm and dry rot treatment as provided by a particular company. Where such a service has been provided by the relevant company it is permissible for anyone to use the service mark to describe the building as having been subjected to the treatment, e.g., 'treated by X' (X represents whatever the service mark is).

Unauthorised use in advertisements

It can be a risky practice to use some else's registered mark in an advertisement without permission. This can still be the case even if the advertisements are to resell the goods concerned or to advertise services related to the goods.

Comparative advertising

Comparative advertising occurs where one trader's product is compared in an advertisement with another's product by reference to a registered trade mark. The sort of thing is where an advertisement makes a comparision like 'The Bentley dishwasher is twice as fast as the Mercedes dishwasher'. If the mark 'Mercedes' is registered and the registration is for the class of goods which includes dishwashers then the advertisment might infringe.

When a mark is used by an advertiser in comparative advertisements, the advertiser is using the registered mark either implicitly or explicitly to say that its businesses, goods or services are as good as or better than those identified by the registered mark. The rationale underlying the protection against comparative advertising seems, from decided cases, to be that

- the advertiser is unjustifiably obtaining the benefit of the image and reputation that is associated with the mark and has been built up in the public's mind by the registered proprietor

Thus, this kind of use of the registered marks of others amounts to infringement.

Altered or adulterated goods and repackaging

It can also be a risky practice to alter trade-marked goods and resell them under their original mark. Once the goods have been altered the proprietor might justifiably object. This sort of infringement is based on the fact that

- the altered goods should no longer be identified by the mark as they are not the same as the goods to which the mark was originally applied

Similarly,

- it can amount to infringement of a service mark to use the mark to indicate a particular service has been carried out when the service was not carried out by the registered proprietor

It can also be infringement if part of what was done was done by the registered proprietor but the remainder of the service was carried out by someone else.

Repackaging goods and applying the original mark to the goods afterwards can amount to infringement. There has been a considerable amount of activity in the courts in relation to goods imported from EEC countries which are repackaged by someone who is not the proprietor of the original mark. The cases have mostly concerned imports of drugs which have to be repackaged

- in some circumstances it can be permissible to repackage goods and apply the original mark to them

However,

- do not try to do this without seeking specialist advice first

Selling accessories and spare parts

It can be permissible to use another's registered mark to sell accessories, spare parts and similar consumables. However, care must still be taken here

- the accessories or spares must be adapted to form part of the trade-marked goods concerned
- it must be reasonably necessary to use the mark in order to indicate that the accessories or spares are so adapted
- no one must be given the impression that the accessories and spares are from the same source as the original trade-marked goods

Thus, if 'Ace' is registered in respect of radios, televisions, spares and accessories, someone selling aerials for Ace televisions and radios which are independently manufactured must take care to ensure the aerials are not described as 'Ace' aerials.

Supplying ancillary services

It can be permissible to use another's service mark to describe services which are available for use with someone else's services.

For example, if a computerised information service is available through a telephone network it would not be an infringement to describe the service as 'X information service available through Y telephone network services', where Y is the registered service mark of the telephone network service provider.

Importing goods

Do not assume that it is permissible to import trade-marked goods from other countries into the UK without risk of infringement proceedings if there is a similar UK mark registered in respect of the goods. First the goods might not be in any way connected with the UK registered proprietor of the mark. Thus, use of the mark in relation to the imported goods would directly infringe the exclusive rights of the proprietor.However, even importing goods into the UK which are sold overseas by a UK manufacturer or by an associated company can still infringe. Goods which are imported under such circumstances are sometimes referred to as 'grey market goods'. With these goods it is not always clear whether the importation infringes.

Imports from the EEC

The position in relation to trade-marked goods from EEC countries is different, as is mentioned in chapter 9. If the trade-marked goods are put on sale in another EEC country by or with the consent of the UK registered proprietor then the importation cannot be prevented. Even so, care needs to be taken because goods sold in other countries with similar marks to UK registered marks may in fact have no connection at all with the UK proprietor, so importation in such a case could still infringe.

The difference in rights between Part A and Part B marks

● for Part A and Part B registrations, the rights are identical with one exception

For marks registered in Part A, use of the mark without consent in relation to the description of goods or services covered by the registration is infringement, whether innocently committed or not. With Part B marks the position is almost exactly the same. There is one significant difference

● if the alleged infringer can show that no confusion or deception is likely to arise from the allegedly infringing use then there is no infringement

The distinction is a reflection of the fact that,

● for marks registered in Part A of the register the law treats them as being 100% inherently distinctive of the goods or services for which they are registered thus, as far as the law is concerned, any use as a mark is infringement irrespective of whether there is any prospect of confusion arising

Part B marks are marks which have low inherent distinctiveness but which have been registered because evidence of distinctiveness through use has been established. If in any particular case it can be shown that no confusion or deception is likely to arise from the alleged infringer's use then this is indicative that the mark has not become sufficiently distinctive through use.

PASSING-OFF AND THE RIGHTS OF THE OWNER OF GOODWILL

In its classic form passing-off occurs where a trader confuses or deceives the public about the identity of his or her business, products or services. Where the public is led to believe that the business, products or services are those of another trader or are connected with another trader, and that other trader's business or trading goodwill is likely to be damaged, this can amount to passing-off.

The law of passing-of may develop and broaden to cover more general situations in which one trader's business is damaged by false representations made by another trader. However, the most instructive guides currently availble to what can amount to passing-off are found in previously decided cases. With the law of passing-off there are no statutory rights set out in an Act of Parliament as there are for registered marks.

Activities that may be passing-off

Passing-off goods

- refilling empty trade-marked containers with goods which are not those of the plaintiff e.g., refilling empty gas cylinders
- representing that goods or services are supplied under licence from the plaintiff
- supplying the plaintiff's goods packaged together with other goods so that the public may think the other goods are also those of the plaintiff
- supplying other goods in substitution for those requested e.g., selling a drink consisting of a different brand of rum and cola when asked for 'Bacardi and Coke'
- supplying the plaintiff's reject or substandard goods which had not been marketed by the plaintiff e.g., obtaining scrapped goods intended for destruction and selling them as the plaintiff's goods
- where two different qualities of the same goods are normally supplied by the plaintiff, representing the lower-quality product is of the higher quality
- selling second-hand, modified or repaired examples of the plaintiff's goods whilst representing they are new
- selling examples of the plaintiff's goods which have deteriorated as if they are of normal quality

Passing-off a business

- representing a business is the plaintiff's business when it is not
- representing a business as being connected with the plaintiff's business, e.g.,
  — an agent
  — an authorised, dealer or distributor
- representing that a business is licensed by or authorised by the plaintiff

Passing-off goods as being of a generic kind
There have been some cases where passing-off has succeeded against traders who misrepresent the character or quality of their goods without actually passing them off as the goods of anyone else. However, where the misrepresentation can damage the general reputation of a generic product then the suppliers of the generic product may be able to succeed in a passing-off action. This can occur

- by passing-off goods as having been manufactured or produced in a particular geographic region when they have not
  e.g., selling a drink as sherry when it has not been produced in the Jerez region of Spain (although because of delay in enforcing their rights, the Spanish sherry producers cannot now stop fortified wine made in the UK being described as British sherry)

- by passing-off goods as champagne which have not been made in the Champagne region of France
- selling a drink as advocaat when it is made with eggs and sherry rather than with eggs and the more expensive spirits of the traditional recipe

Switch selling
The Law of Passing-Off by Christopher Wadlow (London: Sweet & Maxwell, 1990) suggests that it can amount to passing-off to lead potential customers, say by advertisements, to believe that a certain product is available for sale which is not in fact available. If there is no intention to supply the advertised goods but rather to supply an alternative product, Wadlow suggests this may be actionable if the purpose of the misrepresentation is to attract customers in order to offer them an alternative product.

Reverse passing-off
Although the classic form of passing-off is for a trader to represent its goods or business as that of another, passing-off can also work in reverse. It can sometimes also amount to passing-off for a trader to represent that another trader's business, goods or services are its own.

This has happened in one case where the designers represented they were the designers of a cable car system when in fact someone else was the designer (*Bullivant* v *Wright* (1897) 13 TLR 201). In another case recently one company showed prospective customers pictures of conservatories which had in fact been built by another company *Bristol Conservatories Ltd* v *Conservatories Custom Built Ltd* [1989] RPC 455).

CRIMINAL OFFENCES

Counterfeit goods

It is a criminal offence to use a registered mark or something deceptively or confusingly similar to a registered mark in without consent in certain circumstances (TMA 38, s. 58A). Here such a mark will be referred to as a 'counterfeit mark'.

No offence is committed unless

- what is done is done for personal gain or to cause loss to someone else
- it is intended that the goods are to be mistaken for those of the proprietor of the mark

The circumstances in which such an offence is committed are

- applying the mark to goods or using it in relation to goods
- using the mark in advertising goods
- using goods or other material so marked for commercial purposes
- using material bearing the mark for packaging, labelling or advertising

It is also an offence to possess goods or materials bearing a counterfeit mark in the course of business to enable someone else to commit any of the

above-mentioned offences. However, to commit this offence requires knowledge or a reason to believe that

- the other person is not entitled to use the mark and
- that the goods concerned are not connected with the trade mark owner

The penalties for offences are

- fines
- imprisonment for up to 10 years

The court has the power to order that any counterfeit goods are handed over
by the offender. The court also has power to order that any such goods are
either destroyed or handed over to whoever it considers appropriate (this is
likely to be the trade mark proprietor).

Local weights and measures (trading standards) authorities are specifically
given the function of enforcing the provisions concerning counterfeit goods.

Unlawfully representing a mark is registered when it is not

It can be an offence to represent that a mark is registered when it is not.

NO CONFUSION — NO INFRINGEMENT

If there is no prospect of confusion between marks then there can be no
infringement. There are two types of confusion

- marks or get-up being confusingly or deceptively similar
- confusion between the identities of businesses, products or services arising
  from use of similar marks or get-up

Where a mark or get-up is inherently distinctive or is treated as being
inherently distinctive the only question that arises is whether the allegedly
infringing mark or get-up is too similar. If a mark is not inherently distinctive
but has become distinctive through use then the question is whether confusion
of identity is likely to arise.

Thus, the essence of infringement lies in what way a mark or get-up is to be
considered distinctive.

Assessing infringement requires two different kinds of comparisons

Marks and get-up have to be compared in order to ascertain the likelihood of
the two different kinds of confusion arising. Because there are two different
kinds of confusion the assessment requires two different comparisons.

The first kind of confusion requires an examination of

- whether the marks are inherently too similar

The second kind of confusion requires two examinations

- are the marks inherently too similar, and, if so
- is confusion of identity likely to arise?

When the different comparisons are used

Registered marks
Once a mark is registered it is treated as 100% inherently distinctive. The likelihood of confusion of identity is therefore wholly irrelevant.

Thus, there are basically only two questions to ask in assessing registered mark infringement

- is the allegedly infringing mark inherently too similar?
- if so, was it used in respect of the goods or services covered by the registration?

There is only one limited case where the second kind of confusion, confusion of identity, is ever relevant to registered marks. It is open to a defendant to show that in the case of a Part B registered mark, even if the first kind of confusion exists, the second kind of confusion is not likely to arise.

Passing-off
In passing-off not only must marks or get-up be inherently similar, but also, if there is no likelihood of confusion of the identities of the businesses, products or services concerned then there is no passing-off. In other words for passing-off, a mark must be distinctive through use.

Thus, for passing-off not only must the marks be inherently too similar but also there must be a likelihood of confusion of identity.

Comparing for inherent similarity

Comparing marks and get-up to decide whether they are inherently too similar and hence conflicting is not a mathematical exercise of logic. Marks are not examined detail for detail to see what is similar and what is different in order to decide whether on balance they are or are not too similar.

However, the comparison is an objective one. The marks are compared for objective similarities, one against the other. The only exception to this is where there is evidence of actual confusion. Evidence of actual confusion may be relevant in assisting a court to assess whether a mark or get-up is inherently (objectively) too similar to another.

The crucial factor to bear in mind is that

- it is how people are likely to perceive the marks that matters in carrying out a comparison

The whole mark
The marks or get-up should be considered as a whole and not in little bits. This is particularly the case with pictures, logos and the shape, packaging and appearance of products.

Colours
Colour may be particularly relevant. However, strange as it may seem, colour in the case of registered marks is normally ignored. This is because the

registered proprietor's exclusive rights include the right to use the mark in any colour (unless the registration is expressly limited to the use of the mark in only one colour or in particular colours). In passing-off cases colour may be the only significant feature, such as in one case concerning grey Sodastream gas cylinders.

Memorability and imperfect recollection
Some parts of marks may be more memorable than others. Thus, not all aspects of a mark may be as relevant as others. This is particularly significant in relation to imperfect recollection. People may only remember parts of a mark. Where goods of a similar kind are not sold side by side, confusion could easily arise. This also means that marks and get-up are not necessarily to be considered in a side-by-side comparison.

Underlying associations
The idea of the mark may be relevant. In one case a mark which included the picture of a golden fleece prevented the registration of the words 'Golden Fleece' in respect of goods of the same description because of the similarity (*Re Australian Wine Importers' Trade Mark* (1989) 6 RPC 311).

Additionally, people may fail to remember exactly both the visual aspects of a mark or get-up as well as the idea underlying a mark. Some people think that the logo on the packaging of Fox's Glacier Mints includes a picture of a white arctic fox rather than a polar bear. Thus, there could be confusion if someone else used a picture of a white fox on a mint product.

Pronunciation
The pronunciation of marks may be significant because, whilst on paper they may look quite different, they may sound too similar. In such a case confusion could easily arise if goods are ordered verbally.

Don't forget the lazy and illiterate
Do not think that adding disclaimers to the packaging of products like 'This product should not be confused with X product' will help in any way to avoid being held liable in passing-off or registered mark infringement cases. Many people are illiterate; others do not bother to read labels when they buy products.

Comparing marks is not easy
Although all of the above aspects may be taken into account when marks and get-up are compared, they are just guides to considerations to take into account in making a comparison. In difficult cases decisions can go either way so there is no guaranteed formula for assessing beforehand whether a decision is going to take one or other course.

Comparing for confusion of identity

If the evidence in a passing-off action or a Part B registered mark infringement case shows that the public are not likely to be confused about the identity of the business, products or services concerned, then, despite any objective similarity between marks or get-up, the plaintiff's case fails.

The basic issue is

- has a sufficient association between the identity of the business, product or service concerned and the mark or get-up been established so that the public are likely to be confused about the identity by the use by another trader of marks or get-up which are objectively too similar?

This question requires an examination of all of the relevant circumstances. This is the aspect of passing-off protection which is difficult for the plaintiff and why it is far better to have registrations effected where possible. Compiling the necessary evidence can be extremely time-consuming and costly.

Descriptiveness
In carrying out a comparison, the first thing to consider is whether the mark or get-up is descriptive. Although the Jif lemon is an example of a descriptive mark being protected, the courts will not readily afford protection under the law of passing-off to descriptive marks or get-up. Evidence of considerable distinctiveness through use is likely to be required.

Extent of use and strength of image
The extent to which the mark has been used is relevant to the question of strength of image. In other words

- what evidence is there that enough people rely on the mark or get-up to identify the business, product or service concerned?

Evidence of the length of time during which use was made can be relevant as well as the geographical extent of trading, numbers of customers, turnover, and extent of expenditure on advertising and promotion.

Breadth of image
The way the mark or get-up has been advertised and promoted, and the kind of goods in respect of which it has been used are relevant to the question of breadth of image. The image may be sufficiently broad to indicate that confusion could arise even though the kinds of businesses, goods or services of the plaintiff and defendant are quite different and are not naturally associated with each other in any way.

Comparison before registration

When an application is made to register a mark, it is compared with other marks already on the register. The mark will not be registered if it seems to resemble too closely a mark already on the register.

The basis of the comparison is very similar to that used to decide whether infringement has occurred. However, the comparison of classes of goods is not so strictly applied. For the purposes of obtaining a registration a mark will not be registered if it is for *the same description* of goods or services as that of a mark already on the register.

ATTACKING A REGISTRATION OR APPLICATION

Introduction

With registered marks, a defendant does not have the same opportunities that a defendant in a passing-off case has to show that there is no likelihood of confusion. However, unlike passing-off, the defendant does have the opportunity to attack the validity of the registration.

There are basically two stages at which registered marks can be attacked. The first is when the application for registration is made and the second is after the registration has been granted.

It is not necessary to wait for someone to sue you in order to attack a mark. When applications for registered marks are made, the fact that the applications have been lodged and what classes of goods and services are covered by them can be ascertained from searches carried out at the Trade Marks Registry.

The grounds of attack

The following is a list of the grounds on which the various attacks can be based

- the mark is likely to deceive or cause confusion,
- the use of the mark would be contrary to law or morality
- the mark is a scandalous design (TMA 38, s. 11)
- the mark is identical with or nearly resembles an existing registered mark, registered for
  — the same goods or services
  — the same description of goods or services
  — services associated with goods of the same kind
  — goods associated with services of the same kind (TMA 38, s. 12)
- the registration was obtained by fraud (TMA 38, s. 13) (TMA 38, s. 26)
- the mark is wrongly registered (TMA 38, s. 32)

Of the above grounds, the most significant in practice and the ones which will be given some consideration here are that the mark is likely to deceive or cause confusion, it is too like an existing registered mark or it has not been used.

Confusing or deceptive marks

A mark can be confusing or deceptive because it conflicts with a mark someone else uses. It can also be confusing or deceptive because it is misleading in some more general way.

For example, if there is a risk that the use of a mark in relation to goods or services for which registration is sought may amount to passing-off it will not be registered.

A mark might be misleading about the characteristics or quality of the goods in respect of which it is used. A classic example of this is the Orlwoola mark which was sought to be registered for textile goods and would have been misleading if used for non-woollen goods.

The mark is too like an existing registered mark

If a mark is too like an existing registered mark then it will not be registered. This provision is narrower in scope than the previous provision. It only applies where the registration is sought for the same description of goods or services as an existing registration. Alternatively, if the registration is sought for services and there is an existing trade mark registration for goods associated with those services (and vice versa for services associated with goods) registration will not be permitted.

The mark has not been used

There are basically two different categories of objection to the lack of use of a mark

- there was no bona fide intention to use it when the application was made
- there has been no use since registration

No intention to use
When a mark has never been used before it is extremely difficult either to prove or disprove the existence of a bona fide intention to use it when only an application is being made.
   The basic point is that

- the intention at the registration stage needs to be an honest intention. It may not matter that it is vague or indefinite.

Bona fide use after registration
To prove actual use of a mark is not difficult. It should not even matter how little use is made of the mark, provided it is bona fide. However, if a mark is used simply in order to avoid the mark being struck off the register that is unlikely to be treated as bona fide use.

Incorrect registration
If a mark is incorrectly registered because, say, a similar mark is on the register for the same classes or descriptions of goods then the rights of the proprietor of the later mark can be extinguished by an application to rectify the register.

OWNERSHIP OF RIGHTS

Registration of marks

With registered rights, unlike copyright, design right and semiconductor chip protection, nationality and residence are not issues. Anyone can apply regardless of nationality.

Additionally, when applying to register a mark, no one is actually required to produce evidence that they either have used a mark or that they intend to do so. Thus,

- as a matter of practical reality, no evidence of any sort of right to be registered as the proprietor is needed to apply for a registration

It can happen that different people claim to have a better right to apply to register a mark. Although the rights to registration essentially depend on being the first to apply, there are some special circumstances where someone can claim to have a better right to apply for registration.

The first situation is where someone is already using the mark but has not applied to register it.

Another situation is where someone such as an employee obtains confidential information that a particular mark is proposed to be used by his employer. If the employee applies to register the mark in order to pre-empt the employer, the employer can still challenge the registration and claim a better right to be registered than the employee. It is the fact that the information has been obtained and used in breach of confidence that is relevant.

However, a better right to become the applicant for registration does not arise from use overseas. Only use in the UK counts.

A similar mark has previously been used but is unregistered

There is a circumstance in which two different proprietors can obtain registrations of similar marks in relation to similar goods or services. This is where there has been honest concurrent use. The TMA 38 has a specific provision in s. 12(2) permitting this.

Honest concurrent use can apply where use of the mark sought to be registered started

- after the conflicting mark was registered, or
- before the conflicting mark was registered

In the first case the question will be whether the later mark should be registered despite the rights of the existing proprietor. In the second the question will be whether the user of the earlier unregistered mark has a prior right to be the registered proprietor.

In one case the following guidelines were set out in deciding whether to allow registration

- is the possibility of confusion slight?
  - this requires a comparison of the two marks to ascertain whether they are inherently (objectively) too similar. However, two aspects in particular are relevant — how close the marks are phonetically and how likely it is that confusion would arise from inaccurate or imperfect recollection
- was the later conflicting mark honestly chosen?

- how long had the later mark been used before the application for registration was made?
- is there any proof of actual confusion?
- has the extent of use of the later mark been greater than the earlier mark?
- on balance, which would cause greater hardship, allowing the registration or disallowing it?

Of all of the above criteria probably the most important are whether the later mark was honestly adopted and whether there is any proof of actual confusion.

Obtaining rights under passing-off

There are three basic qualifications required to be able to establish the right to control the use of marks and get-up under the law of passing-off. These are

- the existence of trading goodwill
- use (i.e., through use the mark or get-up identifies the business, product or service concerned)
- damage to goodwill

Trading goodwill
The fundamental principle underlying the protection afforded by passing-off is that if other traders are allowed to use confusingly or deceptively similar marks or get-up this can damage the goodwill of the business concerned. The business may lose customers to the competition; the image and reputation associated with its marks may be damaged and it may be difficult to recover a trading position once lost.

What is goodwill?   The concept of goodwill is a difficult one to pin down. It has been described as

> the benefit and advantage of the good name, reputation and connection of a business. It is the attractive force which brings in custom. (Lord Mac-Naghten in *Commissioners of Inland Revenue* v *Muller & Co.'s Margarine Ltd* [1901] AC 217.)

Thus

- the law of passing-off protects a form of property, goodwill, which is created through business and trading activity
- passing-off is about stopping others making use of goodwill or controlling what use they can make of it

No formalities required   To obtain goodwill there are no special rules to follow. Just start trading and, depending upon how much effort you put in, people will come to know of your business, products and services. You cannot help creating an image or reputation if you deal with people. What you can help is what kind of image or reputation you create and how extensively it is known.

No goodwill — no protection Goodwill is a concept which only applies to trading and businesses. If there is no trading or business activity taking place then there is no goodwill to protect.

Thus, it has sometimes proved difficult in the past for voluntary organisations, individuals, churches, political parties and the like to stop others using similar names, marks or get-up because there was no trading or business goodwill to protect or because the alleged infringer was not trading or in business.

In other words,

- there is no general protection for image and reputation under the law of passing-off in the absence of goodwill

Use
It is one thing to show that a business has been trading and that it must have a business goodwill. It is another to show that the goodwill is associated with a particular mark or get-up. In other words, it is necessary to show that the mark or get-up has acquired sufficient distinctiveness through use.

Thus,

- use of a mark or get-up is vital to the success of any passing-off action
  - in establishing that trading goodwill is associated with the mark or get-up
  - in indicating the likelihood of confusion

There must at least be a likelihood of damage to goodwill
What is absolutely vital to understand is that the protection in passing-off is against business or trading goodwill being damaged.

- if there is no prospect of damage to goodwill then there can be no protection

The types of damage which can arise from confusion are as follows

- direct loss of business
- damage to image and reputation from the infringer's inferior goods or services
- damage to image and reputation arising from the infringer wrongfully leading the public to believe there is an association between two non-competing businesses
- exposure to the risk of legal action which might be incorrectly brought against a business because of confusion with the identity of the infringer's business
- damage to business connections with suppliers, other traders and business customers arising from confusion

- the fact that confusion is likely and because of the particular circumstances of the case, damage to goodwill will inevitably result, even though there is no actual proof of damage

- where the plaintiff is in the business of licensing (selling permission) to use intellectual property rights or could be, the damage may be considered to be the loss of an opportunity to sell a licence (permission). For example, the infringer may be selling goods and representing that they are sold under licence when they are not. Alternatively, the image and reputation of the licensing business might be damaged arising from such a representation, say, if the goods are of poor quality

The potential for damage to goodwill is dependent on the likelihood of confusion.

DURATION OF RIGHTS

Registered marks

Proof of entitlement to rights in a registered mark is established by production of the certificate of registration. Thus, although the rights take effect from the date of application and infringements occurring prior to the issue of the certificate are actionable, it is not possible to commence proceedings until the certificate has been issued.

The rights in a registered mark last for ever, provided the renewal fees continue to be paid in order to maintain the registration.

The only way the rights can otherwise come to an end is if the registration can be attacked and expunged.

Passing-off

The rights afforded under passing-off last as long as the goodwill associated with a mark or get-up lasts. In other words, as long as the mark continues to be used, the rights will continue. The rights start as soon as sufficient distinctiveness through use can be demonstrated and there is trading goodwill to protect.

However, goodwill does not necessarily die when a mark or get-up ceases to be used. The image or reputation of a business, product or service lies in what people have learnt of it. Thus, goodwill can last quite some time, even after a business has closed down.

LICENSING, FRANCHISING AND CHARACTER MERCHANDISING

The way the law of registered marks and passing-off works causes difficulties in two particular areas of commercial activity and can cause difficulty in a third. The areas concerned are, respectively, franchising, character merchandising and licensing.

Licensing is the commercial activity of giving others permission to use intellectual property rights for a fee.

Franchising is where a way of doing business is developed together with a name, get-up, image and identity for the business. The way to organise and run the business is part of the confidential know-how of the scheme. The franchisor exploits all of this by selling others the right to use the confidential information and know-how, the right to use the names, logos and get-up for the business and to use the copyright materials developed by the franchisor.

In addition, in order to maintain uniformity between all franchised outlets so that they all have a common image, the people who buy franchises agree to conform to requirements about maintaining the image and reputation associated with the franchise and to use the marks, logos and get-up in the same way as every other franchisee and to maintain particular standards of products and services. An example of a franchise is the Benetton chain of retail outlets. Another is the Pronuptia chain and another is the BSM (British School of Motoring) group of driving schools.

Character merchandising is the exploitation of the image and reputation of real or fictional characters such as characters appearing in books, films, on television, in cartoons and other media. It is the exploitation of fame.

The way character merchandising works is that the originator of the character (or even a real person who has become a 'celebrity') grants others rights to use the character's name, or picture or some other distinguishing feature in relation to goods. The sort of things might be Bugs Bunny 'T'-shirts or Batman bubble gum or Star Wars toys or Mickey Mouse telephones.

The right to sue

In order to be able to license, franchise or character merchandise there must be some intellectual property rights to enforce. This is where the problems arise. The licensor, franchisor or character originator is not necessarily entitled to be the registered proprietor of marks or to sue in passing-off.

In order for a registration of a mark to remain valid, the registered proprietor must have had a bona fide intention to use the mark when applying to register or must actually make bona fide use of the mark. If this is not the case the mark can be expunged from the register leaving it open for someone else to become the registered proprietor. There is one useful exception to this rule which will be examined later in this section.

Only the owner of trading goodwill can sue for passing-off. Not only that, there must be a likelihood of confusion of identity and proof of actual damage or the likelihood of damage. If the licensor, franchisor or character originator has never used the mark then there will be difficulty establishing the existence of trading goodwill associated with it.

The problem under the law of registered marks

The problem with registered marks is that often there is no connection in the way of trade between the person giving permission and the person or organisation which manufactures or supplies the goods or services concerned under licence, in a franchise or makes use of the character. Thus, the franchisor, licensor or character originator may have difficulty establishing use of the mark as registered proprietor. Lack of such use can endanger a registration.

. The people who are actually using the marks are the licensees, franchisees and those exploiting the characters on goods and in relation to services. Any one or all of them might be able to claim a better right to be the registered proprietors of the marks.

Registered user agreements

It is not always essential that the licensor, franchisor or character originator is directly involved in using registered marks. The law is designed so that the owner of registered marks can grant others the right to use them without using the marks personally. There are three crucial factors in ensuring that this can be done without affecting the validity of the registrations of any registered marks

- it is essential that quality control conditions are imposed on all franchisees, licensees and character users and enforced

- an agreement must be entered into setting out the terms on which permission to use the marks is given

- the agreement must be registered at the Trade Marks Registry

The important effects of registering user agreements are that

- the user does not get a better right to be the registered proprietor of the mark through use

- the use of the marks by the registered users is treated as use by the franchisor for all purposes. This is important in relation to rights under the law of passing-off

Trafficking in marks

It is not a foregone conclusion that marks created for use in a franchise operation will be registered. The Registrar of Trade Marks has a wide discretion about whether or not to register marks. One of the grounds on which a registration can be refused or attacked after registration is that the franchisor is in fact 'trafficking' in trade marks.

'Trafficking' in a mark is essentially dealing in the mark as a commodity in itself rather than using it to distinguish your own goods and services or goods and services with which you are connected in some way from those of others. Obtaining a registration for a mark and never using it yourself but instead giving others permission to use the mark can amount to trafficking. The same applies to engaging in a business of registering and buying and selling marks with no intention of actually using them.

As far as registered marks are concerned,

- if there is no real connection in the way of trade between the registered proprietor and the goods or services for which a mark is registered then the registration may be invalid and is liable to challenge and be expunged from the register

● it is irrelevant that the mark is the name of a fictional character which is the creation of the applicant for registration. There still must be a connection in the way of trade

The problem under the law of passing-off

Under the law of passing-off there needs to be the potential for damage to goodwill arising from confusion.

The consequences for licensing, franchising and character merchandising are not good. In these areas of commercial activity the person granting rights often does not have any trading goodwill associated with the marks or get-up concerned. The main area of difficulty is with the absence of the likelihood of confusion.

With passing-off the image of a fictional character from television, films, radio, books, cartoon strip comics, and suchlike is hardly likely to be associated with all of the different kinds of products the character might appear on. If a Mickey Mouse telephone does not work well most people are hardly likely to think of complaining to the Disney group of companies because they would not associate Disney, the cartoon film makers, with the manufacture of telephones.

The problems are not insurmountable

There are ways and means of making licensing, character merchandising, franchising and similar activities work, despite the problems posed by the law of passing-off and registered marks. These include the use of other intellectual property rights such as copyright and confidentiality as well as contractual rights.

Thus, do not assume it is going to be a simple matter to copy franchises or to use the names of celebrities and fictional characters freely.

Before attempting to use a name or likeness of a personality in the UK take advice beforehand and check on the state of the law at the time.

PICKING MARKS AND GET-UP

Introduction

There are very few restrictions on what kinds of things can be chosen as names, marks or get-up. The most likely form of control arises when you receive a solicitor's letter alleging you have chosen a name, mark or logo which infringes a registered mark or the use of which amounts to passing-off.

People get uppity when their reputation is at stake

There is one major difference between copying image, style and presentation and other kinds of copying. People are very touchy about what they consider is their unique identifier, be it a name, a logo or a get-up. They will often fight hard to protect it. However, if you can get as close as lawfully possible to an established name, mark, logo or get-up this can help a great deal in living off an established reputation and the associated goodwill.

It is not always easy to pick a name, mark or logo which is going to be a real winner. When you have got one it is well worth hanging on to. Business names, brand names and trade and service marks are extremely valuable if only because people tend to buy on the strength of a name or mark.

Decide on an image

Before choosing a mark you should be clear about what kind of image you want the business, product or service to have. To a certain extent the image of any business, product or service can be created. The way business is done, the presentation and style of the employees, the premises, the products and the way these things appear to people in general all go to make up the identity and the image. Particular aspects, characteristics or qualities can be emphasised in order to promote the desired image.

It has become common when launching new businesses, products or services to carry out market research beforehand in order to ascertain various things. Companies often want to identify if there are any gaps in market areas which they could fill with a carefully positioned product or service offering. If a market area is already identified it may be desirable for a company to know what characteristics and qualities people who make up the target market either seek in the product or service concerned or which might appeal to them particularly.

Information of this type can help in creating an integrated image for the product or service concerned. The design of a product or the style in which a service is to be presented may be affected. The colour scheme for the product, the design of its packaging and promotional and marketing materials may be influenced and the position can be similar for services.

A great deal may be spent on advertising and promotional campaigns and these may be tailored to the image it is desired to present.

Once all this effort has been put into creating an image, the marks and get-up selected as identifiers come to mean the business, product or service which has that image. Thus, the marks and get-up can be extremely valuable and they need to be selected with care.

Foreign meaning

If the mark is a word mark then it can be important to check what other meanings the word may have in other languages. When considering the different meanings words can have in other languages it is important not just to consider the meaning but also what the word sounds like when it is spoken and what phonetic equivalents there may be or other words or phrases there may be which have a slightly different spelling and not a very appropriate meaning. Care should also be taken with logos and pictures. A logo of a hand giving the 'thumbs up' sign does not go down very well in Iran and would be greeted with much the same sort of enthusiasm that one and two finger gestures might receive in the UK. In fact logos incorporating human gestures like a winking eye are among a number that should be carefully investigated before being adopted.

Why people choose marks

When people adopt marks and get-up they do so in order to achieve several objectives. Sometimes people choose marks and get-up without thinking about what they want to achieve or even without thinking carefully about what they are doing or why they are doing it. However, the following are some of the things people commonly want marks and get-up to do. They want:

- to have an identifying 'label' or get-up
- something different from what others are using
- to have a label that has, as part of its ordinary meaning, some in-built association with the what it is to be used to identify
- to have something that is similar to what everyone else is using because there is a common image in the trade
- a label that is easy for people to use and recognise
- something that is easily remembered
- something that makes an impression so that people will take notice of it

Avoid descriptive and misleading marks and get-up

The one thing that people often fail to take account of is the need to have a mark that is distinctive. This is important in order to obtain the maximum legal protection against copyists.

If a carpentry business is called the Carpentry Shop this name is descriptive of the kind of business concerned. Other people may want to use exactly the same words to describe their own similar businesses. The words are ordinary English words so it would seem somewhat inconvenient if the English language were to be allowed to be monopolised by a few individuals.

Additionally, consider the position where ordinary words are used as a mark but the ordinary meaning of the word is misleading. If a company describes itself as 'The Natural Juice Company' but sells juice which has additives and is reconstituted from concentrated juice by the addition of water the name is then wholly misleading.

In passing-off the courts will not allow the law to be used to protect marks and get-up which are in themselves deceptive, fraudulent or which perpetrate misrepresentations themselves. A registered mark can be attacked if it is deceptive or confusing (in a broad sense).

Invented words lacking subtlety

Often marks are adapted from descriptive words into made-up names. The made-up words are not the same as the descriptive words from which they are adapted. At the same time they retain enough of their visual appearance or their sound when pronounced to maintain a connection with their ordinary meaning or an image associated with them. In the computer industry names are often made up from commonly used computer industry jargon in order to convey a high-tech image through the name. Words like network, telecommunications, link, digital, computer, automatic, system and technology are ordinary words that are often adapted for use in names. Network is abbreviated to 'net', telecommunications is abbreviated to 'tele', 'tel' or 'telecom', computer is abbreviated to 'compu', technology is abbreviated to 'tek' or 'tech'. The end-results are in names like digitek, computel, compunet, digilink, technomatic, micronet, compusys, systel, systek, telecom.

This practice of making up words from ordinary descriptive words is a variation on the situation where ordinary descriptive words are used directly as marks. Consider the position where one company adopts the name comptel as a name and another adopts the name telcomp. Are people likely to be confused? How close should others be allowed to get when choosing names? It is one thing to have exactly the same name. It is another to have one which is not the same but is similar.

Clearly, adopting unsubtle invented word names is not always going to be a good idea when the invented word consists of commonly used terms or is recognisably made up of ordinary descriptive words.

CHOOSING COMPANY AND BUSINESS NAMES

People are legal entities. An individual can set up in business and trade under his or her own name. Apart from formalities such as registering for VAT purposes, conforming with legislation concerning the display of the name and address of the proprietor at the premises and on business stationery and other things which have nothing much to do with the choice of name,

- there are no official formalities to be observed in relation to selecting the name or registering it anywhere
- there is no official register of business names.

Fred Smith the butcher can quite happily trade under his own name, such as 'Fred Smith–Butcher'. There is nothing in general to stop him doing so. The only way he could be prevented from doing so was if someone else had the right to sue him for passing-off or registered mark infringement.

Another kind of legal entity is a partnership. A partnership exists where two or more people carry on business in common with a view to a profit. Except in a few special cases, there are no formalities to be observed in relation to the choice of name.

An incorporated company is a legal entity. There are various kinds of incorporated company. The two most common are the private limited company (designated by 'Limited' or 'Ltd') and the public limited company (designated by 'public limited company' or 'plc'). Unlike sole traders and partnerships, companies are incorporated and registered with the Registrar of Companies. However, it is important to appreciate that incorporating and registering a company at Companies House with a particular name gives no exclusive right to the use of the name. What also needs to be understood is that

- there is no prohibition against the registration of companies with similar names

This means that different companies which are unrelated and which have unrelated shareholders could all be on the Register of Companies with names which are similar, such as Fred Smith Butchers Ltd, Fred Smith Bakers Ltd, Fred Smith Candlestick Makers Ltd or even Fred Smith Butchers (Rotherham) Ltd. The only advantage that incorporating a company with a particular name gives in relation to the use of the name is that it should prevent anyone else incorporating a company with *exactly the same name*. It will not prevent someone incorporating a company with a very similar name.

It is also important to appreciate that when a company name is registered no comparison with or search of registered marks is carried out by the officials at Companies House. The people responsible for incorporating the company like solicitors, accountants or other private advisors may have carried out their own searches and enquiries into conflicting names but no official search is carried out.

With limited exceptions the only thing that can operate to prevent anyone adopting a particular name for a company or business, whether assumed or real, is whether anyone else can stop them using it under the law of passing-off. The law of registered marks could only be used if the name was used to identify goods or services rather than just the identity of the business.

The limited exceptions which can be used to stop people adopting names for incorporated companies or assumed names for businesses are rules which prohibit the use of certain limited categories of words as part of a name. For example, under regulations made under s. 29 of the Companies Act 1985 government consent is required to the use of words such as 'English', 'duke', 'royal', 'trade union', 'trust' or 'insurance' as part of a name, to mention just a few.

In other words,

- anyone can set up in business and trade under any name they please without having to register it anywhere or having to go through any formalities
- they can similarly use any names, marks, logos or get-up for their businesses that they wish without any registration or other formalities

also,

- the incorporation of a company with a particular name neither gives any special right to the exclusive use of the distinctive portion of the name nor any immunity from being accused of registered mark infringement or passing-off

8 Remedies

EXERCISING YOUR RIGHTS

So far the discussion in this book has been about property and rights. These are abstract concepts; how can they be of any practical use? The law itself takes a very practical approach — nothing is recognised as a right unless there is a legal remedy for a wrongful invasion of that right. Rights are enforced by the law through various legal remedies. Those which are relevant to enforcement of intellectual property rights are discussed in this chapter.

In general, you need help from the law to keep people from trespassing on your intellectual property. This usually involves bringing a legal action in the civil courts. The process of doing so is described in chapter 12. This type of legal action is a private action; the person bringing it is entirely responsible for investigating the facts and gathering the evidence needed to prove his case. In addition, certain types of intellectual property infringement are also made criminal acts, which provides at least the theoretical possibility of the government taking action to stop the infringer. However, criminal prosecutions are not common, so in practice you have the responsibility for taking action to protect your intellectual property.

Legal remedies can be divided into three general classes. The first class is court orders which regulate the behaviour of the party who is the subject of the order. The second is orders which deal with things, for example, dealing with possession of disputed property or disposal of infringing goods. The third is the payment of money as a recompense for injury.

When considering the subject of remedies, there are three important questions:

- what are you trying to achieve?
- how quickly can you achieve the desired result?
- what remedies are available to achieve the desired result?

In the rest of this chapter we will first look at the various results that an intellectual property owner may be trying to achieve, and then give the information from which the other two questions can be answered for any particular desired result.

WHAT ARE YOU TRYING TO ACHIEVE?

Before asking for any particular remedy — indeed, before even starting to sue — you must answer the question

● what am I trying to achieve by this lawsuit?

If you have thought this out at the beginning, the litigation procedures and tactics can be streamlined toward achieving that particular goal.

The best result will differ in each case, and depends upon the particular circumstances. The decision about what goal to aim for should be taken in consultation with your legal advisers. Possible goals in an intellectual property infringement suit include the following:

stopping continuing infringements;

preventing or discouraging infringements;

identifying all the participants in a chain of infringing acts;

getting the infringer to take a licence;

preventing infringing goods from reaching the market;

getting a judicial determination of validity which can be used against other infringers;

recovering financial losses;

preventing the infringer from profiting from the infringement.

Of course, in most cases the plaintiff will be trying to achieve several of these goals, and very few of them are mutually exclusive.

GETTING WHAT YOU NEED AS QUICKLY AS POSSIBLE

Sometimes legal remedies are useless unless they can be obtained quickly. For example, suppose you have purchased the exclusive licence to sell 'The Boss' T-shirts at a forthcoming Bruce Springsteen concert at Wembley Stadium. Although this licence was expensive, the enterprise will be very profitable if there is no price-cutting competition. A few days before the concert you learn that unauthorised T-shirts, which are almost identical in design to the authorised merchandise, are already being hawked on the pavement along Oxford Street, and it is likely that a large number of unauthorised traders will be in the Wembley area at the time of the concert. People who sell things from suitcases are most unlikely to have the money to pay any award of damages that you might obtain at the end of any litigation. The only effective relief is to stop the sale of infringing T-shirts immediately.

Even where immediate relief is the only real remedy, it is generally advantageous to get to the desired result as quickly as possible. The longer things drag on, the greater the cost and disruption, and the damage to the plaintiff's business from the infringer's activities is likely to become increasingly serious the longer those activities are allowed to continue. Even if all that is wanted is monetary compensation, delay in getting that compensation causes loss through the effects of inflation.

In many cases it will be possible to achieve at least part of the desired relief, at least if the proper steps are taken. Of course, one way that aims can be speedily achieved is to negotiate a settlement with the other party, before or immediately after litigation is commenced. However, that is not possible in many cases, so the legal routes to speedy relief discussed below will have to be explored.

Interim remedies

The law has long recognised that 'justice delayed is justice denied', and has provided for various kinds of interim relief, that is, legal remedies given before the full trial of the matter. This is usually referred to by lawyers as 'interlocutory' relief.

There are three kinds of interim relief that are important in intellectual property cases, all of which take the form of an order to the defendant

- injunctions
- *Anton Piller* orders
- *Mareva* injunctions

In addition, there is a very limited right to seize articles which infringe copyright without having to get a court order.

General principles
There are some general principles that apply to any kind of interim relief.

Speed   It is vital to keep in mind the old saying 'he who hesitates is lost' when considering interlocutory relief. No order for interlocutory relief will be granted if the plaintiff has delayed unreasonably after learning of the facts on which the application is based.

Evidence   The grant of any of these interim orders can potentially have a serious effect on the person against whom the order is made, who has not yet had the chance to present his case fully. Therefore, they are not lightly granted, and the party asking for the order must produce sufficient supporting evidence. The mere suspicion that the defendant is a shifty character is not enough.

Ability to pay if the order should not have been granted   It may turn out, after a full trial of the matter, that the interlocutory order should not have been granted. The plaintiff is then liable to pay damages to the defendant to compensate him for his losses caused by the grant of the interlocutory order. Therefore, before an interlocutory order is granted, the plaintiff must give an undertaking to the court that it will pay these damages if it ultimately turns out that the order should not have been granted. The court will look for evidence of an ability to pay under such an undertaking, and will refuse to grant the order if satisfactory evidence is not forthcoming.

Types of interim remedies useful in intellectual property cases

Injunctions   The term 'injunction' is used for court orders which are directed to the behaviour of a party to the litigation. Such orders are most commonly couched in the negative, ordering the person not to do something; for example, ordering the defendant to cease manufacturing a part that has been determined to infringe the plaintiff's patent. However, in certain circumstances the court will make a positive order, known as a 'mandatory injunction', which orders a stated act to be done. For example, a defendant who is merely the retailer of infringing goods may be ordered to disclose the source of his supply of the goods.

There are two kinds of interim injunction, the ex parte injunction and the interlocutory injunction, obtained by somewhat different procedures. The term '*ex parte*' means that the application is made without the defendant having the chance to prepare or present evidence. Indeed, generally the application for the injunction is made without any notice to the party against whom the injunction is sought. This type of injunction can only be applied for by the plaintiff. It is only granted when the plaintiff can show real urgency, and is only granted for a sufficient time for both sides to prepare evidence for a full interlocutory injunction hearing.

An interlocutory injunction is only granted after the defendant has been given notice of the application for the grant of the injunction and a reasonable opportunity to prepare evidence to oppose the application. Alternatively, if the defendant believes that it would be a waste of money to oppose the injunction, he may formally agree to refrain from the acts the plaintiff is seeking to have enjoined. Such a formal agreement is called an undertaking.

The modern approach to the question whether to grant an interlocutory injunction was laid down by the House of Lords in *American Cyanamid Co.* v *Ethicon Ltd* [1975] AC 396, a patent infringement case.

1.   The plaintiff must first show that he has an arguable case, that there is a serious issue to be tried.

2.   Can the plaintiff be adequately remedied for any injury done pending trial by money damages, and is the defendant likely to be able to pay those damages? If so, no injunction will be granted. If not, proceed to the next step.

3.   Can the defendant be adequately remedied for any injury done by the grant of the interlocutory injunction if it later turns out that it should not have been granted, and is the plaintiff likely to be able to pay those damages? If so, an injunction will be granted. If not, then proceed to the next step.

4.   The inconvenience caused to the defendant from the grant of an injunction must be balanced against the inconvenience to the plaintiff if an injunction is refused. Almost any factor may be considered in determining where the balance of convenience lies, depending on the facts of the particular case. Where the balance of convenience is close, the court should try to maintain the status quo. This is another reason why it is important to act speedily if you are the plaintiff — if you act fast, the status quo will be that the defendant is not yet in volume production of the infringing goods. If you delay, the defendant will have established production and sales, making refusal of an injunction the way to preserve the status quo.

It is possible for the parties to agree that the interlocutory injunction hearing will be treated as the trial of the action. This resolves the case speedily but is usually appropriate only where there is no real dispute about the facts and the important issue in the case is a question of law.

Anton Piller Orders   These are really a specialised form of injunction, named after the plaintiff in the case in which the Court of Appeal first approved such an order. An *Anton Piller* order is intended to give the plaintiff a remedy in cases where there is a real danger that the defendant will destroy vital evidence if normal litigation procedures are followed. For this reason, it is applied for *ex parte,* and the hearing is closed to the public (called an 'in camera' hearing) so that news of the order cannot leak out to the defendant before the order is served on him. This procedure gives the defendant no chance to dispose of documents or objects that could be important evidence.

This 'search and seizure' order is probably the most Draconian order a civil court can issue. Typically, the named defendant is ordered to permit the plaintiff's representatives (a) to enter his private premises, (b) to search the premises for infringing goods and relevant documents and (c) to remove such goods and documents as they find. Further, the defendant is often ordered to answer specified questions under oath.

The effect on the defendant of such an order can be devastating. There is no warning that this is about to happen. The first he knows of it is when the plaintiff's solicitor turns up at his door with the order. He has to react almost immediately, as he is only allowed a short time to contact a solicitor. Refusal to comply with the order carries the possibility of penalties for contempt of court, as well as the possibility of adverse inferences being drawn against him if the case ever comes to trial. While he has the opportunity to make an urgent application to the court to have the order set aside, if he refuses to comply with the order pending the hearing of this application but loses in court, he is liable to be fined for contempt of court. He cannot refuse to answer the questions on the ground of self-incrimination, although evidence obtained in this way cannot be used in any related criminal proceedings.

The procedure does provide some safeguards for the defendant. First, the court requires actual evidence of a strong case against the defendant, and that there is a real danger that evidence will be destroyed if he is given advance notice, resulting in significant harm to the plaintiff. Secondly, the order must be served by a solicitor, and the inspection carried out under his supervision. All solicitors are by law officers of the court, who can be punished by the court if the procedures are not properly carried out. The solicitor must supply the defendant with a copy of the order and of the evidence the plaintiff put before the court to get the order. The effect of the order must be explained to the defendant, who should be advised to seek immediate legal advice and given an opportunity to consult with a solicitor. The order should provide that the defendant may make an urgent application to discharge or vary the order. Further, the order should not be granted unless the court is satisfied that the plaintiff can meet any obligation to the defendant under the cross-undertaking in damages.

In order to obtain an Anton Piller order, the plaintiff must prove the following:

1. he has a strong prima facie case of infringement or passing off;
2. there is a real danger that the defendant will destroy hide or dispose of infringing goods or relevant documents if he is given notice of the plaintiff's request for an inspection;
3. inspection would do no harm to the defendant;
4. the potential damage to the plaintiff is likely to be considerable;
5. justice requires that the order be granted.

As the courts are aware of the seriousness of these orders and the possibilities for abuse, they require real evidence of these items, not mere assertions or unsupported suspicions.

Mareva injunctions A *Mareva* injunction is an order designed to prevent a defendant from spiriting his assets abroad or otherwise dissipating them or concealing them during the pendency of an action so as to deprive the plaintiff of any monetary compensation should he eventually be successful at trial. This order will only be granted where the plaintiff can show a likelihood that the defendant will be held liable to pay damages or some other monetary award to the plaintiff at the end of the litigation, and that the defendant will transfer assets out of the country or dissipate them to avoid paying that money judgment. The court has power to freeze specified assets to prevent their removal or dissipation until the matter is tried. The court may also order the defendant to swear an affidavit about his finances and assets, and may also order him not to leave the country until the affidavit has been sworn and served.

Like an *Anton Piller* order, a *Mareva* injunction is a very serious imposition on the defendant, and is obtained without notice to the defendant. So the requirements for obtaining a *Mareva* injunction, and the safeguards for the defendant, are very similar to those for an *Anton Piller* order. In addition, the defendant must be left enough money to live on and to carry on his day-to-day business.

A *Mareva* injunction may also affect innocent third parties, such as a bank. In order to protect such third parties, the order must be very specific so the third party will know exactly what it can or cannot do. The bank must be given notice of the order as soon as possible, preferably by telephone, fax or telex, and given the opportunity for a speedy *inter partes* hearing. The plaintiff's cross-undertaking in damages extends to any damage suffered by a third party, and the plaintiff should also be obliged to pay any reasonable expenses of the third party in carrying out the order.

Seizure of infringing goods The Copyright, Designs and Patents Act 1988 has provided a new remedy for the owners of copyrights and performer's and recording rights: seizure of infringing copies without the need to go to court. This goes against the general reluctance of the English law to allow self-help where other people's property is concerned, for fear of breaches of the peace. In

order to allay some of these fears, the Act lays down the following conditions
for seizure:

- before anything is seized, notice of the time and place of the proposed
  seizure must be given to the local police station.

- goods can only be seized on premises where the public have access —
  compare the *Anton Piller* order, which can give access to private premises.
  This limitation would mean, for example, that goods could be seized from
  a shop-floor, but not from the stock-rooms at the back of the shop.

- nothing may be seized from a person who is at his regular place of
  business, which would seem to effectively limit the remedy to seizure from
  street-corner vendors and itinerant salesmen

- no force may be used in any circumstances

If any thing is seized, a notice giving details of who made the seizure and the
reason why it was made must be left on the premises.

Early relief can be final relief

Returning to the example of the Bruce Springsteen T-shirt sellers outside
Wembley Stadium, it is clear the interim relief which prevents them selling their
wares in the period surrounding the concert effectively gives complete relief. In
the unlikely event that any of the hawkers had the money or desire to pursue
the case to trial, which could be about two years later, the merchandise would
have no market.

In practice, a significant proportion of intellectual property infringement
cases settle immediately after the grant of interim relief. The plaintiff should
therefore always look at the possibility of obtaining interim relief at a very early
stage in the litigation preparations, and should make sure that chances of
obtaining such relief are not jeopardised by undue delay.

There is also the possibility that both parties can agree to treat the
interlocutory injunction hearing as the trial of the action, thereby giving a rapid
conclusion to the litigation. This procedure is only suitable where there is no
real dispute over the facts, discovery is not needed to develop important
evidence, and the plaintiff content with injunctive relief.

Blocking infringing imports

A copyright owner can prevent the importation of specific printed material,
films and records which he alleges to infringe his copyright by giving notice to
the customs authorities. This is done by giving written notice to the Commis-
sioners of Customs and Excise that he is the owner of the copyright in the work,
and requesting infringing copies to be treated as prohibited goods and thus
denied entry for a specified period, not to exceed five years. The usefulness of
this provision is limited in the case of sound recordings and films, however,
because there is no blanket period, as there is for printed materials, and the
customs authorities must be told when and where the infringing copies are
expected to arrive in the UK.

REMEDIES IN INTELLECTUAL PROPERTY CASES

Other regulatory behaviour — injunctions

Final injunctions, i.e., injunctions granted at the end of the case, as opposed to interlocutory injunctions, are available for all types of intellectual property actions, including infringement and breach of confidentiality. There are some general principles governing the grant of final injunctions, and then there are some special provisions relating to the grant of a final injunction for some types of intellectual property infringement.

General principles for final injunctions

An injunction is classed by the law as an 'equitable' remedy, which means that it is never available as a matter of right, and the court always has a discretion whether or not to grant it. That being said, in reality final injunctions are rarely refused in intellectual property cases, unless the property right has expired before the date final judgment is given. An injunction must expire at the same time as the intellectual property which it is protecting.

The main consideration in the decision whether to grant a final injunction is whether the plaintiff can be adequately recompensed by money for the wrong done. In intellectual property cases, where a property right has been invaded, the answer to this question is almost always 'no'. This is the case even when an interlocutory injunction was refused on the ground that the defendant could recompense the plaintiff with damages for any injury done pending trial.

An injunction may, very rarely, be refused where the infringement was minor *and* there is no danger that it will be repeated by the defendant. However, the mere fact that the infringing acts ceased prior to trial, even if the defendant asserts that they will not be repeated, is not a ground for refusing to grant an injunction.

In theory, very serious delay under circumstances in which the defendant was led to believe that the plaintiff did not object to his activities and, in reliance on this belief, spent a lot of money on facilities to make the infringing goods would be grounds to deny an injunction, but this does not seem to happen in practice.

Special provisions in intellectual property cases

There are some exceptions to the general rule that a final injunction is normally granted in intellectual property infringement cases. For all kinds of intellectual property, no injunction will be granted if

- the right has expired
- a licence of right is available to the defendant
- the infringing use was by or on behalf of the government

In patent cases in which the defendant made the invention earlier than the patentee, there can be no injunction to prevent the defendant from continuing to do things he was doing or preparing to do in good faith before the patent was applied for. This right cannot be sublicensed, and can only be transferred together with the business to which it relates.

It is sometimes possible for the defendant to a passing-off action to use the mark or name in issue in a way that will not be confusing. For example, it may be possible to add something that will sufficiently distinguish it from the plaintiff's name or mark, or to avoid confusion by a suitably worded disclaimer. In such a case, the court will grant only a qualified injunction, which requires the defendant to take the appropriate steps in the circumstances to prevent passing-off.

Orders relating to property

Delivery up, forfeiture and destruction

The courts have an inherent jurisdiction to order the delivery up to the plaintiff or the destruction of items which came into existence through a breach of the plaintiff's property rights. This is an equitable remedy, so, like an injunction, the plaintiff cannot demand it as a right and the court has a discretion whether or nor to grant it. The purpose of the order is to prevent infringing goods from getting on to the market, and to prevent the defendant from profiting from his infringement by stockpiling goods made during the term of the intellectual property right to sell after that term has expired.

The general principles for the grant of these orders are the same as for the grant of an injunction. The most common reason for refusing an order for delivery up or destruction of the product in issue is that the infringement only involves a small part of that product, for example, infringing circuitry for controlling the windscreen wipers on a Mercedes car. In that case, the court is more likely to order the defendant to replace the infringing part with a non-infringing substitute. An order might also be refused if it would cause a temporary shortage of a life-saving drug, at least until the plaintiff can get sufficient production going to supply the defendant's customers as well as his own.

The remedy is limited to articles in the possession of control or the defendant, so it cannot be used to remove infringing goods from innocent third parties such as independent distributors, unless title to the goods remains with the defendant.

For copyright, designs and performance rights, the Copyright, Designs and Patents Act 1988 has a detailed scheme relating to orders for delivery up and related orders. In the case of copyright and design right, this order can cover infringing works in the possession, custody or control, of a person in the course of a business, or articles specifically designed or adapted for making copies of an infringing work, such as printing plates and moulds. However, for such articles to be subject to delivery up, the plaintiff must prove that the person against whom the order is sought knows or has reason to believe that the article has been or will be used for that purpose.

In the case of performance rights, the articles which are the subject of the order are 'illicit records'. Where breach of a performer's rights is complained of, an illicit recording is one made without the consent of the performer, unless it is made for purely private purposes. In the case of recording rights, the recording is illicit if it is made for other than private purposes without the consent of the owner of the recording rights or of the performer.

In each case, an order cannot be made for delivery up of articles which were made before the start of the six year limitation period.

Provision is made to give notice of the proceedings to other people who may have an interest in the articles, and if it turns out that more than one person is entitled to the articles the court can order them sold and the proceeds divided.

In cases of trade-mark infringement and passing-off, the courts tend not to order delivery up or destruction if the infringement can be remedied by removing labels or markings from the goods.

Declarations and certificates of validity

The owner of the right which has been the subject of litigation not only wants to win against this defendant, but also to be put in a better position to win against other infringers. He therefore will often seek a judicial 'blessing' on the validity of his intellectual property right. This should discourage future infringers, and greatly improves the chances that an interlocutory injunction can be obtained in future cases.

The court has an inherent power to make declarations relating to property rights when those rights have been challenged. For patents, trade and service marks and registered designs, the relevant statutes also provide that the plaintiff who successfully survives an attack on the validity of his patent, mark or registered design may be awarded a certificate of contested validity. The effect of this is that, in any future case in which the defendant unsuccessfully contests validity, the plaintiff will be entitled to costs on the solicitor and client basis, which means that the plaintiff recovers from the defendant a higher percentage of his legal costs than he would under the normal award of costs.

Monetary Remedies

The basic principle behind the various monetary remedies available in intellectual property cases namely, damages, account of profits and costs, is to compensate as far as possible for financial losses. Awards of damages in excess of the financial loss in order to punish wrongdoing or to discourage others, though common in the USA, are very rare in England.

Damages

Damages are available as a remedy in all intellectual property infringement cases, and for passing-off and breach of confidentiality. There are some general principles which apply to all types of intellectual property cases, and then special rules for each type of intellectual property.

Procedure It is the almost invariable procedure in intellectual property cases to separate the issues of liability and damages. Non-monetary remedies, such as injunctions and orders for delivery up or destruction, are made at the time that liability is determined. However, all stages of determining damages, including discovery and the trial, called an inquiry as to damages, take place after liability has been finally determined, including any appeals.

Inquiries as to damages tend to be time-consuming, expensive and rare. Most cases settle after liability has been determined.

Determining the amount of damages   This is a very complex subject. The brief outline given here is of necessity over-simplified. Your legal advisers will be able to give advice on the type and amount of damages likely to be awarded, and the proof needed to obtain that award.

There are some basic principles that are always applied:

1.   Damages are intended as far as possible to put the person awarded the damages in the position he would have been in if the wrongful acts had not occurred.

2.   Damages cannot be awarded if there is no proof of the amount of the loss, so that any award would be purely speculative (although even then, the plaintiff may be entitled to nominal damages in the case of patent, trade mark and copyright infringement and passing-off).

3.   However, there is always some uncertainty in determining loss, and this does not prevent an award of damages. Any guesses that have to be made should always be in favour of the victim and against the wrongdoer.

4.   There cannot be a double recovery for the same damage. For example, if a patentee is fully compensated for his loss by damages paid by the infringing manufacturer, he cannot recover damages from the retailer of the infringing goods.

In the more common type of intellectual property case, where the plaintiff is a manufacturer of goods protected by the infringed intellectual property, there are four possible bases on which damages can be assessed:

1.   Loss of profit on sales lost to the infringer of goods covered by the intellectual property in issue.

2.   Any loss of profit caused by price-cutting by the infringer on goods covered by the intellectual property, which caused the plaintiff to cut its own prices.

3.   A reasonable royalty on any sales made by the infringer of infringing goods which could not have deprived the plaintiff of a sale; for example, because he had insufficient manufacturing capacity to meet demand, or the infringer's sales were in a market the plaintiff did not sell into.

4.   A reasonable royalty on all the defendant's sales.

Basis number 4 is an alternative to the other three. Bases numbers 1 and 2 can always be combined, as these are two different kinds of loss. Use of basis number 3 in addition to numbers 1 and 2 is only possible where it does not result in a double recovery to the plaintiff on any of the infringer's sales.

Special rules   Normally the successful plaintiff in an infringment action has a right to damages, which means the court has no discretion to refuse an award in some amount, even if only nominal. There are some circumstances, however, where the plaintiff is not entitled to any damages at all, and others when the court does have a discretion whether to award damages.

For patents, copyright, design right and registered designs, no damages will be awarded where the infringement was 'innocent', i.e., a person who can prove that he was not aware, and had no reasonable ground for supposing that the particular right in question existed. In practice, this is almost impossible to prove.

For copyright, design right and registered designs, damages are limited in cases where a licence of right is obtained by the defendant.

In patent cases, there are a number of other circumstances where no award of damages can be made, or where the award is discretionary. The most important cases where no damages can be awarded are

- for infringements committed before the patent was amended, in the case where the patentee fails to prove that the original specification of the patent was framed in good faith and with reasonable skill and knowledge (Patents Act 1977, s. 62(3)).

- where the patent is found only partially valid, unless the patentee proves that the specification was framed in good faith and with reasonable skill and knowledge (Patents Act 1977, s. 63(2)).

The most important cases where damages are discretionary are

- in the case of a partially valid patent, even where the plaintiff does prove that the specification was framed in good faith, etc., there is a discretion as to the date from which damages should start to run (Patents Act 1977, s. 63(3)).

- where the infringement started before the patent was granted, damages can be reduced if the court finds that it would not have been reasonable to expect, from the application as published, that the defendant's acts would have infringed the patent as granted (Patents Act 1977, s. 69(3)).

The copyright legislation is unusual in that it provides for 'additional damages'. These can be awarded if the infringement is flagrant, or the defendant has reaped a benefit from the infringement which significantly exceeds the amount of damages payable to the copyright owner (Copyright, Designs and Patents Act 1988, s. 97(1)). There was a similar provision under the Copyright Act 1956, but it was rarely used, and most applications for such damages were refused.

Account of profits
This is an equitable remedy which is probably available in all cases where a property right of the plaintiff has been invaded. The infringer is treated as having been carrying on his infringing business as the agent of the property owner, and is therefore liable to hand over the profits made from this business under the normal agency principles. The plaintiff cannot have both damages and these profits, as that would be a double remedy on the same damage.

As it is an equitable remedy, the court always has a discretion to refuse the plaintiff's request, and to award damages instead. This refusal would be based on one of the recognised grounds for refusal of an equitable remedy, such as excessive delay or the likelihood that it would produce an oppressive result. An account is not available in cases where there is no right to damages.

In practice, an account of profits is very rarely even requested. This is probably because the taking of an account is likely to be very difficult and expensive, and because of the considerable uncertainty in most cases about how much of the defendant's whole profit can be attributed to his misuse of the plaintiff's intellectual property.

Interest
The court has a discretion to award interest on sums awarded for the period between the date of each infringement and the date of judgment. Such interest is usually awarded, at a standard rate of interest used by the court. While this rate varies from time to time, it is usually less than the commercial rate of interest then prevailing. Interest is always payable for the period between delivery of the judgment and payment of the money. No allowance can be made, however, for the effects of inflation.

When assessing damages, the court should also compensate the plaintiff for any adverse tax effects caused by receiving damages instead of receiving the money which he would have received if it had not been for the defendant's activities.

Costs
In general, the winning party is awarded costs. These are not the full amount that he has paid out during the litigation, as there are complicated rules about what kinds of expenses are allowable and how much is a reasonable sum for each expense. The process of deciding what sum the losing party will pay to the winner is called 'taxing', and is done by a court official called a 'taxing master' on the basis of detailed documents submitted by the solicitors.

There are several bases for taxing costs, and the court making the order for costs will specify which level is to apply. The usual basis, called 'standard basis' costs, usually results in the winner getting about three-quarters of his actual costs. When the plaintiff has a certificate of contested validity from earlier proceedings, the court can order costs on the higher 'indemnity' basis.

CRIMINAL OFFENCES

All the intellectual property statutes create criminal offences, but only those in the Copyright, Designs and Patents Act 1988 relating to protection of copyright and performer's rights are of any real relevance to the subject of this chapter. The offences in relation to patents, trade and service marks and registered designs generally relate to falsification of the register and false claims to protection made by marking goods.

In the case of copyright and performer's rights, certain types of infringement are made criminal offences. These include most infringing acts, provided they are done for business purposes and with knowledge that the items concerned are infringing.

Beside the criminal offences specifically provided by the intellectual property legislation, there are criminal offences relating to trading practices, such as misleading trade descriptions, which may be applicable. Normally, local trading standards officers are responsible for instigating criminal proceedings for such offences, usually based in part on information supplied by traders and others who are affected by the activity concerned.

9 Competition Law and Intellectual Property

WHAT IS COMPETITION LAW?

Competition law is the branch of law that deals with how businesses compete in the market-place. Experience shows that competition can be distorted or diminished, for example, by competitors getting together to agree on prices, or by one company becoming so successful that it drives everyone else out of a market. Starting from the premise that the existence of competition is a good thing, competition law attempts to prevent competition being distorted or diminished.

WHAT HAS THIS TO DO WITH INTELLECTUAL PROPERTY?

This question is best answered by a few examples of the effects of competition law on the use of intellectual property rights.

A small company wants to license its patent covering a product it manufactures to a larger company which would be able to manufacture on a much larger scale and sell to a wider market, thereby increasing the income from the patent. However, the larger company would also be able to manufacture more cheaply, thus providing dangerous competition. Can the small company prevent this competition by dictating the price at which its licensee sells? Competition law says no. However, it may be possible to limit the licensee to selling for certain uses only.

In your industry, research and development of new products is extremely expensive, and only the two largest manufacturers can afford to carry on a full R & D programme. Can you get together with other smaller members of the industry to have a joint R & D programme? In these circumstances the answer is probably yes. Can you get the other parties to agree that each of you will limit the output of products developed under this agreement in order to maximise returns on the investment in the R & D for each of you? No. Can the two large manufacturers pool their R & D to save costs? Probably not.

The effects of ignoring the prohibitions of competition law, either deliberately or through ignorance, can be very high. For breaches of EEC competition law rules, you could be fined as much as 10% of entire turnover of the whole group of which your company forms part for the previous year. In addition you will be ordered to cease the prohibited conduct. Any contract terms which breach competition rules will not be enforced by the courts, and the presence of such terms could endanger the validity of the whole contract.

SYSTEMS OF COMPETITION LAW

There are various competition law systems in operation in the world. The UK has some competition laws which apply to all UK manufacturers. Almost every UK manufacturer will also be affected to some extent by the EEC rules. Therefore, in this chapter we will cover UK and EEC competition law in some detail.

Other competition law systems will only be encountered by those who trade in the countries concerned. The oldest system of competition law is that of the US, where it is called antitrust law. Because of the importance of the US market we will briefly outline US law so that you have some awareness of potential pitfalls.

UK COMPETITION LAW

The present law relevant to exploitation of intellectual property

At the time of writing, the following legislation may affect exploitation of intellectual property:

- The Restrictive Trade Practices Act 1976. This applies to restrictive agreements relating to goods or services, and agreements for the supply of information about goods and services
- The Fair Trading Act 1973. This applies to certain monopolistic practices
- The Competition Act 1980 can be used to scrutinise anti-competitive practices falling outside the Restrictive Trade Practices Act 1976

However, the government has proposed a new scheme of competition regulation, which will probably be introduced into Parliament in 1990. This will be discussed briefly at the end of this section.

Agreements
The main UK statute regulating agreements which are restrictive of competition is the Restrictive Trade Practices Act 1976. The term 'agreement' is not limited to formal, written contracts; unwritten, informal 'understandings' are covered. Similarly, the Act cannot be avoided by splitting one agreement up into a series of documents, nor by splitting a multilateral agreement up into a series of bilateral agreements.

It is not a simple matter to determine whether the Restrictive Trade Practices Act 1976 applies to any particular agreement. This is an area where you would be well advised to seek advice from a lawyer with experience in this area of law. However, as general guidance, the application of the Act 1976 to an agreement can be assessed by answering the following series of questions:

- Are there two or more parties carrying on business in the UK?
  If no, the Act does not apply
  If yes, go to next question

- Do two or more parties accept one or more restrictions, i.e., obligations that limit the freedom they had before accepting the restrictions?
  If no, the Restrictive Trade Practices Act 1976 does not apply
  If yes, go to next question

Note that it has been held that restrictive covenants in a lease are not 'obligations' under the Act, because before the lease was granted the lessee had no rights at all with respect to the leased property. The same reasoning should apply to intellectual property licences.

- Are any of these restrictions listed in s. 6 of the Act or art. 3(2) of the Restrictive Trade Practices (Services) Order 1976
  If no, the Act does not apply
  If yes, go to next question

The types of restrictions in agreements relating to goods are set out in s. 6(1) of the Act. They relate to actual or recommended prices, terms and conditions governing the supply or manufacture of the goods, the quantities or descriptions of the goods, the manufacturing processes applied to the goods and the types of persons to whom the goods can be sold or the areas in which they can be sold.

The types of restrictions in service contracts covered by the Act are set out in art. 3(2) of the Restrictive Trade Practices (Services) Order 1976. They cover charges for services, the terms and conditions for the supply of services, the extent to which the services can be supplied, and the types of persons to whom or the areas in which the services can be supplied.

- Do all of the listed restrictions come within the disregarded restrictions of s. 9 or s. 18 of the Act?
  If yes, the Act does not apply
  If no, go to next question

The disregarded restrictions that could apply to agreements involving intellectual property are restrictions relating exclusively to goods or services supplied under the agreement, restrictions to ensure that the goods or services meet officially approved standards such as British Standards, and restrictions on employment.

- After eliminating any disregarded restrictions, are the remaining listed restrictions accepted by more than one party?
  If no, the Act does not apply
  If yes, go to next question

- Is the whole agreement exempted under any one provision of s. 28 of the Restrictive Trade Practices Act 1976 and sch. 3 to the Act?

If yes, the Act does not apply
If no, the Act applies.

The types of agreements between only two parties involving intellectual property which could be exempted agreements are

1. distribution agreements, in which the only relevant restrictions are those controlling the supplier's right to supply the same type of goods to others or those controlling the distributor's right to handle competing goods
2. exchanges of know-how
3. trade or service mark licences where the restrictions only relate to the type of goods or services or the method of producing them
4. patent licences or assignments where the restrictions only relate to articles made using the invention and which are not patent pooling arrangements
5. registered design or design right agreements (other than pooling arrangements) where the restrictions only relate to articles covered by the registered design or design right
6. copyright agreements where the restrictions only relate to the copyright work
7. agreements where the restrictions only apply to goods or services which are or will be made or sold outside the UK

If the Restrictive Trade Practices Act 1976 applies to an agreement, the agreement must be notified to the Director General of Fair Trading. Failure to notify makes the restrictions unenforceable.

After notification, the agreement will then be referred to the Restrictive Practices Court which can declare whether or not the Act applies to the agreement, declare restrictions contrary to the public interest void or order parties to eliminate provisions declared contrary to the public interest.

Monopolies, mergers and anti-competitive practices
Distortions in competitive conditions can come about otherwise than by agreement. This is particularly likely to happen when a significant percentage of a particular type of goods or class of services is supplied by a single company, or a group of related companies. This is a 'monopoly situation'.

Anti-competitive conditions may result from other than monopoly situations. Under the Competition Act 1980, an anti-competitive practice occurs when a person, in the course of business, pursues a course of conduct which alone, or in conjunction with the conduct of his associates, has or is intended to have the effect of restricting, preventing or distorting competition in all or any part of the UK. This could include an agreement which does not fall within the Restrictive Trade Practices Act 1976, for example, because only one party accepts the restrictions.

Therefore, be warned

● just because your intellectual property agreement falls outside the Restrictive Trade Practices Act 1976 does not mean you are home clear. If the agreement results in a monopoly situation or is anti-competitive, you could still be in trouble.

Under the present law, the regime for the control of monopoly situations and other anti-competitive practices is separate from the system for regulation of restrictive agreements which was examined above. The two are mutually exclusive — where the anti-competitive situation arises because of an agreement registered under the Restrictive Trade Practices Act 1976, that is dealt with under that Act by the Director General of Fair Trading and the Restrictive Practices Court. Where there is no registrable agreement, the situation is dealt with by a referral by the Director or the Secretary of State to the Monopolies and Mergers Commission.

The Commission's job is to investigate whether there is a monopoly or anti-competitive situation. The Commission issues a report, and may make recommendations about remedies, but it is for the Secretary of State to take action to remedy the situation.

Proposed new legislation

In July 1989 the government published a White Paper proposing new legislation to deal with anti-competitive agreements. The new legislation will abolish the Restrictive Trade Practices Act 1976 and replace it with a broad prohibition on anti-competitive agreements that will mirror the language of Article 85 of the Treaty of Rome, discussed in the next section.

EEC COMPETITION LAW

Purposes of EEC competition law

Like every other system of competition law, that of the EEC is intended to prevent, or at least reduce, distortions to the competitive process. Unlike most other systems, it has an additional purpose — to foster the establishment of a truly common market by preventing practices which tend to put up barriers to trade between the member States. This can affect the way that intellectual property rights, which are given by national law, can be used.

Rules relating to agreements

Certain types of agreements between competitors can adversely affect competition, and adverse affects can result from consciously concerted practices even when there is no actual agreement between the parties. Article 85 of the EEC Treaty, the full text of which is contained in the appendix 3, prohibits certain types of agreements and concerted practices.

For Article 85 to apply, three conditions must be met:

1. there must be two or more 'undertakings', a term which covers the whole spectrum of business enterprises from companies to individuals, involved in the agreement or concerted practice;

2. the object or effect of the agreement or concerted practice is the prevention, restriction or distortion of competition within the EEC;
3. trade between member States may be affected.

All types of agreement are covered, including 'gentlemen's agreements' and one-sided agreements where only one party accepts competitive restrictions. Further, if there are a series of related agreements, each of which looked at separately is harmless but which taken together have an anti-competitive effect, the agreements will be looked at as a whole. For there to be a 'concerted practice' there must be some deliberate coordination between the parties resulting from direct or indirect contact.

The effect on competition has to be within the EEC. Therefore, an agreement which could only affect competition in, say, India, would not fall within the prohibited category. However, be warned — even indirect effects within the EEC are sufficient.

The third condition, that the agreement or concerted practice 'may affect trade between member States', in practice has generally been given a wide interpretation. Even if trade in only a single member State is directly affected, the situation is analysed to see whether trade with other States could be affected indirectly. Agreements which directly prohibit or limit export to other member States will always meet this condition, however small the effect actually proves to be.

Having set out the general conditions that must be met, the first part of Article 85 then sets out examples of prohibited agreements, those which:

— fix prices and trading conditions, directly or indirectly

— limit or control production, sales markets, development or investment

— share markets

— put other businesses at a competitive disadvantage by discriminatory terms and conditions

— create tie-ins, where the offending party will only deal with third parties if they agree to unrelated obligations.

Please note that this list is not intended to be exhaustive — do not assume that your agreement will escape scrutiny just because it does not come within any of the categories in the list.

How do you determine whether the agreement you propose to sign comes within Article 85(1)? This is not a determination that you should make without expert help, because the consequences of getting it wrong can be serious.

The second paragraph of Article 85 simply states that prohibited agreements are automatically void. In fact, the whole agreement is not necessarily void — if the offending provisions can be taken out without destroying the effect of the whole agreement, then only those provisions will be rendered void.

The provisions of the first two paragraphs are somewhat tempered by the third paragraph of Article 85. This provides an exemption from the effects of the Article for certain types of agreements which fall within the description of prohibited agreements in paragraph 1. These are agreements which overall have beneficial effects, namely, contributing to 'improving the production or distribution of goods or to promoting technical or economic progress', while at the same time allowing consumers a fair share of the resulting benefits. This provision acknowledges that certain agreements, on their face anti-competitive, have benefits to the community which outweigh their effects on competition. When we come to examine competition law aspects of intellectual property licences in chapter 13, the importance of this exemption will become apparent. There are, however, two conditions for its application — the restrictions imposed must be no greater than required to produce the beneficial results, and they must not provide an opportunity to substantially eliminate competition. Even an overall beneficial result does not give you *carte blanche* to restrict competition.

Rules relating to market dominance

In general, one business entity is incapable of having a distorting effect on competition by unilateral action, which is why Article 85 requires the participation of two or more undertakings. This general principle does not apply when that one business entity holds a dominant position in the market in question. Dominance of a market necessarily implies the power to charge excessive prices or impose unnecessarily restrictive trading conditions and get away with it.

EEC competition law does not forbid the acquisition of a dominant position by legitimate means. After all, dominance is often the reward for efficient and effective competition of the type competition law is meant to foster. Instead, the law is directed towards controlling abuses of dominance.

Article 86 of the EEC Treaty prohibits abuses of a dominant position in very general terms. Any abuse is prohibited, provided it is capable of affecting trade between member States, so long as the undertaking holds a dominant position in the whole or a substantial part of the common market. The Article then lists examples of abuse of a dominant position. These correspond to the types of prohibited agreements under Article 85.

The main difficulty in applying Article 86 is in determining whether there is a dominant position. The first step, which is the main source of the difficulty, is to define the relevant product market. The test that is usually applied is whether consumers consider different types of goods to be acceptable substitutes for each other. Decisions under Article 86 have generally used a narrow level of interchangeability to define products forming part of the same market.

The relevant geographical market must also be established, in order to determine whether it constitutes the required 'substantial part' of the common market. It is the area in which the dominant entity faces competition relating to the practices which are alleged to be an abuse of that dominant position. Whether this geographical market is a sufficiently substantial part of the common market as a whole will depend on the facts of the particular case, but several cases have held a single country is enough.

Having defined the market, then it can be decided whether there is dominance. Market share is the most important factor in determining whether there is dominance. Other factors include an extensive sales network, absence of potential competitors, strong trade marks and intellectual property rights giving a technological lead over the competition.

It should be noted that, unlike Article 85, there is no provision for exemption of otherwise prohibited activities on the ground of overall benefit.

Free movement of goods

We have seen that one purpose of the competition rules of the EEC is to promote free trade between member States. There are other provisions of the EEC Treaty which relate to the free movement of goods throughout the common market. While these provisions are not really part of competition law, they do affect the use of intellectual property rights, and it is convenient to discuss them here.

Articles 30 to 36 of the EEC Treaty deal with the free movement of goods. While they are primarily directed to governments, they can affect the rights of individuals. Article 30 sets out the basic principle that member States cannot impose quantitative restrictions or anything with an equivalent effect on imports from other member States. Articles 31 to 35 deal in more detail with this principle and need not concern us.

Article 36 is important because it provides the permissible exceptions to the general principle. One of the permissible grounds for restrictions on imports is 'the protection of industrial and commercial property', which means intellectual property. There is, however, a restriction — the import restriction will not be permitted if it constitutes 'a means of arbitrary discrimination or a disguised restriction on trade between member States'.

At present, all intellectual property rights are given by national law. Although there are proposals for a Community patent and Community trade marks, which would be valid throughout the EEC, it will be some time before these become a reality. It is easy to see how enforcement of national intellectual property rights against importers of goods covered by those rights could lead to a rigid division of the market.

The European Court found a resolution of this conflict by making a distinction between the 'existence' and the 'exercise' of an intellectual property right. The court interpreted Article 36 as protecting only the existence of the right; its exercise is governed by the Treaty rules, including those relating to free trade and competition. The court has laid down the further principle that the exercise of an intellectual property right can only be justified if it is done to protect the 'specific subject-matter' of the particular intellectual property right involved.

The court has developed one further general principle relating to enforcement of intellectual property, the doctrine of 'exhaustion of rights'. This means that the first marketing of products covered by the right in question, if done by the owner of the right or with his permission, 'exhausts' the right so that it cannot be enforced against subsequent owners of the products.

Operation of the EEC competition rules

Who is responsible?
The Commission of the European Communities, based in Brussels, has the primary responsibility for the enforcement of EEC competition law. The Commission is the equivalent of the civil service in the EEC, which derives most

of its power from orders of the Council of Ministers, representing the governments of the member States. Decisions of the Commission can be reviewed by the European Court of Justice (ECJ), based in Luxembourg.

Competition law issues may also come before the national courts of member States. A defendant sued for breach of an agreement which contravenes Article 85 will probably plead that the agreement is therefore void and cannot be enforced against him. The same would be true of an agreement which was forced on him as an abuse of the dominant position of the other party. Abuses of EEC competition law have also been pleaded as defences to actions for infringement of intellectual property rights.

Finding out where you stand with the Commission

You are about to enter into an agreement which could possibly fall within the terms of Article 85. Aware of the potentially heavy penalties for being in breach of the competition rules, you want to know whether or not this is a prohibited agreement before you are committed to it. What can you do?

There are a number of possibilities. In general, the greater the degree of certainty obtained, the more arduous, time-consuming and expensive the procedure.

For certain common types of agreement which tend to fall within Article 85(1), the Commission has issued regulations setting out what terms will be given an automatic exemption under Article 85(3) and what terms will be prohibited unless an individual exemption is obtained from the Commission. These regulations are known as 'block exemptions'. There are block exemptions for patent licences, joint research and development agreements, know-how licences and franchise agreements. Also relevant to our subject- matter is the block exemption relating to exclusive distributor agreements. We will discuss all these block exemptions in detail in chapter 13. You would be well advised to take advantage of a block exemption wherever possible.

If you do not believe that your agreement falls within Article 85 at all, you can improve your peace of mind by applying to the Commission for 'negative clearance'. This involves providing the Commission with the relevant background facts as well as a copy of the agreement. If the Commission agrees with you, it will certify that, on the basis of the facts in its possession, there are no grounds under Articles 85(1) or 86 for it to take any action. This certification can be withdrawn if new facts come to light or the circumstances change.

Where your agreement is probably within Article 85(1) and does not come within any of the group exemptions, then the exemption provisions of Article 85(3) will only apply if you obtain an individual exemption. Only the Commission can grant exemptions, you cannot wait until the agreement is challenged in court and argue that it meets the requirements of Article 85(3). Individual exemptions are applied for through notification of the agreement to the Commission.

The main advantages of notification are that it does provide certainty, and that the parties to an agreement which is found to infringe Article 85(1) and which is not entitled to an exemption under 85(3) will not be liable for fines for the period from notification to the date of a formal Commission decision on the agreement.

The main disadvantages of notification are that it is expensive and time-consuming and there can be a delay of two or three years before the Commission issues a decision. While an exemption, if granted, does apply retrospectively from the date of notification, there is always the uncertainty over whether an exemption will be granted at all.

The Commission has tried to resolve this problem of delay by issuing what are called 'comfort letters'. These are informal statements that the Commission does not believe it has any reason to intervene. The grounds for this statement are given. Alternatively, the letter may state that the Commission would be prepared to grant an exemption were the matter to proceed to a full decision. While this does not give the full protection of a formal exemption, it is not likely that the Commission would take a different position later unless the circumstances had changed.

Enforcement — how the Commission gets its facts

The Commission is the policeman for competition law. Like the police, it needs to know when a 'crime', a breach of the rules, has been committed, and it needs to be able to uncover the facts about that breach.

It can find out about a possible breach of competition law in several ways. It may learn of this through the notification procedure. It may learn through publicity and news reports. Often, someone who believes they have been harmed by anti-competitive behaviour will lodge either a formal or an informal complaint with the Commission, or will complain to their European MP, who will contact the Commission.

The Commission has wide powers to get the information it needs. There is a strong incentive to keep your business behaviour outside the prohibitions of Articles 85 and 86, and to make careful use of available block exemptions — namely, the arduous, time-consuming and expensive procedure of supplying the Commission with information once it decides to investigate you.

The Commission's equivalent of police questioning is the request for information. The usual first step is a letter specifying the information sought, and giving a time-limit for reply. While you are not compelled to reply to this type of request, if you decide to do so you must answer truthfully, fully and carefully. The Commission can impose fines if incorrect information is supplied deliberately or negligently.

The decision whether or not to reply to this informal request should be taken with expert advice. If you do not reply, the official concerned must obtain a Commission decision requiring supply of the information.

If a decision requiring information is issued, then you must supply the requested information within the time allowed, or you will be subject to financial penalties. While there is a right to appeal to the ECJ, such an appeal is almost certain to fail.

The Commission also has the equivalent of the police search warrant. Commission officials can come on to your premises, inspect your documents and take copies and ask knowledgeable employees for oral explanations. One way this is done is by mandate. The inspector with a mandate will normally give several days' notice of his visit and explain what information he is looking for. While there is no power to make you agree to an inspection under mandate, it is not generally a good idea to refuse the inspector entry. It raises immediate suspicion in the Commission that you have something to hide, and will almost certainly simply postpone the evil day.

When inspection under a mandate has been denied, the Commission can then seek to compel an inspection by issuing a decision. Refusal to comply with a decision results in financial penalties, often heavy, and the legal authorities of the member States will normally assist the Commission to gain entry.

In cases where the Commission suspects that a business might destroy damning evidence if it is given notice of an inspection, it will proceed directly by decision. The first that business knows about the inspection is when the inspectors turn up on the doorstep demanding admittance. In this case, the investigators will wait an hour or so in order to allow the firm to bring in its lawyer, but no other time to prepare will be given. While there is a right to appeal the decision to the ECJ, a very short time is allowed for the appeal, and it is almost certain to be unsuccessful.

Assuming you have time to prepare, it is advisable to arrange for the inspector to be dealt with by a group including a lawyer, preferably with previous experience and a knowledge of the company's affairs, a senior member of management who can authorise access to files and to employees, and a court reporter or experienced shorthand writer to keep a record of the proceedings. Do not, under any circumstances, destroy documents before the inspection, even if those documents seem to have only the most trivial relevance to the issues, and do not try to hide documents. It is a good idea to make a photocopier and copying staff specially available, preferably away from the main file area, and keep a copy for your files of every document the inspectors ask to be copied. Use the inspection to give the Commission information favourable to your position, don't just respond to requests.

The only documents which you can refuse to produce are those between an outside lawyer and his client relating to legal advice. Unfortunately, this exempt category does not include legal advice from an in-house lawyer to his employer. It is almost impossible to withhold information from the Commission on the ground that it is confidential, even if it contains trade secrets vital to the company's business. However, the Commission cannot disclose business secrets to third parties, at least not without giving the business a chance to object and to take the matter to the ECJ if necessary.

Enforcement — how the Commission decides

Before the Commission makes a formal decision, either to impose penalties for infringement, or that the agreement is exempted or not within Article 85(1) at all, the parties and other interested parties have a right to a hearing. The Commission must set out its position, and the terms of any proposed condition for an exemption, in a detailed document. The parties are given time to reply in writing, following which an oral hearing takes place.

Enforcement — penalties for breaking the rules

The Commission ensures that the law is obeyed in future by ordering those it has found to be in breach of Article 85 or Article 86 to stop their unlawful behaviour.

Punishment for past unlawful actions, and for ignoring Commission orders, is financial, namely fines. Fines for breaches of Articles 85 or 86, or for breach of a condition for exemption, are set according to the gravity of the offence. The minimum is 1,000 ecu, but a fine can be as much as 10% of the turnover on all products world-wide of the entire group of companies of which the offender forms part. If the agreement was notified, fines cannot be imposed for activities during the period the Commission was considering its response.

Orders to terminate breaches can be enforced by penalties for each day that the order is not carried out after the given date. At present, these penalties are between 50 and 1,000 ecu per day. For failure to supply information when obliged to do so, or for the supply of incorrect information, fines can be between 100 and 5,000 ecu.

US ANTITRUST LAW

The United States has the oldest competition law system in the modern world. It has largely developed through judicial decisions, and has become a complex area of legal specialisation. In a book like this we can give no more than a rough outline of its main provisions. Those doing business in the US should seek advice from a lawyer with experience in antitrust law before entering any agreement which could affect competition.

The foundation on which all US antitrust law has been built is the Sherman Act. Its two main sections sweep broadly over the whole field of business competition:

1. Every contract, combination in the form of trust or otherwise, or conspiracy, in restraint of trade or commerce among the several States, or with foreign nations, is declared to be illegal . . .
2. Every person who shall monopolise, or attempt to monopolise, or combine or conspire with any person or persons, to monopolise any part of the trade or commerce among the several States, or with foreign nations, shall be deemed guilty of a felony . . .

You have probably spotted the similarity of these provisions to Articles 85 and 86; this is not accidental. The US system of competition law was the pioneer which has served as a model for most of the later systems, including that of the EEC.

These provisions are simply stated and comprehensive in their reach. However, a little thought makes it obvious that they also condemn all sorts of things that can benefit competition and the consumer. Very early on the courts perceived that the literal wording of the Sherman Act was too broad, and developed ways of making the provisions sufficiently flexible to permit desirable agreements and behaviour.

The most important of these flexibility factors is the so-called rule of reason. This approach involves dividing business practices into two classes.

(a) Certain business practices are so clearly anti-competitive that they are *per se* illegal. That means that they are held to be illegal without any analysis of their actual effect on competition. An example of a *per se* illegal practice would be all retailers of television sets in an entire region agreeing to charge the same price for each particular model.

(b) All other practices are examined under the 'rule of reason'. This calls for the court to make an economic analysis of the effects of the act in question. The steps of this analysis are similar to those for Articles 85 and 86.

The anti-trust laws are enforced by the government, in both civil and criminal court proceedings and by administrative action. The laws are also enforced by civil proceedings by individuals.

There are two federal government agencies responsible for antitrust enforcement, the Antitrust Division of the Department of Justice and the Federal Trade Commission (the 'FTC').

The Antitrust Division's main function is to enforce the Sherman Act by both civil and criminal court proceedings. In general, criminal proceedings are only brought in the most flagrant cases. The Division also publishes guides to its view of the antitrust implications of certain things, such as mergers and technology licensing, and can give advisory opinions on a proposed course of conduct similar to the EEC comfort letters.

The FTC has powers to enforce other legislation dealing with unfair competition, price discrimination, tie-ins and mergers, using an administrative procedure. After investigation by the FCC's own staff, it holds an administrative hearing, which has many of the characteristics of a court trial but is held within the Commission and presided over by a Commission lawyer. It enforces its orders through the civil courts.

Private individuals can bring civil actions for injury caused by antitrust violations, and any damages are trebled, in effect fining the violator without need for criminal proceedings. While a high proportion of private antitrust actions are unsuccessful, they are very expensive for the defendant, and the US courts rarely order the losing party to pay the winner's costs. When doing business in the United States, it is always wise to consult an experienced antitrust lawyer before starting any activity or entering any agreement with possible effects on competition.

10   Business Approaches to Using Intellectual Property

INTELLECTUAL PROPERTY IS USELESS IF NOT USED

Intellectual property is not some alchemist's magic stone which will automatically turn a leaden, losing business into a golden success. Like any other business property, it must be used properly in order to help your business become more profitable.

It is impossible to give general advice in a book such as this about the best way for any particular business to use its intellectual property. Proper use will depend on many factors, such as the type of business, its size, current income, access to capital, business strategy and long-term plans. Best use of intellectual property is primarily a business decision which each individual business needs to make for itself, with the appropriate professional advice from your lawyers and your financial advisers.

What we can do for you in this book is to give some general guidelines. In this chapter we will examine some important aspects of the four basic approaches to using intellectual property in business. These basic approaches are:

● Keeping it to yourself to gain competitive advantage

● Sharing it with others

● Selling it

● Using intellectual property belonging to other people

In subsequent chapters we discuss in more detail some aspects of using intellectual property which are part of these basic strategies. This should give you enough basic knowledge to begin to make effective use of the intellectual property 'tools' that are described in the first part of this book.

THE FIRST STEP — WHAT DO YOU HAVE IN YOUR TOOL-BOX?

Before you can start making sensible decisions about the best way to use your intellectual property in your business you need to know just what intellectual property your business owns. Despite the importance of intellectual property in the business world, existing accounting and inventory management practices often fail to list intellectual property rights among a company's assets, either in the accounts or in the inventory. If you are in this position, you would be well advised to have an intellectual property audit performed. This should be done by a specialist in intellectual property law who will be able to recognise where there are existing rights, and who can point out steps that need to be taken to obtain or protect intellectual property.

For example, there may be protectable inventions made during the development of a new product. To get either patent or trade secret protection, it is vital that the invention is not disclosed to the public until a decision is made whether or not the invention is protectable and whether to seek protection. This means you need to have an 'early-warning system' set up, so that the research and development departments notify management and/or legal advisers when a possibly protectable idea has been developed, well before the product or product literature is available to the public.

To give another example, are the steps necessary to protect business confidential information always taken? Are employees made aware of what is confidential, and of their duty to maintain confidentiality? Are customers given confidential information without signing secrecy agreements?

Trade marks and other things that the public associates with your business, such as appearance of goods or premises, are things that almost every business owns, and which are frequently undervalued and not given proper protection. The trade and/or service marks that you are using should be registered whenever possible, and should be used consistently in all advertising and promotional activities. When new marks are to be selected, remember that marks which describe the goods, or which are merely laudatory terms are very difficult to protect. It may take more work and money to get the public to remember an unusual mark, but once they do, it is easy to protect. 'Kodak', a word invented by the founder of the Eastman Kodak Company, has become one of the strongest trade marks in the world.

Where there are items that are best protected by copyrights, such as manuals and software, it is very important to ensure that the business actually owns the copyright. Often these items are prepared by outside consultants, and the consultant will own the copyright unless the proper provisions have been made.

These are only a few examples of the steps that need to be taken to identify and protect the intellectual property which, if properly protected and exploited, should be a valuable asset of any business.

To benefit from intellectual property, you must

- know what you have

- take proper steps to protect it

USING INTELLECTUAL PROPERTY FOR COMPETITIVE ADVANTAGE

To get a competitive advantage from your intellectual property, you have to prevent your competitors from using it. This has two aspects. One is passive: you do not license them to use it. The other is active: you must do whatever is necessary to prevent them from infringing your intellectual property rights.

There are a number of factors which must be considered in choosing this strategy. First, do you have suitable intellectual property? Secondly, this strategy is generally more suited to certain types of business. Then, the advantages and disadvantages must be weighed.

Suitable intellectual property

Any of the types of intellectual property described in the first part of this book can be used to gain an advantage over competitors. Although people generally think of patents as the best way of getting a competitive edge, there are many examples of businesses which have kept ahead of their competition without patents. For example, Levi Strauss & Co. have taken and kept a very large market share by making their trade-marks almost universally recognised world-wide, and by aggressively protecting the decorative aspects of their jeans, such as the pocket designs, through copyright or design rights. Ashton-Tate are using copyright to protect their D-Base software. The recipe for Coca-Cola is a trade secret that has been closely guarded for decades.

Types of businesses

Because this strategy generally requires large capital resources in order to fully exploit the intellectual property in manufacturing and marketing the product, and sufficient income to be able to fight off infringers through litigation where necessary, it is generally best suited to large companies with the resources to do these things. The competitive advantage may be lost if even a single infringer is allowed to continue unchecked because the intellectual property owner cannot afford to sue all infringers.

This strategy may also be suitable in the very special case where the intellectual property protects a leading product in a specialised field, which generates high revenues. In this case, even if the owner of the intellectual property is not big enough to fully exploit the market at the beginning, this type of intellectual property can be a good basis for raising the capital to expand the company so that the market can be fully exploited and the competitive advantage maintained by suing all infringers. This has happened in recent years in the US in the case of some biotechnology companies such as Genentech. However, there are many difficulties for a small company in carrying out this strategy, and it probably only succeeds in exceptional cases.

Advantages and disadvantages

The main advantage of this strategy is that you keep control over your intellectual property. By refusing to license others, you do not create competition which did not exist previously. The intellectual property allows you to stop competition from infringers. Further, the profits from manufacturing and distributing the product yourself are usually much larger than the royalty income from licensing someone else to produce the same quantity.

The main disadvantage of this strategy is that it is expensive, and may be beyond the means of many businesses. This strategy will only work if you are prepared to enforce your intellectual property rights against all infringers. If you don't, then you are effectively giving a free licence to compete to anyone who wants it. Another disadvantage is that, in fields where there are a number of companies with intellectual property rights in the same field of technology, a refusal to license will likely make it very difficult to obtain licences for any of that intellectual property that you might need. As a result, in that type of industry, each company must obtain a wide range of intellectual property to ensure as far as possible that it will be free to carry on its business without needing a licence from any of its competitors.

For discussion of issues relevant to this strategy, see chapter 11 on discouraging infringers, chapter 12 on intellectual property litigation, and the section on defensive patenting in chapter 15.

SHARING WITH OTHERS

This most commonly occurs through licensing. This may be a licence where you use the intellectual property yourself and also allow the licensee to use it, or you may agree not to use the intellectual property yourself. The various types of licences are discussed in chapter 13. You may also use the intellectual property to make the products yourself, but allow others to share in the profits by being your distributors. Distribution agreements are also covered in that chapter.

Types of intellectual property

Most types of intellectual property are suitable for this strategy, but there are pitfalls in licensing trade marks and confidential information which must be guarded against.

Trade marks are regarded as being an indication of the origin of the goods they are attached to. The law is therefore very suspicious of any arrangement which could make this indication untruthful or deceptive to the consumer. Indeed, until the 20th century, a trade mark could not be licensed or transferred in any way, unless the business to which it related was also transferred. Under the present legislation a limited form of licensing, called registered user, is permitted. The rules relating to licensing of trade marks are discussed in chapter 13.

Strictly speaking, confidential information cannot be 'licensed', it is communicated under an agreement of confidentiality. However, it is accepted usage to speak of a trade secret or know- how licence. There is danger in widely licensing trade secrets, where so many people are licensed that it becomes difficult for the trade secret owner to police the licensees to ensure that they are keeping the information confidential. If the information leaks out, and the trade secret owner does not promptly act to stop further leaks and to limit the damage done by the disclosure of the information, the confidentiality of the information is lost for ever.

Reasons for licensing

Any type or size of business can use licensing as a valid business strategy under the right circumstances. Where the business does not want or have the resources to use the intellectual property itself, licensing is usually the best way to get a financial return on the intellectual property. Where the business does use the intellectual property itself, but does not have the resources to exploit the whole market, licensing others to supply the rest of the available market increases the return on the intellectual property.

There are other reasons for licensing, not directly linked to a financial return on the intellectual property. Where a technology is covered by numerous patents belonging to many owners — a common situation in the semiconductor and chemical industries — it may be necessary to grant a licence under your patents covering the technology in order to get a licence under other people's patents which otherwise would block your exploitation of your own patents, or make that exploitation more difficult or expensive, or less efficient. Licensing is also a way of avoiding or settling infringement litigation. This is discussed in chapters 11 and 12.

Advantages and disadvantages

The main advantage of this strategy is that it maximises the returns on intellectual property for most companies. Even in the case where the owner does not use the intellectual property himself, it allows him to retain some control over it, and to retain control over the other people using it. In the case of the owner who also uses it himself, licensing does allow a very limited degree of control over these licensed competitors.

The main disadvantage is that the returns are less when others share by licensing or distribution. Licensing also has the disadvantage of creating a competitor. This can be a particularly acute problem where the licensee is much larger than the licensor. A licensee can also be the most dangerous challenger of validity of the licensed intellectual property, as having a financial incentive to get free from the licence, and inside knowledge about the intellectual property.

A licensor must be prepared to enforce his rights against infringers, otherwise his licensees will become resentful of unlicensed competition and will be given an especially strong incentive to challenge the validity of the licensed intellectual property.

SELLING THE INTELLECTUAL PROPERTY

Like any other kind of property, ownership of intellectual property can be transferred. When intellectual property is sold, ownership is transferred to the new owner, and the old owner now has no rights. If he uses the intellectual property, he will be an infringer. Contrast the case of a licence. There is no transfer of ownership, all the licensee has are rights to use. Even where the owner has agreed in the licence agreement not to use the licensed intellectual property himself, if he does so it will not be infringement (although he will be in breach of contract and can be sued for that).

Types of intellectual property

All types of intellectual property can be sold. The transfer of ownership is technically called 'assignment'. When a physical object, such as a piece of furniture, is sold, the law regards change in possession of the object as being all that is needed to show the change in ownership. However, because intellectual property is a bundle of legal rights, not a tangible object, which can affect third parties, the law generally insists that certain formalities are carried out before it recognises the change in ownership. This usually involves a document signed by the seller, and often also involves some form or registration of the assignment. The rules for each type of intellectual property are set out in chapter 14.

This is true even where there is a formal certificate relating to the intellectual property, for example a patent or a trade mark registration certificate. Transferring possession of the piece of paper does not transfer ownership of the rights in the patent or trade mark. The formalities must be gone through before the change in ownership is legally recognised.

Reasons for selling

The most common reason for transferring ownership in intellectual property is when it is an asset of a business which is being sold. While such sales are not within the ambit of this book, this is a good place to point out that, whether you are selling or buying a business, any intellectual property owned by the business should be a listed asset and properly transferred. This is sometimes overlooked when neither the businessmen nor their lawyers have any familiarity with intellectual property law.

The next most common reason for assigning intellectual property rights is because there is some separate obligation to do so, most commonly arising from employment or a contractual relationship. For example, the copyright law permits an agreement for the assignment of future copyright, in other words, an agreement that the author will transfer ownership of the copyright in a work she will create in the future as soon as that work is completed. This can arise from an employment contract, for example, where a teacher agrees to transfer to the school or college the ownership of course materials which are distributed to the students, or it may be a provision in a publishing contract. It should be noted that the Patents Act 1977 has a specific provision that makes void an obligation in an employment contract obliging an employee to assign future inventions which belong to him to his employer. However, an employee is free to assign to his employer any invention once it is made, and this is a common reason for assignment of patents and patentable inventions.

In other cases, it is generally advisable to license rather than sell the rights. However, where the owner of the rights has no interest in exploitation himself, and does not want the trouble and expense of the ongoing licence relationship with its possible obligation of going after infringers, selling the intellectual property provides a way of making some return on the expense involved in developing it.

Advantages and disadvantages

The main advantage of selling the intellectual property is that it provides a quick return on the costs of development. There are no continuing obligations, and in particular there is no risk that you might have to undertake expensive litigation against infringers.

On the other hand, the main disadvantage is that this usually provides the least return, particularly when the intellectual property becomes more valuable as it is exploited. It is very difficult to properly value intellectual property rights, particularly when they relate to a new product or an untried process.

Another consideration is that an assigment and a licence may have different tax treatments, depending on the terms of the licence. The tax effects for your particular business should be explored with your tax or financial advisers.

USING OTHER PEOPLE'S INTELLECTUAL PROPERTY

So far we have discussed business strategies for using your own intellectual property. However, there is the other side to the card. For every licensor there is a licensee. You are not solely dependent on developing your intellectual property, you can and should make use of other people's where this is appropriate.

From the rest of this chapter, you will have seen that you can benefit from other people's intellectual property by buying it, licensing it or becoming a distributor. There is another way: you can learn from it and use that information in developing your own business and in generating your own intellectual property. That process is commonly called 'reverse engineering'. While reverse engineering is a common practice in many industries, it must be done carefully or it carries a risk of infringement litigation from the owner of the rights in the thing that was reverse engineered. Reverse engineering is discussed in chapter 15.

Advantages and disadvantages

This approach is particularly good for small businesses without the means to do the research and development that is needed to produce a new product or a develop a new technology. By taking a licence, particularly where the licensor is already making the product or using the technology and is prepared to share the practical know-how that it has acquired, the licensee can quickly get into a new business with the least possible risk and capital expenditure.

However, any business can make use of other people's intellectual property, and should do so whenever it would be profitable and fit in with the general business strategy.

Of course, making legitimate use of other people's intellectual property will normally involve paying for it. This will affect the profit that you make; though the cost of buying or licensing the intellectual property must be weighed against the costs involved if you had developed it yourself. It may also affect your competitive position, particularly if you are competing against your licensor. While reverse engineering does not involve payment, it does carry the risk of infringement litigation which, even if you succeed in proving that your activities did not constitute infringement, does involve expense and lost time.

the costs involved if you had developed it yourself. It may also deter your competitors position, particularly if you are counting against your license. While reverse engineering does not involve payment, it does carry the risk of infringement litigation which, even if you succeed in proving that your device did not constitute infringement, does involve expense and lost time.

11   Heading Off Infringers (Without Going to Court)

PREVENTION IS BETTER THAN CURE

Using litigation to resolve disputes between individuals or companies is rather like using war to resolve disputes between nations. It is very costly both in terms of time and human resources, it diverts resources that could otherwise be profitably employed, it can expose company practices and confidential documents to hostile scrutiny, it subjects the people involved to a great deal of tension and emotional wear and tear, and it can turn mere disagreements into lifelong enmity. While sometimes there is no alternative, you should consider litigation to be a last resort.

What can be done to avoid litigation over intellectual property? First, you should do everything possible to discourage those who have only just started to infringe, or who might start infringing unless warned off. Secondly, there may be room for negotiation and compromise. Thirdly, there are some ways of resolving disputes short of actually going to court. However, the ostrich method of avoiding litigation — simply putting your head in the sand and ignoring infringements — will generally lead in the end to loss of your intellectual property rights.

HOW TO DISCOURAGE INFRINGEMENT

Quite a lot of intellectual property infringement is the result of sheer ignorance. This can be ignorance of the law, or of the existence of an intellectual property right, or both. This is particularly true in the areas of copyright and trade marks. Educating the public, both about the law and the existence of your intellectual property rights, will warn off the otherwise honest.

The dishonest may take a little more dissuasion. The best protection is a reputation for aggressively protecting your intellectual property. Most deliberate infringers are only out to make a quick profit in the easiest way possible, and will avoid ripping you off if they know that spells certain trouble. You may also deter this type of infringer by a warning letter, but care must be taken in writing such letters, for reasons explained below.

Giving notice of your rights

One of the best ways of discouraging infringement is by putting an appropriate notice on everything that you produce using your intellectual property. What is appropriate depends on the type of intellectual property involved.

Patents
As soon as a patent is applied for, the goods should be marked with words such as 'patent applied for' or 'patent pending' in some place that will come to the attention of a person examining those goods. However, please note that it is a criminal offence under s. 110 of the Patents Act 1977 to represent in any way, including putting such markings on the goods, that an application for a patent has been made in respect of goods sold when this is not true. In the event that an application was made but does not result in a patent being granted, you are given a reasonable time to discontinue such markings.

Once the patent has been granted, the goods should be marked to indicate this. Such marking has two advantages; as well as warning off infringers, it effectively prevents a defendant in an action for infringement of the patent from successfully raising the statutory defence of innocent infringement. This defence, provided by s. 62 of the Patents Act 1977, bars recovery of damages or profits from an infringer who can prove that 'at the date of the infringement he was not aware, and had no reasonable grounds for supposing, that the patent existed'. Merely marking the goods with the word 'patented' without specifying the number of the patent or patents concerned will not automatically bar this defence. Under the statute, you must also include the patent number to make sure that the defendant can't wriggle out of paying you monetary compensation for the infringement.

The Patent Act 1977 also makes it a criminal offence to falsely represent that goods sold are covered by a patent. So be careful about the way you mark the goods before a patent is granted. Once the patent expires or is revoked for some reason, you are given a reasonable time to remove any markings or other indications that the goods are covered by the expired or revoked patent.

Copyright
The UK copyright law does not require a notice of copyright in order to give protection. However, you would be well advised to put a copyright notice on works in which you claim copyright for a number of reasons.

First, such a notice will serve to give warning to infringers. This is particularly important for things that are very easily copied, such as software or musical recordings. Many people are simply unaware that they should not make copies of such things to give to their friends. A notice which not only informs them that this is a copyright work, but also explains that this means that they are not allowed to make copies freely, may deter the honest from copying.

Copyright is now governed by the Copyright, Designs and Patents Act 1988. Section 97 of this Act provides for a defence of innocent infringement very similar to the patent defence discussed above. A copyright notice, placed so that it must come to the attention of anyone who examines the work, should effectively prevent any such defence from succeeding.

There is another reason why you should always include a copyright notice in the proper form. In certain countries, you will not get copyright protection if the work is published anywhere in the world without a copyright notice. Until recently, the most important country of which this was true was the United States. However, in order to allow the US to join the Berne Convention, the previous requirement of a copyright notice on all works, wherever published, was made optional for works first published after 1 March 1989. However, you would be well advised to still put a copyright notice on everything published after this date, as it also prevents the defence of innocent infringement in the US.

That notice must be in a specific form. First must come the word 'Copyright', or the abbreviation 'Copr.' or the symbol consisting of a C in a circle. Use of this symbol could cause problems in the computer software field, because there is no ASCII code to produce this symbol. Some people have substituted '(C)', but the validity of this is undecided — one court has held that a C in a hexagon was an acceptable substitute. Play it safe; if you can't reproduce the C in a circle, use the full word or the official abbreviation. Next must come the year of first publication, followed by the name of the person who owns the copyright.

Confidential information

Whenever you are giving an outsider confidential information, you should always mark all documents which contain such information with a notice of your claim, such as stamping the word 'confidential' or equivalent on at least the front page. Depending on the terms of your confidentiality agreement, you may also wish to add warnings against unauthorised disclosure or copying.

With information that your employees should treat as confidential, it is not always possible or practical to use confidentiality notices. However, you should have a company policy regarding marking of documents that would normally contain confidential information, such as customer lists, lab notebooks and business plans. In places such as research labs, manufacturing plants and any other place where confidential information can be learned by listening and looking, employees should all be identified by wearing badges, they should sign in and sign out, and perhaps even have bags and briefcases inspected on leaving. Further, as discussed below, you should educate your employees about the existence of company confidential information and the need to keep it secret.

When an employee who has had access to confidential information leaves your employ, either voluntarily, by retirement or as a result of being fired or laid off, that employee should be interviewed before leaving, by either his manager or a member of the personnel department. During the interview, the employee should be reminded of his obligations to respect and keep secret the company's confidential information, which continue after he leaves. The types of confidential information to which he has been exposed during his employment should be identified to him. He should be told that he should not take any documents that contain such information with him, unless he has express permission from senior management.

You must also take steps to control access by visitors to your company's premises, where they could learn confidential information. This should involve at the least having all visitors sign in and out. Where employees wear badges, the visitor should be required to wear a badge identifying him as a visitor, and in sensitive areas visitors should always be escorted by an employee. In such areas it may also be desirable to monitor the contents of briefcases etc. on entering or leaving the premises. Particular care may be necessary when the visitor is from a competitor, and sensitive information can be learned just by seeing work in progress or looking at drawings or charts which are open for the use of employees.

Trade marks

There are no statutory requirements for giving notice of trade mark rights, nor is there a statutory innocent infringement defence. However, it is still a good idea to indicate that you regard a name or logo as your trade mark or service mark. The most usual way of doing this is by putting a small 'TM' next to the mark whenever it appears. On literature and advertising you may also want to add a notice at the bottom of the page such as 'GLOPPO is a trade mark of the ABC Company'. However, in the UK do not use the term 'registered', or some other description indicating that the mark is registered, unless the mark has actually been registered. Falsely representing that a mark is registered is a criminal offence under s. 60 of the Trade Marks Act 1938. If you have a foreign registration, you can so indicate, provided you make it clear that the registration is in a foreign country.

You may have seen a symbol consisting of R in a circle placed next to a trade mark. Under US law, that symbol is reserved for use with trade marks and service marks registered with the US Trade mark Office.

Designs

For registered designs, the Registered Designs Act 1949 has provisions about marking and innocent infringement which are very similar to those relating to patents. In particular, any notice or marking should include the registration number in addition to any general indication that the design is registered.

It is also a criminal offence under the Registered Designs Act 1949 to falsely represent that a design is registered.

The Copyright, Designs and Patents Act 1988 also provides a defence of innocent infringement against an award of damages for infringement of a design right. However, there are no provisions relating to marking items in which a design right is claimed. You must be careful not to imply by any marking that the design is registered if it is not. The standard copyright notice would not be suitable, because under the new legislation copyright and design right are two different forms of intellectual property.

Publicity

As well as marking the goods, you should let the existence of your intellectual property rights be as widely known as possible. For example, when you launch a new product covered by a patent, state that fact in all your launch publicity and advertising. Currently, intellectual property is a subject of public discussion, so you may be able to interest the local press or the trade journal for your industry in running a piece on the intellectual property that you have developed, and your company's attitudes towards using and enforcing intellectual property rights.

Education

It is important that you educate your employees about the importance to the company's business of intellectual property rights.

The type of education required will depend on the employee's job. For example, those who are likely to come up with inventions, such as your research staff, must be made aware of the need to keep work confidential, and to promptly disclose to the patent department (if you have one) and to senior management any potentially patentable inventions. Where possible allegations of copying could arise, such as reverse engineering or developing compatible computer hardware or software, the importance of documenting each stage of the development to provide evidence of independent development must be taught. All employees who could possibly have access to confidential information should be informed of their duty of confidentiality and how to put such duty into practice. You should take particular care in training your sales and marketing staff, because experience shows that most leaks of confidential information tend to come from those departments. After all, it is a sales representative's job to sell as much as he can, so naturally he wants to tell the customer of anything that will help him to make the sale.

There may also be a need to educate the general public. For example, many people do not think they are doing anything wrong when they copy a piece of software to give to a friend. One way of dispelling this illusion, and perhaps discouraging some of this type of copying, is to let the public know that this is copyright infringement which can have harmful consequences on the industry when done by many people.

Reputation for protecting intellectual property

Most of us would think twice before picking a fight with a heavyweight champion boxer or a Welsh rugby scrum-half. The people who specialise in quick rip-offs to make easy money will similarly think twice before ripping off your products if you have a reputation for aggressively pursuing infringers. For example, when Snoopy merchandise first became a big selling item, hundreds of rip-off products appeared almost overnight. The copyright owner, United Features Syndicate, sued everyone it could catch who was making or selling such merchandise. As a result, the number of rip-offs declined sharply. Other examples of companies who have aggressively protected their intellectual property would include International Business Machines Corporation (computer patents), The Distillers Company plc (Johnny Walker whisky) and Louis Vuitton (luggage). Although this strategy is expensive at the beginning, it pays off in the long run. Indeed, without aggressive protection, some intellectual property rights can be lost or rapidly become worthless.

Warning infringers

Both the genuinely innocent infringer and the quick rip-off merchant may well be persuaded to stop if they are merely threatened with litigation.

The time-honoured way of providing such a warning is a solicitor's letter before action. However, unless your solicitor specialises in intellectual property matters or has had prior experience, there is a trap that he may fall into. This is the so-called 'threats' action, which is provided by statute in the case of patents, design rights and registered designs. For example, s. 70 of the Patents Act 1977 gives a person who is affected by threats of patent infringement litigation, even if the threats were not made to him directly (for example, they are made to his customers), the right to bring a legal action against the person making the threats to get an injunction against further threats and damages.

Almost any communication from the patentee or his lawyer or other agent, other than the mere notification of the existence of the right in issue, is capable of being a threat on which the action can be based. Basically, all that is required is that the person receiving it perceived it as a threat. However, it must be directed to someone other than the world at large; a general statement by the intellectual property owner that he intends to enforce his rights is not sufficient, but a warning directed to everyone in the trade is sufficient. Further, it must be perceived as a threat of *litigation* — but most threats are.

The person who is directly threatened can sue; the person whose customers are threatened must show that his business will be affected if the customers are affected by the threats; in practice, threats to customers almost always are sufficient basis for the manufacturer to bring a threats action.

The only defence to this is to show that the threats relate to acts which are patent infringement. The effect of this provision is to give the potential defendant to a patent infringement suit the ability to start litigation at the time of his choosing, and to have those procedural advantages that go with being plaintiff.

How do you avoid giving the defendant these advantages? The same section also declares that merely notifying someone of the existence of a patent does not constitute a threat of proceedings sufficient to trigger a threats action. Section 253 of the Copyright, Designs and Patents Act 1988 has similar provisions in respect of design rights. Of course, an infringer who is ignorant of the law and whose legal adviser is not experienced in intellectual property matters may not recognise a letter in such terms as being a threat of litigation at all. If you feel that you must give a more explicit warning, then you had better be sure that you are ready for infringement litigation before you do so.

To summarise, in order to warn off infringers and to discourage others from starting to infringe, you should

- mark goods covered by patents with an indication that patent protection is claimed and the number of the patent(s) concerned

- when a patent has been applied for which covers the goods, mark the goods to indicate this

- put a copyright notice on published items for which you are entitled to copyright protection

- clearly mark confidential documents, educate your employees to respect company confidential information and make sure outsiders can't learn your secrets when visiting your premises

- indicate that you regard names and logos used in business as your trade and service marks

- mark goods covered by registered designs or design right to so indicate

- publicise the fact that you have intellectual property and that you intend to protect it

- educate your employees and the general public about the importance of respecting intellectual property

- cultivate a reputation for aggressively protecting your intellectual property rights

- warn infringers that you intend to protect your rights, and be prepared to follow up on the warning where neccessary

NEGOTIATING WITH INFRINGERS

Unless you are willing to license your intellectual property to all comers, not usually a wise course of action, negotiation is not a universal substitute for litigation. You should, however, consider in each case whether it is possible to do a deal which would further your interests more than litigation would.

One circumstance where this may be the case is where the infringer is very small or has made very few infringing items. Such an infringer would most probably be unable or unwilling to bear any legal costs, and will usually be willing to agree to cease infringement. However, with this type of infringer, the expense of disposing of unsold infringing goods is often of major concern. Where quantities are small and the goods relatively inexpensive, it may be cheaper for you to agree to buy the goods at cost than to launch an action in order to get an injunction, especially as this type of infringer is unlikely to have the means to pay any order for costs. Alternatively, if the sale of the remaining goods would not cause you any real damage, you might agree that the infringer can sell the goods, provided he turns over any profit to you. If you take this route, it would be advisable to set a time-limit for completing such sale.

Another possibility for negotiation is presented when the infringer is a reputable company operating in a field quite separate from your business. Giving that company a licence at a proper royalty to use your intellectual property, but limiting the licence to that non-competing use, increases your income from the intellectual property while protecting your business.

Negotiation may also be the best choice where the accused infringer has extensive intellectual property rights of its own, which you may be infringing or which you need to use to make the best use of your own technology. In those circumstances, it is in the interests of both parties to negotiate a cross-licence of the intellectual property rights that each other needs.

RESOLVING DISPUTES WITHOUT GOING TO COURT

As full-scale litigation in all areas of law becomes more and more expensive, people are looking at other, less expensive ways of resolving disputes. Before launching full-scale litigation, you should consider with your legal advisers whether any of these alternatives would be a satisfactory alternative in the particular circumstances. Many of these alternatives do not bar recourse to full litigation if they fail to resolve the dispute.

Mediation

In mediation, an independent third party assists the parties in resolving their dispute. The mediator has no power to decide issues or to determine the outcome of the dispute. His or her role is to facilitate negotiations between the parties, to cool heated discussions and to suggest compromises.

Needless to say, mediation is unlikely to be successful unless the parties are on relatively good terms and are really anxious to settle their dispute amicably. Obviously, mediation does not prevent either party from going to court.

Mini-trial

A mini-trial in its usual form is a method of helping senior management to settle disputes by making them aware of the strengths and weaknesses of their company's case. The lawyers for each side present arguments based on an agreed set of facts to the members of senior management responsible for making decisions on settlement. This presentation may optionally be presided over by an independent lawyer agreed on by the parties, who acts as 'judge'. Very often the parties agree that the 'judge' should submit his views on the strengths of each party's case in confidence, to assist the negotiators' assessment of their case.

Clearly, use of a mini-trial involves a lot of cooperation between the two sides, and will not be successful unless there are otherwise good relations between the companies. The parties must agree on the conditions under which the mini-trial will be carried out, and must also reach agreement on at least the basic facts. Use of a mini-trial will not prevent either party from later commencing litigation, except in the unlikely event that both parties agreed that this should be so. In the event of litigation following a mini-trial, you have the advantage of having had a good look at the other side's case, but of course they have also had a good look at yours.

Arbitration

Arbitration resembles litigation in that a third party actually decides the dispute for the parties. The difference is that the arbitrator, or a panel of arbitrators, is chosen by the parties themselves. The parties also decide the rules under which the arbitration is conducted.

Arbitration may be either binding or non-binding. In the former case, neither party can bring litigation covering the matters resolved by the arbitrator. Since 1979 it has also been possible for the parties to agree that there will be no appeal to the High Court from an arbitrator's decision.

In general, arbitration is the result of provisions inserted in an agreement between the parties. Thus, in the context of intellectual property, arbitration is most likely in disputes concerning licences. It is unusual, although not unknown, for parties to a dispute concerning intellectual property infringement to agree to arbitration without a prior contract containing an arbitration provision, at least where the arbitration is to be binding. It has been used successfully where the parties and their lawyers were on good terms, and the parties were not direct competitors in the particular technology concerned.

There is probably very little advantage to non-binding arbitration, except where both parties have good reasons not to go to court. In all other cases, the losing party is likely to commence litigation, so the arbitration merely represents additional costs and delay. Depending on the rules governing the arbitration, it can be an expensive process, particularly if there are disputes over relevant facts.

Reference to the Comptroller

The Patents Act 1977 has a little-used provision which allows the parties to refer to the Comptroller General of Patents, Designs and Trade Marks the question of infringement and any issues of validity of the patent. This can only be done if both parties agree. However, the Comptroller is given the discretion to refuse such a reference if it ought to be dealt with by a court, which passes the case to the Patents Court.

This procedure is probably undesirable if there are any issues of law involved in the dispute, or any disputes of fact which would involve extensive and disputed evidence. It is also unlikely to be significantly cheaper in the long run, as there is a right of appeal from the Comptroller's decision to the Patents Court and thence to the Court of Appeal.

THE DANGERS OF DOING NOTHING

Going after infringers is at the very least a nuisance, and generally involves a great deal of time and expense. Why bother?

If you are making no use of the intellectual property and have no plans to make any use of it, then there is no reason to bother. You can abandon intellectual property for anyone to pick up who wants it, just as you can abandon any other kind of property for which you have no further use.

However, if the intellectual property has any present or future value, infringers cannot simply be ignored. Doing so will involve loss of rights, even loss of the intellectual property itself. The following is a list of some of the more serious consequences that can result from inaction.

No interim relief

As discussed in chapter 8, the speed at which you can get relief is often as important as the relief itself. In many cases, an intellectual property owner who cannot obtain an interlocutory injunction or an *Anton Piller* order will be at a serious disadvantage. However, the courts will not grant interlocutory relief unless you have acted fast after first learning of the infringement. Similarly, even though you may have acted speedily against one particular infringer, if you have previously knowingly allowed others to infringe unchecked, it is virtually impossible to get interim relief against the one you have decided to sue.

No relief at all

There is a general principle that the law does not favour long delay in asserting rights. For most legal rights this principle has been given statutory force in the Limitation Act 1980. There are also non-statutory grounds barring relief, based on acquiescence in the wrong, which lawyers call estoppel.

A statutory period of limitation means that no legal action can be brought after the end of a specified period following the event which gives the plaintiff the right to sue. For example, the limitation period for infringement of patents, trade marks, copyrights and designs is six years from the date on which the infringing act was committed. Therefore, if the acts of infringement had stopped completely more than six years before the date the legal action is commenced, this gives the defendant a complete defence to the action. In the more common case, where the infringement may have started more than six years before the suit was brought but continued for some time after that date, an action can be brought and a final injunction obtained, but damages can only be awarded for infringements that occurred after the start of the six-year period.

Where the delay has been particularly long, and the defendant has been led to believe that the intellectual property owner did not object to his activities, the equitable principles of estoppel may apply to stop an infringement suit. This defence is not easy to establish, and in general will only be applied where the defendant can show that he had good reason to think that his activities were not objected to, and in reliance on that belief he has made significant investments for the production of the goods which are belatedly accused of infringement. To prevent the defence of estoppel succeeding, it is important to put possible infringers on notice that you do not agree that they can do what they are doing. This most commonly occurs in the case where there are a large number of infringers, and the property owner sues only a few of them at a time.

Loss of the intellectual property

In two cases, allowing infringing activities to go unchecked can lead to the loss of the intellectual property itself.

With confidential information, this loss can occur very quickly. As the rights depend on the confidentiality, the first unauthorised disclosure which is allowed to occur without action being taken against the disclosure can wipe out the needed confidentiality. Speedy action is imperative for the protection of confidential information.

Intellectual property rights which protect commercial public reputation and attribution, such as trade and service marks, and the action for passing off, are lost more slowly but can also be lost by inaction in the face of infringement. Extreme delay in the face of numerous and open infringements may be held to amount to abandonment of the mark. Even in the case where there is only one infringer, delay may lead to the infringer's use ceasing to be deceptive, and thus ceasing to be an infringement. For example, various brands of 'British sherry' had been on the market for over 100 years before producers of genuine sherry, i.e., produced in the Jerez district of Spain, complained. Although the court found that use of the term 'sherry' to describe the product complained of was not apt, the long use of the term 'British sherry' could not now be stopped.

Encouraging other infringers

There is a basic fact of life we all learned in the school playground — those who do not stand up to bullies are continually picked on. That is also a fact of life in the commercial world. If you are seen to allow one infringer blatantly to get away with his activities, others will also come in. On the other hand, those who acquire a reputation for coming after every infringer find after a while that they are generally left alone, and that those who try to compete with them are careful to do so fairly.

Thus, sticking your head in the sand in the face of infringement does about as much good as it does for the ostrich

- almost certain loss of the chance of a quick termination of any litigation
- possible total denial of a remedy against the infringer
- possible loss of the intellectual property rights themselves
- encourages others to start infringing

12 War on Infringers

Sometimes litigation is unavoidable. The infringer may be a crook, bent on making a quick profit, who will not stop unless things are made too hot for him. Or, the accused infringer may be a reputable company which has grounds for believing that it is not infringing. Or, there may be so much at stake for both parties that only a full determination of the dispute through the legal system will suffice. When the methods of enforcing your intellectual property rights without going to court discussed in the previous chapter are not enough to achieve the desired goal, litigation is the only answer. This chapter is an introduction to litigating intellectual property infringement actions through the entire legal process.

There are six main stages in litigation. In chronological order, they are (1) preparation before litigation, (2) starting the litigation, (3) getting the case to trial, (4) trial, (5) appeal and (6) enforcing the resulting judgment. Only a very small proportion of cases go all the way through the legal procedure. In some, interim relief is obtained in the early stages which effectively decides the action. Most settle somewhere in stage 3. However, once you step aboard the litigation train, there is no guarantee that you will be able to get off before it reaches the end of the line. You need to know what you are letting yourself in for.

PRE-LITIGATION PREPARATION

Most people who have not been personally involved in litigation think of the trial as being the main event in a lawsuit. In reality, litigation is like an iceberg; the trial is only the visible tip, the main bulk is out of view. Most of the time and effort, and a good deal of the cost, has already been expended before the trial starts.

It is a cliché to say that litigation is like war, but it is still true. In particular, good preparation is essential for both a successful military campaign and for successful litigation. Of course, the person planning to launch the offensive, the plaintiff, has generally the advantage of time to prepare, although in some cases he may have to move fast to get interlocutory relief. While the defendant can be taken by surprise, often the likelihood of an infringement action can be anticipated, giving the defendant a chance to make preparations. In this section, we give guidance to both sides about necessary or desirable steps in pre-litigation preparation.

IF YOU ARE THE INTELLECTUAL PROPERTY OWNER

The intellectual property owner is the potential plaintiff in any litigation, although do not forget that you can become the defendant if you give the accused infringer the chance to bring a threats action.

Pre-litigation preparation for the intellectual proeprty owner should include some, preferably all, of these steps

- see whether litigation is likely to be cost-effective
- make sure you have the right to sue
- pick your litigation team
- check for skeletons in the cupboard
- aim for a quick result
- check your weapons — investigate any flaws in your intellectual property
- find out as much as you can about the infringer and the infringement
- anticipate defences

Do a Cost-Benefit Analysis

While this is not a mandatory step, you would be well advised to do a rough cost-benefit analysis before you take any further step towards litigation. Then, if the possible cost clearly outweighs the likely benefit, you will be able to make a rational decision about proceeding any further. There still may be a good reason for starting litigation; for instance, to break a deadlock in licence negotiations. Sometimes there is no alternative, because failure to exert the right against infringers leads to its loss — for example, a trade mark's reputation can become so diluted by unrestrained infringement that it ceases to be distinctive of the owner's goods and is worthless and unenforceable.

The cost of litigation depends largely on how long the process will take. If the case can be effectively terminated at an early stage by obtaining an interlocutory injunction, it will cost a great deal less than if the matter proceeds all the way through to trial. Therefore, the first step in the cost-benefit analysis is to determine with your legal advisers the chances of obtaining an interlocutory injunction, or other interim relief such as an *Anton Piller* order, which will have the effect of terminating the case. This is discussed in more detail below.

You must also factor in the chance that the defendant will not give up if an interlocutory injunction is granted against him, and that the case proceeds through the whole litigation procedure, including trial. While some of the work that was done in preparing for the injunction will be useful in preparing for trial, extra expense will have been incurred. Further, if at trial the court finds that the interlocutory injunction should not have been granted, the plaintiff may be liable for a large sum under its undertaking as to damages which it must give in order to obtain the injunction.

The main cost of litigation is made up of the following:

(a) Legal costs. While it is very hard at this early stage to anticipate what you will end up paying in lawyers' fees and related costs, you should consider that the legal costs of one party could be between £45,000 and £75,000 for a simple infringement case which goes to trial, between £75,000 and £275,000 for the average case, while large, complicated cases, particularly large patent cases can cost £400,000 or more. In the case of an early resolution forced by obtaining interlocutory relief, the costs are likely to be in the range of £12,000 to £35,000, depending on the amount of evidence needed. You must also remember that the loser will pay all his own costs and about two-thirds to three-quarters of the winner's costs.

(b) Internal costs. This would include things like the cost of copying documents and travel expenses for employees to attend the trial to testify or to consult with your lawyers. This is likely to be small compared to item (a), perhaps 5% of that amount.

(c) Lost employee time. This can be an important cost, particularly to a small company. The employees likely to be most involved in the litigation are those who were involved in creating the intellectual property in question, who are often key employees. Besides the fact that these employees will probably need to be present throughout the trial, your lawyers will need to consult with them during all the pre-trial stages. It is very hard to put a number to this cost, as it is not just the hourly rate of that employee multiplied by the number of hours he or she spends on the litigation. You also lose the work that the employee would have contributed to the company during that time. In patent cases where the inventor is often a research scientist or engineer, the demands of the litigation can seriously detract from research efforts.

(d) Diversion of management energies. Intellectual property litigation often concerns a patent, product or trade mark which is of great importance to the company's business. In these circumstances, the company's management is naturally concerned about the outcome of the litigation and becomes involved in the process. While there is nothing wrong with this, it does divert energy from the proper role of management, which is to run a successful and profitable business. Most intellectual property litigators know of cases where a very senior executive became involved in the case to the point of obsession, and the company's business suffered as a result. Again, the cost of this item to the company is impossible to state in figures, but it must be considered as a factor in deciding whether to sue.

To determine the likely benefit from a successful infringement action, you should make an assessment of the effect that the infringer is having on your profits. This will be at least the profit from sales lost to the infringer. In a competitive market, low-price sales by the infringer may also have the effect of lowering the price that you can charge, thus reducing profits on the sales you made. There may also be a loss if the infringer's goods are inferior and are mistaken by customers for your goods, thus causing loss of reputation, but this is hard to assess in money terms. On the other hand, if you contemplate ultimately licensing the infringer, particularly if the infringer does not compete directly with you, then the benefit would be the anticipated royalties.

There are other, intangible benefits which should be considered. If you have licensed the intellectual property, your licensees will become discouraged and unwilling to continue paying royalties if you stand by and allow competition from an infringer. Finally, you should never forget that the strongest deterrent to future infringers is a record of aggressively protecting your intellectual property rights. Most people will stay out of any business that carries an almost certain risk of legal action.

Therefore, to evaluate litigation

- determine the possible length and complexity of the litigation
- estimate the costs, including
  — legal fees and costs
  — internal costs
  — lost employee time
  — diversion of management energies
- weigh the costs against the benefits
  — increased profits from additional sales which would otherwise have been lost to infringer if no injunction
  — increased profits from higher prices obtainable in the absence of infringing sales
  — royalties from licensing infringer
  — discouraging other infringers
  — keeping licensees happy

Make sure you have the right to sue

If you are the original, sole owner of the intellectual property, then you have the right to sue. The 'original' owner of a patentable invention is the inventor, except in the very common case where the inventor is an employee and the invention is owned by the employer. Ownership of inventions is dealt with in chapter 5. An individual inventor may have assigned his right to the invention to another before the patent issues. The 'original' owner of a copyright is the author, except in the case of works made by employees in the course of doing their jobs. The ownership of copyright is dealt with in more detail in chapter 6.

If you own the intellectual property through assignment, or if you are a co-owner or an exclusive licensee, then you must make sure that you can sue and have followed the proper procedure. The statutory rules for each of these categories, for each type of intellectual property, are set out below.

Assignee
Patent. Can sue for infringement occurring after assignment, but can only sue for previous infringement if the assignment gives that right (Patents Act 1977, s. 30(7)). Assignment must be in writing and signed by both parties (Patents Act 1977, s. 30(6)). Registration of the assignment with the Patent Office is evidence

of ownership (Patents Act 1977, s. 32(9)). Failure to register can result in loss of damages, see chapter 8 (Patents Act 1977, s. 68).

Copyright. Can sue if the relevant exclusive right was assigned (Copyright, Designs and Patents Act 1988, s. 90(2)). This means that the assignee of the publishing right can sue for unauthorised publication, but not for unauthorised public performance. If all rights are assigned, obviously the assignee can sue for any infringement.

Trade mark. Can sue if the proper assignment procedure is followed (see chapter 14) and the assignment is registered (Trade Marks Act 1938, s. 22). Registration of the assignment is evidence that the assignment is valid (Trade Marks Act 1938, s. 46).

Design right. Can sue if the relevant right has been assigned and the assignment is in writing, signed by the assignor (Copyright, Designs and Patents Act 1988, s. 222). An exclusive licensee must be joined as a party to the action, either as a plaintiff if the licensee agrees, otherwise as a defendant (Copyright, Designs and Patents Act 1988, s. 238).

Registered design. Assignment must be registered (Registered Designs Act 1949, s. 19(5)).

Co-owner

Patent. Can sue, but the other co-owners must be joined as plaintiffs (if they consent) or as defendants (Patents Act 1977, s. 66).

Copyright. Can sue if the other co-owners are joined as plaintiffs or defendants (Copyright, Designs and Patents Act 1988, s. 102(1)).

Trade marks. The statute permits joint ownership (Trade Marks Act 1938, s. 63), but does not contain provisions as to who can sue. Probably the same rule as for patents and copyright would be applied.

Design right. Can sue (Copyright, Designs and Patents Act 1988, s. 258).

Registered design. Can sue (Registered Designs Act 1949 s. 2(2)).

Exclusive licensee

Patent. Can sue, but must join the owner as plaintiff or defendant (Patents Act 1977, s. 67).

Copyright. Can sue, with same rights as the owner (Copyright, Designs and Patents Act 1988, s. 101).

Trade mark. Registered users (who need not be exclusive licensees) can sue if the owner refuses to do so or neglects to do so for more than two months after the registered user called on the owner to sue (Trade Marks Act 1938, s. 28(3)).

Design right. Can sue, but must join the owner as a plaintiff or defendant (Copyright, Designs and Patents Act 1988, ss. 234 and 235).

Registered design. The statute is silent on the subject. If the owner refuses to take action, the exclusive licensee could try following the patent rule and sue, joining the owner as defendant. As there is no reported case in which that has occurred, it is impossible to predict whether the action would be permitted.

Non-exclusive licensee

Except in the case of a registered user of a registered trade mark, a non-exclusive licensee never has the right to bring an infringement action.

Therefore, if this could be a problem, the licensee must ensure that the licence agreement obliges the licensor to take action.

Pick your litigation team

Almost all intellectual property infringement cases are tried in the High Court. For a trial in the High Court, you are required to have both a solicitor and a barrister (although this may change in the future). In patent cases, you may optionally decide to add to the team the particular expertise of a patent agent. In a case of any size, it is also highly desirable to have someone in your company to liaise with the lawyers. The functions, and criteria for selecting, each of these team members, are as follows.

Solicitor
It is preferable to have a solicitor who has experience in the field of intellectual property litigation. Most of the large City of London firms have their own intellectual property departments, and there are other smaller firms in London that have made this a speciality. There are solicitors outside London that specialise in this area, but they are relatively few in number. If the firm of solicitors that you usually use for the company's business does not have experience in intellectual property litigation, they may be able to refer this matter to another firm that does. Alternatively, if you have a patent agent that your company uses, he or she may be able to recommend an experienced solicitor. It is possible to conduct intellectual property litigation using a solicitor who is not experienced in this area if the solicitor is willing to work closely with a barrister who is an intellectual property specialist, but that can cause problems and probably increases the cost.

Barrister
It is important to select a barrister who is a specialist in intellectual property. A solicitor who specialises in this area will be familiar with all the barristers who practise in this area (a small number of people) and will be able to make an informed recommendation. In a major case your solicitor may also recommend that you use a Queen's Counsel (a 'QC', sometimes referred to as a 'silk' because he or she wears a silk gown in court), a senior barrister who is an experienced advocate, in addition to the so-called 'junior' barrister who will do most of the preparatory work done by barristers.

Patent agent
A patent agent is qualified in a science or technology and in the writing and prosecution of patents but is not a lawyer, and cannot take any steps in litigation without a solicitor. In most kinds of intellectual property cases a patent agent will not be involved. However, in patent cases it is common to have a patent agent as part of the litigation team. He or she will be able to contribute expertise in the area of patent drafting and procedure. This will usually be the patent agent who obtained the patent, or the patent agent whom your company normally uses to obtain patents in the area of technology involved in the case.

In-house liaison

In a case of any size, it is important to have someone who is responsible for day-to-day liaison with the lawyers. If your company has its own legal department, then this person will normally be a member of that department. Otherwise, the liaison person should be someone with a good knowledge of the company and some knowledge of the area of the company's business involved in the case. The person chosen should ideally be from middle management or equivalent, with authority to get employees to do tasks that are necessary for the litigation.

Looking for skeletons in the cupboard

The litigation process includes discovery. Among other things, this will involve showing the other side the documents that you have that are relevant. It is important to understand from the outset that this means that

- you have to show your opponent your company documents *including those that are damaging to your case*

You must also understand that

- hiding or destroying discoverable documents which are damaging to your case is very wrong, and is severely punished by the courts

This rule applies to both parties once litigation has commenced. Indeed, it applies to the plaintiff as soon as the first investigations into whether the plaintiff's intellectual property is being infringed commence. Similarly, it applies to the defendant as soon as he gets a warning letter or has some other good reason to fear litigation. Destruction of damaging documents in these circumstances is generally assumed to be deliberate and to be an attempt to prevent justice being done.

However, this does not mean that you have to keep every scrap of paper for ever. It is advisable to have a formal company policy about retention of documents, to which every employee is required to adhere. For example, this could require routine documents to be destroyed after one or two years, financial and policy documents to be kept for the relevant tax period (usually six years), and very important documents, particularly those recording the development of inventions and other things covered by intellectual property, to be kept indefinitely or for a very long period.

Destruction of documents under such a policy, provided that there is no litigation on the horizon, will not normally attract adverse consequences from the courts.

However, human nature being as it is, no such policy is ever completely carried out. Therefore, before starting the litigation

- check for skeletons in the cupboard

This task is usually done by your solicitor. It is important to identify the files that are likely to contain relevant documents, including the personal files of individuals concerned with the development and marketing of the product in issue. Every company has its hoarders, who keep every scrap of paper — one of those scraps may be the little hole that sinks the whole case. Your solicitor will be able to identify which documents are likely to be relevant, and which of the relevant documents need not be shown to the other side because they are protected as privileged. This is discussed in more detail later in this chapter in the section on discovery.

What happens if you find a skeleton? The situation should be studied by your whole legal team. It is not necessarily fatal to litigation. For example, a document apparently damaging on its face may have an innocent explanation. The document may be explainable, or it may be contradicted by other, more reliable documents. It may be possible to shape the litigation in such a way that the document ceases to be relevant. If the worst comes to the worst, and the document kills the chance of a successful outcome to any litigation, then at least you have been spared the expense and public exposure that would otherwise have been incurred.

Getting a quick result

Generally a plaintiff wants to get relief against infringement as quickly as possible, both to minimise the damage done, and to keep down the cost of litigation. In many intellectual property cases, the dispute is quickly resolved, from a few days to a few months after starting the action, if the plaintiff is successful in getting an interlocutory injunction or *Anton Piller* order.

There is, however, an almost certain killer of the chances of interim relief — delay:

● delay in applying for interim relief is almost always fatal

Therefore, the first thing to do as soon as you have selected an intellectual property lawyer is to assess the chances of obtaining interim relief. For an interlocutory injunction, the best chance of success is when the application is made before the defendant is in full production or marketing, another reason for not delaying. The more damage that you can demonstrate is likely if the defendant continues unchecked, and the more unquantifiable that damage is likely to be, the better the chance of getting an interlocutory injunction. Your chances are also improved in the case of patent, registered design and trade mark infringement if the intellectual property concerned has previously been held valid in litigation.

If the decision is to apply for interlocutory relief, then you may not have the time to fully carry out all the preparatory steps that are suggested in the rest of this section. There will certainly not be time to amend the patent, or to carry out an exhaustive validity search. It is still most advisable to carry out a preliminary validity study of a patent that has not been litigated to look for obvious weaknesses. Even if an interlocutory injunction is granted, a defendant will be more inclined to carry on with the litigation if he sees a good chance of invalidating the patent. If he succeeds, you may be liable to pay him a very large sum of money for losses caused through the grant of the injunction.

In conclusion, interlocutory relief is almost always desirable because it tends to produce a relatively fast and cheap result. Therefore

- consider the chances of interlocutory relief at the earliest possible moment
- act quickly, doing only such preparation as is essential to success

Check your weapons

You would not go into battle without checking that your weapons are in good working order. You should not start intellectual property litigation without checking for any weaknesses that could allow the defendant to make a successful attack on the validity of the intellectual property on which you have based your case. While it is always possible that the defendant will come up with a successful attack that could not have been readily anticipated, you may save yourself a great deal of grief and expense by spending money before you start litigation by making a reasonable check on the validity of the intellectual property concerned.

Of course, the level of checking that can be done will depend on how much time is available. If, for example, there is an immediate threat to start infringing, the chance of obtaining an interlocutory injunction will be enhanced if you bring the action and request the injunction before the defendant actually starts to infringe. This may not give very much time for preparation.

So, before starting litigation, you should check the intellectual property concerned to see

- if there are any possible attacks on its validity which have a chance of success
- whether anything can be done to strengthen validity

What needs to be done will depend upon the type of intellectual property concerned.

Patents: validity study

As discussed in chapter 5, it is possible for a granted patent to be revoked for several reasons as being invalid. If this happens, the patentee not only loses the patent, he also loses the case and has to pay most of both sides' costs.

The grounds for revocation are set out in Patents Act 1977, s. 72(1). The most common grounds raised by defendants in patent infringement cases are

- that the invention is not a patentable invention
- that the specification of the patent does not disclose the invention clearly enough or completely enough for it to be performed by a person skilled in the art.

Other grounds of revocation are that the person to whom the patent was granted was not entitled to it, that the disclosure in the issued patent specification is wider than the disclosure in the patent application, and that the scope of the patent was wrongly extended by an amendment which should not have been allowed. A through patent validity study should consider all possible grounds of revocation.

An invention may not be patentable because it is not new, it is obvious, or is excluded from protection. In most cases, an attack on the patent on this ground is based on prior art, claiming lack of novelty or inventive step. To anticipate such an attack, a good validity study consists of two parts:

- a reasonably thorough prior art search, followed by
- an examination of the patent in the light of that search

However, be aware that there is no such thing as a perfect prior art search. The defendant, who after all has the best motivation to find something, will almost always come up with something he claims to be prior art that you did not find. The inherent incompleteness of any search is the reason why you should not rely on the search made during the examination of the patent application by the Patent Office. Until there is litigation, no one had the incentive or resources to do an exhaustive search.

In addition to looking at novelty and obviousness in light of the prior art, the validity study should also consider whether any of the claims or the specification could be open to attack as being defective. The ways in which the claims and specifications can be defective are discussed in Chapter 5.

Who should do the study? From your litigation team you could select the patent agent, the solicitor or the barrister.

In general, patent agents are the most experienced at doing the patent search, although it may also be done by the solicitor. Both patent agents and solicitors who specialise in patent work are experienced at doing the study. Patent barristers do not have the resources to do the search, but have the expertise to do the study. However, do not give the job to the person who originally prosecuted the patent application; we are all human, and there is always a built-in, unconscious bias against finding that we made a mistake or missed something. Also, the study should be at least reviewed by a person who is familiar with both the Patents Court and the case law, either the barrister or the specialist solicitor.

Obviously, you do not want the validity study falling into the wrong hands, particularly if there is any doubt about the patent. Remember

- discovery includes all relevant documents, even those you would prefer that the other side did not see, unless there is some privilege against disclosure in discovery recognised by the law

Assuming the study was carried out by a barrister or solicitor, it can be protected by professional privilege from disclosure to the other side in discovery. Opinions of registered patent agents which relate to 'protection of any invention, design, technical information, trade mark or service mark, or as to any matter involving passing off' will be similarly protected under the Copyright, Designs and Patents Act 1988, s. 280, but not opinions that relate to matters such as the effect of a patent licence.

Also keep in mind that

- this privilege can be lost if the study is not kept confidential

Any validity study should therefore be treated as a highly confidential document, and the study or its results should only be disclosed to people who need to know the results for the purposes of litigation. In other words, apart from the company's lawyers, only senior management directly involved in the decision to sue or to settle litigation should be shown the study or told its result.

Amendment of patents

The validity study may have turned up something which shows a weakness in the patent as granted. Is there any way of correcting this before beginning litigation?

It is possible to apply at any time after the patent is granted for an amendment, either before the validity has been challenged (Patents Act 1977 s. 27) or after a challenge to validity (s. 75). However, the amendment may be refused if you wait too long before applying. In a recent case, *Smith Kline & French Laboratories Ltd* v *Evans Medical Ltd* (Chancery Division, 24 May 1989), amendment was refused where the patentee waited eight years from learning of the defect in the patent before applying for amendment. Where there are no pending proceedings in which the validity of the patent is challenged, the application is made to the Patent Office, otherwise the application may be made either to the High Court or to the Patent Office. The court or the Patent Office has the right to refuse an offered amendment, unlike amendments before the patent is granted, when the applicant has a right to make any amendment which complies with the rules.

Under the Patents Act 1977 there are two important limitations on any amendment made after grant:

- the amendment must not bring in matter 'which extends beyond' the matter originally disclosed in the patent application when it was filed

- the amendment must not 'extend' the protection given by the patent as originally granted.

These limitations provide a considerable danger in seeking an amendment before litigation, because the court could determine that the Patent Office should not have allowed the amendment on one or both of these grounds — and obtaining an amendment which breaks either of these rules is itself a ground for revocation of the patent. Experience has shown that there is often considerable difficulty in determining whether an amendment has added forbidden matter, and a fair degree of subjectivity is involved in deciding whether an amendment is within these limitations. Whenever subjective judgment is involved in any decision, it is possible for two people, in this case the judge and the Patent Office examiner, to conscientiously come to opposite decisions. Therefore, the decision as to whether to apply for amendment before starting litigation is one that requires careful consideration from your whole team.

A difficult factor to assess is the amount of time that will be needed to get the amended patent. If the application to amend goes through unopposed, the chances are that the amendment will be allowed quickly. However, applications to amend are advertised, and if this produces opposition the procedure can drag on for a very long time. This has serious repercussions on your chances of getting a quick resolution to the matter through an interlocutory order.

Amending a patent after grant may also affect the ability to recover damages for infringement. If the patent is amended successfully before the matter comes to trial, the patentee is entitled to damages, provided the court is satisfied that the patent as originally granted was 'framed in good faith and with reasonable skill and knowledge'. The case law does not provide a clear test of what is needed to meet this requirement, but the patentee will generally succeed if the patent was prepared and prosecuted by a competent patent agent who took the known prior art into account and followed accepted procedures. It is, however, advantageous from the point of view of damages to amend early. If you wait until the patent is found wholly or partially invalid at trial and then amend, there is no right to any damages unless at least one whole claim was held valid and infringed and the good faith and reasonable skill and knowledge requirement is met. Even then the award of damages is in the court's discretion.

To summarise, while it may be possible to cure problems by amending the patent

- if you wait too long the amendment may be refused
- the amendment must not bring in matter 'which extends beyond' the matter originally disclosed in the patent application when it was filed
- the amendment must not 'extend' the protection given by the patent as originally granted
- it may take a long time, removing any chance of interlocutory relief
- it may affect the amount of damages

Copyright and design right

Under both the 1911 and 1956 Copyright Acts it was presumed that copyright subsisted in the work in question and that the plaintiff owned the copyright, unless the defendant challenged the correctness of either or both presumptions.

These presumptions do not appear in the Copyright, Designs and Patents Act 1988. It is too soon at the time of writing to know how the courts will treat this change. However, it would seem prudent for a plaintiff to be ready to come forward with evidence supporting his claims to ownership of a valid and subsisting copyright or design right, even before he knows what challenges the defendant will raise.

Proving ownership involves coming up with admissible evidence of the chain of title. Where ownership is claimed by an employer as a result of the author's employee status, proof of that status at the time the work was created will be needed. Where ownership results from assignment, that will have to be proved, preferably by the assignment document. The various ways that ownership can be acquired are dealt with in chapter 6, and advice on the evidence needed to prove ownership is best given by your barrister or solicitor.

There are three components to subsistence of copyright or design right. These are:

- The work is original. As explained in chapter 6, this basically means that the work was not copied from something else.
- The nationality requirements discussed in chapter 6 are met.

- The protection is still in existence. The periods of protection are discussed in chapter 6.

Proving each of these in any particular case will depend upon the circumstances and the available evidence. If the new law is interpreted as requiring positive proof from the plaintiff, the originality requirement could cause problems, as it essentially requires proof of a negative, i.e., that the work was not copied. Obviously, if the author is available to testify, his testimony that he did not copy should be enough to make a prima facie case. Where the author is not available, then it may be necessary to look for documents relating to the creation of the work, or even call an expert in the field to say that he is familiar with works of this type and that the work in question is not a copy of any work known to him. In some cases, it may prove difficult to establish the nationality qualifications needed for protection of the work in the UK, and this should be investigated before suit is filed. In most cases the work is new enough when sued on for the period of protection not to be a problem, but this is something that should always be checked.

The same general principles will apply to semiconductor chip design protection.

Registered designs

In the case of a registered design, the registration will be invalid if either

- the design was not original at the time the registration was filed, or
- the design was not one that was registrable under the Registered Designs Act 1949

A validity search and study, similar to that for a patent, may be desirable before commencing litigation, particularly if the design is commercially important to both parties so that protracted litigation with high costs is anticipated.

Confidential information

To succeed in an action for breach of confidence, you must be able to prove

- that the information is indeed confidential, and
- that there is an unbroken chain of confidentiality between you and the defendant

Make sure that you have the necessary documents to prove this before you launch your action. If there has been a breach of confidence by someone other than this defendant, you will also have to show that you took steps to remedy the breach.

Trade and service marks: use of the mark

If you propose to sue on an unregistered mark under an action for passing off, you will have to prove sufficient use of the mark commencing before the defendant's use or registration.

If your action is based on a registered mark which you are not currently using, you must be sure that the defendant will not be able have the mark removed from the register for non-use. There are two bases for removal for non-use, either

- the mark was registered with no bona fide intent to use and there has been no bona fide use in fact, or

- there has been no bona fide use for a continuous period of at least five years

There is a trap for the unwary in the use provisions. Trade marks are registered for use in connection with particular types of goods specified in the registration. If the trade mark is not used for the specified goods, or very similar goods, then it is liable to removal for non-use even though it has been used on other goods.

Another trap can be relying on use by licensees. Only use by a registered user will be effective to prevent removal for non-use, and then it must be use in accordance with the terms of the registered user agreement.

Even if you are currently using the mark for the specified goods, there is a possible pitfall. If the registered mark uses a particular typescript or design, you must check that the form of the mark that you are currently using corresponds to or at least closely resembles the one shown in the registration. Marks are often modernised from time to time, without any thought being given to the effect that this might have on the original registration. If more than minor changes have been made since registration, it is wise to register the current mark before taking action, or you may be held not to be using the mark as registered. This is particularly important for marks that were registered 10 or more years ago.

Therefore, before commencing litigation for infringement of registered marks

- check the goods the mark is being used on

- check who is using the mark

- check the form in which the mark is currently being used

Validity of a trade mark or service mark
A trade mark owner faces two validity hurdles. First, the court may hold that the mark as originally registered was not valid, in effect disagreeing with the Trade Marks Registry. This is unlikely to happen to a mark that has been registered in Part A of the Register for more than seven years, for it is protected by a statutory presumption of validity which can only be displaced by proof of fraud or that the mark is somehow contrary to the public interest. Second, a mark that was originally valid may have become invalid if it has become the generally used term in the trade for the article itself; examples are 'shredded wheat' and 'aspirin'. This is explained in chapter 7. It is a good idea to have your barrister or solicitor experienced in trade mark litigation give you an opinion on the likely outcome of any validity challenge before commencing litigation.

Find out as much as you can about the infringer and the infringement

The more information you have managed to gather about the suspect
infringement and the proposed defendants before suing, the more likely it is
that the litigation will proceed smoothly and successfully.

Patent infringement
Where the patent covers a product, the product that is suspected of infringing
should be obtained and studied by a technical expert. At this stage, this expert
can be an employee, although at trial it is preferable to have an outside expert
give evidence showing the defendant's product to infringe the patent, where
infringement is disputed.

Where the patent covers a process, information is generally more difficult to
obtain. It may be possible by studying the product sold by the defendant to
determine the process by which it is made. Other sources of information are the
defendant's sales literature, and technical publications by the defendant's
employees.

Copyright infringement
Assuming the defendant's work is not an exact copy, an analysis of the
similarities between the works is necessary to determine the likelihood of
success in a copyright infringement action. In the case of software, this analysis
will require a technical expert, preferably working in conjunction with a lawyer
who specialises in the law relating to computers.

Where the work was not published, it will be necessary to obtain proof that
the defendant actually had access to the infringed work, for example, that a
former employee of yours who knew about the work is now working for the
defendant. Where you suspect access to the work was obtained by industrial
espionage, the services of an experienced private investigator may be needed to
uncover the necessary evidence.

Infringement of trade and service marks
In order to succeed in either an action for infringement of a registered mark or
for passing off, it is necessary to prove that there is a likelihood that the
relevant public would be deceived or confused by the defendant's mark. If the
two marks are identical and are used on similar goods in the same class, this is
presumed. In any other case, some evidence of confusion should be looked for
before commencing litigation. Often, your attention is drawn to the infringer's
activities because there is actual customer confusion. For example, you receive
complaints about the defendant's goods, or goods bought from the defendant
are returned to you for repair. Where there is no evidence of actual confusion,
it may be advisable before bringing an action to conduct a preliminary public
survey, using an experienced market survey organisation, to see what likelihood
of confusion there is.

Infringement by companies
It is rarely worth suing an infringer unless the infringement is taking place on a
commercial scale. This means that, in most cases, the infringing goods are being

made or sold, or other infringing acts are being done by a company. Companies range in size from huge international conglomerates to one-man businesses running out of a PO box address. However, they have one thing in common — the law treats all of them as 'persons', separate from the human beings that make up their shareholders, directors and employees.

These legal persons can be sued in their own right. Almost always, the company will be named as a defendant in the infringement action. However, it does not necessarily stop there. This may come as a shock to many people, but employees and directors may also be liable as individuals for the infringement and could also be sued.

The plaintiff has two issues to deal with:

● are any individuals liable for the infringement in addition to the company?

● in what circumstances should those individuals be sued along with the company?

Liability of employees

A company may be a legal person, but it can only physically act through its human agents and employees. The actual acts of infringement are carried out by these individuals, who are legally responsible for their acts, even though carried out while they are doing their job under instructions from their employer.

● 'I was just following orders' is not a defence.

This means that the individuals who perform the acts of infringement, such as the engineers who designed the infringing part, the workers who make it and the salesmen who sell it are all liable to be sued as infringers. The law makes the company liable for the acts of its employees when they are done in the course of employment. This is referred to as 'vicarious liability', a principle which applies to all employers whether they be companies, individuals or partnerships.

The question of whether an employee is acting in the course of his employment when he does an act can be a difficult one to answer. Obviously, where he is carrying out his normal job in the way he has been instructed to do it, this is in the course of his employment and his employer will be vicariously liable if that act was wrongful. Could the employer escape liability by telling the engineers to design a part, but to make sure that it does not infringe? The law says no; an employer is still liable for the act when the employee was authorised and instructed to do it, even though the employee carried out the act in an unauthorised way. However, the employer may not be liable if the infringement is the result of a completely unauthorised act outside the sort of things which that employee is employed to do. For example, if a salesman tinkered with a non-infringing machine at the time it was delivered to the customer so as to make it infringing, the salesman's employer may escape liability for that infringement if the salesman was employed only to sell the machines and was not supposed to make any adjustments or alterations to them. It might be different if part of the salesman's duties involved installing the machines in the customer's premises. In practice, it is unlikely that any infringement worth suing over would be one for which the employer is not liable.

Liability of directors

Where a director directly does an infringing act in connection with the company's business, then the same principles apply as apply to employees. The question examined in this section is whether a director can be personally liable for infringements by his company where he has done only those things normally done by directors, such as advising management and participating and voting in board meetings. As we shall see, the issue of directors' liability is much less developed legally than the issue of employee-employer liability, and therefore more uncertain.

One thing is certain — a director is not automatically liable for infringements by his company, even where he approved the activities which resulted in the infringment and even when he is the controlling shareholder. If that were not so, the general principle that the company is a separate legal person, and the limited liability given to the participants in the company by the law, would be meaningless.

The uncertainty arises when trying to decide what is needed above normal activities of a director to give rise to individual liability. One such circumstance is where the company is wholly owned and totally controlled by an individual or a small group of individuals who completely ignore the formalities of the corporate structure and use the company to achieve their own ends. In such circumstances, a court may declare that the company is merely those individuals in disguise, the '*alter ego*' of the individuals to use the technical legal term. In that case, the limited liability is lost and the individuals are liable for all the company's acts. In general, courts are reluctant to find that this has happened except in egregious cases.

The second circumstance where a director may be individually liable is where he has personally ordered or directed the infringing acts. This most commonly arises in the context of a small company where the director is also the owner and managing director. In practice, it is often very difficult to determine on the facts of a particular case whether the director has crossed the line and become personally liable. The mere fact that it is a small company is not enough. In a 1921 case, the House of Lords declined to find two people personally liable for damage caused by an explosion at the premises of a company that made explosives, even though they were the only managing directors and directors of the company (*Rainham Chemical Works Ltd* v *Belvedere Fish Guano Co. Ltd* [1921] 2 AC 465). The requirements for this type of liability were analysed fairly recently in a case involving copyright infringement, *C. Evans & Sons Ltd* v *Spritebrand Ltd* [1985] FSR 267. The judge refused to hold that liability could only be established if the director actually knew that the acts that he had ordered were infringing or if he was reckless whether or not they could infringe. While liability in any case will depend on the particular facts, a director who is involved in directing business activities of the company may be individually liable if those activities are found to infringe another's intellectual property rights.

When should individuals be sued for infringements by companies?
First, it should be stressed that it is unusual in the area of intellectual property
infringement for an individual to be sued along with the company of which he
or she is a director or employee. Perhaps the most common reason for adding
an individual defendant is where the company is in bad financial shape but the
individual is likely to have sufficient funds to pay damages and an award of
costs. Another common reason is where the individual is a determined infringer
who keeps setting up new companies as a vehicle for his unlawful activities. An
injunction against the company alone will be ineffective to prevent future
infringements: an injunction against the individual is the only way to stop the
infringements.

Suing an individual who controls or who has influence over company
decisions may be a way to encourage an early settlement. On the other hand,
this strategy can backfire, as that person may be so angry about being sued
individually that the litigation becomes a personal crusade, and he will not
agree to settlement on any terms.

It is even more unlikely that an employee who is not also a director or major
shareholder will be sued. However, there are some circumstances where this can
be justified in order to provide more effective relief. For example, suppose that
your company is small, and your major competitor is a large company known
for aggressive tactics. You discover that you are losing business because your
competitor's salesmen are telling all your customers that your goods infringe
their company's copyrights. This statement is not true and totally unjustifiable.
A letter from your solicitor to the competitor produces a flat denial that this is
happening, and an assertion that the sales force are specifically instructed not
to make such comments. This makes it clear that the company will fight
litigation aimed at stopping these damaging remarks, and that if the salesmen's
activities continue for as long as it would take to resolve the case through
normal litigation, your company will be out of business. In those circumstances, suing the individual salesmen against whom you have evidence that they
have been making these statements to your customers may be the only course
likely to bring a quick stop to the practice.

To summarise

- individuals are always liable for infringing acts, even when they were
  simply doing their job

- an employer is liable for infringements by employees related to their
  employment

- directors may be liable for infringement by their company if they
  personally ordered the infringing acts

- it is not usual for individuals to be sued for infringements by a company,
  unless this is necessary to get proper relief

Picking which infringer to sue
Apart from employees and directors of companies, there are two circumstances
in which there can be multiple infringers

- several people or companies are independently making infringing products or using infringing processes
- because intellectual property rights cover most activities in the distribution chain, there may be three separate infringers with a single infringing product: the manufacturer, the distributor and the user

In the first case, choosing which of the infringers to sue if they are too numerous or your resources do not permit you to sue all of them simultaneously depends on the circumstances. In general

- pick the one against whom your legal advisers believe you have the clearest case. If you can win the first action, it makes it much more likely that the other infringers will settle or give up

However, where some infringers are much larger operations than others, picking the smallest as being the least likely to put up an effective fight is not always successful in getting the large infringers to settle without a fight.

Where it is important to get a quick result, and it is likely that all other infringers will settle once the first to be sued has done so

- pick the infringer against whom you have the best chance of getting interim relief

For example, if one infringer is already in production, while another is still preparing to go into full production, it is preferable to sue the second infringer first, as your chances of getting an interlocutory injunction are better.

In the second case, it is usually best to go as high up the chain as possible. A successful action against the manufacturer cuts the infringement off at the source. Where the manufacturer is located overseas and is not easily sued in the UK, then you would probably pick the major UK distributors. There are cases, however, where suing a major customer can produce a speedy settlement with the manufacturer.

In both cases, you should also consider which infringers will be able to pay damages and costs if you win. It can be an expensive victory to win against a defendant with no resources, as you are unlikely even to be able to recover your costs, let alone damages.

Jurisdiction
Jurisdiction is the technical term for power of a court over a defendant.

- if the court has no jurisdiction over a particular person or type of case, then you cannot bring an action against that person or for that type of case in that court

The courts which can hear intellectual property cases are discussed below.

Whether the court has jurisdiction over a particular defendant depends on a number of factors. As virtually all intellectual property infringement actions are brought in the High Court, we will here only discuss the jurisdiction of that court. Jurisdiction is primarily defined in terms of service of the official document which commences the action. For defendants who are citizens of or resident in any EEC country, the provisions of the Brussels Treaty control where they can be sued. For infringement of any form of intellectual property which must be registered, namely, in the UK, patents, registered trade and service marks and registered designs, the courts of the country where the intellectual property is registered have exclusive jurisdiction over actions concerning that property. The provision of the Brussels Treaty that appears to be applicable to actions for infringement of non-registrable intellectual property provides that a defendant can be sued in the country where the harm occurred. For breach of an obligation of confidentiality, an EEC defendant can be sued in the country where the obligation was to be carried out — which would normally be where the defendant's business was located.

For non-EEC defendants, if the defendant can be served in England or Wales or their territorial waters, there is automatically jurisdiction, unless the plaintiff tricked the defendant into coming into the jurisdiction so he could serve him. However, the defendant may be able later to persuade the court that it is very unfair on him to try the case in England and there is some foreign jurisdiction where the action really belongs. In any other case the court's permission must be obtained before service is attempted. This permission is likely to be granted for most infringement actions where the acts complained of are committed within England and Wales. In confidential information cases where the action is based on a breach of the contract requiring confidentiality, the action can be brought provided the contract was made in England and Wales or is governed by English law.

Anticipating defences

There are a number of defences that are commonly raised in intellectual property infringement actions. You, as plaintiff, can anticipate likely defences and take steps to assess the chance of success before you make a final decision to start litigation. Defences are of two kinds

- defensive, in which the accused infringer effectively says 'I didn't do it'

- offensive, in which the defendant attacks the intellectual property being used against him

It is particularly important to assess the strength of any possible offensive defence before starting litigation, because if the defendant succeeds with this type of defence, you not only lose the case, you also lose your intellectual property.

One attack is to allege that the intellectual property concerned is invalid. We have already discussed steps you should take to ensure that you are not suing on intellectual property which is vulnerable to such an attack.

A second important offensive defence is the allegation that the enforcement of your intellectual property rights is contrary to EEC law. The law relating to the interaction of national intellectual property rights and the principles of free movement of goods between the member States was mentioned in chapter 9. The basic principle to be learned from the cases is that the owner of intellectual property rights in one EEC country cannot use those rights to prevent or hinder the importation of goods placed on the market in another EEC country by the owner of the rights or with his permission.

The principles discussed in chapter 9 and summarised above only apply to imported goods. If the infringing goods are being made in the UK you do not have to worry about the effects of Article 30. If the goods are imported directly from outside the EEC, Article 30 does not apply. Therefore, it is important to determine where the infringing goods are being made.

Secondly, it is important to determine who is making imported goods you believe are infringements. If these goods were made in the EEC under voluntary licence, then you will be unable to use your UK intellectual property rights to keep them out, unless there has been improper repackaging or application of trade marks by the importer. If the importation is being done by your licensee in breach of an exempted obligation not to make sales in your territory (this type of provision in licence agreements is discussed in chapter 13), then you would have an action for breach of contract, but it is almost certain that the European Court would not allow you to use your intellectual property rights to stop the importation.

IF YOU ARE THE ACCUSED INFRINGER

If the first thing you know about infringement accusations made against you is being served with a writ, or, even worse, someone turning up at your door with a court order to search the premises, you have no opportunity for pre-litigation preparation. However, in a lot of cases, you will have some advance warning of litigation. This may be through any of the approaches to heading off litigation discussed in the previous chapter, ranging from an informal approach offering to discuss a licence to a formal solicitor's letter. If you have a programme to monitor competitors' intellectual property, as discussed in chapter 15, then you may be aware of a possible threat of litigation even before you are approached by the intellectual property owner. Whenever you have some warning of threatened litigation, there are several things that you can do which will considerably increase your chances of a satisfactory outcome.

Pick your litigation team

You will need the same type of team as the intellectual property owner, and the advice on team selection given above applies to the accused infringer as well.

Is your opponent's intellectual property valid?

The best investment you can make is to get the most thorough study possible in the time you have available of the validity of the intellectual property which you are accused of infringing. This study will as far as possible mirror the type of study made by the intellectual property owner, discussed above.

- if this study reveals a good basis for attacking the validity of the intellectual property, you should discuss with your legal advisers the possibility and advisability of launching a pre-emptive strike

While potential defendants are usually content to sit it out and see whether they are sued, there are advantages to seizing the initiative where you have a very good chance of success. First, if you have spotted the flaw in the intellectual property, the chances are that the property owner has too. If so, he may be just using it as a threat with no real intention of suing. Calling his bluff may result in a favourable settlement, getting rid of the cloud over your business. In some circumstances, such as when you are trying to raise finance for the business or sell it, this cloud can have severe financial effects. Secondly, the plaintiff has some procedural advantages in litigation, and an unmeasurable psychological advantage.

The type of action open to you depends on the type of intellectual property which you are accused of infringing. However, if you are going to bring an action

- look primarily for an action that will let you raise allegations of non-infringement as well as invalidity

An attack on validity will often result in the intellectual property owner seeking to narrow the scope of his claimed protection in order to maintain validity — and that narrowing may very well result in your activities being held to be non-infringing. This 'squeeze' on the property owner may persuade him to come to a favourable settlement at an early stage, and increases the chance of your eventual success if he does not settle, so you should strive to keep the advantage by litigating both validity and infringement in the action.

Challenging the validity of a patent

There are three ways of attacking a patent before the patent owner sues you

- threats action
- application for revocation to the Patent Office
- petition for revocation to the High Court

Threats action

Threats actions were discussed in chapter 11. If the patentee has been properly advised, he will not have done anything that counts as a 'threat' on which you can base an action. However, if the patentee has done anything more than merely notify you of the existence of the patent, and you genuinely believe that you are being threatened with litigation, you probably have a basis to bring the action. You should particularly enquire whether the patentee or its representatives have said anything to your customers which carries an express or implied threat of litigation.

As the patentee will certainly plead that the threats were justified and counter-claim for patent infringement, turning the case into a full-blown patent infringement litigation, you should not bring a threats action unless you have grounds for a reasonable hope of success in an infringement action. However, taking this initiative when you have such grounds gives you the tactical advantage of catching the patentee off guard, and starting the litigation before he has finished preparation. It also gives you the advantage any plaintiff has of being able to have a greater measure of control of the litigation than the defendant. If you are hoping to settle the case, it gives you an advantage at the bargaining table. If you are in the process of negotiating a major licence agreement or the sale of your business, any threat of litigation can seriously affect the negotiations, which may make it necessary for you to act quickly to get the issue resolved. These are all factors that your litigation team will take into consideration when advising whether or not to bring a threats action.

Application for revocation

This is made to the Patent Office, and may be made at any time. It is commenced by filing a form and a document called a 'statement of case', which sets out the grounds on which revocation is sought. The Patent Office sends a copy of the form and the statement to the patentee, who replies with a counter-statement. Discovery is rare, and evidence is usually given in written form, by affidavit or statutory declaration, rather than live with cross–examination. After all the written evidence is in, there is a hearing, at which the parties present their arguments to a senior Patent Office official, called the 'hearing officer' who will decide the matter. There is a right to appeal the hearing officer's decision to the Patents Court, and from thence by leave to the Court of Appeal, with further appeal to the House Of Lords possible in cases raising important legal issues.

In most cases an application for revocation to the Patent Office is not a good idea. The Office is not experienced at handling cases where there is disputed evidence, and therefore cross-examination is necessary to get at the truth. Further, in disputed matters under the previous Patents Act, the Office resolved doubts in favour of the patent applicant, and that old thinking may linger on. A tendency to favour the patentee could be particularly damaging because the Office has the same power as the High Court to grant a 'certificate of contested validity', discussed in chapter 8, which will make it harder to attack the patent successfully in subsequent court proceedings. Where you have a good case that you do not infringe as well as grounds for attacking validity, you should not use revocation proceedings in the Patent Office in which only validity questions can be decided. In such a case you should bring an action in the High Court in which both infringement and validity issues can, and usually are, combined. Finally, because of the right of appeal to the Patents Court, the proceedings will probably be no cheaper than High Court proceedings and may even cost more.

Revocation proceedings in the Patent Office are probably most useful where you have a good attack on the novelty of the patent based on prior art that the Patent Office did not consider when it granted the patent, and you want to use the proceedings to bring the patentee to the negotiating table.

Petition for revocation

This is the equivalent action in the High Court to the application for revocation. It also has disadvantages, in particular, the inability to raise any infringement issues, and is rarely used. It cannot be combined with any other action.

It is not possible to bring an action in the High Court merely for a declaration of invalidity. However, validity can be put in issue in an infringement action, an action for threats and an action for a declaration of non-infringement, discussed below.

Challenging copyright

There is no statutory threats action in copyright. However, in cases where the threats are clearly unjustified, are being made publicly and are damaging your business, you may be able to bring an action for slander of title, although this is a difficult action to win and is rarely brought. Alternatively, if the unjustified threats are being made to a customer, distributor or licensee with the intent of getting that person to break his contract with you, you may have a right to sue for inducing breach of contract.

Challenging design right

The Copyright, Designs and Patents Act 1988 does provide for a threats action. Under s. 253, a person who is being damaged by threats of design right infringement litigation can bring an action for a declaration that the threats are unjustified, an injunction against continuation of the threats and damages. There is not yet any case law on this provision, but the courts are likely to apply the rules developed for patents threats actions.

Challenging registered designs

Threats action
Registered Designs Act 1949, s. 26, provides an action for threats of infringement litigation similar to the patent and design right provisions.

Rectification of the register
The Registered Designs Act 1949 allows anyone who is prejudiced by a wrongful registration to apply to the High Court to have the registration removed. One of the grounds for removal is that the design registration is invalid. Where there is a good argument that the registration is invalid, but the case for non-infringement is weak, an application for rectification should be carefully considered.

Challenging trade marks

Threats actions
There is no statutory action for threats of litigation for infringement of a registered trade mark. However, there is the possibility of an action for slander of goods, if the infringement accusations are untrue because there is either no infringement or the trade mark is invalid, and the person making them knows them to be untrue but made them to injure the business of the person he is accusing of trade mark infringement.

Rectification of the register

The statute allows trade marks that have not been used to be registered, but provides for removal from the register in certain cases of non-use. As we have seen above, there is 'non-use' for these purposes if the mark has only been used on goods different from those that it was registered for, or the only use has been by a licensee who is not a registered user, and these facts are readily ascertainable. If the registered mark that you are accused of infringing has not been used at any time up to one month before the application for removal for non-use is filed and was registered with no genuine intent to use, or has not been used for a continuous period of five years, you can apply to the Trade Marks Registry to have the mark removed from the register.

It is also possible to apply to have a mark that should not have been registered removed. However, if the mark has been registered for more than seven years, it can only be attacked if there is proof that the registration was obtained by fraud, or that the mark was confusing, contrary to law or morals, or scandalous. In effect, it is almost impossible to succeed in an application for rectification if the registration is more than seven years old, except on grounds of non-use.

Do you have a good non-infringement argument?

You should also ask your professional advisers to study your product and the intellectual property you are accused of infringing carefully to determine all grounds on which you can argue that you do not infringe. This study is normally combined with the validity study, to give an overall picture of the chance of success at trial.

In the case of patents, the Patents Act 1977 provides for both the High Court and the Patent Office to give a declaration that specified acts or products do not infringe specified patents. Before applying for such a declaration, however, you must have asked the patentee, in writing, for a written acknowledgment that the product or process in question does not infringe the patent, giving the patentee full details of the product or process in question. If the patentee refuses or fails to give the requested acknowledgment, you can then proceed with the action for the declaration.

The advantage of this action is that issues of validity can also be raised. It is clear that you can ask for a declaration of invalidity as well as of non-infringement, but it is not clear whether you can also ask for revocation of the patent in this action.

Where there has been no actionable threat, but the patent is casting a shadow over your business or business negotiations which you believe is unjustified, bringing an action for a declaration of non-infringement should be seriously considered.

There is no specific action for a declaration of non-infringement provided for any other form of intellectual property. It may be that in most cases the accused infringer is content to wait, hoping that he won't be sued. However, there is a general power in the court to grant declarations of legal or equitable rights, which can be used when there is some real question about those rights. There may be cases where it is necessary to get a judicial finding that there is no infringement, rather than waiting to see if you are sued.

Investigate other defences

Beside non-infringement and invalidity, there are a number of other defences that may be open to you. You should investigate the applicability of every possible defence, so your lawyers will have material to plead your defences to the action once the suit is brought.

There are a number of defences that apply generally to any kind of intellectual property infringement action. Those which you should always investigate are:

(a) Expiry of the limitation period. The law does not favour the bringing of very old claims. Therefore, for each type of intellectual property, a limitation period of a specified number of years is established. For example, the limitation period for patent infringement is six years. This means that the patentee cannot sue for any acts of infringement which occurred more than six years before an action is filed. For infringement which continues over a period of time, part of which was before the start of the limitation period and part of which was within the period, the owner can sue, but will only recover damages for the infringements occurring within the period.

(b) Acquiescence or estoppel. If the patentee has deliberately led you to believe that no action will be taken against you, he may be unable later to enforce the patent against you. This is a difficult defence to establish unless you have written agreement from the patentee that he will not sue. However, if you can show that the patentee knew of your activities, and by long inaction or representation led you to believe that you would not be sued, in reliance upon which you invested a lot of money in gearing up to produce the accused product, you may convince the court that the patentee is now estopped, which means legally prevented, from suing for infringement.

(c) Licence. You may have a licence from the intellectual property owner covering the intellectual property in question. This may be an express licence, or it may be implied as a matter of law. An example of an implied licence is the licence to use that automatically comes when you purchase legitimate goods covered by the intellectual property in question.

(d) EEC defences. These have been discussed above. You should investigate whether there are any grounds for claiming that there are competition law grounds for the court to refuse to enforce the intellectual property against you.

(e) Crown use. The extent to which the Crown, i.e., the British government, can use intellectual property without the owner's agreement is governed by the various intellectual property statutes. In general, the property owner cannot obtain an injunction against Crown use, but is entitled to compensation.

Besides the defences which are common to all types of intellectual property infringement litigation, there are defences which are specific to a particular type of intellectual property. We will set out some of the most common of these defences — your legal team will be able to advise you whether there are any others that could apply to your case.

Patent

(a) Statutory defences. The section of the Patents Act 1977 that deals with infringement, s. 60, also contains a list of exempted acts. This means that, if your activities come within one of the listed categories, you have a defence to any infringement action. The two items in the list which are most commonly relied on are private, non-commercial use and use for experimental purposes connected to the subject of the invention. The third exemption is the preparation in a pharmacy of a prescription, and the remaining three relate to use in ships, aircraft and other vehicles which are only temporarily or accidentally in the United Kingdom.

(b) Use before the patent was filed. Section 64 of the Patents Act 1977 gives the person who in good faith used the invention before the priority date of the patent the right to continue using it after the patent is granted. This also covers the situation where serious preparations were being made to use the invention at the time the patent was filed. This right cannot be licensed, but can be transferred with the business. However, it is possible that the section could be interpreted to mean that you can only carry on doing the same thing you were doing before the priority date, making you liable for infringement if you introduce any improvements that would be covered by the patent.

(c) Use after a patent lapses. If you start to use or make serious preparations to use an invention after the patent has lapsed for failure to pay a renewal fee, and the patent is subsequently restored, you are allowed to continue that use.

(d) Repair of patented products. The purchaser of a patented product automatically gets the right to have that product repaired or modified as needed. This repair or modification can be carried out by a third party, who will not be liable for infringement. This right does not extend to replacement of the patented product, and it is not always easy to draw the line between repair and replacement.

(e) Licence of right. As explained in chapter 5, in certain limited cases the patentee can be compelled to grant a licence. If the patent that is being asserted against you is one for which a compulsory licence is obtainable, you should consider applying for such a licence. If granted, there can be no further infringement, and settlement of any litigation is very likely.

(f) Innocent infringement. This is not a complete defence, but it does prevent an award of damages. You have to prove that you were not aware, and had no reasonable grounds for believing, that the patent existed. If there are reasonable grounds for believing that the product might be patented, a proper search to see whether a patent exists must be made. Deliberate ignorance is not innocence. This defence cannot be raised if the patented products were marked with the patent number. The courts have not in general been ready to find that the infringement was innocent.

Copyright: statutory defences

There is a whole chapter of the Copyright, Designs and Patents Act 1988 which deals with acts that are not infringements of copyright although they are within the general scope of the copyright owner's exclusive rights. There is not room here to deal with all of them; the ones most likely to be of use to readers of this book are set out below. The complete list is to be found in ss. 28 to 76 of the 1988 Act.

(a) Fair dealing. There was a great deal of case law under previous Copyright Acts concerning what constitutes fair dealing in various contexts. Basically, use of the work for private study or research, quoting passages in a review or news report, and an incidental inclusion of copyright material in another work are not infringement of copyright.

(b) Educational uses. Sections 32 to 36 of the Copyright, Designs and Patents Act 1988 provide detailed guidance to non-infringing educational uses of various types of work. In general, educational establishments are allowed a broader scope of use than is allowed under the fair dealing provisions.

(c) Libraries. Librarians are given a number of exemptions from copyright infringement, mainly connected with making copies of works.

(d) Public administration. Use of a work in the course of Parliamentary or judicial proceedings, or in a royal commission inquiry is exempt, and there are provisions relating to copying from works that are by statute made open to public inspection.

(e) Designs. The relationship between copyright and design right has been discussed in chapter 6. In order to keep the two rights separate, it is not an infringement of the copyright in a document which embodies a design protected by a design right to make that design, although it will be an infringement of the design right.

(f) Electronic works. Provided there were no licence restrictions on copying or transferring the work, all the original purchaser's rights are transferred to subsequent purchasers, including the right to use back-up copies if the original is no longer usable. All copies made by the original purchaser must be transferred, or they will become infringements if the original purchaser keeps them.

Copyright: other defences

(a) Objectionable work. In rare cases the courts have refused to enforce a copyright on the grounds that the law should not protect a particularly undeserving plaintiff. An example of this is *Spycatcher,* which the House of Lords stated would not be protected from infringement because Peter Wright's publication of the book 'reeked of turpitude'. This is unlikely to happen except in the most egregious circumstances.

(b) Innocent infringement. While there is a defence of innocent infringement provided by the copyright statute to a claim for damages (but not any other remedy), it is very difficult to prove you are entitled to it. You must prove that you did not know, and had no reason to believe, that copyright subsisted in the work. This defence is most likely to succeed in the case of works that appear to be old enough that copyright should have expired. Otherwise, as almost all types of work are capable of being protected by copyright, a defendant should reasonably have expected that the work in question was also protected.

(c) Spare parts. As explained in chapter 6, under the pre-1988 Act law, industrial articles made from a drawing were protected by copyright for the life of the author of the drawing plus 50 years, whereas articles designed to appeal to the eye had a much shorter period of protection. While this anomalous situation has been removed by the Copyright, Designs and Patents Act 1988, there is a transitional 10 years of continued copyright protection for industrial articles made from drawings made before 1 August 1989. The same transitional provisions allow any previous rule of law that prevented or restricted the enforcement of that copyright to continue in operation. This means that the exemption from copyright infringement for the manufacture of spare parts, laid down by the House of Lords in *British Leyland Motor Corporation Ltd* v *Armstrong Patents Co. Ltd* [1986] AC 577, can be raised as a defence to a charge of infringement based on copying of industrial articles for the supply of spare parts.

Design right
(a) Copyright. The design right legislation has the mirror image provision to that in the copyright legislation, namely, that it is not an infringement of the design right in a work which is also covered by copyright to do something which is an infringement of the copyright in that work.

(b) Licences of right. Under Copyright, Designs and Patents Act 1988, s. 237, licences of right are available during the last five years of the design right. In infringement proceedings, if a licence of right is available and the defendant agrees to take such a licence, no injunction or order for delivery up can be made against him, and damages are limited to not more than twice the amount he would have had to pay as licence fees under the compulsory licence.

(c) Innocent infringement. For direct infringements, this is similar to the provisions for patents and copyright, namely, absence of knowledge or reasonable belief. Where the defendant innocently acquired the infringing articles, not knowing or having reason to believe that they infringed a design right, the only remedy that can be obtained is a reasonable royalty on the articles.

(d) Spare parts. The Copyright, Designs and Patents Act 1988 specifically excludes from design protection features of shape which enable an article to fit with another article so that either article can perform their function, and features of an article which is intended to form an integral part of another article which are dependent upon the article they must fit with (see chapter 6). This provision was intended to permit such things as the manufacture and sale of spare parts and to prevent the problems that had developed under the old law which were the subject of *British Leyland Motor Corporation Ltd* v *Armstrong Patents Co. Ltd* [1986] AC 577.

Registered designs
The only statutory defence provided by the Registered Designs Act 1949 is innocent infringement.

Trade marks
(a) Independent rights. Because trade mark and service mark rights can be acquired by use, an earlier, unregistered user may have a better right than the proprietor of a later, registered mark. Further, a user of a concurrently

registered mark for the same class of goods may continue using it, even if that mark is very close to the plaintiff's mark. Instead of suing for infringement, the plaintiff will have to try to have the mark removed from the register for invalidity. Of course, if this is successful, continued use of the removed mark will then attract an infringement suit.

(b) Use of your own name. Anyone is allowed to make bona fide use of his or her own name in connection with his or her business, provided reasonable care is taken to avoid confusion. Bona fide means honest use with no intention to deceive anyone or to make use of any goodwill acquired by another business. You are also allowed to use a bona fide description of your products, provided that description would not be likely to be taken as meaning that the product is somehow connected to the owner of the registered mark. For example, if your name is McDonald, you can sell hamburgers, but you can't call them 'Big Macs', and you can't put a golden arches sign outside your restaurant.

(c) Marks registered in Part B of the Register. Although the definition of infringement is the same for a Part B mark as it is for a Part A mark, Trade Marks Act 1938, s. 5(2), provides that the plaintiff is not entitled to relief if the defendant can prove both (a) that the use the plaintiff complains of is not likely to deceive or cause confusion and (b) that this use is not likely to be taken as indicating a 'connection in the course of trade'. Unfortunately, there is no clear guidance as to what kind of evidence the defendant must provide to establish these two requirements.

Can you make anyone else pay?

If you are not the originator of the infringing products, you should see whether you are indemnified against intellectual property infringement by anyone further up the chain. If you are a licensee or distributor, then if you were properly advised before signing the agreement, you will have ensured that you were given at least some protection against the effects of intellectual property infringement. An innocent purchaser of infringing goods is protected by a warranty that is implied by law that the seller had the right to sell the goods and that the buyer has the right to possess them without assertion of rights by third parties, except those rights that the buyer expressly agreed to be subject to.

You should also examine your insurance policies. Besides any insurance that expressly covers intellectual property infringement that you may have taken out, sometimes general liability policies are so broadly worded that they cover liability for infringement.

STARTING THE LITIGATION

Now the factors have been weighed, the decision to litigate taken and the preparations completed. Before going into the details of the litigation process, let us take a bird's-eye view of what happens between now and the end of the process

- the parties have to tell each other what their case (for the plaintiff) or defence to it (for the defendant) is and what facts they base it on

This is done primarily by formal written documents called pleadings. Once the exchange of pleadings is completed

● the parties have to gather the evidence needed to prove to a court these facts on which their case is built

In intellectual property cases, a great deal of this evidence is either contained in, or based on, documents. As the trial can take place many years after relevant events occurred, most witnesses will not remember a great deal about what happened without being reminded by looking at documents. As documents are so important

● each party must show the other the documents which it possesses or has control over which are relevant to any of the facts which have to be proved by either side

This exchange of documents, the most important part of the discovery process, includes documents which are not favourable to your case. The only exclusion is for documents which the law exempts from disclosure to the other side for specific reasons, called 'privileged' documents. The most important category of privileged documents are those which contain advice from your lawyer.

Once discovery is complete

● each party prepares to prove at trial the facts on which his case is based

This will include selecting documents, finding and preparing suitable witnesses, including experts on specialised subjects relevant to the issues in the case, and preparing any models, graphs or charts which may help to explain the case in court. In patent cases, either party may also want to do experiments, the results of which will be put before the trial judge.

Then follows:

the trial, at which evidence is given, usually through oral testimony of witnesses, and legal arguments are made by the parties' barristers,

judgment,

any appeals,

unless the case settles, which can happen at any stage.

Having taken this quick tour through the litigation process, a more detailed look at the main stages follows. However, this is not a do-it-yourself litigation guide — there are many complicated rules and important details which cannot be covered in this book.

THE COURT

Most intellectual property litigation is brought in the High Court. However, the Copyright, Designs and Patents Act 1988 provides for the creation of a Patents County Court which can deal with matters relating to patents and designs. The first such Patents County Court is at the time of writing being set up at the Wood Green court complex of the Edmonton County Court. Although the legislation envisages a jurisdictional limit for such actions, with those who bring actions in the High Court which could have been brought in the County Court being limited to recovering costs at County Court levels, no such limit is to be set initially. This gives litigants a free choice between the High Court and the Patents County Court. It is also possible to bring copyright and passing off cases in a County Court, provided the sum claimed is less than the general County Court jurisdictional limit (at present £5,000).

County Court procedures are in general intended to make litigation speedier and cheaper. Experience will tell whether that will be the case in patent and design actions in the Patents County Court. Procedures in the Patents County Court will be basically County Court procedures, but subject to special rules which were still being prepared at the time this book goes to press.

High Court actions involving patents, registered designs and registered trade marks must be brought in the Chancery Division. Patent and registered design cases are always dealt with by a specialist Patents Judge, who also usually hears trade mark cases. Other types of intellectual property cases may also be brought in the Queen's Bench Division, but are more commonly started in the Chancery Division because the judges of that division have the greatest experience in dealing with such cases.

Because the High Court is the most common forum for intellectual property cases, the procedure described in the rest of this chapter is the procedure followed in the High Court.

THE WRIT

Litigation in the High Court is started by the issuance and service of a writ. This is a formal document, which informs the defendant that he has been sued, and that he must either satisfy the plaintiff's claim or defend the action. The writ is usually prepared by the plaintiff's solicitor, and is issued by being sealed by an official of the court.

The writ must name the plaintiff(s) and all defendants, and must give an address for communications, which will be the address of the plaintiff's solicitor, and also the plaintiff's address. The writ must also give a statement of the plaintiff's claim. This is called the 'indorsement'. This can either be a full detailed statement or a concise statement of the relief the plaintiff is asking the court to give. For example, in a patent case, a concise statement would say that the plaintiff is claiming an injunction to restrain further infringement of patent No. 123456 and damages for past infringement. In intellectual property cases the concise statement is almost always used.

Once issued, the writ must be served within 4 months. If service was not possible within that time, for example, because the defendant was evading service, then the period can be extended by further 4-month periods. For individual defendants resident in England and Wales, the writ can be served by giving it to the defendant personally, by sending it to his last known address by first-class post or by putting it in an envelope addressed to the defendant and putting it through the letter-box at that address. For corporate defendants, service is at their registered offices.

Where the defendant is not in the jurisdiction of the court, leave must be given before the writ can be served outside the jurisdiction. Service outside the jurisdiction is a complicated subject, and it can be expensive to effect. The acceptable methods vary for different countries, depending in part on the laws of the foreign country and whether there is a treaty in effect between the UK and the country concerned which provides for service of writs when leave is granted. The writ must be served within 6 months of the date it was issued.

With the writ is served a form called an 'acknowledgment of service'. If the defendant wishes to contest the claim he must fill in the form and return it to the court. Failure to do so within the prescribed time entitles the plaintiff to judgment on his claim.

PLEADINGS

It would be most unfair and would not help the cause of justice if parties had to turn up to trial without knowing what the case against them was. In the English system each party has to let the others know what case he intends to try to prove at trial, in sufficient detail to allow everyone to properly prepare. This is done by an exchange of formal documents, called pleadings. The most important pleadings are

- the statement of claim, in which the plaintiff states what he is claiming and the basic facts on which he bases his claim
- the defence, which is the defendant's reply to the statement of claim, responding to each of the plaintiff's allegations and setting out the defences relied upon
- the counterclaim, in which the defendant countersues the plaintiff for any claims he has against the plaintiff. These are usually related to the plaintiff's action, such as a claim for revocation of the patent which the plaintiff claims is infringed, but can be completely separate
- the reply, the plaintiff's answer to issues raised in the defence
- the defence to counterclaim, in which the plaintiff responds in the same way to the counterclaim as the defendant responds to the statement of claim

Statement of claim

If the statement of claim was not indorsed on the writ, after the defendant has given notice of his intention to contest the case, the plaintiff must serve a full statement of claim. This is a statement of the facts on which the plaintiff's claim is based, and which lists the relief that is claimed, such as damages, delivery up of infringing goods or an injunction. In patent cases the plaintiff must also serve a document called 'particulars of infringement', which must specify which claims of the patent are infringed, and give details of at least one example of infringement by the defendant of each of the listed claims. You will appreciate that this requirement means that a lot of investigative work must be done before you can even begin infringement litigation.

Defence

This is the defendant's reply to the statement of claim. Every allegation in the statement of claim must be dealt with in this reply, because failure to deal with any allegation is presumed to be an admission that it is true. Besides denying the plaintiff's allegations, this document also sets out the defendant's positive defences, such as invalidity, unenforceability because of EEC competition law or innocent infringement. If the defence is that a patent is invalid then the defendant must serve at the same time as the defence a document called 'particulars of objections', which states the basis of the invalidity allegation.

Counterclaim

If the defendant also has a cause of action against the plaintiff, he can bring it into the litigation that the plaintiff started, unless it is of a type which cannot readily be tried together with the plaintiff's claim. In intellectual property cases, the most common counterclaim is for the appropriate remedy for invalidation of the intellectual property right concerned, for example, revocation of a patent. Another common counterclaim is an allegation that the plaintiff has infringed the defendant's intellectual property. This is particularly likely where both parties are in the same field of technology and own significant amounts of intellectual property relating to that technology. Such a counterclaim can be a good way of getting settlement talks going. The counterclaim is pleaded in the same way as a statement of claim, and is usually put in the same document as the defence.

Reply and defence to counterclaim

The reply is the plaintiff's answer to issues raised in the defence, and is not strictly necessary when the plaintiff denies everything the defendant has said in his reply. Where there is a counterclaim, the plaintiff must serve a defence to it, which follows the same rules as the main defence.

Further and better particulars of pleadings

If you think that your opponent has not given all the details of his case that the rules of pleading require, you can serve a request for further and better particulars, specifying the areas where you say insufficient detail has been given. In intellectual property cases these requests are widely used to try to pin down your opponent's case as far as possible.

Pleadings timetable

In theory, pleadings are exchanged on a very tight timetable, laid down in the rules of procedure. According to these rules, the statement of claim must be served within 14 days from the service of the writ; the defence and any counterclaim must be served within 14 days from the service of the statement of claim; and the reply and defence to counterclaim served within 14 days from service of the defence. The only exception to this is for patent infringement cases, where the period for service of the defence is 42 days. In practice, this timetable is stretched almost beyond recognition, as the parties can, and almost always do, agree to give each other more time to prepare the pleadings. It is not unusual for the pleading stage to take six months in a patent infringement case and about half that time for other types of intellectual property litigation. Where an application for an interlocutory injunction is made, it is usual to delay all pleadings until after that is decided, which can take several months.

Amendments to pleadings

The pleadings are important, because you cannot raise issues at trial that were not raised in the pleadings unless the judge gives permission to amend the pleadings at trial to raise the new issues. However, an amendment raising new issues may not be allowed at that late stage if it is clear that the pleadings could have been amended significantly earlier in the litigation process. It is usually only allowed on the basis that the amending party pays all the other side's costs occasioned by the amendment, including the costs of preparing for trial on issues that become irrelevant as a result of the amendment.

As it often happens that some important facts may not emerge until discovery, it is common to amend the pleadings at least once. Pleadings can be amended once before the close of pleading without needing any permission to do so. However, after the last of the pleadings has been served, it is necessary to get the court's permission to make an amendment. This permission is rarely refused if the application for leave to amend is made in a timely fashion, although usually on terms that the amending party has to pay the extra costs that the amendment causes the other party.

- don't be afraid to amend pleadings as needed to fit the facts as they emerge, but don't wait until the last minute to do so

TEMPORARY REMEDIES

There are many instances where justice can only be done if the court acts to prevent further damage to the plaintiff pending trial, or to prevent the defendant from doing something that would injure the plaintiff's chance of getting the relief he is entitled to at trial. When you realise that it can often take several years from issuing the writ before the case is finally decided, you can appreciate the importance of the various forms of temporary relief, known by lawyers as 'interlocutory' relief. The nature of and requirements for the forms of temporary relief most common in intellectual property cases have been discussed in chapter 8. Here we look at the procedure for getting this interlocutory relief.

Ex parte injunction

An injunction will only be granted *ex parte* in cases where the plaintiff has shown clearly that there is real urgency making it impossible to give the normal notice, and that he has not delayed in applying for the injunction. While normally the writ should have been issued (but not necessarily served) before the application is made, this is not always possible. For example, the plaintiff may learn at 6.00 p.m. one day, after the court offices are closed, that a licensee intends to disclose the plaintiff's trade secrets in a press conference that has been called for 9.00 a.m. the next morning. In these circumstances an emergency motion for an interlocutory injunction may be made to a High Court judge anywhere (for example, judges often make such orders from home, and there are historical examples of orders being granted by a judge while attending an opera, or while bathing in the Thames!). Under these circumstances, the plaintiff can apply for the injunction with a promise to have the writ issued as soon as possible.

An *ex parte* injunction is normally granted for a short period, usually to the first day on which there can be a hearing of the matter, immediate notice to be given the defendant.

A practice has grown up of giving informal notice to the defendant of an application for an *ex parte* motion, giving him the chance to attend the hearing and argue, although no chance to gather evidence. These are called 'opposed *ex parte* injunctions'. The advantage to the plaintiff of such a proceeding is that the court, if it decides to grant the injunction, will normally set a timetable at the hearing for the full motion hearing, with the injunction to remain in place until that hearing, thus saving the expense of repeated appearances to maintain injunctions granted each time for very short periods. On the other hand, if the defendant's opposition is successful, the court can award him his costs.

Interlocutory injunctions

This is an order from the court which prevents the defendant from continuing the acts that the plaintiff says are infringements until the matter is determined at trial.

The application for the interlocutory injunction is made to the court by notice of motion, which is served on the defendant. This must be accompanied by written evidence supporting the plaintiff's case. This evidence must be sufficient to establish a prima facie case on each of the requirements for the grant of such an injunction, discussed in Chapter 8. The defendant has the opportunity to submit written evidence in reply, if he wishes to contest the motion. If he does not wish to contest the motion, he will normally resolve the matter by giving the plaintiff an undertaking not to do the acts specified in the notice of motion. If he contests the motion, the plaintiff normally has a chance to serve further evidence in reply.

After the written evidence is complete, there is a hearing. It is very unusual for live evidence to be given at the hearing, which normally consists only of legal argument.

In the event that an injunction is granted or the defendant undertakes not to continue the activity in issue, the plaintiff must give a cross-undertaking to pay damages to the defendant if it turns out at trial that the injunction should not have been granted at all, or that it was too broad in light of the scope of the intellectual property coverage determined at trial. Where the plaintiff is not a

UK resident or British company, the court may require that some security for this undertaking be given, such as by placing funds in a bank account under the joint control of the parties' solicitors.

There are a number of tactical considerations to be weighed when deciding whether to apply for an interlocutory injunction. For example, the gain to you, the plaintiff, from having the defendant out of the market pending trial must be weighed against the danger of having to pay damages to the defendant if at trial it is determined either that no injunction should have issued, or that the one that issued was too broad. The cost and trouble of gathering the usually considerable evidence needed for the application is another factor to be weighed. Also, while winning an interlocutory injunction application is likely to improve the chances of settling the case, losing it is likely to encourage the defendant to go on fighting.

Where the defendant believes that it is almost certain that the plaintiff will get the interlocutory injunction, he can offer to give an undertaking in lieu of an injunction. Such an undertaking has the same effect as if the court had granted an injunction in the same terms. This has the advantage of saving both parties the expense of the hearing. It also has the advantage for the defendant that he does not have a formal court order on the record against him.

The court, instead of granting an interlocutory injunction in a case where the balance of convenience is only very slightly tilted to the plaintiff, may instead order a speedy trial. This means that the case will be set for trial significantly earlier than if no such order is made. It is also possible for the interlocutory injunction hearing to be treated as the trial of the action, if both parties agree. This is only likely if there is no dispute over the facts, and the case resolves to a pure legal issue.

Anton Piller orders

An *Anton Piller* order is intended to give the plaintiff a remedy in a case where there is a real danger that the defendant will destroy vital evidence if normal litigation procedures are followed. It is perhaps most commonly used in intellectual property cases, particularly copyright and trade mark infringement cases and passing off. The principles governing the grant of an *Anton Piller* order are set out in chapter 8.

In order to obtain an *Anton Piller* order, the plaintiff must have strong evidence that the defendant is committing acts of infringement. The plaintiff must also satisfy the court that, if the defendant is given notice of the action, the infringing goods and incriminating evidence are likely to promptly disappear. Thus, these orders are most commonly given in cases where the goods which the plaintiff says are infringements are easily transportable, and the defendant is not a major established business with a good reputation. They have been effective against small businesses dealing in bootleg cassettes, videos and character merchandising articles such as T-shirts.

The plaintiff first has the writ issued, and then makes his application before the writ is served. The application is made *ex parte,* in a hearing closed to the public, called an 'in camera hearing', so that news of the order should not leak out. The plaintiff supplies written evidence showing a strong case for infringement and the reasons why he believes the defendant is likely to destroy or dispose of infringing goods and relevant documents. Because of the serious nature of the order, the plaintiff must make full disclosure, including any relevant facts that do not favour his case. Failure to do so can result in the order being discharged, regardless of the merits, and an award of damages against the plaintiff.

If the court finds that the plaintiff has made out his case, an injunction is issued, ordering the defendant to permit the plaintiff's representatives to enter the defendant's premises and remove specified goods and documents. The defendant can also be ordered to answer specified questions, usually about the source of the infringing goods. The defendant cannot refuse to answer on the ground of self-incrimination, but any answers cannot be subsequently used against him in any related criminal proceedings. The order can even be granted for the search of premises located abroad, so long as the defendant is personally in the jurisdiction of the court.

As this order is Draconian, the court usually requires certain safeguards against abuse. The order is limited to specified premises and must specify exactly what the defendant is to do. The plaintiff's solicitor is usually required to attend, to serve the order and copies of the evidence submitted to the court in the application for the order, and to ensure that the proper procedures are followed. He is also made responsible for the safe-keeping of the seized items. If the defendant refuses entry, force cannot be used, although that refusal is a contempt of court which can be dealt with by penalties or even imprisonment. The defendant is usually given an opportunity to contact his solicitor before the search commences, and to apply immediately to have the order discharged. Further, the plaintiff must give an undertaking as to damages, and an undertaking that the seized material will only be used in the case in which the order is obtained.

Mareva injunctions

Where the plaintiff can show that there is a real danger that the defendant will transfer his assets out of the jurisdiction in order to avoid paying a money judgment to the plaintiff, the court has power to order a freezing of specified assets to prevent their removal until the matter is tried. The court may also order the defendant to provide an affidavit detailing his assets, and may even order the defendant not to leave the country until this is done. The requirements for the grant of a *Mareva* injunction are discussed in chapter 8.

A *Mareva* order can be made at any time after the writ is issued, or, in cases of extreme urgency, with an undertaking to issue the writ as soon as possible. It is usual to apply for a *Mareva* order *ex parte* because if the defendant has notice of the application he could dispose of the assets in question before the order can be granted. The plaintiff must have sufficient evidence to establish each of the requirements for the grant of the injunction, and must give a cross-undertaking in damages.

The injunction should not normally be issued against a responsible company with a history of paying its debts, nor should it be so Draconian that it puts the defendant out of business. An individual defendant should be allowed sufficient money to live on and to pay the costs of defending the plaintiff's action against him. An English court cannot grant an order relating to assets outside the court's jurisdiction.

When considering whether to apply for a *Mareva* injunction, the cross-undertaking should be carefully considered, because the injunction can have serious financial effects on the defendant if it turns out to have been wrongly granted. In a recent case, a defendant who succeeded in the action, but who claimed to have lost his very lucrative job and to have been unable to get another as a result of the injunction, was given damages in excess of £1 million.

GETTING THE CASE TO TRIAL

Between starting the litigation and the trial a lot of work has to be done. This falls into two stages. In the first stage, certain information is obtained from the other side, who can also obtain similar information from you. This process is called discovery. The second stage is trial preparation.

As this is the stage of litigation where settlement most frequently occurs, we will also look at the ways of terminating the litigation before trial.

Discovery

Discovery is the process of obtaining relevant evidence from the other side. This is a two-way process — you have to give discovery too. This includes the documents which are not helpful or even damaging to your case as well as those that are favourable. There are only very limited types of relevant documents that you can refuse to produce in discovery, which are discussed below. The only type of discovery which occurs routinely is the production of documents. Other forms of discovery, such as having the other side respond to written questions, require the court's permission unless the parties voluntarily agree to some other form of discovery.

Documents

After the pleadings are closed, each side must prepare a list of the documents that are relevant to the pleaded issues which are or have been under its control. Your list will be prepared by your solicitor.

Obviously, your solicitor must know what documents you have or had in order to prepare this list. The job of identifying where relevant documents are likely to be located and finding those documents will be the responsibility of the in-house liaison, if you have one. Otherwise, your solicitor will have to interview the people in the company most likely to know about the matters in issue in the case in order to determine where relevant documents may be found. The determination of what is relevant involves an understanding of the legal issues, and should be made by your solicitor, not by you or your employees.

When you are the plaintiff, you should have gone through at least the first sweep of document gathering before you started the litigation, to make sure that there were no discoverable documents lurking in your files which could seriously damage your case. If you are the defendant, you will have to work fast to find the documents. While the rules provide only 14 days for preparation of the lists, in practice the parties usually agree between themselves to a considerably longer time. This is particularly true in intellectual property cases, which tend to involve a lot of documents.

There are certain documents that you do not have to show to the other side, although they must be included in the list. These are documents that are protected from disclosure by a legal privilege. The main privilege that is likely to arise is the privilege given to communications between a lawyer or patent agent and his or her client. Both outside and in-house lawyers are covered by this privilege under English law. This class of privilege also includes communications between the lawyer or client and third parties when the communication is connected with litigation and is made when the litigation has commenced or is at least imminent. This covers such things as reports from experts who are advising on technical matters raised in the intellectual property litigation. Other classes of privilege which may arise are the privilege against self-incrimination, documents arising from an attempt to settle which are made 'without prejudice', and documents which it is not in the public interest to make available. Your solicitor will decide which documents privilege can be claimed for. The claim of privilege by either side can only be challenged in a court hearing. The documents for which privilege is claimed are listed in one section of the list, and in each case there must be a brief statement of the ground for claiming privilege for that document.

The documents for which no claim of privilege is made are listed under two headings, those which you still have control over and those which are now in the control of others. In the latter case, the list must state where those documents are now.

After the lists are exchanged, the parties are given an opportunity to inspect the listed documents for which no claim of privilege has been made, and to take copies of any of them. It should be noted that documents obtained through discovery can be used only in connection with that particular case, and the court has power to restrain abuses of discovery through contempt proceedings. The court can order that only limited access is given to documents containing trade secret information, and the parties normally agree on the terms of such an order.

If you have good reason to believe that there are relevant documents which your opponent has not put in his list, then you can apply to the court for an order that he produce these documents. You must be able to give some details of the missing documents, so you cannot apply just because you think your opponent is a crook who would stop at nothing to hide evidence. Most commonly, you learn of the missing document because it is referred to in some other document.

There is in general no right to obtain discovery from an independent third party. If a third party has relevant documents, they can be obtained by a court order called a subpoena *duces tecum,* which orders that person to attend the trial and bring the named documents with him. There is one exception to this rule which was laid down by the House of Lords in a patent infringement case, which is where a third party innocently assists in the wrongdoing, justice can only be done by the third party giving information about the wrong and the wrongdoers, and there is no general public interest in keeping this information confidential. The original case involved customs information identifying the importer of infringing goods.

- WARNING — the *only* use that can be made of documents that are obtained in discovery is for that particular piece of litigation. It is contempt of court, which can be punished severely, to use those documents for any other purpose whatsoever.

Interrogatories
These are written questions which the other party must answer under oath, and they provide discovery of facts which cannot be found from the documents. Two sets of interrogatories may be served without a court order, provided that the interrogatories are relevant to the case in which they are asked and will help to dispose fairly of the case or save time and costs. Interrogatories are not usually allowed about the contents of documents unless there is evidence that the document has been lost or destroyed. They cannot be used to 'fish' for something that will help you make out your case; they can only be used where there is good ground for believing that the matters enquired about actually occurred. It is also possible to apply to the court for leave to serve interrogatories.

Where interrogatories are served without order, the party on whom they are served can apply to the court for an order varying or withdrawing any interrogatories which it believes are not proper. Otherwise, the interrogatories must be answered within the period (not less than 28 days) specified by the party serving the interrogatories.

In answering interrogatories ordered by the court, you must answer where you or those under your control have the information, unless it is protected by the same privileges that apply to documents.

Settlement and termination

After the pleadings are completed and discovery has taken place, both parties have a better idea of the strengths and weaknesses of their respective cases. This makes it a good time to seriously consider the possibility of settlement. In extreme cases, one party may have concluded it has no real chance of success, so the case should not proceed any further.

Settlement
People are often afraid to initiate settlement negotiations because they think they will look weak, but

- in reality, a settlement is almost always a better result for business than going through the whole legal procedure of trial and appeal

Whether you are plaintiff or defendant, after the main round of discovery has been completed you should consult with your legal team to review the chances of success. This will give you a realistic assessment of what settlement offer should be made. This is also a good time to do a further cost-benefit analysis. Settlement negotiations are most likely to succeed where both sides have a realistic estimate of the probable outcome if the case were to proceed to the end.

Who should initiate a settlement approach? In general, the first approach is best made by the person who has the best rapport with his opposite number in the other side's team. For example, if senior management from both the defendant and the plaintiff know each other and have not become emotionally embroiled in the litigation, then the first approach comes best from contacts at that level. Unfortunately, however, it is common for senior management on at least one side to be emotionally involved, and emotional involvement tends to make settlement very difficult. Often, the first settlement overtures are made by the barristers for each side; they are members of a small profession, particularly in the intellectual property field, who generally know and trust each other, and who do not usually have a long history of representing the client and therefore identifying with him, as solicitors often have.

If a settlement is reached, the litigation must then be terminated. This is most commonly done by a consent order for a stay (indefinite suspension) of the litigation. Both parties agree on the terms of the order which the court is then asked to enter. The settlement terms may be made part of the order, or the publicly available order may say that the proceedings are stayed on terms of the settlement agreement which is referred to in the order but not part of it. This procedure allows the parties to keep the settlement terms secret, and is often used in intellectual property cases. The advantage of having an order for stay of the proceedings provided the settlement terms are complied with rather than simply dismissing the case is that, if either party refuses to comply with its agreement, compliance can be enforced by contempt proceedings in the same case. If the case has been dismissed, it would be necessary to begin a new action for breach of contract in order to enforce the settlement agreement.

Termination

A realistic assessment may be that you have no real chance of success. If you are the plaintiff, you should then look for a way of terminating the case as soon as possible, without adding to your costs or causing the defendant to incur further costs which you will be liable to pay. One way of doing this is simply to take no further action — many defendants will be happy to let sleeping dogs lie. However, a company may have to make provision for the potential liability of a pending legal action in its accounts, and will not be content to let this state of affairs continue indefinitely. If the plaintiff does not proceed, the defendant can apply for the case to be dismissed for want of prosecution with an order for its costs to be paid by the plaintiff. Unfortunately, the English courts have shown a considerable reluctance to dismiss for want of prosecution unless the defendant can prove that his defence is being prejudiced by the delay, e.g., important witnesses may die or forget. The defendant may also try to force the case to trial.

Once the pleadings are closed, the plaintiff cannot terminate the case without the leave of the court unless all parties consent in writing. Leave will normally be given, but on terms that the plaintiff pay the defence costs. Further, if the defendant had a counterclaim against the plaintiff, this will continue as an independent action unless it is also settled.

If the defendant decides his chances are not good, but cannot get an agreed settlement, he can attempt to force the plaintiff's hand by paying money into court. Under this procedure, he deposits with a court office a sum of money for damages and interest. This may be done in respect of all the plaintiff's grounds of action for which he is claiming damages or other monetary relief, or only on some of them, and may also take into account the effects of any counterclaim. This procedure is of limited applicability in intellectual property cases, because the plaintiff is usually seeking an injunction.

The plaintiff is given notice of the payment in, and has a short time to make up his mind whether or not to accept it. If he does accept it, then the case is terminated and he goes through the procedure to get his costs up to the date of the payment in. If he does not accept it, and after trial gets the same or a lesser amount, then he is liable to pay the defendant's costs from the date of the payment in. The trial judge must not be told that there has been a payment into court.

Trial preparation

Trial preparation starts at an early stage, and can involve a great deal of work and expense

- the real issues in the case must be identified
- the evidence needed to prove your case must be gathered and prepared for use in court
- the relevant law must be researched for the preparation of the legal arguments

Summons for directions

The first step in trial preparation is an application to the court for directions on matters relating to trial preparation, called a summons for directions. It is the plaintiff's responsibility to take out this summons, which is done at a fairly early stage. If the plaintiff neglects to do so, the defendant can do it instead.

The order sought from the court, called the order for directions, is usually in a standard form agreed upon by the parties. One area dealt with is discovery; this is where issues arising out of the initial round of documentary discovery are dealt with. Where the infringement is a process, or is a very large piece of machinery, the plaintiff may seek an order for inspection of the plant where the process is carried out or of the machinery.

The order for directions is also concerned with limiting the issues in dispute. This may be done by amendments to pleadings, or by the use of notices to admit facts. These notices are appropriate where you believe that your opponent has no reasonable grounds on which to dispute the existence of a relevant fact. If your opponent improperly refuses to admit a fact, then he is liable to pay the costs of proving that fact at trial.

The order will also deal with issues relating to the trial evidence. A recent rule requires that an outline of the expected testimony of each witness who is to be called to give evidence at trial be given to the other side before the trial. In patent cases, either side may want to put in evidence of experiments done to prove or disprove infringement. The order will provide for the service of notice of such experiments, and for the carrying out of the experiments and any experiments in reply that the other party may want to carry out. If it is proposed to use models, photographs or charts at trial, the other side are given a chance to inspect them before the trial.

The order may also limit the number of expert witnesses to be used. There is power to order an exchange of expert witness's reports prior to trial, but in practice this is normally done by agreement between the parties. The rules also provide for appointment of an independent court expert, although this is unusual, and either party wanting such an expert will raise the matter at the summons for directions.

Preparing the evidence

Advice on evidence   In intellectual property cases it is usual for the barrister to prepare a written opinion, outlining all the evidence that will be needed to prove the case at trial. This will include documentary evidence and evidence to be obtained from testifying witnesses. The barrister will also try to anticipate the opponent's case, and advise on evidence that will be needed to refute the defendant's evidence.

Witnesses   The solicitor finds the witnesses, and finds out what evidence they will be able to give. The solicitor does this by interviewing the witness and showing him relevant documents.

Witnesses are divided into two types: fact witnesses and expert witnesses. An expert witness is someone who is qualified to give evidence about a subject beyond ordinary common knowledge, but who does not know the particular facts of this case from first-hand experience. For example, in a patent infringement case involving a detergent, the inventor of the detergent would be a fact witness when he testifies about how the invention was made. Another chemist, with a lot of experience in detergent chemistry but who was not involved in making this invention, could testify as an expert witness about detergent chemistry in general, and how this patent relates to what was known before. In patent cases, and cases of infringement of copyright in software, expert witnesses tend to play a major role.

It is important to know whether a witness is an expert or a fact witness for two reasons; first, the rules of evidence which apply to trials allow expert witnesses to give opinions on matters within their area of expertise, while a fact witness can rarely give an opinion. Secondly, under professional rules, a barrister cannot interview a fact witness before that witness gives evidence, but he can speak to his client and to expert witnesses about their evidence before they testify. The solicitor can speak to the fact witnesses and prepare an account of the evidence that they can give for use by the barrister when asking them questions to bring out their evidence in court.

Documents   The barrister will also identify the documents that will be needed for the trial. So that each document can be readily identified during the proceedings, the solicitors for each party will agree on a single set of documents, containing all the documents that any party wants to use. Each page of this set, called the 'agreed bundle', is numbered, allowing ready identification of that page at trial.

Models, charts and photographs These are of great assistance in explaining technical concepts, and are of particular use in patent cases. They are also useful to provide comparisons of similarities between the original and the accused infringement in trade mark and copyright cases. Where they are used, they should be professionally prepared so as to make the best impact.

Under the order for directions, a time will be set in advance of trial for the other side to inspect any model etc. that is to be used at trial, to give them time to produce models or charts in response or to prepare objections to the admissibility of the item. For example, the model may not be to scale, which could produce a false impression, or the chart may not be based on accurate information.

Experiments In patent infringement cases, it may be necessary to carry out experiments to prove infringement. This is normally done by giving the other side formal notice of the experiment, giving details of the proposed experiment, and the time and place where it is to be carried out. The defendant is given an express invitation to attend, usually represented by the defendant's solicitor and expert witness(es). Indeed, the court normally does not permit evidence of experiments unless such a notice has been served and opportunity to attend given. This may also be a way of inducing a settlement, if the experiment provides strong proof of infringement. Conversely, the defendant may believe that an experiment will clearly prove that he is not infringing, and therefore serves his own notice of experiment. Having seen the experiment, the other party may then wish to perform its own experiment in reply, to try to show that the original experiment was flawed.

Surveys In cases for infringement of registered marks or for passing off, it is necessary to have evidence of actual confusion, or of a real likelihood of confusion. It is always best to have evidence of actual confusion, if it is available. Where there is no clear evidence of actual confusion, or the evidence is weak, then the use of a public survey to prove likelihood of confusion should be considered.

The courts tend to view these surveys with suspicion. It is therefore important that the survey is very carefully carried out by experienced professionals in public surveys. However, the questions to be used in the survey should be drafted or carefully reviewed by your lawyers, who must have the final say on the matter. This is because public opinion poll experts are not familiar with the relevant law or with the rules of evidence, and may ask questions that would not be admissible in court, invalidating the whole survey.

TRIAL

Getting a trial date

The process of getting a trial date is started by the plaintiff formally setting the case down for trial. The order for directions usually contains a provision for setting the case down for trial after certain specified steps have been completed, although the time for doing so specified in the order is often extended by agreement. Once the action is set for trial, the solicitors can have the action put in the list of actions waiting to be tried. An estimate has to be given of the length of the trial — usually the lengthier trials have to wait longer to get a trial date. A date will then be fixed, usually well in the future.

The given date may be postponed, usually by agreement, if the parties are not ready for trial. In intellectual property cases, where there are so few barristers specialising in the area, a postponement may also be sought if the barrister who prepared the case is unavailable at the given date because another case has gone on longer than expected, or because of illness. While technically the convenience of the barrister is not a reason for postponement, it does happen in intellectual property cases.

Procedure at trial

The case will be tried by a judge, there being no right to a jury trial for intellectual property cases. It will normally be tried in public, but the trial judge does have the power to exclude the public when confidential technical information is being disclosed in evidence. This is called an 'in camera' hearing.

Separation of issues of liability and damages
It is the universal practice in the Chancery Division of the High Court, where patent and trade mark cases and most other intellectual property cases are tried, to fully determine issues of liability before having a trial on the amount of damages. This means not only a separate trial on liability, but taking that issue all the way through the appeal process before starting to prepare for trial on the amount of damages, called 'an inquiry as to damages'. This procedure can save a lot of time and money if it is determined that there is no liability, or that the plaintiff's case has only been partially made out. In practice, inquiries as to damages are rare, because once liability is determined the parties usually settle. In infringement cases, it can be very expensive to prepare and try the damages issues.

Order of proceedings
Except in certain very unusual cases, the plaintiff starts. Leading counsel for the plaintiff, the QC if the plaintiff has one or otherwise the senior barrister, makes an opening statement, taking the judge through the plaintiff's version of the case. No facts can be referred to in this statement unless the plaintiff expects to produce evidence of these facts. Because witnesses do not always remember when in the witness box everything that they said when giving their proofs of evidence to the solicitor, or because their testimony may be shaken by cross-examination, the opening statement is usually pitched at a relatively low key. The client is often disappointed by the opening statement, feeling that his barrister has not put his case forcefully enough. However, be patient; the proper place for a forceful statement is at the close, when all the evidence is in.

After his opening statement, the plaintiff's counsel then calls the witnesses for the plaintiff, in the order which has been decided upon by the lawyers. Each witness's testimony in support of the plaintiff, called the 'evidence in chief', is elicited by questioning by the barrister, using the material supplied by the solicitor who interviewed that witness. Usually, the witness will be able to look at documents from the agreed bundle to help his recollection.

The barrister for the other side then gets to question the witness, called 'cross-examination'. The purpose of cross-examination is to test the reliability of the witness's testimony, and to try to get further evidence from the witness which may be helpful to the defendant's case. Even if your witness ends up giving evidence which harms your case, you cannot do anything to discredit him unless very exceptionally the witness is so clearly biased against you that the judge rules he is a 'hostile' witness.

If you are going to be a witness, there a few important things to bear in mind

● you are not expected to remember everything without help

Thus when you are giving evidence for the side that called you, you will have already gone over the evidence with the solicitor; you will be asked questions by a barrister who has the solicitor's written account of the evidence you can give, and you will be able to look at relevant documents
However

● if you are genuinely unable to remember, you should say so

Most witnesses who are made to look bad on cross-examination get into that position, not because they were dishonest, but because they were afraid to say 'I don't remember'. Instead of giving that true answer, they try to reconstruct what they think probably happened, and then talk about that speculation as if it were a fact.

Therefore, the golden rule for all witnesses is

● don't worry that you might look foolish, just always tell the truth, even if that involves saying 'I don't remember'.

When all of the plaintiff's witnesses have testified, the defendant's counsel then makes an opening statement of his case. The defence witnesses are called and examined in the same way. Then the defence makes a closing statement, followed by the plaintiff's closing statement. These statements will contain legal arguments as well as discussion of how the evidence supports that party's case. The defence only has a right to reply if the plaintiff's counsel cites new cases that had not previously been discussed. This means that the plaintiff has the important advantage of having both the first and the last word in the trial.

Judgment
The judge may either give his judgment immediately after the end of counsels' closing statements, or he may take time to consider the case. It is the practice for the judge to deliver his judgment orally in open court, even though he may have prepared it in writing. When he has prepared a written judgment, the parties may be given a copy of it immediately before the oral pronouncement.

Reference to the European Court
If a question arises in the case relating to interpretation of EEC law, the court has power to refer that question to the European Court of Justice. This should

normally not be done until the facts are determined, and only if the ruling is necessary for the English court to render judgment. There is no need to refer a question where there is a previous decision of the European Court on the point, or where the law is so clear there can be no reasonable dispute about its meaning. In the early days of British membership in the EEC, the English courts showed reluctance to refer matters to the European Court, but references are being made more frequently now.

APPEAL

To the Court of Appeal

There is a right to appeal the final judgment of a High Court judge to the Court of Appeal. This appeal can be on both issues of fact and issues of law.

There is a limited time after judgment is given to file an appeal. The appeal process is started by filing a notice of appeal, which lists the grounds on which the judgment is appealed and states how the decision of the trial court should be varied. The party who files the notice of appeal is called the appellant. If the other party, called the respondent, also wishes to contend that the decision should be varied, he can file a cross-appeal.

After the notice of appeal, and the notice of cross-appeal, if any, are served, the appeal is set down for hearing. Before the date the appeal is likely to be heard, the appellant's solicitor must provide three sets of papers for the appeal judges, which include the notice of appeal and any cross-appeal, the judgment appealed from, the pleadings, the trial transcript or the judge's notes of the evidence and all relevant documents from the trial.

In patent cases, where there has been an order for revocation of the patent that is appealed from, the Comptroller of Patents must also be given notice of the appeal. The purpose of this provision is to prevent patentees buying off defendants so that the appeal against revocation goes unchallenged, leading to a strong possibility that an invalid patent will remain in force. This result is deemed to be contrary to the public interest, so the Comptroller is given the ability to appear to contest the appeal on revocation when the defendant does not.

The appeal is heard by three Court of Appeal judges. No new evidence is heard, and no oral evidence is given. The counsel read to the court the parts of the evidence that are relevant to their case, and argue the law. While the judges can rule orally immediately after the hearing is concluded, it is usual for them to delay giving judgment, and to provide a written judgment to the parties.

To the House of Lords

There is no right to appeal to the House of Lords. To appeal from the Court of Appeal, either the Court of Appeal or the House of Lords must give permission. In general, this permission will only be given if there is an important point of law involved. There is a possibility of appeal directly to the House of Lords from the High Court, but only where the appeal is on a point of law of general public importance on which there is good reason for a direct appeal. This provision is very little used, being mainly of use where there are irreconcilably conflicting appellate decisions on the same point of law.

Even the process of merely applying for leave to appeal can be expensive, so your legal team will carefully consider whether an adverse result in the Court of Appeal should be taken any further.

ENFORCING THE JUDGMENT

Once you get the litigation train to the end of the line, and have a judgment which has survived the appeal process, you then have to enforce that judgment

● it is the winning plaintiff's responsibility to make sure that the defendant complies with the court's order

However, the court has certain powers to ensure this compliance. Generally, the successful plaintiff in intellectual property cases is more concerned with the injunction that has been obtained than with damages, although the latter can be sizeable sums of money in a case where the infringer operated on a large scale and there was no interlocutory injunction.

Injunctions

When the plaintiff has reason to believe that the defendant is not obeying an injunction, the remedy is to bring the defendant back before the court by a motion for contempt of court. The motion must be accompanied by supporting written evidence. The defendant is given an opportunity to put in evidence of his own, to which the plaintiff can reply. There is then a hearing for argument. If the court decides that the defendant has disobeyed its order, then it can try to enforce obedience. In some cases the disobedience may have been merely the result of a failure to understand the original injunction, in which case the court will clarify its order. Where the disobedience was deliberate, the court may impose fines or even imprison the offender until its order is obeyed. Imprisonment is usually a final resort after more than one contempt proceeding has been brought.

Money judgments

The law provides various ways of enforcing money judgments, including seizure of the defendant's property. However, it is very unlikely that you will fully recover the money from a defendant who either does not have the money, or who is prepared to go to any lengths to avoid paying. If money damages and recovering your costs are important to you, then only sue reputable defendants who are good for the money.

13   Sharing Intellectual Property

SHARING YOUR TECHNOLOGY WITH OTHERS

There are very few companies with the resources to fully exploit the world market for their technology by themselves. The vast majority of intellectual property owners will need the assistance of others to obtain the maximum return on their investment in developing that intellectual property.

There are two ways of using your technology in markets which you cannot reach with your own resources — granting licences and appointing distributors.

- a licence gives a third party permission to do something that is by law an exclusive right of the intellectual property holder

A licence may be granted by an agreement between the holder of the intellectual property rights and the third party (called the 'licensor' and 'licensee' respectively), or it may be implied as a result of some act by the intellectual property owner. A common implied licence arises whenever patented goods are sold; even without anything being said or written, the purchaser gets permission to use those goods.

- a distributor is someone who sells goods manufactured by another

When those goods are covered by a patent, which gives its owner the exclusive right to sell or use the goods, the distributor obviously has to be licensed to exercise those rights. However, in the intellectual property world it is most usual to reserve the term 'licensee' for one who is given the right to manufacture the goods covered by the intellectual property being licensed.

LICENSEE OR DISTRIBUTOR

Assuming that the decision has been made to enlist the aid of others in exploiting your technology, the decision arises — licensees or distributors? The two are not mutually exclusive and a firm often uses both. The choice should be carefully considered in each individual situation.

- granting a licence is the best choice for markets where you do not have the capacity to competitively supply goods of your own manufacture or services by your own employees

This most commonly occurs when the market concerned is geographically distant from your home base. For example, the goods may be bulky and expensive to transport. Or, a foreign country may have technical regulations which you find it difficult to meet in your own manufacturing process without considerable extra expense. Another reason for foreign manufacture is provided by customs barriers; if they are high, it will be difficult for foreign manufactured goods to compete with locally produced goods.

You may also want to use a licence to reach a different type of user than your business is geared for. For example, manufacturing a drug for human use may require different procedures, controls over the manufacturing process and packaging than the manufacture of the same drug for veterinary purposes.

- using a distributor when you do not need the manufacturing abilities of a licensee is generally advantageous

First, you have direct control over the quality of the goods. Secondly, you can make a normal profit on the goods, rather than the usual licence payment of a royalty of a few per cent of the wholesale price of the goods sold by the licensee. Thirdly, you have not put your technology into the hands of a potential competitor, because a distributor needs to be given much less confidential information than a manufacturing licensee.

You should also investigate whether there are any tax or other financial effects that might affect the choice between a licensee and a distributor. For example, the profits from goods sold to a distributor would be ordinary income, but payments from a licensee may be treated as capital, depending on how the licence is structured. You should also investigate the liability for VAT that possible alternative transactions incur. Financial considerations can be particularly important when dealing with overseas markets. Certain countries may make it very difficult for a licensee in that country to pay royalties to a foreign licensor, but more readily allow a distributor to pay for imported goods. Taxation and foreign export controls are outside the scope of this book to discuss in any useful level of detail, and you are strongly advised to consult your professional financial advisers about the effects of the particular arrangements you are considering.

LICENSING

What is a licence?

To the man in the street, the term 'licence' is most often associated with selling alcohol. We go to our local licensed premises for a drink, where we may have a chat with the licensee, and then stop off at the off-licence on the way home for some wine to have with dinner. Here, the term licence refers to a permission granted to sell alcoholic beverages, something that the law does not allow the rest of us to do. The licensee is the person given that permission.

In the field of intellectual property, the term 'licence' has the same meaning.

- a licence gives the licensee permission to do something which the law says is the exclusive right of the owner of the intellectual property which is licensed

For example, the copyright law says that the copyright owner has the exclusive right to do certain listed acts, which include copying the work, issuing copies to the public and making adaptations of the work. A publisher needs a copyright licence from the copyright owner, normally the author, to print and sell copies of a book. A film producer needs a copyright licence to turn that book into a film or television show.

However, there is a trap for the unwary in thinking of a licence as permission to do something

- just because you have a licence under a patent that covers a particular item does not mean that you are automatically free to produce that item

The item may also be covered by a different patent owned by someone else; for example, a car is composed of a large number of components, each of which may be covered by a different patent. Another example would be a chemical which is covered by one patent, made by a process that is covered by another. You may also have a licence that covers the goods, but you are prevented from producing them because of government regulation, because it would put you in breach of a court order or a contract with another person or for a variety of reasons.

A more accurate description, therefore, is

- a licence is an immunity from being sued for infringement of the intellectual property rights which are covered by the licence

The Patents Act 1977 makes this very plain — it nowhere defines positively the rights of the patentee. Instead, it provides that a person infringes the patent by doing certain acts without the consent of the patent owner.

A licence is also a contract, and is governed by all the legal rules and principles that apply to contracts in general. Some basic contract principles that are important to our discussion here are set out in chapter 3.

What can be licensed?

As we have seen, a licence gives permission to do something which the licensor has the right to exclude others from doing. Therefore,

- any right to exclude can be the subject of a licence

The only things that are discussed in this book that cannot be licensed are moral rights and performers' rights. Note that what is actually licensed is the right — while we often talk loosely of a patent licence, what is actually licensed is one or more of the exclusive rights owned by the patentee. The patent itself is only a piece of paper.

While we talk of licensing confidential information, that is really a contract for the disclosure of the secret information under terms which include the recipient keeping the information secret, and not a licence within the strict definition given above. However, in this chapter we will follow the usual practice and refer to such contracts as licences.

In general, intellectual property law does not place restrictions on how the intellectual property rights are licensed (restrictions on licensing arising from competition law are discussed later in this chapter). There are exceptions to this rule.

First, the Patents Act 1977, s. 44, renders void provisions in a patent licence which require the licensee to acquire any non-patented product from the licensor or another source selected by the licensor, or which prohibits the licensee from using non-patented products not supplied by the licensor or other nominated source. The only exception to this ban on tying clauses is where the licensee opted to obtain such products on reasonable terms, and the contract gives the licensee the right to terminate this provision on three months' notice.

The licensing of marks and get-up is also subject to restrictions. These originally arose from the principle under which the common law came to protect trade marks, that the mark indicated to the purchasing public that the goods originated from a particular business. It followed that use by some other business was regarded as being potentially deceptive and contrary to the basis for protecting marks. Unfortunately, the present state of the law on licensing of marks is far from clear.

For registered trade and service marks, the Trade Marks Act 1938 provides a system of registered use by persons other than the owner of the mark. The proprietor of the mark and the proposed user apply jointly to the Trade Marks Registry for registration, providing certain information required under the Act. Registration will not be granted unless it is shown that the proprietor is able to control the use of the mark by the user, including control over the quality of the goods or services that the licensee will supply under the mark. While the Trade Marks Act 1938 is silent about the effect of an unregistered user agreement, a court has held that a use under a licence which would have been registrable but in fact was not registered did not invalidate the mark (*'Bostitch' Trade Mark* [1963] RPC 183).

Registered use under the Trade Marks Act 1938 also requires that there is a sufficient business connection between the proprietor of the mark and the licensee or his goods or services. This requirement comes from statutory prohibition of the quaintly entitled activity, 'trafficking in a trade mark'.

No one was sure what this phrase in the Act meant until a recent case involving the modern practice of character merchandising. An American greetings card company had developed a character called 'Holly Hobbie', a little girl in a demure Victorian sun-bonnet. She caught the public's imagination, and her owner began to make money from licensing other companies to make dolls, games, children's clothing and similar goods using this character and her fictional companions. The greetings card company decided to protect its position in Britain, where it had licensees. It applied for registration of the name 'Holly Hobbie' as a trade mark in various categories, and for registration of user agreements with licensees for each of these categories. The agreements appeared to satisfy the control requirements.

Registration was refused on the grounds that this was trafficking in a trade mark, and the House of Lords agreed. They said that there must be a 'trade connection' between the proprietor of the mark and his licensee. This is on a sliding scale; at one end is the proprietor who uses the mark himself in exactly the same way as the licensee, at the other is the 'dealer' in marks, who registers them with no intent to use them but merely to make money by selling or licensing them to others. The greetings card company was too close to the dealer end of the scale, as it was not in any of the businesses for which it had granted licences. Quality control provisions alone were not enough to give the needed trade connection.

These registered user provisions do not apply to unregistered marks. Under the old common law principle, these could not have been licensed. However, the rationale of certain modern cases dealing with unregistered user agreements for registered marks could be used to argue that it is possible to license the goodwill in an unregistered mark so that the licensee's use of the mark would be protected by passing off.

As explained in the first part of this book, the owner of a piece of intellectual property may have more than one exclusive right in respect of that property. For example, the owner of a copyright has the exclusive right to make copies, to distribute copies to the public, to publicly perform the work and to make adaptations of the work. A copyright licence does not have to be for all of these rights. For example, the author of a novel will typically license to his publisher the rights to make copies and distribute them to the public. If he has any negotiating power at all, he will reserve (i.e., keep for himself) the rights to make a stage play, film or television show from the book, all of these being adaptations of the copyright work. Then, if the novel is a best seller, he will be able to license any of these adaptation rights separately. He may also separately license the right to translate the novel and to publish translations. Similarly, a patent owner may allow a licensee to make goods for use in its own business, but not give the licensee the right to sell the items covered by the patent. Indeed, every time a patent owner sells goods covered by the patent, it is implied that the purchaser is given a licence to use those goods, but not to exercise any other right under the patent.

A licence need not be confined to a single piece of intellectual property, or to a single type. For example, it is common when patents are licensed by a patent owner who is using the patent in its own business for the licence to also cover confidential information relating to the practical use of the patents. A patentee is not required to give every detail of commercial production in the patent specification, but may have discovered that in practice certain manufacturing conditions or starting materials produce the best result. A licensee of the patent will normally be willing to pay extra for such information, which otherwise it would have to spend a great deal of time and money discovering for itself.

To summarise

● any intellectual property right other than moral rights and performer's rights can be licensed

In general, there are no restrictions on how intellectual property is licensed, apart from competition law restraints. However

● licensing of registered marks is subject to several conditions

— the owner of the mark must be able to control the use made of the mark by the licensee
— the quality of goods or services supplied by the licensee under the mark must be specified and controlled
— there must be a trade connection between the owner of the mark and the licensee or his goods or services

- it is uncertain whether and how an unregistered mark can be licenced

Where the intellectual property gives the owner more than one exclusive right

- those rights can be separately licensed
- a licence can cover more than one type of intellectual property

Who can license?

Where the intellectual property rights are owned by one person or other legal entity, such as a company, whether the original owner or an assignee, that person has full rights to license the intellectual property.

Where the intellectual property is owned by more than one person, for example, the copyright in works of joint authorship (see chapter 6), all the co-owners must agree on the licence. Therefore, if you are taking a licence of intellectual property in circumstances where co-ownership is a possibility, particularly in copyright licences, you should make enquiries about ownership and get a written warranty that there are no other persons having a claim to ownership.

A licensee may have the power to grant sub-licences, depending on the terms of his licence.

- it is advisable to provide expressly whether or not a licence carries the right to sublicense, to avoid later disputes

Types of licence

You have now decided whether to license and what to license. This is not the end, as you now have to decide what type of licence best suits your needs. The most important things to decide upon are

- degree of exclusivity
- scope
- period
- method of payment

Degree of exclusivity
A licence can be exclusive, sole or non-exclusive.

- an exclusive licence means that no one apart from the licensee can exercise the licensed rights in the territory covered by the licence. Even the licensor is excluded

- a sole licence means that the rights are exercisable by the licensor, the licensee and no one else

- a non-exclusive licence means that the licensor can compete itself and grant as many other licences as it wishes

In general, a licensee will want the greatest degree of exclusivity it can get, while a non-exclusive licence gives the licensor the greatest degree of flexibility. If you grant an exclusive licence, your return on your intellectual property depends entirely on the success of that licensee. With a non-exclusive licence, you can remedy the failings of your licensee by finding another who can perform better or reach markets your first licensee could not. Another disadvantage of exclusive licences are that they attract the most competition law problems. An exclusive licence is most commonly appropriate where the licensed technology is new, and the licensee will have to develop the market in the licensed territory for the product. Another reason for giving exclusivity would be that all the licensor has is a patent or secret idea, and the licensee has to develop the licensed technology for commercial production. A sole licence is appropriate where the licensor is already operating in the territory. It may also be an acceptable compromise with a licensee who wants exclusivity in a territory, but you want to be able to enter that territory yourself if the licensee fails to perform satisfactorily.

Scope
There are two components to scope

- territory

- type of end use

It is a common practice to grant a licence for a geographical area smaller than the area in which you have exclusive rights. For example, where you hold patents in several countries, you may want to license the patents in countries where you cannot effectively exploit the patented technology yourself. After all, an important reason for licensing is to take advantage of local manufacturing and knowledge of the local market. While intellectual property law allows such subdivision of rights, there are competition law effects to be considered. These are dealt with below in detail, but can be reasonably accurately summarised by the following principle: you cannot divide up the Common Market by granting a series of exclusive licences which keep each licensee's territory safe from any competition by the licensor or other licensees.

Intellectual property law also allows you to limit a licence to a particular end use of the licensed property. For example, a licence to make a patented chemical could limit sales of that chemical to the steel industry, while another licensee could be limited to selling to the petroleum refining industry. A copyright licence could limit one publisher to sales to education authorities and institutions, while another sells only through bookshops. Again, any competition law effects of such a limitation must be looked at before the licence is finalised.

Period

Most intellectual property rights only last for a limited time. For example, a patent is granted for 20 years, a copyright for the life of the author plus 50 years. Therefore, third parties only need permission to do things covered by the intellectual property rights while the owner has exclusivity. As soon as that patent or copyright has expired, anyone may practise the invention or copy the work. Indeed, if a patent is declared invalid by a court, the patent owner's exclusive rights will terminate even earlier. Therefore, in general

● an intellectual property licence can only last as long as the exclusive rights of the licensor

This simple principle is not easy to apply in real life because a licence often covers more than one piece of intellectual property. For example, a patent may be licensed with confidential information. That information may remain secret after the expiry of the patent, and the licensee may still need to use it. Or, several patents may be needed to use the licensed technology, those patents expiring at different times. It is also common in a manufacturing licence for the licensor to agree to include any patents covering improvements in the licensed technology that it may subsequently obtain.

Intellectual property law provides very little guidance on the period of a licence. The Patents Act 1977 does provide that a licence to work a patented invention may be terminated by the licensee after all the patents relating to the invention which were in force at the time the licence was granted have ceased to be in force. Alternatively, a court can vary the terms of the licence if they would be unfair after the patents in force at the time of the licence have expired or been revoked. On the other hand, competition law is concerned to prevent an intellectual property owner trying to extend his period of exclusivity by agreement, and will normally invalidate any attempt to do so. For instance, payment of royalties must cease when the intellectual property right to which they relate expires. This means that, when several pieces of intellectual property with different expiry dates are included in the licence, separate royalties should be assigned to each or no royalty may be collectible after the first one expires. This is discussed further below in the section on competition law.

In general, a licensee will want as long a licence period as possible. However, a licensor is not obliged to license for the whole term of its exclusive right, and is given more flexibility by granting licences for shorter periods. Then, if the technology proves to be more successful than originally envisaged, or if the licensee proves to be less successful, a new licence can be negotiated on better terms. A compromise would be to grant a licence for a short term, with a provision making it renewable on certain conditions. In general, in cases where the licensee is taking a commercial risk, either by developing the commercial manufacturing technology or by opening up a market for a new product, it will not be possible to get a licensee unless he is given a long period which gives him a chance to recoup his expenses in getting the licensed business up and running.

Payment

While the most common method of payment for a licence is a royalty on products produced under the licence, that is not the only alternative. For example, where both parties have proprietary technology in the area, it is common to cross-license each other, with payment only if one party has significantly more to license than the other. Where the licence is incidental to some other transaction, such as a joint venture, the licence may be royalty-free, the intellectual property owner getting its return through the joint venture profits. A licence can also be paid for by a lump sum, or by some combination of a lump sum and royalties. In general, a lump-sum payment carries risks for both parties, except in the rare case where the potential return from the licence can be anticipated with reasonable accuracy. It may be advantageous where the licensor has no real interest in the licensed technology but needs immediate capital to develop some other technology which it does need.

Important licence provisions

Licences can vary from a simple letter agreement to a document the size of a telephone book. There are, however, some important provisions which should be included in even the simplest licence. There is not room in this book to provide a detailed guide to intellectual property licensing, for which you should consult an experienced lawyer or one of the treatises on licensing which are available. However, we want to draw your attention to some things that you must get right or trouble is likely to follow.

Defining the subject-matter

Where the licence covers a single piece of intellectual property, defining the subject-matter is not difficult. However, when a technology is being licensed, this may include several patents, confidential manufacturing information, copyright plant drawings, and disclosure of future improvements. It then becomes very important to define accurately the technology that is being licensed, which is more than a list of individual pieces of intellectual property. Failure to do so is likely to give rise to disputes about what future developments by the licensor are covered by the licence, or what products are subject to royalty payments.

Defining the rights granted

As we have seen, the intellectual property owner does not have to license all of its bundle of exclusive rights. This means that it is important that the licence is clear about which rights are granted, otherwise it will be assumed that all rights are covered. Particular attention must be paid to this point when the licence covers multiple intellectual property rights. Taking the example used in the previous paragraph, when the licence includes copyright plant drawings, the licensee should have the right to make copies only for its use in exploiting the licensed technology.

Rights to improvements

Practical experience in using the licensed technology usually leads to improvements in the technology and the way it is used. It is in both parties' interests to make the best use of the technology, as this is likely to produce increased returns. Subject to the competition law concerns discussed below, there should be provision for a two-way flow of information between licensor and licensee, with rights for each to use improvements developed by the other.

Payment

The various forms of payment, and factors for choosing between them, have already been discussed. The question of determining the level of payment remains, and is one of the most difficult in the practice of licensing. It is influenced by many factors — published lists of factors influencing licence pricing contain as many as 100 items. Also, like any other form of pricing, it depends on the relative bargaining strengths of the parties and the going market rate. A number of major factors are discussed briefly below.

Degree of exclusivity It should be obvious that an exclusive licence is more valuable than a non-exclusive licence because the exclusive licensee is being guaranteed a freedom from direct competition. The licence payment may also be affected by the presence of active, non-infringing competitors in the same market.

Degree of protection This is a question of both quantity and quality. An example of the importance of quantity would be where the licensor has a large number of patents in the licensed technology. This means that there is very little chance of a third party being able successfully to design around the patents and thereby compete with the licensee without the burden of royalty payments. Similarly, a technology which is protected in many aspects, for example, the ideas are protected by patents, the manufacturing know-how by confidentiality, and drawings and manuals by copyright, is a better prospect for a licensee than one which is vulnerable to having important aspects freely copied by competitors.

Regarding quality, a patent on a pioneering invention which opens up a new field is generally more valuable than one which is a slight improvement on an existing technology. A trade secret which is very difficult to reverse engineer is clearly more valuable to a licensee than one which could be successfully reverse engineered in a few months. A patent which has survived litigation may be worth more than one which has not had its validity tested. A licensor who has a reputation for enforcing his intellectual property against infringers is more likely to command high royalties than one who does not.

State of development A technology which is already running successfully presents less of a risk to the licensee than one which is in early stages of development. Royalties will reflect this relative risk, as well as any costs of development borne by the licensee. In particular, a licensee will usually be prepared to pay more when the licensor can guarantee the quality and rate of production of the licensed product. On the other hand, a well-developed technology which is becoming outdated is unlikely to command high royalties.

Value to the licensee The licence must generate some increase in income to the licensee for him to be willing to take the licence and pay a royalty. This can be from increased profits, perhaps because the goods produced under the licence command higher prices, or from cost savings resulting from use of the licensed technology. The licensor can only expect a minor share of these increased profits or cost savings, because the licensee has incurred most of the risk and capital expenditure in operating under the licence. It is rare that a licensee will be willing to pay more than 25% of the increased income resulting from use of the licensed technology to the licensor.

Importance of future developments   In most industries, the technology used must be regularly upgraded in order to remain competitive. When that upgrading is done by the licensor, a licensee should be prepared to pay more in order to stay current. Conversely, if the licensee will be the party to do most of the upgrading, which the licensor will benefit from by either using it itself or transmitting it to other licensees, the licensee's payments should be less to reflect the value of those improvements.

Market factors   The size and profitability of the market into which the licensee will sell have an obvious effect on the level of royalties the licensee will be willing to pay. The market for licences may also affect the price; in an industry where royalties have generally been a few per cent of sales, it will be virtually impossible to persuade a licensee to pay 20 per cent, even if the invention is worth it.

Reason for licensing   The price of a licence which has been sought by the licensee is likely to be higher than one where there is some pressure on the licensor, for example, a licence to settle infringement litigation. On the other hand, where the licensor has a strong case for validity and infringement, the licence fee may be higher if he has been forced to spend money on litigation before the infringer will take a licence. Similarly, a licensee who has something that the licensor needs, such as manufacturing or marketing ability, is likely to pay less for a licence than one who has nothing to offer.

There are some 'rules of thumb' that are used in intellectual property licensing, although like all such rules there are probably more exceptions, and they should be no more than the crudest guide to setting a licence fee. One commonly used rule is that the licensor should get at least one third of the licensee's profit.

The licence should also provide the details of how the royalties are to be calculated, when they should be paid, and give the licensor the ability to check the licensee's figures. The first point is particularly important, as several issues must be settled. For example, is the price on which the royalty is to be based the wholesale or retail price, how are volume rebates to be dealt with, can the licensee deduct overhead, packaging and shipping or advertising costs and, if so, how are those costs to be determined? Who bears any taxes on the royalty payments? These are factors which, if not clearly agreed to by the parties, can give rise to disputes later.

Warranties, limitations of liability and indemnities
A warranty is the legal term for something that non-lawyers usually call a guarantee. The person giving the warranty is stating that something is true or

will happen, and is liable to put right any damage that the person to whom the warranty is given suffers if that statement turns out to be incorrect. At the very least, the licensee will want the licensor to warrant that it owns the intellectual property that is the subject of the licence. Where a developed technology is being licensed, the licensor may also provide warranties that the process works, and that it will produce goods of a certain minimum quality. Obviously, the licensee would like to get as many warranties as possible so as to reduce its risk of loss, while the licensor wants to give as few as possible.

It is usual for parties to a contract to provide that their liability if something goes wrong will be limited in some way. As between parties of equal bargaining power, this practice is a reasonable way of allocating risk. Such limitation of liability could obviously be used oppressively in contracts where one party is much stronger than the other, particularly in consumer transactions, and there is legislation in the UK severely limiting the use of such provisions in this type of contract. Most intellectual property licences will fall outside this legislation, in which case the licensor should seek to put a reasonable limit on its liability. For example, liability should be limited to paying for the direct consequences of the breach of a promise, excluding liability to pay for injury that resulted indirectly. The licensor should also disclaim or limit liability for damage which was caused by the deliberate or careless act of the licensee or its employees. This may not help when the damage is suffered by third parties, such as the people killed and injured when a poisonous chemical leaked from the Union Carbide plant at Bhopal.

The licensor is not in a position to be able to promise that using the licensed technology will not infringe some third party's rights. What the licensee should demand is an indemnity against any loss that it might suffer through being sued for infringement of any third-party rights which were not disclosed by the licensor before the licence was entered into. This normally takes the form of the licensor agreeing to defend against charges of infringement, to repay the licensee for reasonable legal costs and fees that it may incur and to pay any damages awarded against the licensee. The licence should also provide what is to happen if an injunction is issued which prevents the licensee from continuing to use the licensed technology.

The licensor may in turn require the licensee to provide indemnity when damage is done to third parties caused by some fault of the licensee, and that third party sues the licensor. For example, Union Carbide has asserted that the disaster at Bhopal was caused by the actions of those running the plant, and was not the result of a defective design. If the licence contained a provision of this type, proof of the alleged facts would have shifted the loss to the licensee. In this case, that would not have helped Union Carbide much, because the plant was jointly owned by a Union Carbide subsidiary and the Indian government.

Providing for disputes

Going to court is not the only way to resolve disputes. In particular, parties to a commercial contract such as a licence should seriously consider whether to provide that all disputes over the licence should go to arbitration. The main advantage of arbitration for licence disputes is that an arbitrator with experience in the particular field involved may be able to produce a better resolution than a judge who knows nothing about the technology or the business except what the parties tell him. Arbitration may also be cheaper and quicker than litigation, although this is not always true.

When the licensee is in a different country from the licensor, it is important to provide which country's law will govern the agreement. A licensor should try to ensure that all its licence agreements are governed by the same law, as this makes administration of the agreements easier. It is also possible to agree where any litigation should be brought, provided the country chosen has some relationship to the licence.

Termination

For a number of reasons, one or both parties may want the licence to terminate before the full term has expired. For example, the licensor will probably want to protect himself against a licensee who does not pay royalties by terminating the licence if the payment is late by a specified period. Because termination tends to take place under circumstances in which the relationship between the parties is not very good, the licence should have clear provisions as to the reasons why the licence can be terminated by each of the parties, and the exact procedure for doing so.

The licence should also provide for what is to happen after termination. For example, if confidential documents were given to the licensee as part of the exchange of know-how, the licensor should require these to be returned. In general, a former licensee who continues to use the intellectual property after the licence has been properly terminated is an infringer. There are, however, circumstances in which confidential information can still be used after termination, particularly where the agreement is governed by European competition law. This is examined in more detail in the next section.

To summarise, a licence should

- define what is being licensed
- define the rights granted
- deal with rights to improvements made by both parties during the licence period
- provide clear payment provisions
- provide carefully thought-out warranties, limitations of liability and indemnities
- provide for resolution of disputes
- deal with how and for what reasons the licence can be terminated

COMPETITION LAW AND LICENSING

As a general principle, licensing of intellectual property rights is pro-competitive. It provides wider public access to the benefits of the licensed intellectual property, and contributes to the development and utilisation of new technologies. The European Commission has recognised this, and so has the European Court of Justice.

However, this does not mean that anything goes in intellectual property licensing. Exclusive rights carry the possibility of abuse, and quite detailed rules about what is and is not permissible have been worked out. We look in this section at the European rules in detail, and also briefly mention the application of US antitrust law to intellectual property licensing. Underlying all these rules is a basic principle

- owners of intellectual property must not try to take more than the law has already given them

For example, they cannot take something that has become freely available to the public, for example, by imposing restraints which would extend to a country where they have no rights, or to a time after their rights have run out. They are not allowed to use their exclusive rights as leverage to get advantages the law does not give them, for example, an exclusive right to provide a licensee with unpatented raw materials, or a right to insist that any improvements to the licensed technology made by the licensee shall be the licensor's property.

European and American law also prevent intellectual property owners from being greedy, by saying that their reward comes the first time things covered by the intellectual property are put on the market, and that thereafter the owner cannot restrict what happens to the goods. This is the principle of 'exhaustion of rights', which was discussed in chapter 9.

It is very rare that a piece of intellectual property provides a monopoly in the true sense. Usually, there are competing, non-infringing products and technologies on the market. However, a true monopoly could be created by competitors cross-licensing each other and agreeing to conditions that would restrict competition. For that reason, cross licensing, and the creation of patent 'pools' where more than two parties participate, are carefully scrutinised under competition law.

Licensing in Europe

The main competition law provision governing intellectual property licensing is Article 85, which we discussed generally in chapter 9. Most of the work of applying Article 85 to licences has been done by the Commission, as there have been comparatively few European Court cases dealing with licensing.

As a general principle, the Commission has tended to give Article 85(1) a broad scope, and then provided flexibility by granting exceptions under Article 85(3). When you are considering the possible competition law effects of any licence agreement you are planning to enter into, you must perform a two step analysis

- first step: is this agreement within Article 85 (1)?
- second step: if yes, then can I come within any relevant block exemption?

As we saw in chapter 9, if the answer to step two is no, then you either have to abandon the provisions that resulted in that negative answer, or go through the arduous notification procedure.

There are at present four block exemption regulations that are relevant to intellectual property licensing. These cover patents, know-how, franchising and joint research and development agreements. The relevant sections of these block exemption regulations can be found in appendix 6.

Patent and know-how licensing
It is appropriate to consider the patent and know-how licence exemptions together, because it is very rare for there to be either a pure patent licence, i.e., one with no associated know-how, or a pure know-how licence, one with no associated patents. The two block exemptions are also very similar in structure, and in the types of provisions allowed and not allowed.

The introduction to the know-how Regulation makes it clear that the two block exemptions are mutually exclusive. Therefore, your first task is to determine which of the two your mixed patent/know-how licence comes under.

The patent licensing Regulation states that it extends to:

> patent licensing agreements which also contain provisions assigning, or granting the right to use, non-patented technical knowledge . . . Such agreements can only be regarded as fulfilling the conditions of Article 85(3) for the purposes of this Regulation where the communicated technical knowledge is secret and permits a better exploitation of the licensed patents (know-how). Provisions concerning the provision of know-how are covered by the Regulation only insofar as the licensed patents are necessary for achieving the objects of the licensed technology and as long as at least one of the licensed patents remains in force.

As the know-how Regulation provides that it applies to mixed patent and know-how licences that are not exempted under the patent licensing Regulation, the critical distinction will be the requirement that

● the licensed patents are *necessary* for achieving the objects of the licensed technology

Presumably, when the licensed patents are not necessary for this purpose the know-how exemption will apply. But how do you determine what is 'necessary for achieving the objects of the licensed technology'? The preamble to the know-how licensing Regulation provides some guidance, suggesting that patents are 'necessary' when they 'afford effective protection against exploitation of this technology by third parties'.

This test may not always be as clear in practice as the Commission thinks it will. Because there are some significant differences between the two block exemptions, discussed below, it is important to know which one your agreement comes under. It is to be hoped that a mistaken choice, if made in good faith, will not be punished if the validity of the agreement is later challenged.

Both Regulations start with a long preamble, consisting of a large number of clauses preceded by the word 'Whereas'. This preamble sets out the background for the Regulation's provisions, and provides useful insight into how the Commission will interpret the Regulation. The provisions relating to which regulation applies, discussed above, appear in the preambles.

One important preamble in the know-how Regulation is the definition of 'know-how'. As we saw in chapter 4, there are a large variety of kinds of confidential information, not all of which may be covered.

- for a licence to qualify under the know-how block exemption, the licensed information must be both secret and 'substantial'

The Regulation defines 'substantial' as:

... information which is of importance for the whole or a significant part of (i) a manufacturing process or (ii) a product or service, or (iii) for the development thereof and excludes information which is trivial. Such know-how must thus be useful, i.e., can reasonably be expected at the date of conclusion of the agreement to be capable of improving the competitive position of the licensee, for example by helping him to enter a new market or giving him an advantage in competition with other manufacturers or providers of services who do not have access to the licensed secret know- how or other comparable secret know-how.

The know-how Regulation adds another requirement for qualification which does not apply to know-how in a mixed agreement coming under the patent Regulation. That is that the licensed know-how, including communicated improvements, must be 'identified in any appropriate form'. The know-how must be identified at the time it is transferred or shortly afterwards. The stated purpose of this requirement is to permit verification that the transferred know-how does in fact qualify as being secret and substantial, and that the licensee is not unduly restricted from using his own technology. In some instances this requirement may be very onerous; for example, where the means of transferring the know-how to the licensee is by knowledgeable employees of the licensor working alongside the licensee's employees while getting the licensed technology up and running. Much know-how that is both secret and substantial may be transferred in this way, but it would be difficult to put it all into writing, or even to videotape it.

The body of each Regulation follows the same pattern.

- Article 1 sets out certain provisions which, although apparently limiting competition, will be exempted under Article 85(3) of the EEC Treaty
- Article 2 sets out provisions which are not considered generally restrictive of competition

Together, these two Articles contain the 'white' provisions.

- Article 3 is the list of 'black' provisions, the presence of any of which will prevent the licence from benefiting from the block exemption

Article 4 provides a speeded-up notification system for agreements which contain provisions not specifically mentioned in the Regulation, and the remaining Articles deal with applicability of the Regulation and confidentiality of information supplied under Article 4.

- both block exemptions only apply to two party agreements

The know-how exemption has the further precondition that there must be a detailed identification of the licensed know-how in some suitable form.

Article 1   The patent Regulation contains a list of seven exempted provisions, six of them relating to territorial exclusivity. The same seven provisions are listed in Article 1 of the know-how Regulation. The first two allow sole and exclusive licences. The licensee can agree not to exploit the licensed technology in territory reserved for the licensor. Numbers 4, 5 and 6 deal with other licensees' territory. Agreements not to make or use in another licensee's territory and not to sell actively into another licensee's territory are exempted for the full allowable period of the agreement. However, agreements not to sell passively outside the licensed territory can be for no more than five years from the first sale in the Common Market of the goods concerned. Active selling means taking positive steps to sell outside the licensed territory, such as by sending in sales representatives, setting up distribution centres or advertising. Passive selling means supplying unsolicited orders from outside the territory. The seventh item on the list covers obligations on the licensee to use the licensor's trade mark on the licensed goods.

The know-how Regulation contains an additional exempted provision, an obligation on the licensee to manufacture only for his own needs and to sell the licensed product only in connection with sales of his own products, for example, as an integral part.

These are the broadest provisions that will be exempted under the block Regulation. Narrower provisions along the same lines will also be exempted.

Exclusive licences, agreements not to exploit the patent in the licensor's territory, and obligations not to sell in another licensee's territory are only exempted when the licensee is manufacturing or having the goods manufactured, or intends to do so, thus not covering distributorship type of agreements.

In the case of licences under the patent Regulation, the exemption can only last while at least one of the licensed patents is still in force.

For agreements governed by the know-how Regulation, the exemption lasts only so long as the know-how remains secret and 'substantial'. For provisions in the first three listed categories, exemption lasts a maximum of 10 years from the signing date of the first licence in the territory concerned covering the same technology. For classes 4 and 5 the maximum period is 10 years from the date of signing the first licence for the technology anywhere in the EEC, while the sixth class of provision can only last five years from the same date. However, where there are other licences of the same technology which are covered by the patent Regulation, sales into those licensees' territories can be forbidden for the period of patent protection in that territory. The requirement that the know-how remain secret and substantial injects a real uncertainty into licensing under this Regulation, as it may be very difficult to determine the point at which the remaining secret know-how has ceased to be sufficiently substantial.

Article 2   Most of the Article 2 provisions are common to both Regulations. They include such things as an obligation to keep know-how secret even after termination, prohibition of assignment or sublicensing, field-of-use limitations and minimum royalty or quantity requirements. Quality specifications and a requirement that the licensee purchase certain supplies or services from a source designated by the licensor come within the 'white' list only when they are necessary for satisfactory technical operation of the licensed technology, or, for know-how licences only, if they are necessary to ensure that the licensee's production meets quality standards followed by the licensor and other licensees. Otherwise, such obligations are in the Article 3 blacklist.

Mutual communication of improvements with a licence to the other party to use the communicated improvements is included, but is subject to conditions. For licences under both Regulations, the licence must be non-exclusive. Additionally, under the know-how Regulation, where the licensee's improvements are severable from the licensed know-how, the licensor must not be able to use the licensee's improvements for a longer period than the licensee can use the licensed know-how, unless the licence is terminated for breach by the licensee. The licensee can agree to give the licensor the right to continue using those improvements in return for either a lifting of a post-termination ban on the licensee's use of the licensed technology or for payment of royalties. The licensee must be free to use and license his severable improvements (but not with the licensor's know-how unless he is allowed to sublicense).

The know-how Regulation provides one item on the white list that is not in the patent Regulation, namely, an obligation to continue paying royalties on turnover after the know-how has become public other than by the licensor's actions.

Article 3 Most of the 'blacklist' provisions are common to both Regulations. These include indisputably anticompetitive provisions such as prohibiting licensee challenges to the validity of the licensed intellectual property and price fixing.

However, there are other blacklisted provisions which are more controversial. For example, customer and quantity restrictions are outlawed, as are provisions that the licensee must refuse to sell to customers outside his territory, or prolongation of the term of the licence by automatic inclusion of later patents and know-how, unless both parties have a regular right to terminate after the initial term has expired. The licensee cannot be charged royalties on products not covered by the licensed patents or secret know-how, and cannot be required to assign improvements to the licensor.

The know-how Regulation differs in having more complicated provisions about what is not allowed in the grant back of rights to licensee improvements, and also forbids a post-termination ban on use of the licensed technology by the licensee after the know-how has ceased to be secret, unless the licensee himself wrongfully made the know-how public.

There has been trenchant criticism of the blacklisting of some of these provisions, in particular the quantity restrictions or the charging of royalties on non-covered goods. It is not difficult to envisage circumstances in which such provisions are generally beneficial and not anticompetitive. However, if you want to include such provisions you will have to persuade the Commission of their benign effect in your case by going through the individual notification procedure.

Article 5 This lists the types of agreements that are excluded from the Regulations. For both Regulations, patent and know-how pools, agreements between joint venturers, and cross-licences between competitors *unless* there are no territorial restrictions are excluded. Licences of plant breeders' rights are not included in the patent Regulation, and the know-how Regulation excludes copyright and design right licences, and software licences unless the software is required to exploit the licensed know-how.

Research and development agreements

Unlike the patent and know-how Regulations, the block exemption Regulation for research and development agreements is non-exclusive. Covered agreements may also take advantage of any other relevant block exemption.

Joint ventures purely for research are unlikely to fall within Article 85(1) at all, unless they restrict the parties from carrying on other independent research. However, an agreement which also provides for joint exploitation of the fruits of the joint research is more likely to come within Article 85(1).

Article 1 This lists the types of agreements covered by the Regulation and defines certain terms used.

Article 2 This sets out the preconditions for the exemption to apply. There must be a defined research and development programme, and all parties must have access to the results. Where the agreement is for joint research only, all parties must be free to exploit the results, and provisions for joint exploitation can relate only to results protected by intellectual property rights or which constitute significant and substantial know-how. All parties must be able to obtain supplies of the goods where not all parties have the right to manufacture.

Article 3 The allowable period of an exempted research and development agreement depends on whether the parties were previously competitors or not. For non-competitors, the maximum period is five years from the first marketing of the products produced from the research, plus any further period where the combined market shares of the parties for the goods and equivalent goods does not exceed 20 per cent of the relevant market.

For competitors, the five-year period only applies if their combined shares in the relevant products at the time the agreement was entered into was 20 per cent or less, and the agreement may last so long as that combined market share is not reached. The Article also provides for transitional periods when the market share total is exceeded.

Article 4 This is the list of exempted provisions which restrict competition. These include obligations not to carry on or contract with others to carry on closely related research during the term of the agreement, territorial restrictions on exploitation and active sales, field-of-use restrictions, and an obligation to communicate and non-exclusively licence improvements.

Article 5 This is the 'white list', and includes obligations to communicate knowledge necessary to carry out the research and development agreement and not to use such information communicated by the other party except for the purposes of the agreement, and provisions for the maintenance of intellectual property rights arising from the research. Royalty sharing, and the obligation to supply minimum quantities and to observe quality standards are also on this list.

Article 6 This is the 'blacklist', and contains many provisions also found in the patent and know-how blacklists. Outlawed are quantity, price and customer restrictions, and exclusive sales territories after the expiry of the period allowed by Article 4. The parties must be free after the completion of the research and development programme to challenge the validity of any intellectual property rights held by the parties which are relevant to the programme, or to challenge the validity of intellectual property rights arising from the programme after termination of the agreement. The parties cannot be prohibited from licensing third parties to manufacture if there is no joint manufacture. Any attempt to prevent parallel imports into exclusive sales territories will exclude exemption.

Franchising
This Regulation covers two kinds of franchise agreements

- agreements with individual franchisees

- master franchising arrangements

where the franchisor contracts with a master franchisee who is then responsible for granting individual franchises in his territory. The terms used in the Regulation are defined in Article 1.

Article 2 This lists the exempted restrictive provisions. These are exclusivity, an obligation on a master franchisee to grant franchises only in his territory, and requirements that the individual franchisee operate only from agreed premises, not make active sales outside his territory and not deal in competing goods or services (except spare parts).

Article 3 This is the 'white list', and is divided into two groups. Group 1 is provisions that are only included to the extent they are necessary to protect the franchisor's intellectual property or to maintain the common identity and reputation of the franchised network. There are no conditions attached to the group 2 provisions.

Group 1 includes quality requirements, agreements not to compete, customer restrictions and an obligation to contribute to the franchisor's advertising. Group 2 includes provisions to protect intellectual property, communication and non-exclusive licensing of improvements, non-use of franchisor's know-how after termination and compliance with franchise rules.

Article 4 This contains general conditions for exemption of franchise agreements. The franchisee must be able to obtain the franchised goods from other franchisees or authorised distributors. Guarantees on the goods must apply throughout the Common Market, regardless of where the goods were purchased. The franchisee must indicate to customers that it is an independent business, although this need not detract from the common franchise appearance.

Article 5 This is the 'blacklist', and includes 'fake' franchise agreements where existing direct competitors enter into a 'franchise' agreement in an attempt to restrict competition. Attempts to prevent the franchisee from obtaining satisfactory goods from alternative sources, or to prevent the use of know-how after it becomes public (unless by the franchisee's actions) will exclude exemption under this Regulation, as will price restrictions and limitations on end customers based on their place of residence.

Other intellectual property licences

There are other types of intellectual property licences which are not at present covered by a block exemption, including copyright and trade mark licences. For these, it is necessary to look at Court of Justice decisions and previous Commission actions on such licences to determine whether notification is needed.

Trade mark licences There have been comparatively few court and commission decisions relating to pure trade mark licences. As the franchise trade marks are often an important part of the bundle of rights licensed by the franchisor, some guidance can be obtained from the block exemption and the Court decision in the *Pronuptia* case, case 161/84.
    One thing is clear

- the main principle governing the application of Article 85 is the prevention of division of the Common Market

One of the earliest cases where the European Court had to balance the territorial rights of intellectual property owners against the need to unify the market concerned trade marks. In *Consten and Grundig,* cases 56 & 58/64, Grundig had set up a network of exclusive distributors for its radios and televisions, with each licensee being promised absolute territorial protection, and agreeing not to sell directly or indirectly to anyone outside its territory. Consten was the exclusive distributor for France. Grundig used the trade mark GINT in addition to its 'Grundig' mark, and assigned this trade mark to Consten, so allowing Consten to prevent third parties importing Grundig goods into France by suing for trade mark infringement. The court held that this arrangement fell under Article 85(1) because the absolute territorial bans meant the agreement had the object of distorting competition.
    Because of the nature of trade marks, provisions for quality control will not fall under Article 85(1), unless they are more restrictive than is necessary. Requirements that the licensee purchase supplies from the trade mark owner are only permissible when this is necessary for quality control. For example,

licensees who produce the Campari aperitif using local wine and the licensor's secret recipe, and then sell it under the Campari trade mark, could be required to purchase the secret ingredients needed, but not readily obtainable ingredients such as orange essence.

It is common to settle trade mark disputes by an agreement that one party will not use the mark, or will only use it on certain goods or in certain markets. These agreements are very carefully scrutinised, because they can easily lead to an unjustified dividing up of the market and lessening of competition. First, there must be a genuine dispute. In *BAT Cigaretten-Fabriken GmbH* v *Commission* (case 35/83), BAT had opposed registration in Germany of the mark 'Toltecs' by a small Dutch company because it had a registration for 'Dorcet' which it had not used. The Dutch company could have started proceedings to have BAT's mark removed, but to avoid the cost of the proceedings they decided to accept a settlement agreement proposed by BAT, limiting their use of 'Toltec'. The conditions imposed by BAT proved so restrictive the Dutch gave up sales in Germany, and complained to the Commission about the agreement. The Commission found that there had been no genuine dispute because the 'Dorcet' mark was clearly removable for non-use, and the 'settlement' was merely an attempt to limit competition, and invalid under Article 85. The European Court agreed. Secondly, the settlement must be the least restrictive solution to such a genuine dispute. For example, an agreement not to use a mark at all may be too restrictive if consumer confusion could be avoided by the addition of a distinguishing mark.

Both the patent and the know-how block exemption Regulations expressly state that they apply to agreements that contain ancillary provisions relating to trade marks.

Copyright licences   There is virtually no EEC case law on copyright licences. The only court decision concerned exclusive film distribution rights, which they held did not come within Article 85(1). There have been some Commission decisions, which indicate that the same rules as apply to other forms of intellectual property licensing will apply to copyright licences. In particular, division of markets, non-competition clauses, no-challenge provisions, royalties on unprotected items and transfer of rights to improvements will almost certainly fall under Article 85(1).

Licensing under US antitrust law

There have been some quite violent swings of the pendulum in the view taken under the antitrust laws of intellectual property licensing. In the first part of the century, Supreme Court decisions allowed almost anything to pass muster if it was contained in a patent licence. Round about the Second World War, this attitude began to change, and intellectual property licences began to be scrutinised more closely. The peak of that attitude was reached in the 1970s, when Antitrust Division officials promulgated a list of intellectual property licence provisions that would be treated as *per se* antitrust violations, known as the 'nine no-nos'. When the Reagan administration came into office in 1981, it was quick to dissociate itself from this attitude, and Antitrust Division officials instead made speeches decrying the nine no-nos and stating that almost everything in intellectual property licensing, except naked price-fixing, would be treated under the rule of reason.

Despite this more relaxed attitude, there are some provisions that should be avoided or treated carefully to avoid antitrust problems.

Pricing

Although there is an early Supreme Court case which says that it is not an antitrust violation for a patent licensor to dictate the prices that its licensees should charge for goods covered by the licence, that rule has been so limited by later cases that it should not be relied upon unless the circumstances are very unusual. It is best to play safe and not dictate your licensee's prices.

Tying

The US law relating to tying in intellectual property licences is very complicated. Courts faced with an allegation of an antitrust violation because of tying go through an analysis of the facts, the numbers of steps varying between courts.

The first step is to determine whether there are in fact two separate items in the circumstances of the case; for example, a leg of lamb and a jar of mint sauce are separate items when you buy them at the supermarket, but no one would say that a restaurant is unlawfully tying when they serve mint sauce with your order of roast lamb. If they are two separate items, the court must then determine whether they really were tied, i.e., there was no choice but to take the tied item if you want the tying item. Where both are separately available at reasonable prices, the fact that there may be some advantage to taking both of them is not enough to constitute tying.

In recent cases the enquiry does not stop there. For there to be an antitrust violation, it must be demonstrated that the seller has market power in the market for the tying object. The tying object in the case of licensing is usually the licence itself. In the case of a patent licence it will be very hard to persuade a court that the 'monopoly' rights of a patent do not constitute market power. The situation is less clear in the case of know-how and copyrights, where no monopoly is conferred, although one appeals court held that a copyright gave the necessary market power. The courts have also started to look for significant adverse effects of the tying before finding that the antitrust laws have been broken.

In the case of patent licences, the law makes a distinction between 'staple' and 'non-staple' items. A staple item is one that is readily available on the open market, which has substantial uses which do not infringe the patent, and a non-staple item is the opposite. If it is a non-staple item there is no antitrust violation

Quantity restrictions

In general licensors have been able to impose restrictions on the quantities of licensed goods produced by their licensees. However, the courts are increasingly looking at the circumstances surrounding the agreement to see if the restriction is unjustified. There are circumstances where a quantity restriction would seem to be justified, for example, where a small company which is manufacturing under the patent licenses a very large company. Without a quantity restriction, the giant licensee would quickly put the small licensor out of business. Therefore, a quantity restriction would increase competition in this case.

Territorial restrictions
This is where US law differs most from European competition law. In the case of patent licences, the patent law specifically allows licences for only part of the United States, and a patentee can divide the US up into a number of exclusive territories. However, absolute protection cannot be given because the US also has an exhaustion of rights doctrine, so purchasers from the licensees can resell the goods in other parts of the United States free from restrictions. The same is not true of trade marks, know-how or copyrights. Supreme Court decisions in the 1960s and 1970s, the extreme of the antitrust pendulum swing, held that territorial divisions through patent licences were *per se* illegal, but more recent cases have tended to use a rule of reason analysis.

Field of use
Granting licences limited to a particular field of use is legal, unless it has the effect of dividing a naturally competitive market. For example, if a patented drug can be used for both humans and animals, those are not naturally competitive markets and separate licences can be granted. On the other hand, selling the drug for human consumption in the form of either tablets or capsules is a naturally competitive market, and cannot be divided by a field-of-use restriction.

DISTRIBUTION AGREEMENTS

If you have decided to use a distributor in a particular market rather than a licensee

- select a suitable distributor
- decide whether that distributor will have exclusive distribution rights in the territory
- negotiate a distribution agreement

Finally, the validity of that agreement under competition law must be considered.

Selecting a distributor

It is particularly important when you are going to appoint an exclusive distributor for a territory to make a careful choice of distributor. You should ideally appoint someone with a proven record of selling into the market in which your product will compete, and with the resources to provide any necessary technical after-sales service.

Before entering a distribution agreement, you should be aware of the sad fact that there is probably more litigation over these agreements than over any other type of contract involving the sale of goods. The relationship only works with a degree of trust on both sides. In particular, disappointing sales by the distributor quickly sour the relationship. In addition, the parties are at least potential competitors, and disgruntled distributors often accuse the manufacturer of breaches of competition law when things go wrong.

If your product is likely to be successful, any potential distributor should be willing to give you a history of its business. That will give you an idea how successful this distributor has been at selling other products. If you find a history of selling many different products, each for a short period, you would be wise to look elsewhere. Where yours is a new, unproven product, and you do not have an existing reputation in the market concerned, you may have to be less selective about picking a distributor as the field of applicants is likely to be much smaller. At the very least, you should look for a satisfactory credit history where it is possible to check that.

Finding distributors abroad is not an easy task. You may locate one by attending a trade show for your business in the country concerned, or by reading the trade press. The trade attaché to your country's embassy may be able to help, as one of their tasks is to promote your country's goods. If you use one of the large international accounting firms, they can often use their overseas offices to provide suggestions on suitable distributors. In any event, you must be prepared to travel to the country concerned to meet with potential distributors before making a choice. This is too important a relationship to the growth of your business to be carried on exclusively by post and phone.

Exclusive or non-exclusive?

Having a non-exclusive distributor may seem to be the least risky way of proceeding. If he does not perform to your satisfaction you can simply appoint another distributor, there are unlikely to be any competition law problems, and you have retained flexibility in your marketing arrangements.

On the other hand, a non-exclusive distributor is usually less motivated to work hard promoting your goods and, with a new product or an untried technology, you may not be able to find a distributor to take the risk unless you give exclusivity.

Important contract provisions

Many of the contractual provisions discussed above in connection with licences also apply to distribution agreements, in particular, defining the scope in terms of both territory and goods or services, warranties and liability and provision for disputes. There are some other provisions that are important in distributorship agreements.

Performance
When you decide to give exclusivity,

● performance standards must be built into your agreement

You must be able to terminate if the distributor does not perform satisfactorily, or you will have shut yourself out of full exploitation of that territory.

However, without some kind of objective standard, termination for insufficient performance by your distributor is almost certain to generate trouble, possibly litigation.

Competing goods
An exclusive agent should generally be required not to handle directly competitive goods, and a non-exclusive agent should preferably be under the same obligation.

- the handling by an exclusive distributor of competing goods is the source of a great deal of friction unless it has been possible to devise a set of detailed, objective performance standards

As we shall see, this restriction is permissible under the block exemption for exclusive distribution agreements.

Pricing
- you cannot restrict the price at which your distributor sells

The agreement should provide the price at which you sell to the distributor, rather than listing end sale prices and giving the distributor a discount off those prices, which could be treated as coercing the distributor to sell at those prices.

The manufacturer must be able to raise prices as costs increase, while the distributor needs prices to be as stable as possible. This is generally dealt with by providing that the prices will remain the same for an initial period, which should be reasonable in the light of prevailing economic conditions, and thereafter are only raised on reasonable notice, usually at least 30 days. A distributor with a strong bargaining position may also require a limitation on the frequency of price rises and the amount of each price increase. The latter is usually achieved by referring to some acknowledged published economic indicator related to inflation.

Trade and service marks
In some countries it has become the practice of exclusive distributors to register the manufacturer's trade marks in their own name. This can provide many problems when that distributor is terminated. You should do at least two things to protect your mark

- register it in the countries where you have distributors as soon as the law of that country allows

In many countries you can register before you begin to use the mark, in some you must wait until there has been some commercial use.

- the agreement should provide that the distributor uses the marks only on the manufacturer's behalf, and agrees not to register them in its own name or assert any other ownership rights

It is important to provide also that the distributor will cease using the marks when the distributorship is terminated, and will not afterwards use the marks or any confusingly similar marks.

Termination

You should be aware that some countries, for example, Belgium, protect their local distributors by making it very difficult to terminate distributorships. As laws can change, you should investigate the local laws on this subject immediately before entering into a distributorship agreement, and tailor the termination provisions to be as favourable to you as those laws allow.

DISTRIBUTORSHIPS AND COMPETITION LAW

In general, non-exclusive distributorships will fall outside Article 85(1) of the EEC Treaty, unless they contain a serious competitive restraint such as price-fixing or no-challenge clauses. For exclusive distributorships there is a block exemption.

Exclusive distribution block exemption

Because exclusive distribution agreements are so common, and so frequently have pro-competitive effects, the first block exemption Regulation, issued in 1967 by the Commission, dealt with exclusive distribution and purchasing agreements. In 1983 this Regulation was replaced by two block exemption Regulations, one for exclusive distributorships and one for exclusive purchasing agreements. Only the former affects dealings in intellectual property, so the exclusive purchasing exemption will not be discussed here.

Article 1 is the basic exemption for agreements between only two parties for the exclusive supply for resale of goods within the whole or a defined area of the Common Market.

Article 2 lists the permissible restrictions. The only competitive restriction on the supplier is the obligation not to supply to others in the assigned territory. The only permissible restrictions on the distributor are not to deal in competing goods, to obtain the goods only from the supplier and the obligation to refrain from active sales outside the territory. In addition, there are a few 'white' clauses listed; obligations on the distributor to purchase complete ranges or minimum quantities of goods, to sell under trade marks or in specified packaging and to promote sales.

Article 3 contains the 'blacklist'. The exemption does not apply to exclusive distribution agreements between direct competitors, nor to non-exclusive arrangements between competitors unless at least one of them has a relatively small *total* annual turnover (100 million ecu). The arrangement must not prevent or hamper end users from obtaining the goods from outside the territory, for example, by use of intellectual property rights or preventing passive sales by distributors.

14 Selling Intellectual Property Rights

Intellectual property, like any other form of property, can be sold or given away. Unlike licensing, where the original owner retains ownership rights and merely allows the licensee to use the property, the transfers dealt with in this chapter result in all rights passing to the new owner.

Why should anyone want to transfer all rights, which lawyers call 'assignment', instead of licensing them? A common reason to transfer ownership of intellectual property is that it is part of the assets of a business that is sold. Employees often assign to their employers' rights in inventions or works which they own but which relate to their employer's business. An individual or a small business may have no interest in using the intellectual property right and may prefer to sell outright. On the death of the original creator, the heirs may prefer to sell the rights to obtain cash.

The choice between assignment and licensing is one that can only be made after considering the particular circumstances. There may be significant tax consequences, and you should consult your financial advisers before making the decision. If you decide to transfer ownership rather than license, there are legal formalities that must be complied with to make the transfer effective, and other factors that should be considered in negotiating an agreement to sell intellectual property rights.

ASSIGNMENT DISTINGUISHED FROM LICENCE

We have seen in chapter 13 that a licence is permission to do something with respect to someone else's property that you could not otherwise lawfully do. The licensor retains ownership, that is, the right to exclude everyone other than his licensees from use of the property. On the other hand,

- assignment is the transfer of the ownership, so that after the transfer the original owner is now himself excluded from using the property unless the new owner gives him a licence

For example, you may let a friend borrow your car (a licence); that car must be returned to you and your friend cannot lawfully let someone else borrow it unless you agree. On the other hand, if you sell your car to your friend, he can let anyone he wants drive it, and you will need his permission to drive it yourself.

Unfortunately, the distinction between assignment and licence is not always so clear-cut. Consider an exclusive licence of all rights to run until the rights expire. There is no practical difference between such a licence and outright ownership. However, for tax and other reasons, casting the transaction as one rather than the other could have very different consequences. For this reason, a court faced with deciding whether a document transferred ownership or is only a licence looks at the substance of the transaction, not the words used. Because a licence is generally more advantageous than an assignment, most of the cases consider documents that were called licences. Factors that have been considered to indicate that the transaction was really an assignment include an inability of the 'licensor' to terminate the agreement, giving the 'licensee' unlimited rights to modify and adapt the work, and an intention that the 'licensee' could freely transfer or license his rights without needing the 'licensor's' consent. The courts tend to be ready to find that a 'licence' is really an assignment where they think the naming was purely for tax purposes.

So

- it's not what you call the document, but what the effect of the transaction is that decides whether there is an assignment or a licence

MAKING THE TRANSFER LEGALLY EFFECTIVE

The law requires formalities to make the transfer of many kinds of property legally effective. For example, transferring ownership of land requires a deed and may require registration in the Land Registry. Transferring ownership of a cheque requires endorsement. Other things which require some kind of formality for the transfer of ownership are shares and bonds.

In general

- ownership of property in things which are not physical objects requires a document for transfer to be effective

This is true of intellectual property rights. Rights which only arise after application to a government authority, such as patents and registered designs, generally also have a registration requirement for transfer of ownership.

Agreements transferring ownership are also contracts, governed by the general law of contracts which was outlined in chapter 2. If the contract is invalid, then the transfer will not be legally effective. In this chapter, we will not consider those general rules, but we will look at special rules relating to assignment of inventions by employees to their employers, and at the case law relating to publishing and recording contracts.

Where the intellectual property is jointly owned by two or more people, all the owners must join in the assignment for the assignee to receive the ownership of the intellectual property. Otherwise, all that the assignee receives is the share owned by the persons who join in the transfer agreement.

Formalities

The formalities required for the transfer of intellectual property are as follows.

Patents

Assignments and mortgages of patents and patent applications are void unless they are in writing and signed by *all* the parties to the transaction (Patents Act 1977, s. 30(6)). The assignment may be of only part of the patent rights.

The initial ownership of the patent is recorded on the Register of Patents which is maintained by the Patent Office. All subsequent transactions which affect ownership of or interests in the patent should be entered in the Register. There are two possible penalties for failure to register. If the owner of the patent makes conflicting transactions with the patent, for example, assigns all rights to A and then assigns the rights for Scotland to B, B's right will prevail over A, unless A had applied for registration before the assignment to B (or unless B knew about the assignment to A).

The right to damages for infringement is also affected by registration. Under Patents Act 1977 s. 68, where the infringement occurred after the transfer of title, damages cannot be given for the period before the transfer is registered, unless the transfer is registered within six months of its date, or the court is persuaded that registration within that six months was not practicable, and registration was effected as soon as possible.

The person shown in the Register as being the owner is presumed to be the legal owner, but this can be refuted by evidence that this person is not the true owner.

Copyrights

Assignment of copyright must be in writing, but, unlike patents, need only be signed by the person making the assignment, called the 'assignor'. The assignment can be of only part of the rights of the copyright owner, for example, an author may assign only the publishing rights, or it may be for only part of the copyright period (Copyright, Designs and Patents Act 1988, s. 90). It is particularly common for the right to perform the work publicly to be separately assigned to a copyright collective society such as the Performing Rights Society, which has the means to police public performances effectively and ensure that those performances are licensed, something an individual copyright owner is rarely able to do.

The Copyright, Designs and Patents Act 1988 also permits the assignment of future copyright (s. 91). The effect of such an assignment is that the copyright in such a future work is immediately owned by the assignee as soon as the work comes into existence.

As might be expected, there is no requirement for registration of transfers of copyright ownership.

Moral rights

These are not assignable. On the death of the owner, his moral rights pass under his will if specifically bequeathed. If the moral rights are not specifically bequeathed then they pass to the person to whom the underlying copyright is bequeathed. Otherwise they are exercisable by his personal representatives who administer his estate. (Copyright, Designs and Patents Act 1988, ss. 94 and 95).

Performer's rights

Like moral rights, these are not assignable, but pass under the owner's will, if specifically bequeathed, or are exercised by his personal representatives (Copyright, Designs and Patents Act 1988, s. 192).

Recording rights

As explained in chapter 6, recording rights belong to the person who has an exclusive recording contract with the performer to make commercial recordings of one or more of his performances, provided that that person is a 'qualifying person' as defined in the Copyright, Designs and Patents Act 1988, and discussed in chapter 6. If the exclusive recording contract is assigned, the assignee will get the recording rights, provided the assignee is a 'qualifying person' (Copyright, Designs and Patents Act 1988, s. 185(2)). However, the recording rights can only pass with the recording contract, they cannot be separately assigned (s. 192(1)). If the owner of the exclusive recording contract is not a 'qualifying person', there will be no recording rights, unless a licence under the contract to make recordings has been granted to a qualifying person, who will then have the recording rights (s. 185(3)).

This complicated scenario could result in recording rights appearing and disappearing like the ghost of Hamlet's father, as the exclusive recording contract changes hands between qualifying and non-qualifying persons. It will be interesting to see how the courts deal with an infringer who is caught by a recording right suddenly appearing out of thin air when the recording contract is licensed or assigned.

No special formalities are required by the Copyright, Designs and Patents Act 1988 for assignment or licensing of the recording contract. Dealings with recording contracts will be governed by the normal rules about creation and assignment of contracts, which are discussed in chapter 3.

Design rights

The provisions relating to transfer of design rights in Copyright, Designs and Patents Act 1988, s. 222, are identical to the provisions relating to copyrights.

Registered designs

The Registered Designs Act 1949 does not specifically provide how an assignment must be made. However, under general law, transfer of such a right must be made in writing, signed by the assignor, in order to be legally effective. However, the assignment must be registered, as only the registered owner can sue for infringement of the registered design. Further, an unregistered assignment cannot be used as proof of title, except in proceedings to rectify the register.

The amendments to the Registered Designs Act 1949 made by the Copyright, Designs and Patents Act 1988 include provisions under which the design right associated with any registered design are to be kept in the same hands as the registered design. Under s. 19(3B), any assignment of a registered design is also an assignment of the associated design right, unless the parties express a contrary intention in the assignment. However, if the registered design is assigned without the design right, s. 19(3A) states that an interest under s. 19(3) will not be registered unless the person entitled to that interest is also entitled to a corresponding interest in the design right. Section 19(3) provides for registration (a) where the applicant for registration 'is entitled to a registered design or a share in a registered design' and (b) 'where that person is entitled to any other interest in the registered design'. The term 'any other interest' seems to imply that ownership is one of the 'interests' that, under subsection (3A), cannot be registered unless the corresponding interest in the design right is owned by the same person. If this is the correct interpretation of this subsection, then effectively the design right will never be separated from the associated registered design.

Trade marks and service marks

Assignment of trade and service marks is complicated by the fact that they are something which can indicate to the public that the goods or services in question come from a particular source. Allowing unfettered assignment of marks could cause consumer deception or confusion.

- unregistered marks must be assigned together with the the business in which they are used, including the goodwill associated with the mark

As unregistered marks and get-up are only protected in passing-off if they are used in a business which has goodwill, assigning the marks without a transfer of the business and goodwill transfers nothing. There would be no protection for the mark unless and until the assignee of the mark built up sufficient goodwill through his own use of the mark.

The Trade Marks Act 1938, s. 22 does allow assignment of registered marks without any assignment of the associated goodwill, subject to certain restrictions. Where there are unregistered marks used in the same business and for the same goods, they can be assigned together with the registered marks without an assignment of goodwill, but this does not apply if they are assigned on their own.

The restrictions on assignment contained in s. 22, are designed to prevent customer deception or confusion arising from assignment.

- assignments which would result in more than one person owning marks which are identical or confusingly similar for use on the same type of goods sold in the same market are not permitted

Where there is any question that these restrictions might apply, the owner can ask the Trade Marks Registry to rule whether or not the proposed assignment will be valid. Similarly, an assignment that would allow different individuals the exclusive right to use the same or a similar mark on the same goods in different parts of the UK is invalid.

If it is proposed to assign the mark without the associated business goodwill, the Act sets out a procedure which must be followed or the assignment does not take effect. The person to whom the mark is assigned must apply within six months from the date of the assignment for directions as to how the assignment is to be advertised, and then carry out those directions.

Any assignment of a registered mark must be entered on the register. While registration is not expressly required to sue for infringement of a registered mark, the owner is not allowed to prove title, which is required to bring an action, except by the entry on the register.

Failure to comply with formalities
A purported assignment which does not comply with the requirements of writing and a signature, but which meets the general contract law requirements for an enforceable contract, will be treated as an agreement by the owner to assign the rights at the request of the other party. Such an agreement is said to give an equitable title to the property, because its owner is entitled to the equitable remedy of specific performance, forcing the legal owner to transfer legal title. While the equitable owner has an acknowledged claim over the intellectual property, he cannot enforce his rights against third parties until he obtains legal title.

The results of failure to register have been dealt with above in respect of each type of intellectual property.

EMPLOYEE INVENTIONS — ASSIGNMENT TO THE EMPLOYER

The Patents Act 1977 contains several new provisions which are apparently aimed at protecting employees who are not employed to invent but who come up with inventions useful to their employers.

The ownership of patentable inventions has been explained in chapter 5. For a limited class of employees, inventions they make automatically belong to their employers. However, employees who do not come within these limited categories may also come up with inventions that relate to their work. Before the 1977 Act, ownership of these inventions was governed by the employee's employment contract, which usually provided that all inventions relating to the employee's business made during the term of employment would be assigned to the employer. Now, for employees mainly employed in the UK.

● any agreement by the employee to assign future inventions to the employer is unenforceable, although the employee is free to assign each invention to his employer after it has been made

The employee remains, however, under any duty of confidentiality owed to his employer, which could make it difficult to exploit an invention made using confidential information gained in employment, if the employer is not interested in exploiting it.

PUBLISHING CONTRACTS

It is well known that it is very difficult for an unknown author, songwriter or musician to get his or her work published or recorded. As a result, such people will generally sign any contract put before them by a publisher or recording company. The courts have acknowledged that this great disparity in bargaining power can produce very unfair contracts. For example, in *A. Schroeder Music Publishing Co. Ltd* v *Macaulay,* Macaulay was an unknown songwriter who had entered into a publishing contract with A. Schroeder Music Publishing Co. Ltd, a well known music publisher. He agreed to assign copyright in all his songs, including those written during the agreement, for a £50 'advance on royalties'. On the other hand, the publisher had no obligation to publish his work. The House of Lords held that the contract was invalid as being in restraint of trade, as the terms were forced on the songwriter, who was left unable to exploit his work if the publisher chose not to do so.

● The moral is, do not be greedy

If you are the party with economic power dealing with an intellectual property owner who has no bargaining power, make your agreement fair. If, as in the case of a publishing contract with an unknown, you do not want to oblige yourself to undertake the expense of publishing and promoting something that may not sell, have terms that allow the author to take his rights and try elsewhere without a long wait for the contract to expire.

OTHER PEOPLE'S RIGHTS AFFECTING ASSIGNMENT

There are two categories of people who have rights relating to the intellectual property which can impinge on assignment:

● existing licensees
● creators

The effect of assignment on existing licences

Under the general law of property, a licence will be binding on any assignee of the property, unless that assignee in good faith paid value for the property, did not know of the licence and had no reason to suspect that a licence existed. This rule has been made expressly applicable to assignments of copyright and design rights by Copyright, Designs and Patents Act 1988, ss. 90 and 222.

In cases where there is a register for dealings in the intellectual property, and licences are registrable, this rule is modified. For patents, if the earlier licence is inconsistent with the terms of the assignment, then the later assignment will prevail unless the licensee had applied for registration before the date of the assignment, or the assignee had knowledge of the licence at the time of the assignment (Patents Act 1977, s. 33). The provisions of the Registered Designs Act 1949 have the same effect for licences of registered designs.

As the only way a trade mark can be licensed is by a registered user agreement, the provision of the Trade Marks Act 1938 s. 24, that the owner of the right is subject to any right appearing on the register, means that any assignee will be bound by the rights of a registered user.

Rights of creators

There are two kinds of creator's rights which are independent of the intellectual property rights attaching to the creation:

- the right of an employee inventor to receive compensation for his employer's use of the invention
- the moral rights of creators of certain copyright works

Employee inventors

If a patented invention made by an employee is used by the employer and proves to be of 'outstanding benefit' to the employer, then the Patents Act 1977 provides that the employee must be compensated if the existing benefit that the employee has gained from the invention is 'inadequate'. These provisions apply both to employees whose inventions automatically belong to the employer, and employees who have assigned or licensed their own inventions to their employer after the Act came into effect in June 1978. These compensation provisions cannot be contracted away, although they will not apply where there is a collective trade union agreement covering the matter.

As these provisions only apply to the employer, a bona fide assignee from that employer will not be affected. However, it is likely that a court would look very carefully at an assignment to a related entity at a low price, to ensure that it was not simply an attempt to get out of paying this compensation. The main effect on the employer who assigns is that the price obtained for the assignment will be a major component of the 'benefit' from the patented invention.

Moral rights

The author's moral rights in a copyright work are not assignable, survive his death and are not affected by the author's transfer of all rights under the copyright. This means that

- the effect of moral rights must be taken into consideration every time a work subject to the moral rights provisions is transferred

As the Copyright, Designs and Patents Act 1988 permits waiver of the author's moral rights, the original assignee should attempt to negotiate such a waiver as part of the original assignment. However, if this provision is used oppressively, there is a good chance that the courts would take the same attitude they have taken in the publishing contract cases and make the waiver unenforceable. For this reason, it would be advisable to provide separate, significant, compensation for the waiver, and undue pressure to get the waiver should not be applied.

EFFECTS OF AN ASSIGNMENT ON THE ASSIGNOR

Beside the obvious effect that he no longer owns the intellectual property and needs a licence to use it, there are some other things that can affect an assignor after the transaction is completed

- the assignor may be unable to challenge the validity of the transferred intellectual property
- warranties and other obligations undertaken in the assignment agreement may return to haunt the assignor

Assignor estoppel

We would all agree that it is not fair for a person to give with one hand and take back with the other. Uncle John's gift of a box of chocolates loses its value to the recipient if Uncle John proceeds to sit there and eat all the soft centres when he knows you hate the hard ones. It would be even worse if the landlord let a second-floor flat to you, but then refused to let you use the stairs while still collecting rent. This activity is known to the law as 'derogation from grant', and is not allowed.

- derogation from grant applies whenever rights have been legally granted, and the grantor then does something to make the granted rights less valuable or worthless

The principle has been applied to patent assignments. The assignment only has value to the assignee if the patent is valid, so the assignor cannot voluntarily transfer his rights, then turn round and attack the validity of the patent in the courts. This can occur when the assignor does something which infringes the transferred patent, and is sued by the assignee. In such a case, assuming the assignment was voluntary, the assignor is not allowed to challenge the validity of the patent, although he can defend on grounds of non-infringement. This is called 'assignor estoppel'.

Under common law a licensee was also estopped in some circumstances from challenging the validity of the licensed rights, although this was based on a different principle than derogation from grant. Under EEC competition law, a licensee under any agreement governed by that law cannot be prevented from challenging validity. This does not necessarily mean that the doctrine of assignor estoppel, based on a different principle and involving different considerations, is also outlawed. In the United States, with a similar competition law, a licensee cannot be prevented from challenging validity but nevertheless the doctrine of assignor estoppel has recently been held to apply.

Assignor warranties

The continuing obligations of the assignor will primarily be governed by the terms of the assignment agreement. The purchaser, before paying his money, needs some assurance that he is getting something of value in return. These assurances will be in terms of

- warranties, which are guarantees from the seller that certain things are so, and

- indemnities, which promise to make good any loss

A common warranty is that the seller has the legal right to make the transfer, and that there are no adverse third-party rights which would affect the seller's enjoyment of the property. A common indemnity in intellectual property contracts is against the effects of being sued by a third party for infringement for operating under the contract.

Even without express terms, the law may imply certain terms. Most commonly, there will be an implied promise by the assignor that he has title to the property being transferred and the right to make the transfer. The assignor will also be held to an obligation to take all necessary steps to make the transfer legally effective. As we have seen, the law will also normally imply a promise not to derogate from the grant. However, the law will not imply a warranty that the intellectual property is valid, and the assignor should strenuously resist giving such a warranty.

PRICING THE PROPERTY

This is the most difficult aspect of selling intellectual property. Unlike selling your house, it is not possible to hire a surveyor to give a valuation before putting your intellectual property on the market. Because no rights with independent value are retained, it is even harder than pricing an intellectual property licence, although many of the same considerations apply.

Methods of payment

Although the most common method of payment for the assignment of intellectual property rights is a lump sum paid at the time of transfer, this is not the only possibility. Particularly in cases other than sale as part of a business, it is advantageous to provide for a series of payments, related at least in part to the assignee's exploitation of the property. This can be advantageous to both parties. If the property turns out to be valuable, this will increase the assignor's return; if it turns out to be a flop, it reduces the assignee's financial risk.

Methods of valuation

When you get a valuation prior to selling your house, the valuer's approach is largely based on market value of comparable properties. This type of valuation can be done fairly accurately because there are relatively few factors affecting price and there are a lot of data on market prices of houses. In the case of intellectual property, there are a lot of factors affecting value, and there are very little available data on current prices. Most intellectual property that is sold rather than licensed is transferred as part of the assets of a business, and it is very difficult or impossible to determine how much of the price for the whole business is attributable to the intellectual property.

Probably the simplest method of assessing a price is to base it on the cost of developing the intellectual property concerned. However, in order to find a buyer, this cost must be less than it would cost the likely purchaser to develop a similar technology itself. Obviously, if you have broad patents, or the technology is based on confidential information which is very hard to reverse engineer, this cost will be high. However, this is also usually the least desirable way of doing it, because cost of development can have no relationship to economic benefit from the exploitation of the property. Particularly in the patent and confidential information field, some very simple inventions that cost very little to come up with can produce considerable profits, while inventions on which great sums have been spent prove to be of no commercial value by the time they are finished. The US government and the oil companies spent huge amounts to develop synthetic fuels during the oil crisis of the late 1970s, but the collapse of oil prices following the weakening of the OPEC cartel have made this technology unlicensable in the foreseeable future.

Obviously, the best way to produce a price that is fair to both parties is to estimate the economic benefit that can be expected from using the technology. Unfortunately, this process is, in the case of new and undeveloped technology, almost impossible to predict. For such technology, the seller may be wise to consider a low initial payment, with the remainder of the payment to be assessed in an agreed manner after the licensee has commercialised the technology. Of course, this payment will have to take into account the fact that the licensee took most of the risk and bore most of the expense in making this a commercially viable technology. Readers who are interested in investigating this approach further are referred to *Valuation of Intellectual Property and Intangible Assets* by Gordon V. Smith and Russell L. Parr (New York: Wiley, 1989).

15 Avoiding Problems With Other People's Intellectual Property

KEEPING OUT OF TROUBLE

If you have read all the way through this book to this chapter, you will be well aware of the dangers of ignoring the intellectual property rights of others. For example, you know that a whole business can be shut down for infringing patents, as in the case of the Kodak instant camera business which infringed Polaroid's patents. This can happen even if you acted in good faith and in complete ignorance of those patent rights. You also know that you may have to pay damages which could exceed the profit you made on the goods that were found to infringe another person's intellectual property rights. You have learned that the litigation leading up to these serious consequences is itself very expensive and time-consuming.

On the positive side, you should now be able to anticipate where there could be intellectual property rights that might affect a present or planned product, which enables you to take steps to avoid trouble. You should also understand what constitutes infringement of any particular right that you learn about.

This chapter summarises ways of avoiding trouble with other people's intellectual property rights. Some have already been discussed from the point of view of the owner of the rights, such as buying the rights or taking a licence. The others involve a knowledge of the scope of the various intellectual property rights and what constitutes infringement, discussed in the first part of this book. For example, you are a manufacturer of hi-fi equipment. Your main competitor comes out with a new amplifier which has very good performance characteristics, and you want to reverse engineer it to find out what your competitor has done, hoping to learn something useful.

First, can you reverse engineer a competitor's product? (Reverse engineering is the process of studying a product in every way necessary to determine how it works and how it is put together.) Yes, unless you acquired the item you intend to study under a contractual agreement forbidding reverse engineering; such provisions are common in software licences. However, you should be aware that by reverse engineering you may make it easier for your competitor to win a copyright or patent infringement suit against you. In the case of copyright, where copying must be proved, reverse engineering of the product covered by copyright shows that you had access to the plaintiff's copyright work, and is prima facie evidence of copying. You can take steps to provide counter-evidence of no copying, described in the section of this chapter on reverse engineering. In the case of patent infringement, although copying is not required for infringement, evidence of deliberate copying does make a finding of infringement more likely.

Secondly, what can you do with the information you get through reverse engineering? That will depend on what kind of intellectual property protection your competitor has used. If the key circuit is patented, then all you can do is seek a licence or use the information to try to design around the claims of the patent. On the other hand, if your competitor was only relying on confidentiality, then you can use the ideas embodied in the circuit. However, directly copying the circuit itself could possibly be an infringement of the design right, as discussed in chapter 6.

You can avoid trouble with other people's intellectual property by

- getting permission from the intellectual property owner by taking a licence
- buying the intellectual property
- designing around patents and designs
- taking proper precautions when reverse engineering
- not copying copyright works
- selecting trade and service marks that are distinctive, not descriptive, and which are not readily confused with those of your competitors
- getting intellectual property rights to prevent others from getting the same rights and blocking what you want to do

KEEPING AN EYE OPEN

First, how do you find out what intellectual property rights owned by others are out there so you can take steps to avoid trouble?

With rights that are registered, such as patents, marks and registered designs, you can look for things that could be troublesome. This is done by searching the appropriate registers, all of which are open for public inspection. However, it is not easy to do an adequate search unless you are experienced at searching the relevant register. It is highly advisable to have such searches done by a patent agent. In the case of registered marks, a trade mark agent can also perform searches.

Further, it is possible to learn about pending UK and European patent applications, which are published about 18 months after they were filed. Regular monitoring of published patent applications in your field, again preferably done by a patent agent, will give advance warning of what is pending in the UK and European Patent Offices.

Applications for a registered mark are also published after they have been accepted for registration. As applications for registered marks are only published shortly before registration, there is not so much advance warning. The main reason monitoring this publication of pending applications for registration is that there is a month from publication in which to file a formal notice with the Trade Marks Registry objecting to registration of the mark. While an opposer can object on any ground, it is unlikely that he would go to the trouble of opposing registration unless he believes the mark will conflict with one he uses, whether registered or unregistered.

It is much harder to monitor unregistered intellectual property rights consistently. The best that can be done is to watch what is appearing in the market from your competitors, and to watch the general and trade press for new product announcements.

TAKING A LICENCE

This is one of the most common ways of avoiding trouble. As explained in chapter 13, a licence is really an agreement by the intellectual property owner not to sue. In that chapter, we looked at licences primarily from the licensor's point of view. While everything that was said there is relevant here, in this chapter we will concentrate on the things that the licensee needs to be concerned about.

Obviously

● price is of prime importance

The licensee will also be concerned about

● the degree of exclusivity, and the protection he will receive from competition by unlicensed infringers

He also needs to know whether this licence is all he needs, or whether there are yet other third-party rights covering his product.

Price

● if the licence fee is so high that the goods cannot be made at a competitive price, then the licence is worthless to the licensee

Before entering negotiations to take a licence, the licensee needs to do a great deal of homework in order to know what he can afford to pay. First, it is essential to know as accurately as possible what the product will cost to manufacture. Even with established products this is not easy to do, as the true cost is not just the incremental cost of producing one more item, but must include a proper share of the overhead costs of the business. When the product is not yet in production, accurate costing is obviously more difficult. For example, there may be difficulties in manufacturing on a commercial scale which were not encountered in making the prototypes and which have the effect of increasing the cost. For this reason, the nearer you are to full production at the time you negotiate the licence, the more likely you are to end up with an affordable licence fee. Of course, leaving negotiations until you are on the verge of full production carries the risk of considerable wasted effort if you are unable to obtain a licence.

The licensee must also know how much he can sell the product for. This will entail market research and a survey of competitive products. From the difference between the sale price and the manufacturing cost must come both the licence fee and the licensee's profit. Having an accurate estimate of this amount gives you the boundaries for negotiation with the licensor. Obviously, the licensee wants to make the profit proportion as large as possible, while the licensor wants the opposite result. Where the balance is reached will depend on the negotiating power and skills of the two parties.

Protection from unlicensed competition

This is very important to a licensee paying more than a nominal licence fee.

- if you are paying a significant fee to the licensor, but you are facing direct competition from infringers who can sell at lower prices because they are not paying tribute to the intellectual property owner, you will likely either lose sales or suffer reduced profits

As we have seen, you will be unable to go after infringers yourself unless you have an exclusive licence. It is therefore important to have the licensor contractually obliged to take action against infringers who refuse to take a licence. If he fails to do so, then the licence should provide for a reduction in the licence fee to enable you to compete against the infringers.

If the licensor does take action, but some or all of the licensed intellectual property is held to be invalid, the obligation to pay licence fees in respect of that property should cease immediately. In fact, this is required by the EEC competition rules, which prohibit agreements for the payment of royalties on expired or terminated intellectual property rights. Where the licence includes more than one piece of intellectual property, this could mean that the whole obligation to pay royalties ceases on the expiry or termination of any one of them if the licence does not apportion the royalties between the licensed properties.

Protection from infringement actions by others

Before entering a licence,

- the licensee needs to know whether this is the only licence he needs in order to operate

In the case where the licensor is familiar with the industry but the licensee is seeking a licence in order to enter that industry, the licensor is in a much better position to know what third-party intellectual property rights exist which affect the licensed technology. The licensee should try to get the licensor to state either that no other licence would be needed or to specify what other licences would be needed. Where the licensor does not know of any conflicting third-party rights he will normally indemnify the licensee against the effects of infringement litigation brought against the licensee as a result of practising the licensed technology.

● if your licensor refuses to give such an indemnity, you should immediately become suspicious about the value of the licence you are being offered

Collective licensing

In many everyday circumstances there are activities which need to be licensed because they would otherwise be copyright infringements, but where obtaining a licence from the individual copyright owners is impracticable if not impossible. For example, think of all the public places where background music is played; restaurants, clubs, supermarkets, pubs are just a few examples. Playing this music is generally an infringement of the right of public performance which needs a licence from all the owners of the relevant copyrights in each of the works played. Similarly, a great deal of photocopying which is not covered by any of the exceptions to infringement goes on, particularly in schools and universities.

The great difficulty in obtaining licences from each copyright owner in these cases, and the near impossibility for the individual copyright owners of policing this kind of use, have given rise to copyright collectives. The oldest of these in the UK is the Performing Right Society (PRS), an association of composers, authors and publishers of music, who assign to the PRS their rights relating to public performance. The PRS collects royalties for use of these rights through a number of blanket licensing schemes for various types of use. The licensees must submit regular information on the works they have played, and the PRS apportions out the revenue it receives in proportion to the use made of the various works. An association of record companies, Phonographic Performance Ltd (PPL), performs a similar role for the performance of sound recordings. Much more recently, the Copyright Licensing Agency (CLA) was set up to provide blanket licences to education authorities and other educational establishments for photocopying of copyright material.

The Copyright, Designs and Patents Act 1988 has set up a body called the Copyright Tribunal to oversee these copyright collectives, and to provide a means of 'appeal' on licence terms for the licensees. This body replaces the Performing Rights Tribunal, which had a similar role under the previous Copyright Act but which was limited to dealing with licences of performing rights only. Licensing schemes by copyright collectives ('licensing bodies') may be generally referred to the Tribunal by an organisation representing licensees, although the Tribunal may decline to look at the scheme on the ground that the reference is premature. In the case of a dispute with the licensing body, an individual licensee may refer his particular licence to the Tribunal. The Tribunal can confirm or vary any scheme referred to it. The Tribunal also has power to examine individual licences granted by a licensing body which are referred to it by the individual licensee concerned. The provisions relating to the Copyright Tribunal and collective licensing schemes are found in ss. 116 to 152 of the Copyright, Designs and Patents Act 1988.

BUYING THE INTELLECTUAL PROPERTY

It is less common to buy up conflicting rights than it is to take a licence. Purchasing the rights is most likely to occur when the intellectual property in question is owned by an individual or by a small company with no business in the technology concerned. Indeed, in certain circumstances, it may be more advantageous for a large company to purchase a small business in order to get intellectual property it needs than to take a licence.

Most of what was said in chapter 14 about selling intellectual property is also applicable to its purchase. In addition, the purchaser must be concerned that it is getting something for its money. That involves two matters that need investigation

- the validity of the intellectual property
- the seller's ability to sell it

The seller must also be concerned that the property is transferred as far as possible free from any rights of third parties.

Validity

It is amazing how often an otherwise astute businessman will agree to purchase intellectual property for large sums of money without making any investigation of its validity, although that same person would not dream of signing a contract to buy a house without making extensive checks on the state of the property.

Carrying out a validity investigation is particularly important in the case of patents. As we have seen, a patent may be invalid because of prior art that was not discovered during the process of obtaining the patent. Therefore, at least where significant sums are to be paid, a full validity study should be made at an early stage. This study will be similar to the validity study that should be made prior to commencing litigation, as described in chapter 12.

Title

Ownership of the various types of intellectual property has been discussed in the first part of this book. Understanding these rules will help you to know when issues of ownership can arise. For example, ownership of a copyright work may depend on the employment status of the person creating the work.

When investigating the seller's title, the possibility of earlier sales of all or part of the intellectual property rights should be borne in mind.

For the intellectual property that requires registration, namely patents, registered designs and registered trade and service marks, the purchaser is primarily concerned with what is shown on the relevant register. In the case of registered designs and registered trade and service marks, the legislation states that the person named in the register as the proprietor has the power to assign the registered design or mark, and to give legally effective receipts for any consideration paid for the assignment. This power is subject only to interests in the design or mark belonging to other people which appear on the register.

These provisions mean that a purchaser of a registered design or a registered trade or service mark can take the entry on the register as adequate proof of title, and will not be bound by any rights of other people which do not appear on the register unless he actually knows about them before the transaction takes place.

In the case of purchase of a registered design, the sale will automatically include any associated design right. The purchaser should not agree to any attempt by the seller to exclude the design right from the assignment because, as discussed in chapter 14, this could prevent the purchaser from becoming registered as the owner of the registered design.

The situation is a little more complicated in the case of patents. Section 33(1) of the Patents Act 1977 provides that the later purchaser will get ownership free from the interest of anyone claiming under an earlier transaction who did not register his interest, unless the later purchaser actually knows about the earlier transaction. However, subsection (4) provides that an application for registration shall, for the purposes of subsection (1), be treated as registration. This means that a purchaser cannot be absolutely certain of getting clear title by simply looking at the register just before the transaction is completed, as an earlier application to register may still be in the pipeline. The safest course of action is to obtain a warranty from the seller that there have been no transactions involving the patent that do not appear on the register on a fixed date — which should be a little earlier than the date of the assignment so that the purchaser has time to search the register. Where there is any possibility that the seller may not be financially sound, and an earlier transaction may be in the process of registration so it becomes necessary to rely on the warranty, the purchaser should negotiate to withhold part of the purchase price until his assignment appears on the register. Once this happens, there should be no earlier transactions still in the registration pipeline.

Whenever you acquire a registrable interest in a patent, registered design or registered mark

● it is important for your own protection to apply immediately to have your interest registered

Proof of title for the unregistered rights, copyright, design rights (except where there is a corresponding registered design), unregistered trade marks and confidential information, is more complicated. For copyright and design right, proof of the following facts should be required:

(a)   where the assignment is taken from the original author:
   (i)   date the work was created
   (ii)   nationality and residence of the author at the time the work was created
   (iii)   that the copyright did not automatically vest in another because of employment, commission (for design rights) or an agreement to assign future rights.
(b)   in any other case:
   (i)   and (ii) as in (a)
   (iii)   the means by which ownership was acquired

Moral rights

The new law relating to moral rights is discussed in chapter 6. As the author's moral rights are independent of the copyright, this means that

- the purchaser of a copyright must consider whether his use of that copyright could be affected by the exercise by the author or his heirs of any moral right

If it could, then the purchaser must determine whether he can avoid the effects of that moral right.

What is affected by moral rights?

First, moral rights attach to all copyright works completed on or after 1 August 1989, the date on which the relevant parts of the 1988 Act came into effect. However, in the case of the right to be identified as author or director, the right must have been asserted.

For literary, dramatic, musical or artistic works completed before 1 August 1989, there will be moral rights provided the author was still alive on that date. However, the moral rights will not apply to acts done under an assignment or licence made before 1 August 1989. Where the copyright vested initially in someone other than the author, no moral rights will apply to anything done by the owner or with his consent. There are no moral rights attaching to films completed before 1 August 1989 or records made under the Copyright Act 1956 statutory recording licence.

Avoiding moral rights

From the point of view of authors, s. 87 of the 1988 Act considerably watered down the moral rights provisions. This first provides that a moral right is not infringed if the author consents to the act in question. Secondly, the author can waive his moral rights, either specifically or in general, including future works. This will probably mean that in future most assignments and licences from authors will contain such a waiver, except in the rare case where the author has sufficient bargaining power to refuse to sign a waiver. If you are purchasing the copyright from the author you should attempt to obtain a waiver of moral rights. If you are purchasing the copyright from some other owner, you should enquire as to whether there is a written waiver of moral rights. If not, you could try to locate the author and negotiate a waiver. As this will require giving the author some consideration for signing the waiver, which will probably involve paying the author money, the cost of the copyright should be appropriately reduced.

DESIGNING AROUND PATENTS AND DESIGNS

A patent has come to your attention which you are advised could cover something you are doing or propose to do. You do not want to take a licence, or the patentee refuses to license or demands a licence fee which is more than you can afford to pay. What can you do, apart from abandoning your product or process?

Remember

● the scope of a patent is governed by the claims

These set out the boundaries of what the patentee says is covered by his invention. If you can design your product or process so that it does not stray across these boundaries, you will not be infringing the patent. This is called designing around the patent.

● this course of action is not without risk; if a judge thinks that you got it wrong, and that your activities do fall within the patent claims, then the fact that your intentions were good does not help at all

Care must also be taken that, by getting outside the claims of the patent you are concerned about, you do not fall within the claims of another current patent. You can minimise this risk by following the procedure described below.

(a)   Obtain an independent and detailed analysis of the scope of the claims. This should be done by someone outside your organisation, who should be experienced in preparing such an analysis. This person should be a patent agent, or a solicitor or barrister specialising in patent law. In particular, it is vital that this analysis should not be left to your technical staff or anyone who will be involved in the design process.

(b) Instructions for the design team must be prepared. These should include at least the following items:

(i)   The requirements for the product or process, including any things that must be avoided.

(ii)   A detailed description of what must be avoided. This is taken from the claims analysis; while the analysis itself could be given to the design team, it is probably better to translate it into terms clearly understood by people with the technical background of the team members.

(iii)   It must be made clear to the team that they must try to get as far away from the things to be avoided as is compatible with the requirements they have to meet.

These instructions must be reviewed and approved by the person who prepared the claims analysis before it is given to the design team.

Because of the possibility of copyright in the patent drawings, they should not be given to the design team. In fact, it is preferable that they do not look at any part of the patent. To avoid any problems with any copyright or design right, the design team should not be allowed to see any equivalent product produced by the patentee.

(c)   The design team's proposals must be submitted to the person who prepared the claims analysis, or to another lawyer specialising in patent law, for an infringement analysis and opinion. If that opinion is that the design could be found to infringe, the design team should not be shown the opinion or even told its effect. Instead, a further set of instructions to the design team should be prepared, reviewed and approved by the lawyer, telling the team exactly what is unacceptable about the design. This process should be repeated until the lawyer is satisfied that there is a low chance that the design will be found to infringe (as litigation is such an uncertain activity, there is always some possibility that infringement will be found, although it may be sufficiently small as to be an acceptable risk).

(d)   When the final design has been reached, the lawyer should prepare a detailed written opinion as to why this design does not infringe the patent.

(e)   A search for related patents should be carried out, and the outside patent expert should study these patents to ensure that the final design should have no infringement problems with these patents.

All written communications should be dated and carefully preserved. Communications with the design team should be kept to a minimum and should be in writing.

* the products sold commercially, or the process as practised, must correspond exactly to the approved design

This means that, if problems in production necessitate a change to the design, any change must be approved by the same process described above. It is also important to impress on those involved in production that they cannot make any changes in the design without first getting proper approval.

Similar principles apply to designing around registered designs, which, like patents, protect against independently created designs which come within the scope of the registration. Less stringent precautions will normally be sufficient for designing around designs protected by design right, where copying is required for infringement. It is, however, important that the designer does not see the original design, because of the dangers of unconscious copying.

REVERSE ENGINEERING

The term 'reverse engineering' is here used to mean

* the process of studying a competitor's products to gain useful information

In this section 'information' is used in a very broad sense. This information could be technical, such as the ingredients, the way in which a particular feature has been achieved, or how the competitor overcame certain problems. Alternatively, the information could relate to design features or appearance. The information can be used for a number of different purposes. For example, it could be used in sales and advertising of your own products, providing reasons why your product is superior. To give an everyday example, such advertising has become common in the food industry — less alcohol, less salt, more vitamin C. Or, the information could be incorporated into your own product, although improved upon. In the riskiest case, it is used to short-cut development in order to meet a competitive situation where you are rapidly losing market share to the competitor's product.

While reverse engineering is a widely used and perfectly respectable activity, it carries heavy risks of intellectual property infringement unless it is carried out with great care.

Is reverse engineering permissible?

In most cases the answer is yes, unless you are under a contractual obligation not to do it. For example, the object you want to reverse engineer may have been acquired under a licence that has a term forbidding such activities. If the licence is valid and binding — something that is questionable in the case of shrink-wrap licences of software — then reverse engineering would be a breach of contract. A confidentiality agreement could also contain a prohibition on reverse engineering.

The legality of reverse engineering is more questionable where the item is protectable by copyright and the reverse engineering process involves making a copy. The obvious examples of this are computer programs which are distributed only in object code form, and the control software stored in certain semiconductor devices such as microprocessors. As the object code is usually supplied only on magnetic media such as a disk or magnetic tape, in order to produce a copy of the object code which can be studied by the people who are doing the reverse engineering, the code must be printed out on to paper, called a 'listing'. This is obviously a copy of the software under the copyright law.

Further, in almost every case, before the software can be studied for reverse engineering processes a version which is easier for humans to understand must be produced. This can be done by a process called decompiling, normally performed by one of the commercially available computer programs which can convert the 1s and 0s of machine code into a higher-level language that can be more readily studied. Under the new copyright law this higher-level language version is a 'translation' of the original object code version, as the Copyright, Designs and Patents Act 1988, s. 21(4), defines translation of a computer program as including a conversion 'into or out of a computer language or code or into a different computer language or code'.

This means that the very act of reverse engineering the software will be an infringement of copyright unless it comes within one of the statutory exceptions. The only one that would be applicable is the exemption for fair dealing for the purpose of research, which is dealt with in Copyright, Designs and Patents Act 1988, s. 29, and Copyright Act 1956, s. 6(1). Unfortunately, there is no case law on the meaning of the term 'research' in these provisions which would give guidance whether making copies in the process of reverse engineering would be treated as fair dealing. Anyone involved in a reverse engineering programme which involves making copies, transcriptions or adaptations of the thing being studied should only do so in the context of a programme which a court is likely to believe is a genuine research programme. For example, the study should be limited to determining ideas and principles, not to preparing a detailed description of the way those principles were expressed. There should be an ongoing programme of studying all available software which is likely to yield relevant ideas, not just the one commercially successful program, particularly when the aim is to produce a rival version. Evidence that you were simultaneously doing your own research and development in the same field is also likely to be persuasive.

Despite taking all precautions, you must be aware that the unsettled state of the law means that there is a definite risk in reverse engineering software whenever that involves preparing a listing or decompiling the object code. The law is no clearer in the United States, although there have been some decisions on the subject. One trial court, in *Hubco Data Products Corp.* v *Management Assistance Inc.* (1983) 219 USPQ 450, held that Hubco's modification of the operating system software produced by MAI was an infringement of the copyright in the operating system because, in making the modification, a listing of the object code was prepared. However, in the recent decision in *NEC Corp.* v *Intel Corp.* (1989) 10 USPQ2d 1177, NEC's activities in preparing a listing of Intel's 8086 and 8088 microcode from the chips and then disassembling the code were not even discussed as possible infringements.

While there is widespread opinion that proper reverse engineering is a socially desirable activity, it would seem that in the case of software which is only publicly available in object code or embedded in a semiconductor device where a copy must be made and then 'translated' before it can be studied, reverse engineering involves copyright infringement under the present law. Of course, if the software produced using the information obtained through reverse engineering does not infringe the copyright in the original software, as in the case of NEC's microcode, then any damages for the infringement during reverse engineering will probably be minimal.

Using the Information

One reason for reverse engineering is that you suspect that your competitor is infringing your intellectual property and you are looking for proof. In that case, you will use the information in the litigation process. However, in most cases the purpose of reverse engineering is to get information to use in your own business. This is the type of reverse engineering that carries a real risk of falling foul of your competitor's intellectual property rights.

First

● weigh the benefits of using the information against the possible risks

If the value of the information is trivial, you are probably better off not using it, because merely trying to determine whether the information is covered by some intellectual property right can be expensive. On the other hand

● using the information could save a lot of development time and expense

making it worthwhile to run some risk. The purpose of this section is to tell you how to minimise the risk, but following the steps set out below is no guarantee that you will not be successfully sued for infringement. Further, a book like this can only give very general advice, and you should always consult a lawyer specialising in intellectual property for guidance on your particular reverse engineering project.

Assessing the risk
Assessing the risk involved in using something learned from reverse engineering a competitor's product involves two steps. First, you must find out whether the thing you want to use is protected by any form of intellectual property.

Secondly, if there is intellectual property protection, you must determine whether the use that you want to make is an infringement of that intellectual property.

To carry out the first step involves investigating the competitor's ownership of intellectual property related to the product. This would include patents, copyright, design rights, registered designs and trade marks. If the product has been obtained on the open market, confidential information will not be a problem, but it could be if the product was obtained in some other way. There could also be a potential passing-off action if you intend to imitate the get-up of the product. For patents it is necessary to search for both issued patents and published patent applications issued to the competitor. The register should also be checked for relevant patents assigned to the competitor. A similar search for registered designs should be carried out. The Register of Trade Marks should be searched to see whether the marks that the competitor is using in connection with this product have been registered, and whether the competitor has any other registered marks for the same class of goods. For unregistrable rights, copyright and design right, you should assume that anything that could be a copyright or design right is a valid right and is owned by the competitor.

Having determined what intellectual property is owned by the competitor, you must next determine whether any of that intellectual property could cover any of the information derived from the reverse engineering that you are interested in using. For example, if the only intellectual property your search turned up relating to your competitor's amplifier was a registered design on the casing, then you would know that the only rights the competitor could possibly have covering the circuitry that you are interested in would be copyright or design right.

Once you know what types of intellectual property you need to be concerned about, it must next be determined whether the use you want to make of the information could be an infringement of the right concerned. This determination should be made by a person experienced in carrying out such studies, a patent agent or solicitor or barrister specialising in intellectual property.

Avoiding infringement

If you have determined that the information you are interested in using is, or is likely to be, covered by some intellectual property of the competitor, and that there is a real risk of infringement if you simply go ahead and use the information, that does not mean that there is nothing you can do. There may be ways of avoiding infringement if the right precautions are taken.

Patents   It may be possible to design around a patent, using the techniques described in the previous section.

Registered designs   These can also be designed around, using a similar technique to that used for patents. However, the existence of a corresponding design right must be borne in mind, particularly as it is too soon to tell whether the courts will apply the case law defining infringement of a registered design to the new design right.

Copyright and design right Because infringement of both these rights must involve copying, your chances of avoiding a successful action for infringement depend directly on the degree to which you avoid copying from the competitor's product. There is a particular danger which is hard to avoid, that of unconscious copying. If the people who produce your product have had any chance to study the competitor's product, there is a real danger that any similarities between the two will be held to be the result of such copying, even if you have proof of no deliberate copying.

This means that you must try to put together a design team which knows as little as possible about the competitor's product. It is particularly important that no one on the team had any involvement in the reverse engineering. Preferably, no one on the team will have even seen the other product, although that may be difficult where the product has been on the market any length of time.

The preferable course of action is to hire outside designers to do the design, if you can find suitably qualified people who are not familiar with the competitor's product. If this is not possible, then you should decide on the design team before the reverse engineering even begins, and segregate them from the reverse engineering team. This will not be easy, because these people will almost certainly be colleagues who are used to meeting in the corridors or cafeteria and discussing their work. Everyone involved in the project must be made aware of the importance of no contact between the two groups until at least the final design has been approved, and preferably not until it has been put into production.

Once the reverse engineering is complete, a design brief for the design team must be prepared. It is very important that this document contain no description of the competitor's product. The design objectives must be set out as far as possible in terms of the functions the design is to perform. For example, if the purpose of the reverse engineering was to get the information needed to design a product that will work successfully with the competitor's product as an 'add-on', the design brief should describe the characteristics the add-on will need in order to be compatible, rather than the characteristics of the competitor's product that it must be compatible with. If what is desired is a 'work-alike' product, then the functions the product is to perform should be described, with no reference to how the competitor's product performs those functions.

Once the design brief has been prepared, it should be reviewed by an intellectual property lawyer before being submitted to the design team. All communications with the design team regarding the design should be in writing, and any communications to the design team originating from anyone with knowledge of the competitor's product should first be reviewed by the lawyer. All communications should be dated, and copies kept in a safe place. An example of a use of this technique, sometimes referred to as a 'clean-room' technique, which helped to persuade a judge that there had been no copying, is found in the case in which Intel sued NEC for infringement of copyright in the microcode for its 8086 and 8088 microprocessor chips. Microcode is the instructions that are programmed into the chip to make it work. NEC makes two chips, the V20 and the V30, for which it has a patent licence from Intel for the circuitry, but no copyright licence covering the microcode. The versions of microcode that Intel claimed NEC had copied were written by someone who had helped reverse engineer the Intel code, thereby raising a strong suspicion of copying. However, after Intel accused NEC of copying, NEC had a 'clean-room' code written from functional instructions by someone who had not seen the Intel microcode. The judge found that the similarities between this 'clean-room' code and the accused NEC code were at least as great as the similarities between the Intel code and the accused code. From this, the judge deduced that the similarities must be attributable to the constraints imposed by the hardware specifications, and were not the result of copying the way Intel's code was expressed.

If the first design does not meet all requirements, a supplemental design brief must be prepared, following the same procedure as the original brief. This process is repeated until the team produces a satisfactory design.

Semiconductor chip topography The scheme of protection for semiconductor topography is the only form of intellectual property law that has express provisions relating to reverse engineering. Under the Design Right (Semiconductor Topographies) Regulations 1989, one of the exceptions to the exclusive rights of the owner of the semiconductor topography design right is

- the reproduction of a design for the purpose of analysing or evaluating the design or analysing, evaluating or teaching the concepts, processes, systems or techniques embodied in it.

This clearly permits normal reverse engineering activities. Further, the Regulations provide that it is not an infringement of a semiconductor topography design right to:

(a) create another original semiconductor topography as a result of an analysis or evaluation of the first topography or of the concepts, processes, systems or techniques embodied in it, or

(b) reproduce that other topography.

This provision distinguishes between direct copying of the first topography, which is an infringement, and using the information obtained by the reverse engineering to make your own design and make chips to that design, which is permitted.

The reason for this unusual provision is to be found in the history of this legislation. The UK Regulations are the direct result of an EEC Directive, which required the member States to enact legislation protecting semiconductor topographies. The reason for the EEC action is the US legislation protecting semiconductor chip layouts, the Semiconductor Chip Protection Act of 1984. That Act offered protection in the US to foreign semiconductor chip designs only if the country of origin provided US chips with similar protection. The EEC Directive, and therefore the UK Regulations, are intended to gain that reciprocal protection, and are strongly modelled on the American legislation, which has very similar provisions relating to reverse engineering. Why are these provisions in the American legislation? Because the US semiconductor industry demanded them, and lobbied strongly against an earlier version of the legislation that had normal copyright-type infringement provisions. The industry wanted reverse engineering to be clearly legitimised because everyone in the industry did it.

In the first court decision under the US legislation, the defendant, Advanced Micro Devices Inc., commonly known as 'AMD', successfully used these provisions to fight off an application for an interlocutory injunction. The plaintiff, Brooktree Corporation, accused AMD of copying two of its chips used in high resolution computer displays. AMD admitted studying the Brooktree chips, but produced evidence indicating that their design was made independently and not simply copied from Brooktree (*Brooktree Corp.* v *Advanced Micro Devices Inc.* (1988) 705 F. Supp 491.

SELECTING A TRADE MARK

Because unregistered marks can be enforced through a passing-off action, it is not always easy to avoid problems with other people's marks. However, careful searching before a mark is selected, and care in selecting the mark, can do a great deal to minimise the risk of infringing on other people's marks.

The best way of avoiding trouble is to devise a mark that is inherently distinctive, as that term is explained in chapter 7. Such marks may be much more expensive to come up with and initially promote than ones that are at least partially descriptive, but they pay off in the long run. First, if the mark is truly inherently distinctive, then there is no risk of infringement, because no one has used it previously. Certainly, the risk that there is an existing user of a very distinctive mark in a related field is likely to be low. Secondly, such a mark is much easier to protect against others once you have started to use it, as the only meaning that it has is the one you have given it.

On the other hand, if the mark is at least partially descriptive of the goods or services, there is a real risk that someone else thought of it first. Such marks are also weaker because they can be difficult to protect without first spending a lot of time and effort in developing an image in the mind of customers and potential customers.

Once a preliminary choice of mark has been made, a search should be made try to determine as far as possible whether it is the same as or confusingly similar to an existing mark used in the same field. The first step is to search the Register, both parts A and B, in the class or classes for the goods or services on which the mark is to be used. It is also advisable to search related classes, as the registered proprietor may have started to use the mark on additional goods but not yet registered in those classes. Further, even without a registration in the additional classes, the goods may be sufficiently similar to produce customer confusion and ground a passing-off action.

Simply searching the Register is not enough to ensure that you will be able to use your chosen mark without fear of litigation. A mark does not have to be registered to be the subject of a passing-off action. What is more, an earlier unregistered mark which has been used sufficiently to have the reputation needed for a successful passing-off action will prevail against a later mark, even though the later mark is registered. Therefore, the search should include an attempt to identify unregistered marks being used in the same field. This could be done, for example, by searching trade directories, looking at catalogues and monitoring advertising in the media most likely to carry advertisements for the goods or services in question.

It is harder to say in general where a search for get-ups used by others should be made. Generally, for consumer goods, those in the business monitor their competitors' products and will be aware of the various get-ups that are in use. If you are just entering the business concerned, then some field research may be required. Get-up tends to have much less importance outside the consumer products field and is less likely to be the basis of a successful passing-off action.

Suppose that your searches do not turn up any identical marks, but that there are one or more marks which are fairly close to the one you want to use. As the test for infringement is presence or likelihood of customer confusion, it is hard to tell whether there is an infringement problem without trying your proposed mark or get-up out on the consuming public. The best way of doing this is by a public survey, designed and carried out by an independent organisation specialising in such surveys, although a good survey is expensive. If you decide not to use a survey, at least obtain the advice of a lawyer familiar with the way the courts compare marks in infringement and passing-off cases.

DEFENSIVE PATENTING

Suppose you are in the chemical industry. One of your researchers has come up with a patentable variation on the process you are currently using to produce polypropylene. The variation does not produce a sufficient improvement to justify the cost of converting your process to use it, but it is sufficiently better than any of the processes that your competitors are using that you have no intention of licensing it to them. Why should you go to the bother and expense of applying for a patent on the variation?

Although patenting something that you have no intention of using may seem pointless, it is commonly done in industries, such as the chemical industry, where all the members of the industry do extensive research. In such industries, inventions are often made independently by more than one company. The purpose of such patenting is to prevent a competitor from getting his own patent, which he might be able to use to block some later development that your researchers have come up with and you want to use. This process is sometimes called 'defensive patenting'. This method of avoiding problems with other people's intellectual property should be used in any industry where competitiveness is largely dependent on technological advances, where members of the industry constantly carry on research to come up with these advances, and where patent protection is often relied upon to protect those advances. Typical examples would be the chemical, pharmaceutical, biotechnical and semiconductor industries.

Appendix 1
Example of a Patent

(12) **UK Patent Application** (19) **GB** (11) **2 138048 A**

(43) Application published 17 Oct 1984

(21) Application No **8408025**

(22) Date of filing **28 Mar 1984**

(30) Priority data
(31) **8308899** (32) **31 Mar 1983** (33) **GB**
  8314955   **31 May 1983**

(71) Applicant
  Cyril Deeley,
  Holmwood, Wigan Lane, Chorley,
  Lancashire PR7 4DD

(72) Inventor
  Cyril Deeley

(74) Agent and/or Address for Service
  Wilson Gunn Ellis & Co,
  41-51 Royal Exchange, Cross Street,
  Manchester M2 7BD

(51) INT CL³
  EO04H 12/22

(52) Domestic classification
  E1D PB

(56) Documents cited
  GB 1227920   GB 0657597   GB 0443806
  GB 1187604

(58) Field of search
  E1D

(54) **Post support structure**

(57) A ground-engaging post support structure (10) includes a tube (11) sunk into the ground, usually but not necessarily vertically, and a separate stabilizer (12) which engages the tube (11) at ground level and has outwardly extending arms (14) which are engaged with the ground and can apply a force to the tube (11) tending to resist departure of the tube (11) from its desired disposition. The lower end of the tube (11) can have an inwardly extending flange or rim or can have a pointed cap to make sinking easier. The arms (14) can be in the form of vertical blades. A variety of stabilizers are described and shown in the drawings.

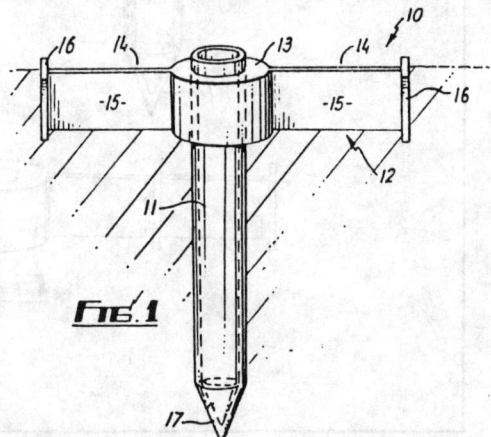

FIG. 1

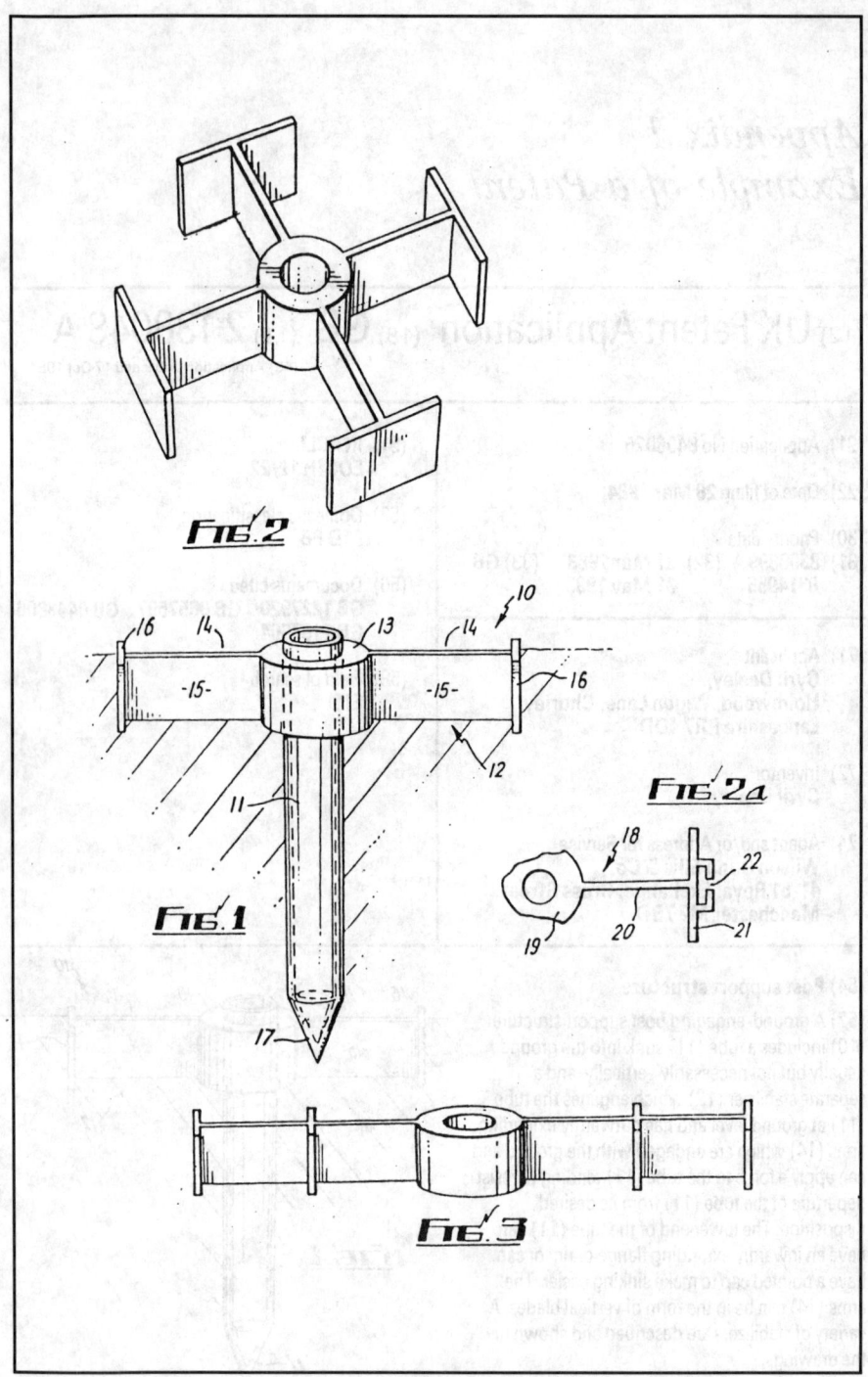

FIG.2

FIG.1

FIG.2a

FIG.3

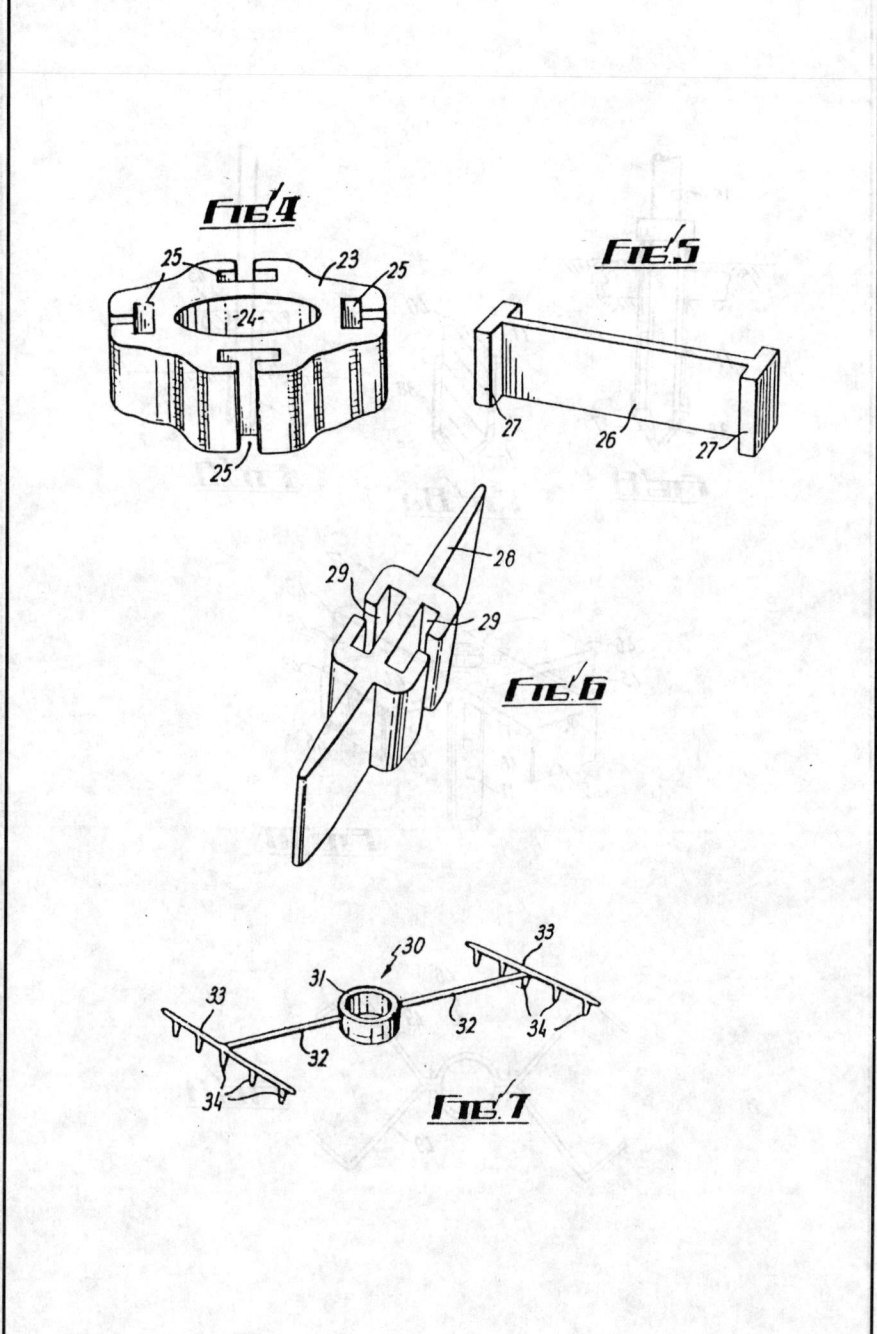

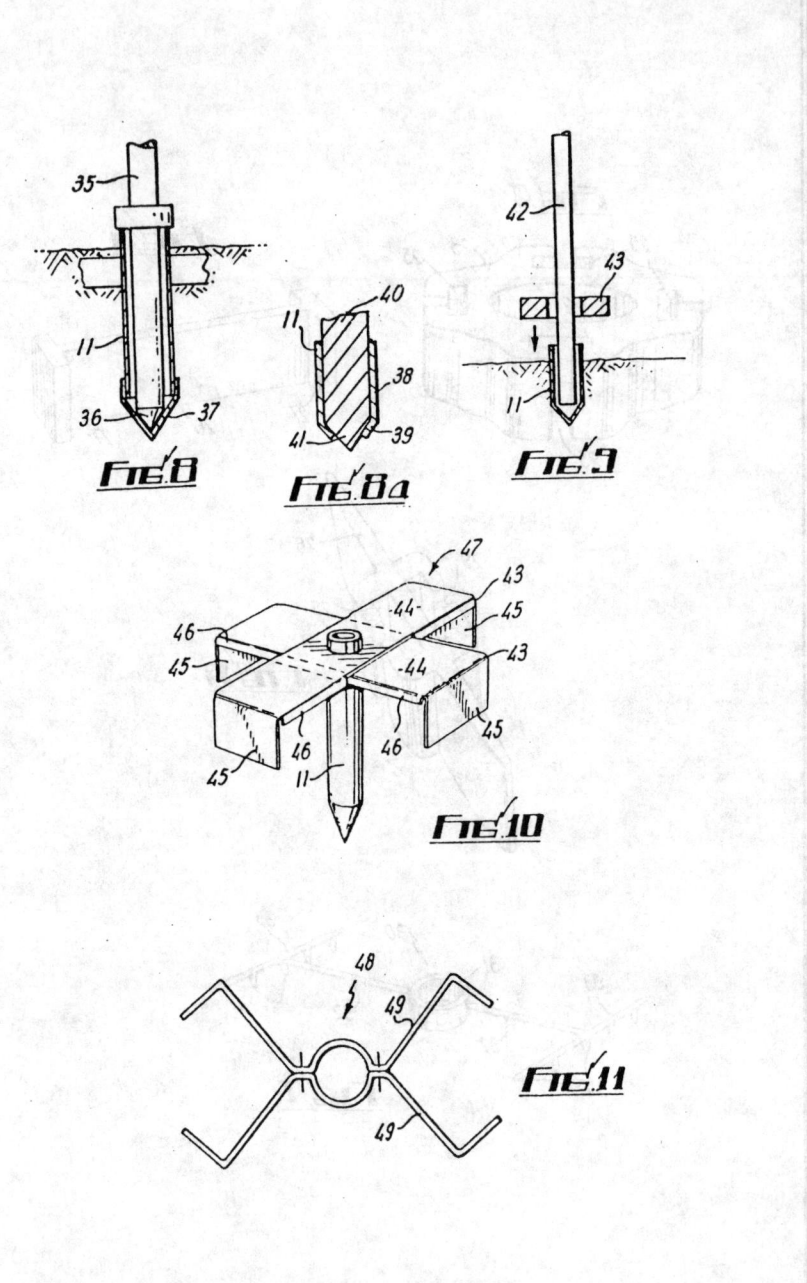

FIG.8

FIG.8a

FIG.9

FIG.10

FIG.11

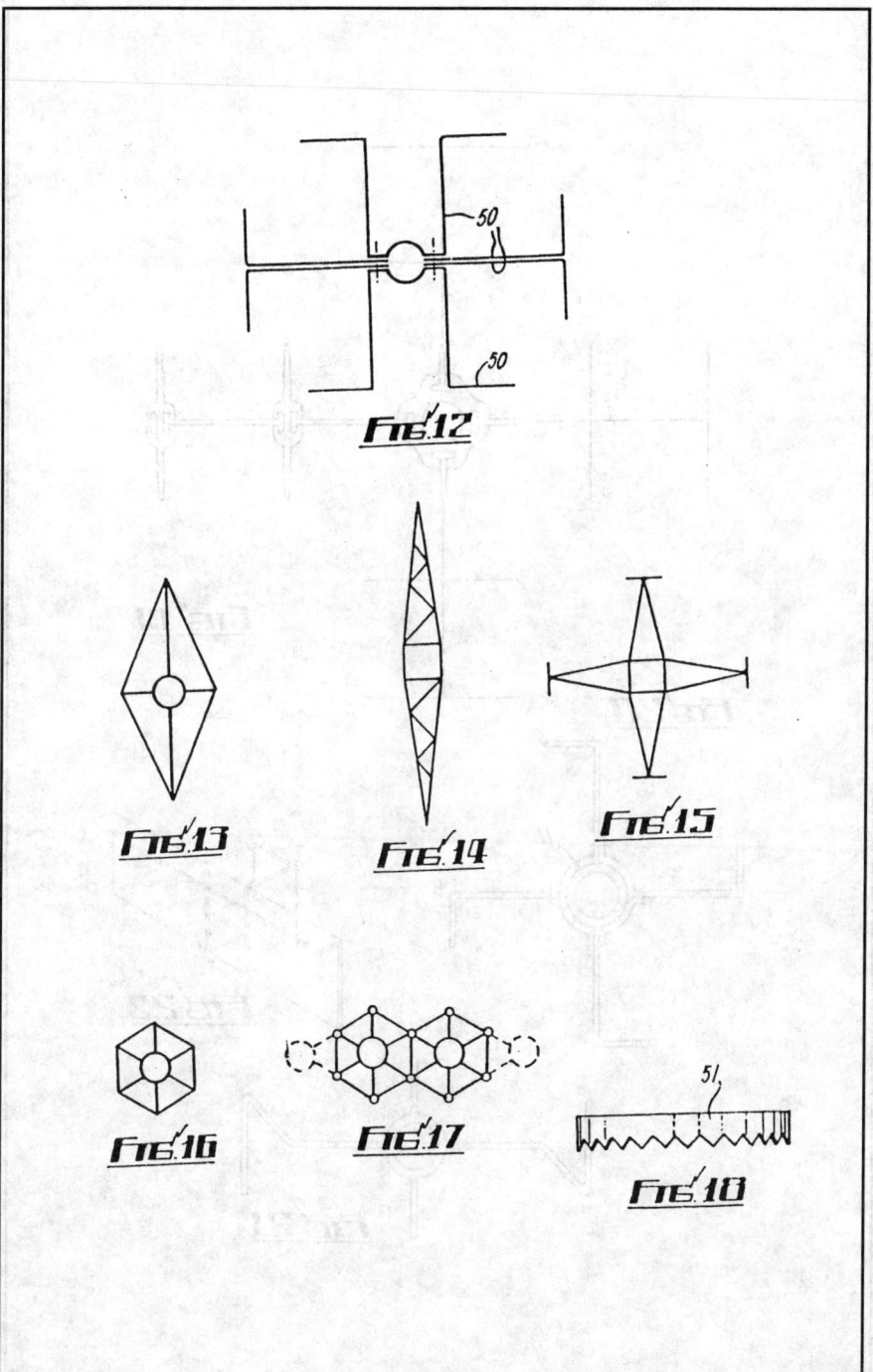

Fig. 12

Fig. 13

Fig. 14

Fig. 15

Fig. 16

Fig. 17

Fig. 18

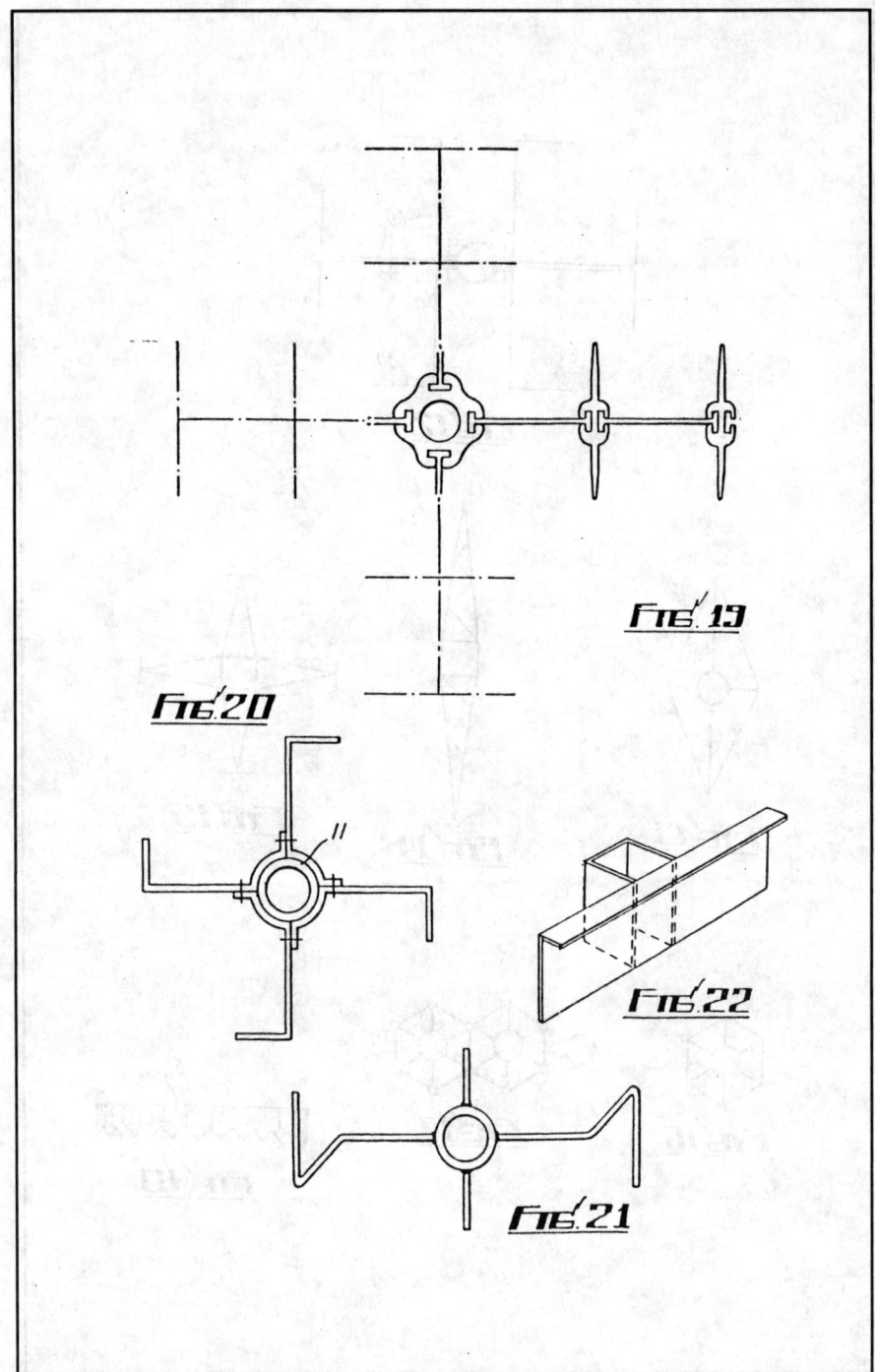

Fig. 19

Fig. 20

Fig. 22

Fig. 21

SPECIFICATION

Post support structure

5 The present invention relates to a structure which can be engaged with the ground to provide a support for a post which can support a sign or the like or can be part of a fence or similar arrangement.

10 Such structures are known, for example from the following prior patent specifications.

EP 11197 (SILBERNAGEL)
WO 80/2173 (TRAUFLER)
15 UK 2104935 (HOWSON)
UK 2068037 (KINGSMERE)
UK 2032486 (HUNTING)
1227920 (NUNEATON)
1112918 (COPPEL)
20 1098555 (BERAERT)

The structures disclosed in these documents all have drawbacks of various kinds. For example, simple steel sockets, although easy to sink, may well be driven in
25 at an angle to the vertical; straightening after sinking usually loosens the socket and encourages failure of the anchorage in use. Structures having integral ground-penetrating blades or ground engaging
30 flanges are bulky and relatively heavy and if not driven vertically are difficult to straighten without disturbing the ground sufficiently to weaken the anchorage.

An object of the present invention is to
35 provide an improved post supporting structure.

Accordingly the invention provides a ground engaging post support structure comprising a tube sunk into the ground to
40 provide a socket and a separate stabilizer surrounding and engaging the tube at ground level and including a plurality of arms extending extending outwardly of the tube and penetrating the ground to be
45 capable of applying a movement resisting force to the tube.

The invention provides a method of forming a post support structure comprising sinking a tube into the ground to form a
50 socket and subsequently arranging a separate stabilizer to engage the socket at ground level and compelling outwardly extending arms of the stabilizer into

engagement with the ground.
55 The invention will be described further, by way of example, with reference to the accompanying drawings, wherein;

Figure 1 is an elevation of a first preferred structure of the invention;
60 Figure 2 is a perspective view of a stabiliser of a structure of the invention;

Figure 2a illustrates a modification of the stabilizer of Figure 1 or 2;

Figure 3 is a perspective view of a further
65 stabilizer;

Figures 4, 5 and 6 are perspective views of components of a composite stabilizer;

Figure 7 is a perspective view of a further possible stabilizer;
70 Figure 8 shows a step in the sinking of a tube of a structure of the invention;

Figure 8a shows a variation wherein the lower end of the tube has an inwardly extending skirt;
75 Figure 9 shows the tube sunk, a post inserted and a stabilizer being added;

Figure 10 shows a further combination of tube and stabilizer;

Figure 11 shows another possible
80 stabilizer construction;

Figure 12 is a schematic plan view of yet another possible stabilizer;

Figures 13 to 16 show further possible composite stabilizer arrangements;
85 Figure 17 shows a network of interconnected composite arrangements;

Figure 18 is a side elevation of an annular outer stabilizer part;

Figure 19 shows schematically a further
90 variation of stabilzer;

Figure 20 shows a yet further possible stabilizer; and

Figures 21 and 22 show further forms of stabilizers.
95 Referring firstly to Figure 1, a preferred post-supporting structure 10 of the invention is comprised of a tube 11 and a stabilizer 12. The tube 11 is driven into the ground by means of drift or podger (Figure
100 8) and forms an upright socket for receipt of the lower end of a post. The tube 11 will normally be sunk vetically for supporting a post for a notice board or fence, but for some purposes, for example a sound-deflecting
105 fence, the tube may be sunk at an angle to

the vertical. For a tube about 35 or 50 mm in diameter or side and normal soil the tube can be driven directly into the ground. For larger sizes, e.g 75 mm diameter or side, an auger

5   or the like may be used to pre-drill a receiving hole somewhat smaller than the tube cross-section. The tube 11 may be circular in cross-section, rectangular, or of any other convenient shape. The tube 11 is

10 sunk so that its upper end is level with or just above the ground. A projection of the upper end above the ground protects a wooden post against rotting at ground level.

After sinking, the orientation of the tube

15 10 can be checked and adjusted to be vertical if necessary. Next the stabliser 12 is assembled to the tube 10 with a central boss 13 thereof closely surrounding the tube 10. Arms 14 of the stabilizer 12 extend

20 outwardly and are in the form of vertical blades 15, having cross-pieces 16, which can be of sheet metal and sharpened and/or serrated along their lower edges. The stabilizer 12 is pressed or driven

25 downwardly to penetrate the ground and form a firm anchorage which resists tilting of the tube 11 due to wind or other forces applied by the post. The fact that the stabilizer 12 is separate from the tube 11

30 means that the stabilizer 12 can be very easily installed without disturbing the tube 11. The central boss or collar 13 can be of a size to effect compaction of loosened soil closely surrounding the tube 11 to make a

35 more secure support.

Figure 1 shows the bottom of the tube 11 in the form of a conical point 17 integral with the tube 11. This can be omitted in some circumstances, for example in light soils

40 when the tube can be easily sunk whilst simply surrounding a drift or podger. Alternatively, a cap can be provided or the tube can have an inwardly extending skirt. These possibilities will be described later.

45 Figure 2 shows a cruciform stabilizer comparable in construction to that of Figure 1.

Figure 2A shows a different type of stablizer 18 have a central boss 19 and a

50 plurality of radial arms 20 having cross pieces 21 and sockets 22 for receipt of additional stabilizer parts.

Alternative configurations of sockets may be provided to cooperate with triangular,

55 cylindrical, Z-shaped or other shaped additional stabilizer parts.

Figure 3 shows a stabilizer similar to that of figure 1 but having additional cross-pieces.

60 Figures 4, 5 and 6 show components of a composite stabilizer comprising: a boss 23 having a central bore 24 and angularly spaced T-slots 25; an arm 26 having T-shaped ends 27; and a cross piece 28

65 having T-slots 29. A plurality of arms 26 can be assembled to boss 23 and have cross pieces 28 attached thereto. The individual components of this stabilizer can be driven into the ground separately, requiring less

70 force individually and not disturbing other parts of the stabilizer.

The slots 25 and ends 27 may have different configurations to those shown in the Figures. For example, the ends may be

75 cylindrical, spirally coiled, Z-shaped or triangular, the slots 25 being correspondingly shaped to engage the ends. Furthermore the boss is not restricted to provisions of four slots.

80 A kit of interchangeable components may be provided in accordance with this invention. Diffferent arrangements of stablizers may be constructed *in situ* from such a kit without any need for elaborate

85 tooling.

Figure 7 shows a stabilizer 30 having a boss 31, to radial arms 32 and spiked cross pieces 33. Spikes 44 of cross pieces 33 can be driven into the ground when the stabilizer

90 30 has been placed over the tube 11.

Figure 8 illustrates a tube 11 being sunk into the ground 12 by means of a drift or podger 35 having a conical point 36. The lower end of the tube 11 has been closed by

95 a sheet metal cap 37 which need not have any great strength, but sufficient to prevent earth from entering between podger 35 and tube 11. Figure 8a illustrates in a cross-sectional sketch how the lower end of

100 the tube wall 38 can have an inwardly extending skirt 39 for the same purpose and for use with a podger 40 having a point 41.

Figure 9 shows a post 42 installed into the

socket formed by the tube 11 and having a schematically illustrated stabilizer 43 being installed.

Figure 10 shows a modified structure comprising a tube 11 and a stabilizer 47 comprised of a pair of inverted U-shaped sheet metal members 43 each having a flat horizonal body 44 and depending limbs 45. Lateral edges of the bodies 44 can have depending flanges 46. The structure of Figure 10 is used in precisely the same way as the earlier described structures.

Figure 11 shows in plan view, a further possible stabilizer construction 48 made of sheet metal components 49.

Figure 12 shows a stabilizer in plan view made from sheet metal blade-like components 50 united by bolts or by welding.

Figures 13 to 16 show further possible composite stabilizers consisting of lattices assembled from separate components in the manner described in relation to Figures 4, 5 and 6.

Figure 17 shows a network of components assembled to form a chain of stabilizers. The network not only serves to support a line of posts but also serves to stablise the soil in the vicinity of the posts. This is useful to restrain erosion on embankments and in other exposed locations.

The arms may form a modular interconnected lattice secured laterally to the surface of the ground by embedment and by tines (e.g. spikes, screws, spades etc), which extend through the lattice into the ground from the surface. Such a lattice may provide a surfaceable or mechanically mountable ground gripping mat of any size that may be required.

Figure 18 shows an annular component 51 which can form a periphery of such a lattice, being united by arms (not shown) to a central boss like that of Figure 4; Figure 19 shows a modified form of composite stabilizer made up from the components of Figures 4 to 6; and Figures 20 and 21 show variations of stablizers comparable in construction and function to those of Figures 11 and 12.

Figure 22 shows a further variation which may be easily constructed from sheet material. A horizontal flange is provided to strengthen the stabilizer against lateral forces.

The arms of stabilizers in accordance with this invention may be arranged to be rigid or flexible. A degree of flexibility is useful for many applications, because lateral forces applied to the post do not usually dislodge the ends of the arms. The flexibility of the latter serves to return the post to the original position when the force has been removed.

Post supporting structures in accordance with this invention may be constructed from metal, plastics, or other materials. In particular the different components of the structures may be composed of different materials according to their mechanical requirements.

The intention is not restricted to the embodiments illustrated and described above; modifications and alterations of detail can be made within the scope of the invention defined in the appendent claims.

CLAIMS

1. A ground engaging post support structure comprising a tube sunk into the ground to provide a socket and a separate stablizer surrounding and engaging the tube at ground level and including a plurality of arms extending outwardly of the tube and penetrating the ground to be capable of applying a movement resisting force to the tube.

2. A structure as claimed in claim 1 wherein the tube is sunk into the ground in a vertical position.

3. A structure as claimed in claim 1 or 2 wherein the tube is circular in cross-section.

4. A structure as claimed in claim 1 or 2 wherein the tube is rectangular in cross-section.

5. A structure as claimed in any preceding claim wherein the lower end of the tube is shaped to make ground penetration easier.

6. A structure as claimed in claim 5 wherein the lower end of the wall of the tube is inwardly and downwardly inclined.

7. A structure as claimed in any of claims 1 to 4 wherein the lower end of the tube has a pointed cap.

8. A structure as claimed in claim 7, wherein the cap is of sheet metal.

9. A structure as claimed in any preceding claim wherein the arms have spikes extending downwards into engagement with the ground.

10. A structure as claimed in any of claims 1 to 8, wherein the arms are in the form of or incorporate vertical blades.

11. A structure as claimed in claim 10 wherein the or each blade is serrated.

12. A structure as claimed in claim 10 or 11 wherein one arm has one or more cross pieces in the form of a blade or blades.

13. A structure as claimed in any preceding claim wherein the stabilizer includes a central collar having a through-hole for the tube and operative, upon installation of the stabilizer to compact earth immediately surrounding the top of the tube.

14. A structure as claimed in claim 10, 11 or 12 wherein each blade is generally L-shaped in cross-section, having a major vertical limb in the ground and a minor horizontal limb on the ground surface limiting ground penetration of the vertical limb.

15. A structure as claimed in any of claims 1 to 8, wherein the stablizer comprises a plurality of inverted-u-shaped members of sheet material having a major horizontal body centrally perforate and surrounding the tube and minor downwardly extending and ground engaging blade-fform limbs.

16. A structure as claimed in claim 15, wherein two such members are provided and arranged at right angles to each other.

17. A structure as claimed in claim 15 or 16, wherein one or both lateral edges of one or more of the members has a short vertical skirt.

18. A structure as claimed in any preceding claim, wherein two or more of the arms are interconnected by one or more further ground-engaging integrers to form a lattice.

19. A structure as claimed in claim 18 wherein the further integers are separate from and attached to the arms.

20. A structure as claimed in claim 18 or 19 wherein one such further integer extends between the arms of two spaced apart structures to form a link between adjacent structures in a fence line of posts.

21. A method of forming a post support structure comprising sinking a tube into the ground to form a socket and subsequently arranging a separate stabilizer to engage the socket at ground level and compelling outwardly extending arms of the stablizer into engagement with the ground.

22. A method as claimed in claim 21 wherein the tube is sunk directly into the ground.

23. A method as claimed in claim 21, wherein a hole is drilled before sinking the tube.

24. A method as claimed in claim 23 wherein the hole has a smaller cross-section than the tube.

25. A method as claimed in any of claims 21 to 24 wherein the tube has its lower side walls inwardly and downwardly inclined and driving is effected to using a pointed drift within the tube.

26. A method as claimed in any of claims 21 to 24 wherein the lower end of the tube has a pointed cap and driving is effected using a drift having a point complementary to the cap.

27. A method as claimed in any of claims 21 to 26 including the step of changing the disposition of the tube after sinking and before installing the stablizer.

28. A method as claimed in any of claims 21 to 27 wherein the stablizer has a central boss which is driven into the ground upon installation to compact earth immediately surrounding the tube.

29. A post supporting structure substantially as hereinbefore described with reference to and as illustrated in the accompanying drawings.

30. A method of making a post supporting structure substantially as hereinbefore described.

Printed in the United Kingdom for
Her Majesty's Stationery Office, Dd 8818935, 1984, 4235.
Published at The Patent Office, 25 Southampton Buildings, London, WC2A 1AY, from which copies may be obtained.

Appendix 2
Protecting Form and Appearance —
Reciprocal Protection Rules

COPYRIGHT WORKS

The two basic ways in which a copyright work can qualify for protection is for the author to meet the nationality requirements or to first publish the copyright works in (or in the case of broadcasts and cable programmes to transmit from) the UK or a country given reciprocal protection.

The transmission/first publication requirement is the simpler to understand and less legally technical of the two. The transmission/first-publication requirement is also in practice more significant simply because commercial people are likely to do things like putting products on the market without knowing about complicated legal technicalities such as the copyright nationality requirements. Furthermore,

- if the rules for the transmission/first-publication requirements are followed then the requirements about the author's nationality become less significant

The old law versus the new

The rules for works under the 56 Act are generally similar to those under the 88 Act but there are some differences. Additionally

- works protected by copyright before 1 August 1989 are deemed to satisfy the requirements of the 88 Act (88 Act, sch. 1, para. 35)

However, this does not do away with the 56 Act requirements. It means that:

- the 56 Act requirements still apply because they need to be referred to in order to ascertain whether the the works were protected by copyright before 1 August 1989 in order to be protected afterwards

The nationality requirements

A copyright work can satisfy the nationality requirements if the author is a 'qualified person' (56 Act) or a 'qualifying person' (88 Act). The following is a brief summary of the first three ways in which the author can be treated as a 'qualified/qualifying person' under the 56 Act (s. 1) and the 88 Act (s. 154):

- the author falls into one of certain specified categories of British nationals
- the author was domiciled or resident
  - in the United Kingdom or
  - in a foreign country which obtains reciprocal treatment under UK law for copyright purposes
- a corporation incorporated
  - under UK law or
  - under the law of a foreign country which obtains reciprocal treatment under UK law for copyright purposes

Alteration of reciprocal protection
It is always possible for the categories of persons given reciprocal protection or the countries afforded reciprocal protection to be extended by what is called an 'order in Council'. This can be done by virtue of s. 159 of the 88 Act.

Reciprocal protection can also be cancelled for certain countries and nationals. This can be done also by order in Council under s. 160 of the 88 Act. Copyright is unique in this respect because there is no corresponding express provision made in any of the legislation concerning rights in performances, design rights (including design right in semiconductor chip designs) or registered designs. Thus, *do not assume that the list of countries at the end of this appendix is comprehensive.*

When do the nationality requirements have to be met and is first publication an alternative?

Literary, dramatic, musical and artistic works
The provisions concerning when literary, dramatic, musical and artistic works must meet the nationality requirements are the most complicated. Fortunately, the relevant time for the author to meet the nationality requirements is the same under the 56 and 88 Acts so at least one level of additional complexity is avoided.

If the work is unpublished then the author must be a qualified/qualifying person:

- when the work was made or
- over a substantial part of the time when the work was made (56 Act, ss. 2(1) and 3(2); 88 Act, s. 154(4))

If the work is published but did not previously meet the nationality requirements when it was an unpublished work then it can still qualify for protection in three different ways on first publication:

- *first publication* has to take place in the UK or a country given reciprocal protection (56 Act, ss. 2(2) and 3(3); 88 Act, s. 155(1))
- if the author becomes a qualified/qualifying person at the time of first publication (56 Act, ss. 2(2) and 3(3); 88 Act, s. 154(4))
- if when first publication takes place the author had become a qualified/qualifying person immediately before death (56 Act, ss. 2(2) and 3(3); 88 Act, s. 154(4))

(The concept of what amounts to 'first publication' is dealt with later in this appendix.)

Typographical editions of published works
The nationality requirements for typographical editions of published literary, dramatic and musical works can be met in two ways. If the publisher is a qualified/qualifying person on first publication the requirements are met. Alternatively, if first publication takes place in the UK or a country afforded reciprocal protection the work can qualify for protection (56 Act s. 15(1); 88 Act s. 154(5) and 155).

Sound recordings
For a sound recording to meet the nationality requirements the author must be a qualified/qualifying person when the recording is made (56 Act s. 12(1); 88 Act s. 154(5)). Alternatively, if first publication occurs in the UK or a country given reciprocal protection then the sound recording will obtain protection on first publication regardless of whether the author meets the nationality requirements (56 Act, s. 12(2); 88 Act s. 155).

Films
A film meets the nationality requirements if the author (88 Act) or maker (56 Act,) is a qualified/qualifying person at the time it is made (56 Act, s. 13(1); 88 Act, s. 154(5)). Alternatively, if first publication takes place in the UK or a country afforded reciprocal protection then the film qualifies for protection (56 Act s. 13(2); 88 Act, s. 155(1)).

Broadcasts
Under the 56 Act there were no nationality requirements to be met by broadcasts. This was simply because only the BBC or ITA could own copyright in broadcasts. Consequently, there was no need for any nationality requirements under which foreign broadcasts could obtain copyright protection. Under the 88 Act, a broadcast obtains protection if the author is a qualifying person (88 Act, s. 154(1)). The author must be a qualifying person at the time the broadcast is made (88 Act, s. 154(5)). As an alternative, a broadcast can obtain protection if it is made from a place in the UK or a country which is afforded reciprocal protection under the 88 Act (s. 155).

Cable programmes
Under the 56 Act the only way a cable programme could meet the nationality requirements was if the provider of the cable programme service in which the

cable programme was included was a qualified person under the 56 Act (56 Act, s. 14A(1)). For this to apply the 56 Act *also required* the cable programme service to be provided either in the UK or in a country afforded reciprocal protection.

Under the 88 Act a cable programme obtains protection first if the author is a qualifying person (88 Act, s. 154) regardless of where the cable programme service is provided. The second way in which a cable programme can obtain protection under the 88 Act is for the cable programme to be sent from a place in the UK or a country afforded reciprocal protection.

Qualifying by first publication/transmission

As can be seen from the above

- an *alternative* to the authors meeting the nationality requirements is for a work to be *first* published in the UK or a country covered by the 56 or 88 Acts

- this obviates the need for any of the authors to meet the nationality requirements on first publication or at all

However,

- if a work is first published in the wrong country it cannot obtain copyright protection by virtue of first publication

The nationality requirements would have to be met on first publication in such a case. Just in case first publication is made in the wrong country, there is a 30-day period of grace (88 Act, s. 155(3)). Provided publication takes place in a country afforded reciprocal protection within 30 days, the previous publication will not affect the qualification for protection. Additionally, unauthorised publication does not count as publication (88 Act, s. 175), so if someone publishes without permission, a later authorised publication in an appropriate country will still be effective to ensure reciprocal copyright protection can be obtained.

What is publication

Publication means

- the issue of copies of the work to the public (88 Act, s. 175)

This applies to all copyright subject-matter, whether created before or on or after 1 August 1989.

Publishing a cable programme

How can a copy of a cable programme, or even a broadcast be issued to the public? The answer lies in the definitions of what can be considered a copy and this is covered below.

Publishing a building

In the case of a work of architecture which is a building, construction of the building is to be treated as equivalent to publication. The same applies to an artistic work which is 'incorporated' into a building (88 Act, s. 175(3)). However, this rule only applies where the construction of the building began after 1 August 1989 (88 Act, sch. 1, para. 45).

Publication must satisfy reasonable public demand

Publication must be intended to satisfy reasonable public demand. In one case under the 56 Act, solely for the purpose of publishing to obtain copyright protection, six copies of a song were put on sale, one copy was put in the British Museum and four were made available to university libraries. One copy of the song was filed in a London office of the publishers. The song was not advertised or promoted initially.

The song concerned was entitled 'You Made Me Love You (I Didn't Want To Do It)'. The 12 copies were sufficient as:

- the intention to satisfy reasonable public demand if it arose existed at the time of publication.

The song later became highly successful and large sales were made (*Francis, Day & Hunter* v *Feldman & Co.* [1914] 2 Ch 728).

What is a copy?

A copy of an artistic work includes

- a three-dimensional copy of a two-dimensional work and vice versa (88 Act, s. 17(3))

So making cuddly toys based on drawings of a cartoon character and issuing them to the public amounts to publishing the drawing.

A copy also includes:

- a 'transient' copy (88 Act, s. 17(6))

In relation to cable programmes a 'copy' includes:

- a photograph of the whole or any substantial part of an image forming part of a cable programme (88 Act, s. 17(4))

Thus, a copy of a cable programme made on videotape is a copy even though most people would think of this as a film. Furthermore, if the cable programme consisted of a film then the videotape copy would be treated as a copy both of the film and of the cable programme. The position in relation to broadcasts and films is the same.

Electronic Publishing

Publication includes:

- making a literary, dramatic, musical or artistic work available to the public by means of an electronic retrieval system (88 Act, s. 175)

This means that publication by inclusion in a system like a computer database qualifies.

Memory chips, magnetic and optical computer tapes, discs
The term 'copy' in relation to a literary, dramatic, musical or artistic work includes:

- recording the work in any material form and this includes storing the work in any medium by electronic means (88 Act, s. 17(2))

Thus, issuing copies of these particular kinds of works on magnetic or optical disc, or stored in semiconductor chips can amount to publication.

What is not publication

The following acts do not count as first publication.

General provisions for all works

- unauthorised publication does not count (88 Act, s. 175)

In this context something is unauthorised if it is done without the permission of the copyright owner (88 Act, s. 178).

Literary, dramatic, musical and artistic works
Performing a literary, dramatic or musical work or broadcasting it or including it in a cable programme service does not amount to publication (88 Act, s. 175(4). So:

- to amount to publication, the issue of copies is essenial

The same applies to broadcasting or including an artistic work in a cable programme service (88 Act, s. 175(4)). The artistic work is not published by this means. However, it should be noted in relation to electronic publishing that where a cable programme service is an electronic retrieval system like a computer database system, then including a literary, dramatic, musical or artistic work in it *can amount to publication* (88 Act, s. 175(4)).
Exhibiting an artistic work is not publication (88 Act, s. 175(4)).
Publishing a film which includes an artistic work is not publication of the artistic work (88 Act, s. 175(4)).
Issuing copies to the public, in the form of graphic works or photographs, of certain kinds of artistic works does not amount to publication of the artistic works. The types of artistic works concerned are works of architecture in the form of buildings or models for buildings, sculptures and works of artistic craftsmanship (88 Act, s. 175(4)).

Sound recordings and films
Playing or showing a sound recording or film in public or broadcasting it or including it in a cable programme service does not amount to publication of the sound recording or film (88 Act, s. 175(4)).

MORAL RIGHTS

There are no nationality requirements to be satisfied for authors or directors in relation to moral rights. There are no nationality requirements to be satisfied for the right to privacy in photographs and films.

PERFORMANCES

There are essentially two different sets of rights in performances:

- the performer's rights and
- the recording rights

Because there are two sets of rights there are also two sets of nationality requirements:

- those to be satisfied by the performer in order for the performer's rights to be recognised under UK law and
- those to be satisfied by the people having the recording rights for the recording rights to be recognised by UK law

Nationality requirements of the performer

For the purposes of the 88 Act a performance meets the reciprocal protection requirements if it is:

- made by a 'qualifying individual' or
- if it takes place in a 'qualifying country' (88 Act, s. 181)

Thus, protection can be given to a performance on the basis of the performer's nationality, which is similar to copyright. Alternatively and by analogy with copyright a performance can obtain protection on the basis of the country in which the performance takes place.

'Qualifying individual' and a 'qualifying country'

For the purposes of rights in a performance, a 'qualifying individual' is

- a citizen or a subject of or
- an individual resident in

certain countries — 'a qualifying country' (88 Act, s. 206)

As regards subject and citizen status for the UK and colonies, the performer must be either:

- a British citizen or
- a British Dependent Territories citizen

'Qualifying countries' are defined as including:

- the UK,
- member States of the EEC and
- any other country to which reciprocal protection is extended

A current list of countries to which reciprocal protection is extended for the purposes of rights in performances is set out at the end of this appendix. Remember that the list can be added to so do not consider that it is comprehensive.

Nationality requirements for recording rights

Recording rights are recognised under UK law if the person who is the prospective owner of the rights is a 'qualifying person'. This applies:

- regardless of whether a performer meets the nationality requirements and
- regardless of the country in which the performance takes place

The most important point to note is that:

- recording rights are obtained under the 88 Act only if there is an exclusive recording contract in existence between the prospective owner of the recording rights and the performer

There is a fundamental distinction which must be understood. The distinction is between:

- the rights which arise under the contract and
- the rights that arise because they are conferred by law under the 88 Act

The contractual rights between a performer and, say, a recording company are legal rights which exist irrespective of any of the 88 Act's provisions. The performer can enforce the contractual rights against the other parties to the contract and vice versa but:

- the contract itself does not entitle the performer or any of the other parties to it to take action against the world at large for infringing recording rights

However, once an exclusive recording contract exists, and provided the person with the benefit of the recording rights is a 'qualifying person', then the 88 Act confers rights (recording rights) on that person which can be enforced against anyone in the UK.

What is an exclusive recording contract?
Exclusive rights arise where the performer has entered into a contract giving someone the right to record one or more performances *to the exclusion of everyone else*. This also must be to the exclusion of the performer (88 Act, s. 185(1)).

The rights follow the contract not the person
Where the person who has the benefit of the exclusive recording contract sells the contractual rights under the contract then the person who purchases the contractual rights also gets the recording rights conferred by the 88 Act (provided the purchaser or acquirer satisfies the nationality requirements).

What if the nationality requirements are not met?
If the person who has the exclusive recording contract does not satisfy the nationality requirements this is not necessarily fatal. The 88 Act provides an alternative way for the recording rights to be recognised. The person who has the exclusive recording contract can give someone else a licence (permission) to record and commercially exploit some or all performances or just to exploit pre-existing recordings of performances. Provided whoever has acquired the licence satisfies the nationality requirements then:

- *that person* will be recognised as having the recording rights conferred by the 88 Act

However, whoever is potentially entitled to the recording rights, that person must be a 'qualifying person' (88 Act, s. 185). A 'qualifying person' is either:

- a 'qualifying individual' or
- a legal entity formed under the law of the UK or a 'qualifying country' (88 Act, s. 206)

The person or legal entity concerned must also satisfy a second requirement. That requirement is:

- to have a place of business in *any* qualifying country at which substantial business activity is carried on (88 Act, s. 206)

Examples

The performer
Assume a performer is from country A that does not get reciprocal protection. Assume a performance by the performer is carried out in country B which is also not a qualifying country. Therefore, as the performance does not take place in a qualifying country and the performer is not a qualifying individual:

- the performer obtains no rights under UK law in relation to controlling recordings and broadcasts of the performer's performances

The exclusive recording company
Now assume the performer enters into an exclusive recording contract with a recording company and the recording company is incorporated under the law of A. A is not a qualifying country but say the recording company has a place of business in France and substantial business is carried on there. France is a qualifying country.

However, as only the second of the nationality requirements is met (substantial business carried on through a place of business in a qualifying country) and not the first (formed under the law of a qualifying country) the recording company may not have recording rights recognised under UK law.

The recording company grants a licence
As a further alternative, assume that the recording company in the previous example either sells all its exclusive recording rights to a German recording company or it gives it a licence (under its rights in the exclusive recording

contract) to record performances and commercially exploit the recording. In either case, as the German recording company is:

- formed under the laws of a qualifying country and
- provided it has a place of business in Germany, France or some other qualifying country
- where substantial business activity is carried on

then it will be a qualifying person.

This will mean that as far as UK law is concerned, the German company will have the statutory recording rights conferred by the 88 Act.

What if there is no exclusive recording contract?

There is something special about the statutory rights a performer has in performances:

- the rights the 88 Act confers on the performer are personal to the performer

This means that the performer cannot sell the statutory rights to anyone else. Although the performer can enter into exclusive recording contracts with others, the performer cannot transfer the statutory performer's rights given under the 88 Act. This also means that, apart from those who may inherit the rights of the performer on his or her death,

- the performer is the only person who can enforce the performer's rights

Any person having the benefit of the exclusive recording contract with the performer must qualify in his or her own right in order to obtain the benefit of the recording rights conferred by the 88 Act on *people having rights in exclusive recording contracts*.

NATIONALITY REQUIREMENTS FOR DESIGNS OF PRODUCTS

Copyright protection for product designs

The provisions concerning reciprocal protection for copyright works which embody designs are the same as for copyright works (see above).

Design right protection

Because design right is not dependent upon registration and because it potentially applies to all mass-produced goods (including things like the shape of packaging), it is likely to be the most significant of the rights for protecting designs in the UK.

One other factor makes design right of potentially greater significance than the other rights:

- design right is unique to the UK

There is no comparable right covered by any international conventions. This means:

- there is unlikely to be any reciprocal or corresponding protection under the laws of other countries for UK designs

The equivalent of registered design protection would have to be relied on.

Few foreign countries get reciprocal protection
What is far more important in relation to the protection of foreign designs in the UK is that:

- the range of countries for which reciprocal protection is afforded is far narrower than for comparable rights like copyright and registered design protection.

A current list of countries is set out at the end of this appendix.

Protection for foreign designs by first marketing
The only way for the many foreign designs to obtain protection is for first marketing to be carried out in the EEC. Protection can be afforded provided certain conditions are met.

UK distributors should note the position
As a consequence of the potentially more limited protection for foreign designs under design right, where rights to distribute a product of foreign design are obtained, reciprocal protection may be important to ensure that others in the UK are not free to copy it.

How can you tell a design is protected?
For those who need to copy to compete, it may prove invaluable to know whether they can copy freely. Unfortunately for those who need to copy:

- the 88 Act does not provide any direct means of ascertaining whether a design is or is not protected by design right

It can be a question of educated guesswork on the basis of knowledge about what designs can and cannot be protected and knowledge about where a product originated from. Clearly also, when buying or obtaining rights in a foreign design, care should be taken in this area.

Indigenous and EEC designs qualify
The nationality requirements are complicated, but one thing is clear in relation to UK and EEC designs created by employees acting in the course of their employment and in relation to designs created under commissions:

- if a design is created under a commission from a company formed under UK law or the law of any EEC country or
- is created by the employees of such a company in the course of their employment

then the design is likely to be covered by the reciprocal protection provisions of the 88 Act.

This is so provided the company is substantially carrying on business in the UK or any country covered by the reciprocal protection provisions. In other words:

- there may be problems for designs from countries outside of the UK and the rest of the EEC, but
- indigenous UK and EEC designs should be covered (provided of course that the information is available to prove the nationality requirements are met)

Ways of obtaining reciprocal protection
There are four basic ways in which a design can qualify under the reciprocal protection provisions of the 88 Act for design right protection:

- the designer is a 'qualifying individual'
- the designer is commissioned by or employed by a 'qualifying person'
- if neither of the above apply then protection may be afforded if articles made to the design are first marketed by a 'qualifying person'
- reciprocal protection is extended to nationals of further countries

The nationality requirements for the designer
The nationality requirements to be met by the designer are only relevant to obtaining protection if the designer *did not* create the design either:

- under a commission, or
- in the course of employment (88 Act, s. 218(1))

If the design was not commissioned or created by an employee, protection may be afforded to a design if the designer is a 'qualifying individual' (88 Act, s. 218).

A 'qualifying individual' is someone who is either:

- a citizen of or a subject of a 'qualifying country' or
- someone *habitually* resident in a 'qualifying country' (88 Act, s. 217)

As regards subject and citizen status for the UK and colonies, the designer must be either:

- a British citizen or
- a British Dependent Territories citizen

'Qualifying Countries' are defined as including:

- the UK
- member States of the EEC
- any other country to which reciprocal protection is extended

A current list of countries to which reciprocal protection is extended is set out at the end of this appendix. Citizenship and being a subject of a country normally depends upon the local law of the country concerned. This aspect will not be considered in detail in this book.

What 'habitual' residence amounts to will be up to the courts to decide but it suggests something more than just occasional or temporary residence or the place where someone eats and sleeps. The requirement of *habitual* residence indicates more than temporary residence or the residence of, say, a person during a visit to another country.

When must the designer be a 'qualifying individual'?
A further problem with relying on the designer's residence or nationality to obtain design right protection is that it is not clear when the designer must be a qualifying individual or a qualifying person. If the designer's status is being relied on to obtain design right protection, all the 88 Act says is that:

- a design obtains protection if the designer *is* a qualifying individual (or in the case of a computer-generated work, a qualifying person)

Advice
When rights in designs are being obtained:

- try to ensure the designs were made by EEC nationals or by permanent residents of EEC countries

otherwise

- ensure the first marketing requirements are met
- keep business records of the nationality, citizenship and residence of designers

If rights in designs are obtained, it is prudent to try to

- ensure suitable contractually binding obligations are obtained from the person selling the rights to provide assistance later if required in proving a design qualifies for protection

At the time of purchase it would be prudent also to try to

- ensure that the seller of the rights meets the relevant nationality requirements if the design was commissioned by the seller or made by an employee of the seller

It would also be prudent to

- check who the designer is and whether that person meets the relevant nationality requirements

The nationality requirements for the designer's employer or the commissioner of the design
A design meets the nationality requirements if it is created:

- in the course of a commission from, or

- in the course of employment with

a 'qualifying person' (88 Act, s. 219)

If the design is a joint commission, the nationality requirements will be met if any one of the persons giving the commission is a qualifying person. The position is similar if there are joint employers. However, in either case only the qualifying persons will be entitled to design right (88 Act, s. 219).

A 'qualifying person' is:

- a 'qualifying individual', or
- legal entity formed under UK law or the law of a qualifying country

In the latter case the legal entity must carry on substantial business activity from a place of business in a qualifying country (88 Act, s. 217). In assessing whether business activity is substantial, no account is taken of dealings in goods which stay, at all material times, outside the qualifying country where the place of business is situated (88 Act, s. 217).

First-marketing nationality requirements

A design can only meet the 'first-marketing' nationality requirements if it does not already meet the nationality requirements laid down for:

- the designer, or
- the designer's employer, or
- the person commissioning the design (88 Act, s. 220(1))

Thus, this section is only relevant if the requirements dealt with in the previous sections have *not* been met, *but*

- it is likely to be of considerable importance as a 'back-stop' way of ensuring the nationality requirements are met

So what are the first-marketing nationality requirements?

First:

- articles made to the design must be first marketed by a qualifying person. (A 'qualifying person' has the same meaning as set out in the immediately preceding section.)

In turn the qualifying person:

- must have the *exclusive rights* to put the articles on the market in the UK.

This means that the qualifying person must either be:

- the design right owner, or
- the exclusive licensee, or
- the exclusive distributor *for the UK*

This applies regardless of where the articles are first marketed, even if the exclusive licensee or distributor first markets the articles *outside* the UK.

Additionally, first marketing must take place either:

- in the UK or
- in a member State of the EEC, or
- in essence what are UK colonies.

'Marketing' means:

- selling,
- hiring or
- offering for sale or hire

in the course of business.

However, no account is to be taken of marketing which is merely colourable and not intended to satisfy reasonable public demand (88 Act, s. 263(1)). The 'merely colourable' condition and the condition that there must be an *intention* to satisfy reasonable public demand will be likely to have the same meaning as for copyright.

Reciprocal protection can be extended to further countries

Reciprocal protection can be extended from time to time to further countries so the list of countries at the end of this appendix is subject to change and must not be considered comprehensive.

Computer-generated designs and the nationality requirements

For computer-generated designs, if the nationality requirements of the designer are relied on, the designer must be a 'qualifying person'. The designer of a computer-generated design is 'the person by whom the arrangements necessary for the creation of the design are made' (88 Act, s. 214).

For the other ways of satisfying the nationality requirements, whether a design is computer-generated or not is of no relevance.

Registered design nationality requirements

The scheme of reciprocal protection for registered designs is quite different to copyright, performers' rights and design right. Anyone from any country may apply to register a registrable design in the UK regardless of whether that person's country permits any similar kind of protection locally for UK designs (RDA 49, s. 1(2)):

- there are no nationality requirements

Designs for which reciprocal protection is available

The reciprocal protection applies to designs for which an application for registration has been made in a 'convention country'. In essence, certain countries have broadly similar arrangements for the protection of certain kinds of designs by registration. These arrangements have, in general terms, arisen through the making of international agreements which have been implemented under the law of the countries concerned.

For reciprocal protection to apply:

- an application must be made in the UK within six months of the first foreign application for registration (RDA 49, s. 14(1))

The effect of the protection is twofold. First, if the foreign registrable design is used or disclosed in the UK within the six-month period this will not prevent it from being treated as new for the purposes of the UK registration. Secondly, the date of the first foreign application for registration operates as a priority date (RDA 49, s. 14(2)). The UK application to register the design is treated as having been made on the date of the first foreign application rather than on the date the application was actually made in the UK. This means that it will be given precedence over any similar applications for registration made in the UK by anyone else after the date of the first foreign registration. Furthermore, the later similar application made by someone else might not be treated as new.

This kind of protection also operates in reverse for UK designs in convention countries. UK designs should obtain a similar priority period of protection upon an application for registration being made in a foreign country following an application made in the UK. The exact form in which protection is given and the priority period will, of course, be subject to the local law of the country concerned and it must not be assumed this is the same as UK law.

Some designs are likely to fall within a class of designs relevant for UK defence purposes:

- it can be a criminal offence for anyone resident in the UK to apply for registration of such a design outside the UK without permission (RDA 49, s. 5)

This applies to anyone who is resident in the UK and not just resident UK nationals. It does not apply to anyone who is resident abroad, even UK nationals.

SEMICONDUCTOR CHIP PROTECTION

The nationality requirements for semiconductor chip designs are not exactly the same as for design right. The New Chip Regulations vary the 88 Act. There are still four basic ways in which a semiconductor chip design can qualify under the reciprocal protection provisions of the 88 Act for protection by design right:

- the designer is a 'qualifying individual'
- the designer is commissioned by or employed by a 'qualifying person'

if neither apply then:

- protection may be afforded if articles made to the design are first marketed by a 'qualifying person,
- reciprocal protection is extended to nationals of further countries

Nationality requirements for the designer

Again, the nationality requirements to be met by the designer are only relevant if the designer *did not* create the design under a commission or in the course of employment (88 Act, s. 218(1)). However, there is a change from the ordinary rules. Despite being an employee or commissioned to produce a semiconductor chip design the designer can be the owner of the design right. This is different to the normal design right ownership rules. If the designer is the *first owner* of the design right in the semiconductor topography the designer may need to meet the nationality requirements for the design to obtain protection (New Chip Regulations, reg. 4(3)).

Thus, if the designer is the owner of the design rights or was not commissioned or employed to produce it then protection may be afforded to a design if the designer is a 'qualifying individual' (88 Act, s. 218). The definition of 'qualifying individual' is the same as for design right but the countries concerned are changed. Fewer countries are covered currently. Only the UK and member States of the EEC count. In other words:

- fewer chip designs will qualify as protectable on the basis of the nationality requirements for the designer

The nationality requirements for the designer's employer or the commissioner of the design

A design meets the nationality requirements if it is created:

- in the course of a commission from, or
- in the course of employment with

a 'qualifying person' (88 Act, s. 219).

This is so provided the designer is not the first owner of design right (dealt with in the previous section). If there is more than one commissioner or employer the nationality requirements will be met if any of them are qualifying persons but only the qualifying persons will be entitled to design right (88 Act, s. 219).

A 'qualifying person' is either:

- a 'qualifying individual' or
- a legal entity having a place of business
  - in a qualifying country or in Gibraltar
  - at which substantial business activity is carried on
- or a person who comes within the description in the schedule to the New Chip Regulations (New Chip Regulations, reg. 4)

The descriptions in the schedule to the New Chip Regulations are set out at the end of this appendix.

There will be fewer qualifying persons because, first:

- the definition of 'qualifying individual' covers fewer nationalities namely:

— only British citizens, EEC citizens and subjects and anyone habitually resident in the UK or EEC

Secondly:

- the places at which a qualifying person must have a business are limited to just the UK and other EEC member States

Thirdly

- the list of people or other legal entities from non-UK or EEC countries who might be qualified persons is far shorter than for ordinary design right

In assessing whether business activity is substantial, no account is taken of dealings in goods which, at all material times, are outside the qualifying country where the place of business is situated (New Chip Regulations, reg. 4).

First-marketing nationality requirements

Like design right for ordinary designs, a semiconductor chip design can only meet the first-marketing nationality requirements if it does not already meet the nationality requirements laid down for:

- the designer
- the designer's employer or
- the person commissioning the design (88 Act, s. 220(1))

Thus, as with ordinary design right:

- this section only applies to semiconductor chip designs if they can only obtain protection by meeting the first marketing requirements
- *all* of the first marketing provisions must be met for a foreign semiconductor chip design to meet the requirements for protection. If they are not then protection is lost.

First, articles made to the design must be first marketed by a qualifying person. The qualifying person must have the exclusive rights to put the articles on the market in the whole of the EEC. This means that the qualifying person must either be:

- the design right owner or
- the exclusive licensee or
- the exclusive distributor *for all of the EEC*

Additionally:

- first marketing must take place in the UK or other EEC States. First marketing in any other place will not be adequate

'Marketing' has the same meaning as for ordinary design right. However, there is a specific provision concerning confidentiality. If an obligation to keep information about the semiconductor chip design confidential is imposed, then any sale or hire, or offer for sale or hire, in such a case is to be ignored for the purposes of deciding whether the design has been marketed (New Chip Regulations, reg. 7).

Reciprocal protection is extended to further countries

Reciprocal protection can be extended from time to time to further countries so the list of countries set out at the end of this appendix is subject to change.

Computer-generated semiconductor chip designs

For computer-generated semiconductor chip designs, if the nationality requirements of the designer are important for the purposes of obtaining protection, the designer must be a 'qualifying person'.

For the other ways of satisfying the nationality requirements, whether a design is computer-generated or not is of no relevance.

LISTS OF COUNTRIES AFFORDED RECIPROCAL PROTECTION

Copyright works

Not all countries obtain full copyright protection. There are four schedules setting out the countries to which different categories of protection apply (see below). Remember that, for any country protection is afforded to:

- nationals
- corporations incorporated under the law of the relevant country
- works first published in the relevant country

The following text is substantially taken from the text of statutory instrument 1989 No. 1293. In addition to the lists of countries, arts 1 to 7 of SI 1989 No. 1293 are set out in full. These articles specify in detail the extent to which UK copyright law is to be applied to the lists of countries set out in the Schedules.

Articles 1 to 7 of SI 1989 No. 1293

1.—(1) This order may be cited as the Copyright (Application to Other Countries) (No. 2) Order 1989 and shall come into force on 1st August 1989.

(2) In this order—

'the Act' means the Copyright, Designs and Patents Act 1988, and

'first published' shall be construed in accordance with section 155(3) of the Act.

2.—(1) In relation to literary, dramatic, musical and artistic works, films and the typographical arrangements of published editions, sections 153, 154 and 155 of the Act (qualification for copyright protection) apply in relation to—

(a) persons who are citizens or subjects of a country specified in schedule 1 to this order or are domiciled or resident there as they apply to persons who are British citizens or are domiciled or resident in the United Kingdom;

(b)   bodies incorporated under the law of such a country as they apply in relation to bodies incorporated under the law of a part of the United Kingdom; and

(c)   works first published in such a country as they apply in relation to works first published in the United Kingdom
but subject to paragraph (2) and article 5 below.

(2)   Copyright does not subsist—

(a)   in a literary, dramatic, musical or artistic work by virtue of section 154 of the Act as applied by paragraph (1) above (qualification by reference to author) if it was first published—

(i)   before 1st June 1957 (commencement of Copyright Act 1956), or

(ii)   before 1st August 1989 (commencement of part I of the Act) and at the material time (as defined in section 154(4)(b) of the Act) the author was not a relevant person; or

(b)   in any work by virtue of paragraph (1) above if—

(i)   a date is, or dates are, specified in schedule 1 to this order in respect of the only country or countries relevant to the work for the purposes of paragraph (1) above, and

(ii)   the work was first published before that date or (as the case may be) the earliest of those dates;
and for the purposes of subparagraph (a)(ii) of this paragraph, a 'relevant person' is a Commonwealth citizen, a British protected person, a citizen or subject of any country specified in schedule 1 to this order, or a person resident or domiciled in the United Kingdom, another country to which the relevant provisions of part I of the Act extend or (subject to article 5 below) a country specified in schedule 1 to this order.

(3)   Where copyright subsists in a work by virtue of paragraph (1) above, the whole of part I of the Act (including schedule 1 to the Act) applies in relation to the work, save that in relation to an artistic work consisting of the design of a typeface—

(a)   section 54(2) (articles for producing material in particular typeface) does not apply,

(b)   section 55 (making such articles not an infringement) applies as if the words in subsection (2) from the beginning to 'marketed' were omitted, and

(c)   paragraph 14(5) of schedule 1 (transitional provision) does not apply,
and subject also to articles 5 and 7 below.

3.   In relation to sound recordings, article 2 above shall apply as it applies in relation to films, subject to the following modifications:

(a)   sections 19, 20, 26 and 107(3) of the Act (infringement by playing in public, broadcasting or inclusion in a cable programme service and related provisions) apply only if—

(i)   at least one of the countries relevant to the work for the purposes of article 2(1) above is specified in schedule 2 to this order, or

(ii)   the sound recording in question is a film sound-track accompanying a film; and

(b)   paragraph (1) of article 2 shall (subject to article 5 below) apply as if Indonesia were specified in schedule 1 to this order.

4.—(1)   In relation to broadcasts, sections 153, 154 and 156 of the Act (qualification for copyright protection) apply in relation to—

(a)   persons who are citizens or subjects of a country specified in schedule 3 to this order or are domiciled or resident there as they apply to persons who are British citizens or are domiciled or resident in the United Kingdom;

(b)   bodies incorporated under the law of such a country as they apply in relation to bodies incorporated under the law of a part of the United Kingdom; and

(c)   broadcasts made from such a country as they apply to broadcasts made from the United Kingdom;

but subject to paragraphs (2) and (3) and article 5 below.

(2)   If the only country or countries relevant to a broadcast for the purposes of paragraph (1) above are identified in schedule 3 to this order by the words' TV only', copyright subsists in the broadcast only if it is a television broadcast.

(3)   Copyright does not subsist in a broadcast by virtue of paragraph (1) above if it was made before the relevant date.

(4)   Where copyright subsists in a broadcast by virtue of paragraph (1) above, the whole of part I of the Act (including schedule 1 to the Act) applies in relation to the broadcast, save that for the purposes of section 14(2) (duration of copyright in repeats)—

(a)   a broadcast shall be disregarded if it was made before the relevant date, and

(b)   a cable programme shall be disregarded if it was included in a cable programme service before the later of the relevant date and 1st January 1985; and subject also to article 7 below.

(5)   For the purposes of paragraphs (3) and (4) above, the 'relevant date' is the date or (as the case may be) the earliest of the dates specified in schedule 3 to this order in respect of the country or countries relevant to the broadcast for the purposes of paragraph (1) above, being (where different dates are specified for television and non-television broadcasts) the date appropriate to the type of broadcast in question.

(6)   In respect of Singapore, this article applies in relation to cable programmes as it applies in relation to broadcasts, subject to article 5 below.

5.   Schedule 4 to this order shall have effect so as to modify the application of this order in respect of certain countries.

6.   Nothing in this order shall be taken to derogate from the effect of paragraph 35 of schedule 1 to the Act (continuation of existing qualification for copyright protection).

7.—(1)   This article applies in any case in which—

(a)   a work was made before 1st August 1989 (commencement of part I of the Act) and copyright under the Copyright Act 1956 did not subsist in it when it was made, or

(b)   a work is made on or after 1st August 1989 and copyright under the Act does not subsist in it when it is made,

but copyright subsequently subsists in it by virtue of article 2(1), 3 or 4(1) above.

(2)   Where in any such case a person incurs or has incurred any expenditure or liability in connection with, for the purpose of or with a view to doing of an act which at the time is not or was not an act restricted by any copyright in the work, the doing, or continued doing, of that act after copyright subsequently subsists in the work by virtue of article 2(1), 3 or 4(1) above shall not be an act restricted by the copyright unless the owner of the copyright or his exclusive licensee (if any) pays such compensation as, failing agreement, may be determined by arbitration.

SCHEDULE 1

COUNTRIES ENJOYING PROTECTION IN RESPECT OF ALL WORKS EXCEPT BROADCASTS AND CABLE PROGRAMMES

(The countries specified in this schedule either are parties to the Berne Copyright Convention and/or the Universal Copyright Convention or otherwise give adequate protection under their law.)

Algeria (28th August 1973), Andorra (27th September 1957), Argentina, Australia (including Norfolk Island), Austria, Bahamas, Bangladesh, Barbados, Belgium, Belize, Benin, Brazil, Bulgaria, Burkina, Cameroon, Canada, Central African Republic, Chad, Chile, Colombia, Congo, People's Republic of, Costa Rica, Côte d'Ivoire, Cuba (27th September 1957), Cyprus, Republic of, Czechoslovakia, Denmark (including the Faeroe Islands), Dominican Republic (8th May 1983), Ecuador (27th September 1957), Egypt, El Salvador (29th March 1979), Fiji, Finland, France (including all Overseas Departments and Territories), Gabon, German Democratic Republic (and Berlin (East)), Germany, Federal Republic of (and Berlin (West)), Ghana, Greece, Guatemala (28th October 1964), Guinea, Republic of, Haiti (27th September 1957), Holy See, Hungary, Iceland, India, Ireland, Republic of, Israel, Italy, Japan, Kampuchea (27th September 1957), Kenya, Korea, Republic of (1st October 1987), Laos (27th September 1957), Lebanon, Liberia, Libya, Liechtenstein, Luxembourg, Madagascar, Malawi, Mali, Malta, Mauritania, Mauritius, Mexico, Monaco, Morocco, Netherlands (including Aruba and the Netherlands Antilles), New Zealand, Nicaragua (16th August 1961), Niger, Nigeria, Norway, Pakistan, Panama (17th October 1962), Paraguay (11th March 1962), Peru, Philippines, Poland, Portugal, Romania, Rwanda, St. Vincent and the Grenadines, Senegal, Singapore, South Africa, Soviet Union (27th May 1973), Spain, Sri Lanka, Suriname, Sweden, Switzerland, Taiwan, territory of (10th July 1985), Thailand, Togo, Trinidad and Tobago, Tunisia, Turkey, United States of America (including Puerto Rico and all territories and possesions), Uruguay, Venezuela, Yugoslavia, Zaire, Zambia, Zimbabwe.

SCHEDULE 2

COUNTRIES ENJOYING FULL PROTECTION FOR SOUND RECORDINGS

(The countries specified in this schedule either are parties to the Rome Convention for the Protection of Performers, Producers of Phonograms and

Broadcasting Organisations or otherwise give adequate protection under their law.)

Australia (including Norfolk Island), Austria, Barbados, Brazil, Burkina, Chile, Colombia, Congo, People's Republic of, Costa Rica, Czechoslovakia, Denmark (including the Faeroe Islands), Dominican Republic, Ecuador, El Salvador, Fiji, Finland, France (including all Overseas Departments and Territories), Germany, Federal Republic of (and Berlin (West)), Guatemala, India, Indonesia, Ireland, Republic of, Italy, Luxembourg, Mexico, Monaco, New Zealand, Niger, Norway, Pakistan, Panama, Paraguay, Peru, Philippines, Sweden, Taiwan, territory of, Uruguay.

SCHEDULE 3

COUNTRIES ENJOYING PROTECTION IN RESPECT OF BROADCASTS

(The countries specified in this schedule either are parties to the Rome Convention for the Protection of Performers, Producers of Phonograms and Broadcasting Organisations and/or the European Agreement on the Protection of Television Broadcasts or otherwise give adequate protection under their law.)

Austria (9th June 1973), Barbados (18th September 1983), Belgium — TV only (8th March 1968), Brazil (29th September 1965), Burkina (14th January 1988), Chile (5th September 1974), Colombia (17th September 1976), Congo, People's Republic of (18th May 1964), Costa Rica (9th September 1971), Cyprus, Republic of — TV only (5th May 1970), Czechoslovakia (14th August 1964), Denmark (including the Faeroe Islands) (1st February 1962 — television; 1st July 1965 — non-television), Dominican Republic (27th January 1987), Ecuador (18th May 1964), El Salvador (29th June 1979), Fiji (11th April 1972), Finland (21st October 1983), France (including all Overseas Departments and Territories) (1st July 1961 — television; 3rd July 1987 — non-television), Germany, Federal Republic of (and Berlin (West)) (21st October 1966), Guatemala (14th January 1977), Ireland, Republic of (19th September 1979), Italy (8th April 1975), Luxembourg (25th February 1976), Mexico (18th May 1964), Monaco (6th December 1985), Niger (18th May 1964), Norway (10th August 1968 — television; 10th July 1978 — non-television), Panama (2nd September 1983), Paraguay (26th February 1970), Peru (7th August 1985), Philippines (25th September 1984), Singapore (1st June 1957), Spain — TV only (19th November 1971), Sweden (1st July 1961 — television; 18th May 1964 — non-television), Uruguay (4th July 1977).

SCHEDULE 4

MODIFICATIONS

1. In respect of Indonesia, article 2(1)(a) above as applied by article 3(b) above shall apply as if the reference to persons domiciled in Indonesia were omitted.

2. In respect of Singapore—

(a) articles 2(1)(a) and (2) and 4(1)(a) above shall apply as if the references to persons domiciled in Singapore were omitted, and

(b) in the application of article 4(3) above in relation to cable programmes by virtue of article 4(6), the relevant date is 1st January 1985.

3. In respect of the territory of Taiwan—

(a) article 2(1)(a) and (2) above shall apply as if the references to persons domiciled or resident in the territory of Taiwan were limited to such persons who are also citizens or subjects of China, and

(b) in the application of Part I of the Act by virtue of article 2(3) above, subsection (1) of section 21 (infringement by making adaptation) applies as if subsection (3)(a)(i) of that section (translation of literary or dramatic work) were omitted.

RECIPROCAL PROTECTION FOR RIGHTS IN PERFORMANCES
SI 1989 No. 1296

The following countries are designated as enjoying reciprocal protection under part II of the Copyright, Designs and Patents Act 1988 (rights in performances):

Austria, Barbados, Brazil, Burkina, Chile, Colombia, Congo, People's Republic of, Costa Rica, Czechoslovakia, Denmark (including the Faeroe Islands), Dominican Republic, Ecuador, El Salvador, Fiji, Finland, France (including all Overseas Departments and Territories), Germany, Federal Republic of (and Berlin (West)), Guatemala, Ireland, Republic of, Italy, Luxembourg, Mexico, Monaco, Niger, Norway, Panama, Paraguay, Peru, Philippines, Sweden, Uruguay.

RECIPROCAL PROTECTION FOR PRODUCT DESIGNS UNDER
DESIGN RIGHT SI 1989 No. 1294

The following countries are designated as enjoying reciprocal protection under part III of the Copyright, Designs and Patents Act 1988 (design right):

Anguilla, Bermuda, British Indian Ocean Territory, British Virgin Islands, Cayman Islands, Channel Islands, Falklands Islands, Gibraltar, Hong Kong, Isle of Man, Montserrat, New Zealand, Pitcairn, Henderson, Ducie and Oeno Islands, St Helena and Dependencies, South Georgia and the South Sandwich Islands, Turks and Caicos Islands.

RECIPROCAL PROTECTION FOR SEMICONDUCTOR CHIP
DESIGNS: ADDITIONAL CLASSES OF 'QUALIFYING PERSON'

A semiconductor chip design may be protectable by design right if

● the designer was employed or commissioned by a 'qualifying person', or

● articles made to the design were first marketed by a 'qualifying person'

The categories of 'qualifying person' have been extended. the definition of a 'qualifying person' now includes the following categories

- British Dependent Territories citizens

- citizens, subject or habitual residents of Japan, Switzerland, the USA, Sweden, Austria, Finland, French overseas territories (French Polynesia, French Southern and Antarctic Territories; Mayotte; New Caledonia and dependencies; Saint-Pierre and Miquelon; Wallis and Futuna Islands), Iceland, Norway

- firms and bodies corporate formed under the law of, or any part of, the UK any other EEC State or Gibraltar and having a place of business in Austria, Japan, Switzerland, the USA or Sweden, at which substantial business activity is carried on

- firms and bodies corporate formed under the law of, or any part of Austria, Japan, Switzerland, the USA or Sweden and having in any such country a place of business at which substantial business activity is carried on

Appendix 3
Rules Regulating the Duration of Copyright in Copyright Works

This Appendix sets out in detail the rules governing the duration of copyright in the various types of copyright works. The rules include both the old and new law.

Literary, dramatic, musical and artistic works — existing on and before 1 August 1989 — the old rules

Under the 56 Act there was a difference in the periods of protection for works depending on whether they were published or unpublished. What amounts to publication as well as what is not publication has been dealt with in Appendix 2.

Under the 56 Act copyright in *unpublished* literary dramatic, musical and artistic works lasted indefinitely (56 Act, s. 2(2)). Once literary, dramatic, musical and artistic works were published copyright protection under the 56 Act lasted for the life of the author plus 50 years from the end of the calendar year of death (56 Act, s. 2(3)).

If there was more than one author, copyright lasted for the life of the last to die plus 50 years from the end of the calendar year of death (56 Act Schedule 3). The only exceptions to these 56 Act rules related to photographs and engravings. If an engraving had not been published during the author's lifetime then copyright in an engraving lasted for 50 years from the end of the calendar year of first publication rather than from the end of the calendar year of the author's death (or the end of the calendar year of death of the last surviving author if more than one (56 Act, s. 3(4)). If a photograph was published then copyright lasted for 50 years from the end of the calendar year of first publication regardless of whether this was before or after the author's death (56 Act, s. 3(4)).

With the exception of photographs, if the work was published anonymously or under a pseudonym copyright lasted for 50 years from first publication (56

Act, Schedule 2). This was provided that during those 50 years it was not possible by reasonable enquiry to identify one or more of the authors. If it was possible then the full period of the life of the author plus 50 years applied.

The new rules for the duration of copyright in pre-August 1989 literary, dramatic, musical and artistic works

Again, there is a distinction between published and unpublished literary, dramatic, musical and artistic works which existed before 1 August 1989.

In general, under the 88 Act if a work was published before August 1989 then the 56 Act rules continue to apply to it for the purposes of calculating the duration of copyright (88 Act, Schedule 1 para 12).

For unpublished works, however, the 88 Act has some specific transitional rules. If a literary, dramatic, or musical (but not artistic) work was unpublished or no copies had been issued to the public, or it had not been performed in public, or broadcast or included in a cable programme service and the author, or the last surviving author died before 1 August 1989, copyright lasts for 50 years from the end of 1989 (88 Act, Schedule 1 para 12). If the author or the last surviving author is still alive on 1 August 1989 the new provisions of the 88 Act apply (88 Act, Schedule 1 para 12(6)) and these are dealt with later in this section.

For unpublished artistic works, where the author died or the last surviving author died before 1 August 1989, the new provisions of the 88 Act apply (88 Act, Schedule 1 para 12). The same applies to any other literary, dramatic, musical and artistic works if none of the specific transitional rules of the 88 Act described above cover them (88 Act, Schedule 1 para 12(6)).

For anonymous works or works created under a pseudonym, if these were unpublished on 1 August 1989 copyright lasts for 50 years from the end of 1989 (88 Act, Schedule 1 para 12(3)(b)) unless the work is published during that 50 year period. If the work is published during that 50 year period then copyright lasts for 50 years from the end of the calendar year in which it is first made available to the public (88 Act, Schedule 1 para 12 and 88 Act, s. 12(2)). However, if the identity of the author or any one of them becomes known during the 50 year period then the general rule applies (copyright lasts for the life of the author plus 50 years from the end of the calendar year of death of the last known surviving author).

Rules for duration of copyright in literary, dramatic, musical and artistic works created on and after 1 August 1989

For works created on or after 1 August 1989, there is no distinction between published and unpublished works. The general rule is that copyright in all such literary, dramatic, musical and artistic works lasts for the life of the author (or the life of the last surviving author whose identity is known if there is more than one author) plus 50 years from the end of the calendar year of death of the author (or death of the last surviving author if more than one) (88 Act, s. 12(1) and (4)).

The exceptions relate to works of unknown authorship, computer generated works, and joint authorship. This will be considered here.

Period of protection where the work is of unknown authorship

Where the identity of the author (this means *all* of the authors if there is more than one author) is unknown, copyright lasts for 50 years from the time the work is first made available to the public (88 Act, s. 12(1)). This does not apply if the identity of the author or any one of the authors becomes known during that 50 year period (88 Act, s. 12(2)).

Period of protection for computer generated works

For computer generated works copyright lasts for 50 years from the end of the calendar year in which it was made (88 Act, s. 12(3)).

Period of protection for works of joint authorship

For works of joint authorship where the period of protection is calculated to run from the death of the author the period is to be calculated from the death of the last author to die whose identity becomes known (88 Act, s. 12(4)).

Duration of copyright in typographical arrangements of published editions

Under the 56 Act copyright lasted for 25 years from the end of the calendar year of first publication (56 Act, s. 15(2)). This rule continues to apply to publications occurring before 1 August 1989 (88 Act, Schedule 1 para 12). For publications occurring on or after that date the rule remains the same (88 Act, s. 15).

Duration of copyright in sound recordings

Under the 56 Act copyright in sound recordings lasted forever until publication. After publication copyright lasted for 50 years from the end of the calendar year of first publication (56 Act, s. 12(3). Under the 88 Act these rules continue to apply to sound recordings published before 1 August 1989 (88 Act, Schedule 1 para 12(2)).

For unpublished sound recordings made after 31 May 1957 which remain unpublished on 1 August 1989, copyright lasts for 50 years from the end of 1989 (88 Act, Schedule 1 para 12(5)). If the sound recording is published within the 50 year period then copyright lasts for 50 years from the end of the calendar year of publication (88 Act, Schedule 1 para 12(5)).

For sound recordings created on or after 1 August 1989 copyright lasts for 50 years from creation unless released during that time. If released during the initial 50 year period copyright lasts for 50 years from the end of the calendar year of first release (88 Act, s. 13).

A sound recording is 'released' when first published, broadcast or included in a cable programme service or shown to the public in a film unless any of these acts are done without authorisation (88 Act, s. 13). Thus, any of the acts described as amounting to 'release' do not count if done without authorisation. It will be possible to obtain one hundred years or more protection for recordings of the same event or substantially the same event. How this can be achieved is described in the section on 'Release' (below) in relation to films and sound recordings.

Duration of copyright in films

Copyright in films under the 56 Act lasted for 50 years from the end of the calendar year of registration where the film was required by law to be registered (eg under the Cinematograph Films Act, 1938). Otherwise copyright lasted forever unless the film was published and, once published, copyright lasted for 50 years from the end of the calendar year of first publication (56 Act, s. 13).

However, if the film was a foreign film and obtained copyright protection only because of first publication in a country covered by the 56 Act's reciprocal protection provisions then it was not protectable by copyright. Once published in a country covered by the 56 Act copyright lasted for 50 years from the end of the calendar year of first publication (56 Act, s. 13(3)(b) and 13(2).

Under the 88 Act, for films existing before 1 August 1989 the 56 Act provisions continue to apply if they were registered or published before 1 August 1989. Otherwise copyright lasts for 50 years from the end of 1989 unless the film is published within that 50 year period. If it is published during that period copyright lasts for 50 years from the end of the calendar year of first publication (88 Act, Schedule 1 paras 12(2) and 12(5)).

For films created on or after 1 August 1989 copyright lasts for 50 years from the end of the calendar year in which it was made unless it is released during that 50 year period. 'Release' means publication, broadcast, inclusion in a cable programme service or the first public showing unless any of these acts are done without authorisation. Thus, any of the acts described as amounting to 'release' do not count if done without authorisation (88 Act, s. 13).

Where a film is released, copyright lasts for 50 years from the end of the calendar year of first release (88 Act, s. 13).

'Release' in relation to films and sound recordings

Although publication (the issue of copies to the public) amounts to 'release'

● a film or sound recording can be 'released' without being published

'Release' includes publication but it also includes acts which do not involve the issue of copies of a sound recording or film to the public. For example, 'release' includes the first broadcast, or first inclusion in a cable programme service and, in the case of a film or film sound-track, the first public showing (88 Act, s. 13). So,

● the only way anyone else might have a copy of a film or sound recording is by making a copy in infringement of copyright

Thus, it may be that 50 years after first release of the first of two versions of a recording or film no-one has a lawful copy of the first version. It has frequently been the case that films are put on release without ever being published. The advent of the video may however, see more films and sound recordings being released than before. It also may be thought that a recording or film in 50 year's time will have little value. However, recordings and films of performances of famous performers of yesteryear like Charlie Chaplin and Billie Holiday, have proved to have considerable commercial value now.

Creating two different versions of the same film or sound recording leaves open the possibility of releasing the 'previously unreleased version' of some very old and very famous film and still getting 50 years protection after having had 50 years protection for the previous version. The possibility of 100 years protection does not apply just to films and sound recordings made on or after 1 August 1989. It can also apply to certain films and to sound recordings which have not been published prior to 1 August 1989.

Duration of copyright in broadcasts and cable programmes

Under the 56 Act copyright in broadcasts lasted for 50 years from the end of the calendar year of first broadcast. Where a broadcast was repeated the copyright in the repeat broadcast did not extend beyond the initial 50 year protection (56 Act, s. 14). For cable programmes under the 56 Act copyright lasted for 50 years from the end of the calendar year in which the cable programme was first included in a cable programme service. Where a cable programme was repeated the copyright did not extend beyond the initial 50 year protection (56 Act, s. 14A).

For all broadcasts and cable programmes the 88 Act rules now apply (88 Act, Schedule 1 para 12(6)). The 56 Act rules are gone but the 88 Act rules are the same. Under the 88 Act copyright lasts for 50 years from the end of the calendar year of first broadcast or inclusion in a cable programme service and copyright in repeats expires at the same time as for the original broadcast or cable programme (88 Act, s. 14).

Appendix 4
Classes of Goods and Services for which Marks may be Registered

PART I GOODS

Class 1. Chemicals used in industry, science and photography, as well as in agriculture, horticulture and forestry; unprocessed artificial resins, unprocessed plastics; manures; fire extinguishing compositions; tempering and soldering preparations; chemical substances for preserving foodstuffs; tanning substances; adhesives used in industry.

Class 2. Paints, varnishes, lacquers; preservatives against rust and against deterioration of wood; colourants; mordants; raw natural resins; metals in foil and powder form for painters, decoarators, printers and artists.

Class 3. Bleaching preparations and other substances for laundry use; cleaning, polishing, scouring and abrasive preparations; soaps; perfumery, essential oils, cosmetics, hair lotions; dentifrices.

Class 4. Industrial oils and greases; lubricants; dust absorbing, wetting and binding compositions; fuels (including motor spirit) and illuminants; candles, wicks.

Class 5. Pharmaceutical, veterinary and sanitary preparations; dietetic substances adapted for medical use, food for babies; plasters, materials for dressings; material for stoppin teeth, dental wax; disinfectants; preparations for destroying vermin; fungicides, herbicides.

Class 6. Common metals and their alloys; metal building materials; transportable buildings of metal; materials of metal for railway tracks; non-electric cables and wires of common metal; ironmongery, small items of metal hardware; pipes and tubes of metal; safes; goods of common metal not included in other classes; ores.

Class 7. Machines and machine tools; motors (except for land vehicles); machine coupling and belting (except for land vehicles); agricultural implements; incubators for eggs.

Class 8. Hand tools and implements (hand operated); cutlery; side arms; razors.

Class 9. Scientific, nautical, surveying, electric, photographic, cinematographic, optical, weighing, measuring, signalling, checking (supervision), life-saving and teaching apparatus and instruments; apparatus for recording, transmission or reproduction of sound or images; magnetic data carriers, recording discs; automatic vending machines and mechanisms for coin-operated apparatus; cash registers, calculating machines, data processing equipment and computers; fire-extinguishing apparatus.

Class 10. Surgical, medical, dental and veterinary apparatus and instruments, artificial limbs, eyes and teeth; orthopaedic articles; suture materials.

Class 11. Apparatus for lighting, heating, steam generating, cooking, refrigerating, drying, ventilating, water supply and sanitary purposes.

Class 12. Vehicles; apparatus for locomotion by land, air or water.

Class 13. Firearms; ammunition and projectils; explosives; fireworks.

Class 14. Precious metals and their alloys and goods in precious metals or coated therewith, not included in other classes; jewellery, precious stones; horological and chronometric instruments.

Class 15. Musical instruments.

Class 16. Paper, cardboard and goods made from these materials, not included in other classes; printed matter; bookbinding material; photographs; stationery; adhesives for stationery or household purposes; artists' materials; paint brushes; typewriters and office requisits (except furniture); instructional and teaching material (except apparatus); plastic materials for packaging (not included in other classes); playing-cards; printers' type; printing blocks.

Class 17. Rubber, gutta-percha, gum, asbestos, mica and goods made from these materials and not included in other classes; plastics in extruded form for use in manufacture; packing, topping and insulating materials; flexible pipes, not of metal.

Class 18. Leather and imitations of leather, and goods made of these materials and not included in other classes; animal skins, hides; trunks and travelling bags; umbrellas, parasols and walking-sticks; whips, harness and saddlery.

Class 19. Building materials (non-metallic); non-metallic rigid pipes for building; asphalt, pitch and bitumen; non-metallic transportable buildings; monuments, not of metal.

Class 20. Furniture, mirrors, picture frames; goods (not included in other classes) of wood, cork, reed, cane, wicker, horn, bone, ivory, whalebone, shell, amber, mother-of-pearl, meerschaum and substitutes for all these materials, or of plastics.

Class 21. Household or kitchen utensils and containers (not of precious metal or coated therewith); combs and sponges; brushes (except paintbrushes); brush-making materials; articles for cleaning purposes; steel wool; unworked or semi-worked glass (except glass used in building); glassware, porcelain and earthenware not included in other classes.

Class 22. Ropes, string, nets, tents, awnings, tarpaulins, sails, sacks and bags (not included in other classes); padding and stuffing materials (except of rubber or plastics); raw fibrous textile materials.

Class 23. Yarns and threads, for textile use.

Class 24. Textiles and textile goods, not included in other classes; bed and table covers.

Class 25. Clothing, footwear, headgear.

Class 26. Lace and embroidery, ribbons and braid; buttons, hooks and eyes, pins and needles; artificial flowers.

Class 27. Carpets, rugs, mats and matting, linoleum and other materials for covering existing floors; wall hangings (non-textile).

Class 28. Games and playthings; gymnastic and sporting articles not included in other classes; decorations for Christmas trees.

Class 29. Meat, fish, poultry and game; meat extracts; preserved, dried and cooked fruits and vegetables; jellies, jams; eggs, milk and milk products; edible oils and fats; salad-dressings; preserves.

Class 30. Coffee, tea, cocoa, sugar, rice, tapioca, sago, artifical coffee; flour and preparations made from cereals, bread, pastry and confectionery, ices; honey, treacle; yeast, baking-powder; salt, mustard; vinegar, sauces (except salad-dressings); spices; ice.

Class 31. Agricultural, horticultural and forestry products and grains not included in other classes; living animals; fresh fruits and vegetables; seeds, natural plants and flowers; foodstuffs for animals, malt.

Class 32. Beers; mineral and aerated waters and other non-alcoholic drinks; fruit drinks and fruit juices; syrups and other preparations for making beverages.

Class 33. Alcoholic beverages (except beers).

Class 34. Tobacco; smokers' articles; matches.

PART II SERVICES

Class 35. Advertising and business.

Class 36. Insurance and financial.

Class 37. Construction and repair.

Class 38. Communication.

Class 39. Transportation and storage.

Class 40. Material treatment.

Class 41. Education and entertainment.

Class 42. Other services.

Appendix 5
Article 85 of the EEC Treaty

1. The following shall be prohibited as incompatible with the common market: all agreements between undertakings, decisions by associations of undertakings and concerted practices which may affect trade between member States and which have as their object or effect the prevention restriction or distortion of competition within the common market, and in particular those which:

    (a) directly or indirectly fix purchase or selling prices or any other trading conditions;

    (b) limit or control production, markets, technical development, or investment;

    (c) share markets or sources of supply;

    (d) apply dissimilar conditions to equivalent transactions with other trading parties, thereby placing them at a competitive disadvantage;

    (e) make the conclusion of contracts subject to acceptance by the other parties of supplementary obligations which, by their nature or according to commercial usage, have no connection with the subject of such contracts.

2. Any agreements or decisions prohibited pursuant to this Article shall be automatically void.

3. The provisions of paragraph 1 may, however, be declared inapplicable in the case of:

— any agreement or category of agreements between undertakings;
— any decision or category of decisions by associations of undertakings;
— any concerted practice or category of concerted practices;

which contributes to improving the production or distribution of goods or to promoting technical or economic progress, while allowing consumers a fair share of the resulting benefit, and which does not:

(a)   impose on the undertakings concerned restrictions which are not indispensable to the attainment of these objectives;

(b)   afford such undertakings the possibility of eliminating competition in respect of a substantial part of the products in question.

Appendix 6
EC Block Exemptions

COMMISSION REGULATION 418/85 OF DECEMBER 19, 1984
On the application of Article 85(3) of the Treaty to Categories of Research and Development Agreements

(OJ 1985, L53/5)

ARTICLE 1

1. Pursuant to article 85(3) of the Treaty and subject to the provisions of this Regulation, it is hereby declared that Article 85(1) of the Treaty shall not apply to agreements entered into between undertakings for the purpose of:

(a) joint research and development of products or processes and joint exploitation of the results of that research and development;

(b) joint exploitation of the results of research and development of products or processes jointly carried out pursuant to a prior agreement between the same undertakings; or

(c) joint research and development of products or processes excluding joint exploitations of the results, in so far as such agreements fall within the scope of Article 85(1).

2. For the purposes of this Regulation:

(a) *research and development of products or processes* means the acquisition of technical knowledge and the carrying out of theoretical analysis, systematic study or experimentation, including experimental production, technical testing of products or processes, the establishment of the necessary facilities and the obtaining of intellectual property rights for the results;

(b) *contract processes* means processes arising out of the research and development;

(c) *contract products* means products or services arising out of the research and development or manufactured or provided applying the contract processes;

(d) *exploitation of the results* means the manufacture of the contract products or the application of the contract processes or the assignment or licensing of intellectual property rights or the communication of know-how required for such manufacture or application;

(e)   *technical knowledge* means technical knowledge which is either protected by an intellectual propery right or is secret (know-how).

3.   Research and development of the exploitation of the results are carried out *jointly* where:

(a)   the work involved is:
—   carried out by a joint team, organization or undertaking,
—   jointly entrusted to a third party, or
—   allocated between the parties by way of specialization in research, development or production;

(b)   the parties collaborate in any way in the assignment or the licensing of intellectual property rights or the communication of know-how, within the meaning of paragraph 2(d), to third parties.

ARTICLE 2

The exemption provided for in Article 1 shall apply on condition that:

(a)   the joint research and development work is carried out within the framework of a programme defining the objectives of the work and the field in which it is to be carried out;

(b)   all the parties have access to the results of the work

(c)   where the agreement provides only for joint research and development, each party is free to exploit the results of the joint research and development and any pre-existing technical knowledge necessary therefor independently;

(d)   the joint exploitation relates only to results which are protected by intellectual property rights or constitute know-how which substantially contributes to technical or economic progress and that the results are decisive for the manufacture of the contract products or the application of the contract processes;

(e)   any joint undertaking or third party charged with manufacture of the contract products is required to supply them only to the parties;

(f)   undertakings charged with manufacture by way of specialisation in production are required to fulfil orders for supplies from all the parties.

ARTICLE 3

1.   Where the parties are not competing manufacturers of products capable of being improved or replaced by the contract products, the exemption provided for in Article 1 shall apply for the duration of the research and development programme and, where the results are jointly exploited, for five years from the time the contract products are first put on the market within the common market.

2.   Where two or more of the parties are competing manufacturers within the meaning of paragraph 1, the exemption provided for in Article 1 shall apply for the period specified in paragraph 1 only if, at the time the agreement is entered into, the parties' combined production of the products capable of being improved or replaced by the contract products does not exceed 20 per cent. of the market for such products in the common market or a substantial part thereof.

3.   After the end of the period referred to in paragraph 1, the exemption provided for in Article 1 shall continue to apply as long as the production of the contract products together with the parties' combined production of other products which are considered by users to be equivalent in view of their characteristics, price and intended use does not exceed 20 per cent. of the total market for such products in the common market or a substantial part thereof. Where contract products are components used by the parties of the manufacture of other products, reference shall be made to the markets for such of those latter products for which the components represent a significant part.

4. The exemption provided for in Article 1 shall continue to apply where the market share referred to in paragraph 3 is exceeded during any period of two consecutive financial years by not more than one-tenth.

5. Where market shares referred to in paragraphs 3 and 4 are exceeded, the exemption provided for in Article 1 shall continue to apply for a period of six months following the end of the financial year during which it was exceeded.

ARTICLE 4

1. The exemption provided for in Article 1 shall also apply to the following restrictions of competition imposed on the parties:

(a) an obligation not to carry out independently research and development in the field to which the programme relates or in a closely connected field during the execution of the programme;

(b) an obligation not to enter into agreements with third parties on research and development in the field to which the programme relates or in a closely connected field during the execution of the programme;

(c) an obligation to procure the contract products exclusively from parties, joint organizations or undertakings or third parties, jointly charged with their manufacture;

(d) an obligation not to manufacture the contract products or apply the contract processes in territories reserved for other parties;

(e) an obligation to restrict the manufacture of the contract products or application of the contract processes to one or more technical fields of application, except where two or more of the parties are competitors within the meaning of Article 3 at the time the agreement is entered into;

(f) an obligation not to pursue, for a period of five years from the time the contract products are first put on the market within the common market, an active policy of putting the products on the market in territories reserved for other parties, and in particular not to engage in advertising specifically aimed at such territories or to establish any branch or maintain any distribution depot there for the distribution of the products, provided that users and intermediaries can obtain the contract products from other suppliers and the parties do not render it difficult for intermediaries and users to thus obtain the products;

(g) an obligation on the parties to communicate to each other any experience they may gain in exploiting the results and to grant each other non-exclusive licences for inventions relating to improvements or new applications.

2. The exemption provided for in Article 1 shall also apply where in a particular agreement the parties undertake obligations of the types referred to in paragraph 1 but with a more limited scope than is permitted by that paragraph.

ARTICLE 5

1. Article 1 shall apply notwithstanding that any of the following obligations, in particular, are imposed on the parties during the currency of the agreement:

(a) an obligation to communicate patented or non-patented technical knowledge necessary for the carrying out of the research and development programme for the exploitation of its results;

(b) an obligation not to use any know-how received from another party for purposes other than carrying out the research and development programme and the exploitation of its results;

(c) an obligation to obtain and maintain in force intellectual property rights for the contract products or processes;

(d) an obligation to preserve the confidentiality of any know-how received or jointly developed under the research and development programme; this obligation may be imposed even after the expiry of the agreement;

(e) an obligation:

  (i) to inform other parties of infringements of their intellectual property rights,

  (ii) to take legal action against infringers, and

  (iii) to assist in any such legal action or share with the other parties in the cost thereof;

(f) an obligation to pay royalties or render services to other parties to compensate for unequal contributions to the joint research and development or unequal exploitation of its results;

(g) an obligation to share royalties received from third parties with other parties;

(h) an obligation to supply other parties with minimum quantities of contract products and to observe minimum standards of quality.

2. In the event that, because of particular circumstances, the obligations referred to in paragraph 1 fall within the scope of Article 85(1), they also shall be covered by the exemption. The exemption provided for in this paragraph shall also apply where in a particular agreement the parties undertake obligations of the types referred to in paragraph 1 but with a more limited scope than is permitted by that paragraph.

ARTICLE 6

The exemption provided for in Article 1 shall not apply where the parties, by agreement, decision or concerted practice:

(a) are restricted in their freedom to carry out research and development independently or in cooperation with third parties in a field unconnected with that to which the programme relates or, after its completion, in the field to which the programme relates or in a connected field;

(b) are prohibited after completion of the research and development programme from challenging the validity of intellectual propery rights which the parties hold in the common market and which are relevant to the programme or, after the expiry of the agreement, from challenging the validity of intellectual property rights which the parties hold in the common market and which protect the results of the research and development;

(c) are restricted as to the quantity of the contract products they may manufacture or sell or as to the number of operations employing the contract process they may carry out;

(d) are restricted in their determination of prices, components of prices or discounts when selling the contract products to third parties;

(e) are restricted as to the customers they may serve, without prejudice to Article 4(1)(e);

(f) are prohibited from putting the contract products on the market or pursuing an active sales policy for them in territories within the common market that are reserved for other parties after the end of the period referred to in Article 4(1)(f);

(g) are prohibited from allowing third parties to manufacture the contract products or apply the contract processes in the absence of joint manufacture;

(h) are required:

— to refuse without any objectively justified reason to meet demand from users or dealers established in their respective territories who would market the contract products in other territories within the common market, or

— to make it difficult for users or dealers to obtain the contract products from other dealers within the common market, and in particular to exercise intellectual property rights or take measures so as to prevent users or dealers from obtaining, or from putting on the market within the common market, products which have been lawfully put on the market within the common market by another party or with its consent.

ARTICLE 7

1.   The exemption provided for in this Regulation shall also apply to agreements of the kinds described in Article 1 which fulfil the conditions laid down in Articles 2 and 3 and which contain obligations restrictive of competition which are not covered by Articles 4 and 5 and do not fall within the scope of Article 6, on condition that the agreements in question are notified to the Commission in accordance with the provisions of Commission Regulation 27 (OJ 1962, 35/118/62), and that the Commission does not oppose such exemption within a period of six months.

2.   The period of six months shall run from the date on which the notification is received by the Commission. Where, however, the notification is made by registered post, the period shall run from the date shown on the postmark of the place of posting.

3.   Paragraph 1 shall apply only if:

   (a)   express reference is made to this Article in the notification or in a communication accompanying it, and

   (b)   the information furnished with the notification is complete and in accordance with the facts.

4.   The benefit of paragraph 1 may be claimed for agreements notified before the entry into force of this Regulation by submitting a comunication to the Commission referring expressly to this Article and to the notification. Paragraphs 2 and 3(b) shall apply *mutatis mutandis.*

5.   The Commission may oppose the exemption. It shall oppose exemption if it receives a request to do so from a Member State within three months of the forwarding to the Member State of the notification referred to in paragraph 1 or of the communication referred to in paragraph 4. This request must be justified on the basis of considerations relating to the competition rules of the Treaty.

6.   The Commission may withdraw the opposition to the exemption at any time. However, where the opposition was raised at the request of a Member State and this request is maintained, it may be withdrawn only after consultation of the Advisory Committee on Restrictive Practices and Dominant Positions.

7.   If the opposition is withdrawn because the undertakings concerned have shown that the conditions of Article 85(3) are fulfilled, the exemption shall apply from the date of notification.

8.   If the opposition is withdrawn because the undertakings concerned have amended the agreement so that the conditions of Article 85(3) are fulfilled, the exemption shall apply from the date on which the amendments take effect.

9.   If the Commission opposes exemption and the opposition is not withdrawn, the effects of the notification shall be governed by the provisions of Regulation 17

ARTICLE 8

1.   Information acquired pursuant to Article 7 shall be used only for the purposes of this Regulation.

2.   The Commission and the authorities of the Member States, their officials and other servants shall not disclose information acquired by them pursuant to this Regulation of a kind that is covered by the obligation of professional secrecy.

3.   Paragraphs 1 and 2 shall not prevent publication of general information or surveys which do not contain information relating to particular undertakings or associations of undertakings.

ARTICLE 9

1.   The provisions of this Regulation shall also apply to rights and obligations which the parties create for undertakings connected with them. The market shares held and the

actions and measures taken by connected undertakings shall be treated as those of the parties themselves.

2. Connected undertakings for the purposes of this Regulation are:

(a) undertakings in which a party to the agreement, directly or indirectly:

— owns more than half the capital or business assets,

— has the power to exercise more than half the voting rights,

— has the power to appoint more than half the members of the supervisory board, board of directors or bodies legally representing the undertakings, or

— has the right to manage the affairs;

(b) undertakings which directly have in or over a party to the agreement the rights or powers listed in (a);

(c) undertakings in or over which an undertaking referred to in (b) directly or indirectly has the rights or powers listed in (a);

3. Undertakings in which the parties to the agreement or undertakings connected with them jointly have, directly or indirectly, the rights or powers set out in paragraph 2(a) shall be considered to be connected with each of the parties to the agreement.

ARTICLE 10

The Commission may withdraw the benefit of this Regulation, pursuant to Article 7 of Regulation 2821/71, where it finds in a particular case that an agreement exempted by this Regulation nevertheless has certain effects which are incompatible with the conditions laid down in Article 85(3) of the Treaty, and in particular where:

(a) the existence of the agreement substantially restricts the scope for third parties to carry out research and development in the relevant field because of the limited research capacity available elsewhere;

(b) because of the particular structure of supply, the existence of the agreement substantially restricts the access of third parties to the market for the contract products;

(c) without any objectively valid reason, the parties do not exploit the results of the joint research and development;

(d) the contract products are not subject in the whole or a substantial part of the common market to effective competition from identical products or products considered by users as equivalent in view of their characteristics, price and intended use.

ARTICLE 11

1. In the case of agreements notified to the Commission before March 1, 1985, the exemption provided for in Article 1 shall have retroactive effect from the time at which the conditions for application of this Regulation were fulfilled or, where the agreement does not fall within Article 4(2)(3)(b) of Regulation 17, not earlier than the date of notification.

2. In the case of agreements existing on March 13, 1962 and notified to the Commission before February 1, 1963, the exemption shall have retroactive effect from the time at which the conditions for application of this Regulation were fulfilled.

3. Where agreements which were in existence on March 13, 1962 and which were notified to the Commission before February 1, 1963, or which are covered by Article 4(2)(3)(b) of Regulation 17 and were notified to the Commission before January 1, 1967, and amended before September 1, 1985 so as to fulfil the conditions for application of this Regulation, such amendment being communicated to the Commission before October 1, 1985, the prohibition laid down in Article 85(1) of the Treaty shall not apply in respect of the period prior to the amendment. The communication of amendments shall take effect from the date of their receipt by the Commission. Where the communication is sent by registered post, it shall take effect from the date shown on the postmark of the place of posting.

4.   In the case of agreements to which Article 85 of the Treaty applies as a result of the accession of the United Kingdom, Ireland and Denmark, paragraphs 1 to 3 shall apply except that the relevant dates shall be January 1, 1973 instead of March 13, 1962 and July 1, 1973 instead of February 1, 1963 and January 1, 1967.

5.   In the case of agreements to which Article 85 of the Treaty applies as a result of the accession of Greece, paragraphs 1 to 3 shall apply except that the relevant dates shall be January 1, 1981 instead of March 13, 1962 and July 1, 1981 instead of February 1, 1963 and January 1, 1967.

6.   As regards agreements to which Article 83 of the Treaty applies as a result of the accession of the Kingdom of Spain and of the Portuguese Republic, paragraphs 1 to 3 shall apply except that the relevant dates should be January 1, 1986 instead of March 13, 1962 and July 1, 1986 instead of February 1, 1963, January 1, 1967, March 1, 1985 and September 1, 1985. The amendment made to the agreements in accordance with the provisions of paragraph 3 need not be notified to the Commission.

ARTICLE 12

This Regulation shall apply *mutatis mutandis* to decisions of associations of undertakings.

ARTICLE 13

This Regulation shall enter into force on March 1, 1985.

It shall apply until December 31, 1997.

This Regulation shall be binding in its entirety and directly applicable in all Member States.

Done at Brussels, December 19, 1984.

COMMISSION REGULATION (EEC) No 4087/88
OF NOVEMBER 30, 1988
on the application of Article 85(3) of the Treaty to categories of franchise agreements

ARTICLE 1

1.   Pursuant to Article 85(3) of the Treaty and subject to the provisions of this Regulation, it is hereby declared that Article 85(1) of the Treaty shall not apply to franchise agreements to which two undertakings are party, which include one or more of the restrictions listed in Article 2.

2.   The exemption provided for in paragraph 1 shall also apply to master franchise agreements to which two undertakings are party. Where applicable, the provisions of this Regulation concerning the relationship between franchisor and franchisee shall apply *mutatis mutandis* to the relationship between franchisor and master franchisee and between master franchisee and franchisee.

3.   For the purposes of this Regulation:

(a)   'franchise' means a package of industrial or intellectual property rights relating to trade marks, trade names, shop signs, utility models, designs, copyrights, know-how or patents, to be exploited for the resale of goods or the provision of services to end users;

(b)   'franchise agreement' means an agreement whereby one undertaking, the franchisor, grants the other, the franchisee, in exchange for direct or indirect financial consideration, the right to exploit a franchise for the purposes of marketing specified types of goods and/or services; it includes at least obligations relating to:

— the use of a common name or shop sign and a uniform presentation of contract premises and/or means of transport,

— the communication by the franchisor to the franchisee of know-how,

— the continuing provision by the franchisor to the franchisee of commercial or technical assistance during the life of the agreement;

(c) 'master franchise agreement' means an agreement where one undertaking, the franchisor, grants the other, the master franchisee, in exchange of direct or indirect financial consideration, the right to exploit a franchise for the purposes of concluding franchise agreements with third parties, the franchisees;

(d) 'franchisor's goods' means goods produced by the franchisor or according to its instructions, and/or bearing the franchisor's name or trade mark;

(e) 'contract premises' means the premises used for the exploitation of the franchise or, when the franchise is exploited outside those premises, the base from which the franchisee operates the means of transport used for the exploitation of the franchise (contract means of transport);

(f) 'know-how' means a package of non-patented practical information, resulting from experience and testing by the franchisor, which is secret, substantial and identified;

(g) 'secret' means that the know-how, as a body or in the precise configuration and assembly of its components, is not generally known or easily accessible; it is not limited in the narrow sense that each individual component of the know-how should be totally unknown or unobtainable outside the franchisor's business;

(h) 'substantial' means that the know-how includes information which is of importance for the sale of goods or the provision of services to end users, and in particular for the presentation of goods for sale, the processing of goods in connection which the provision of services, methods of dealing with customers, and administration and financial management; the know-how must be useful for the franchisee by being capable, at the date of conclusion of the agreement, of improving the competitive position of the franchisee, in particular by improving the franchisee's performance or helping it to enter a new market;

(i) 'identified' means that the know-how must be described in a sufficiently comprehensive manner so as to make it possible to verify that it fulfils the criteria of secrecy and substantiality; the description of the know-how can either be set out in the franchise agreement or in a separate document or recorded in any other appropriate form.

ARTICLE 2

The exemption provided for in Article 1 shall apply to the following restrictions of competition:

(a) an obligation on the franchisor, in a defined area of the common market, the contract territory, not to:

— grant the right to exploit all or part of the franchise to third parties,

— itself exploit the franchise, or itself market the goods or services which are the subject-matter of the franchise under a similar formula,

— itself supply the franchisor's goods to third parties;

(b) an obligation on the master franchisee not to conclude franchise agreement with third parties outside its contract territory;

(c) an obligation on the franchisee to exploit the franchise only from the contract premises;

(d) an obligation on the franchisee to refrain, outside the contract territory, from seeking customers for the goods or the services which are the subject-matter of the franchise;

(e)   an obligation on the franchisee not to manufacture, sell or use in the course of the provision of services, goods competing with the franchisor's goods which are the subject-matter of the franchise; where the subject-matter of the franchise is the sale or use in the course of the provision of services both certain types of goods and spare parts or accessories therefor, that obligation may not be imposed in respect of these spare parts or accessories.

ARTICLE 3

1.   Article 1 shall apply notwithstanding the presence of any of the following obligations on the franchisee, in so far as they are necessary to protect the franchisor's industrial or intellectual property rights or to maintain the common identity and reputation of the franchised network:

(a)   to sell, or use in the course of the provision of services, exclusively goods matching minimum objective quality specifications laid down by the franchisor;

(b)   to sell, or use in the course of the provision of services, goods which are manufactured only by the franchisor or by third parties designed by it, where it is impracticable, owing to the nature of the goods which are the subject-matter of the franchise, to apply objective quality specifications;

(c)   not to engage, directly or indirectly, in any similar business in a territory where it would compete with a member of the franchised network, including the franchisor; the franchisee may be held to this obligation after termination of the agreement, for a reasonable period which may not exceed one year, in the territory where it has exploited the franchise;

(d)   not to acquire financial interests in the capital of a competing undertaking, which would give the franchisee the power to influence the economic conduct of such undertaking;

(e)   to sell the goods which are the subject-matter of the franchise only to end users, to other franchisees and to resellers within other channels of distribution supplied by the manufacturer of these goods or with its consent;

(f)   to use its best endeavours to sell the goods or provide the services that are the subject-matter of the franchise; to offer for sale a minimum range of goods, achieve a minimum turnover, plan its orders in advance, keep minimum stocks and provide customer and warranty services;

(g)   to pay to the franchisor a specified proportion of its revenue for advertising and itself carry out advertising for the nature of which it shall obtain the franchisor's approval.

2.   Article 1 shall apply notwithstanding the presence of any of the following obligations on the franchisee:

(a)   not to disclose to third parties the know-how provided by the franchisor; the franchisee may be held to this obligation after termination of the agreement;

(b)   to communicate to the franchisor any experience gained in exploiting the franchise and to grant it, and other franchisees, a non-exclusive licence for the know-how resulting from that experience;

(c)   to inform the franchisor of infringements of licensed industrial or intellectual property rights, to take legal action against infringers or to assist the franchisor in any legal actions against infringers;

(d)   not to use know-how licensed by the franchisor for purposes other than the exploitation of the franchise; the franchisee may be held to this obligation after termination of the agreement;

(e)   to attend or have its staff attend training courses arranged by the franchisor;

(f)   to apply the commercial methods devised by the franchisor, including any subsequent modification thereof, and use the licensed industrial or intellectual property rights;

(g) to comply with the franchisor's standards for the equipment and presentation of the contract premises and/or means of transport;

(h) to allow the franchisor to carry out checks of the contract premises and/or means of transport, including the goods sold and the services provided, and the inventory and accounts of the franchisee;

(i) not without the franchisor's consent to change the location of the contract premises;

(j) not without the franchisor's consent to assign the rights and obligations under the franchise agreement.

3. In the event that, because of particular circumstances, obligations referred to in paragraph 2 fall within the scope of Article 85(1), they shall also be exempted even if they are not accompanied by any of the obligations exempted by Article 1.

ARTICLE 4

The exemption provided for in Article 1 shall apply on condition that:

(a) the franchisee is free to obtain the goods that are the subject-matter of the franchise from other franchisees; where such goods are also distributed through another network of authorised distributors, the franchisee must be free to obtain the goods from the latter;

(b) where the franchisor obliges the franchisee to honour guarantees for the franchisor's goods, that obligation shall apply in respect of such goods supplied by any member of the franchised network or other distributors which give a similar guarantee, in the common market;

(c) the franchisee is obliged to indicate its status as an independent undertaking; this indication shall however not interfere with the common identity of the franchised network resulting in particular from the common name or shop sign and uniform appearance of the contract premises and/or means of transport.

ARTICLE 5

The exemption granted by Article 1 shall not apply where:

(a) undertakings producing goods or providing services which are identical or are considered by users as equivalent in view of their characteristics, price and intended use, enter into franchise agreements in respect of such goods or services;

(b) without prejudice to Article 2(e) and Article 3(1)(b), the franchisee is prevented from obtaining supplies of goods of a quality equivalent to those offered by the franchisor;

(c) without prejudice to Article 2(e), the franchisee is obliged to sell, or use in the process of providing services, goods manufactured by the franchisor or third parties designated by the franchisor and the franchisor refuses, for reasons other than protecting the franchisor's industrial or intellectual property rights, or maintaining the common identity and reputation of the franchised network, to designate as authorised manufacturers third parties proposed by the franchisee;

(d) the franchisee is prevented from continuing to use the licensed know-how after termination of the agreement where the know-how has become generally known or easily accessible, other than by breach of an obligation by the franchisee;

(e) the franchisee is restricted by the franchisor, directly or indirectly, in the determination of sale prices for the goods or services which are the subject-matter of the franchise, without prejudice to the possibility for the franchisor of recommending sale prices;

(f) the franchisor prohibits the franchisee from challenging the validity of the industrial or intellectual property rights which form part of the franchise, without prejudice to the possibility for the franchisor of terminating the agreement in such a case;

(g)   franchisees are obliged not to supply within the common market the goods or services which are the subject-matter of the franchise to end users because of their place of residence.

ARTICLE 6

1.   The exemption provided for in Article 1 shall also apply to franchise agreements which fulfil the conditions laid down in Article 4 and include obligations restrictive of competition which are not covered by Articles 2 and 3(3) and do not fall within the scope of Article 5, on condition that the agreements in question are notified to the Commission in accordance with the provisions of Commission Regulation No. 27 and that the Commission does not oppose such exemption within a period of six months.

2.   The period of six months shall run from the date on which the notification is received by the Commission. Where, however, the notification is made by registered post, the period shall run from the date shown on the postmark of the place of posting.

3.   Paragraph 1 shall apply only if:

(a)   express reference is made to this Article in the notification or in a communication accompanying it; and

(b)   the information furnished with the notification is complete and in accordance with the facts.

4.   The benefit of paragraph 1 can be claimed for agreements notified before the entry into force of this Regulation by submitting a communication to the Commission referring expressly to this Article and to the notification. Paragraphs 2 and 3(b) shall apply *mutatis mutandis.*

5.   The Commission may oppose exemption. It shall oppose exemption if it receives a request to do so from a Member State within three months of the forwarding to the Member State of the notification referred to in paragraph 1 or the communication referred to in paragraph 4. This request must be justified on the basis of considerations relating to the competition rules of the Treaty.

6.   The Commission may withdraw its opposition to the exemption at any time. However, where that opposition was raised at the request of a Member State, it may be withdrawn only after consultation of the advisory Committee on Restrictive Practices and Dominant Positions.

7.   If the opposition is withdrawn because the undertakings concerned have shown that the conditions of Article 85(3) are fulfilled, the exemption shall apply from the date of the notification.

8.   If the opposition is withdrawn because the undertakings concerned have amended the agreement so that the conditions of Article 85(3) are fulfilled, the exemption shall apply from the date on which the amendments take effect.

9.   If the Commission opposes exemption and its opposition is not withdrawn, the effects of the notification shall be governed by the provisions of Regulation No. 17.

ARTICLE 7

1.   Information acquired pursuant to Article 6 shall be used only for the purposes of this Regulation.

2.   The Commission and the authorities of the Member States, their officials and other servants shall not disclose information acquired by them pursuant to this Regulation of a kind that is covered by the obligation of professional secrecy.

3.   Paragraphs 1 and 2 shall not prevent publication of general information or surveys which do not contain information relating to particular undertakings or associations of undertakings.

ARTICLE 8

The Commission may withdraw the benefit of this Regulation, pursuant to Article 7 of Regulation No. 19/65/EEC, where it finds in a particular case that an agreement exempted by this Regulation nevertheless has certain effects which are incompatible with the conditions laid down in Article 85(3) of the EEC Treaty, and in particular where territorial protection is awarded to the franchisee and;

(a)   access to the relevant market or competition therein is significantly restricted by the cumulative effect of parallel networks of similar agreements established by competing manufacturers or distributors;

(b)   the goods or services which are the subject-matter of the franchise do not face, in a substantial part of the common market, effective competition from goods or services which are identical or considered by users as equivalent in view of their characteristics, price and intended use;

(c)   the parties, or one of them, prevent end users, because of their place of residence, from obtaining, directly or through intermediaries, the goods or services which are the subject-matter of the franchise within the common market, or use differences in specification concerning those goods or services in different Member States, to isolate markets;

(d)   franchisees engage in concerted practices relating to the sale prices of the goods or services which are the subject-matter of the franchise;

(e)   the franchisor uses its right to check the contract premises and means of transport, or refuses its agreement to requests by the franchisee to move the contract premises or assign its rights and obligations under the franchise agreement, for reasons other than protecting the franchisor's industrial or intellectual property rights, maintaining the common identity and reputation of the franchised network or verifying that the franchisee abides by its obligations under the agreement.

ARTICLE 9

This Regulation shall enter into force on 1 February 1989.

It shall remain in force until 31 December 1999.

This Regulation shall be binding in its entirety and directly applicable in all Member States.

Done at Brussels, 30 November 1988.

COMMISSION REGULATION 1983/83 OF JUNE 22, 1983
On the Application of Article 85(3) of the Treaty to Categories of Exclusive
Distribution Agreements
(OJ 1983, L173/1)

ARTICLE 1

Pursuant to Article 85(3) of the Treaty and subject to the provisions of this Regulation, it is hereby declared that Article 85(1) of the Treaty shall not apply to agreements to which only two undertakings are party and whereby one party agrees with the other to supply certain goods for resale within the whole or a defined area of the common market only to that other.

ARTICLE 2

1.   Apart from the obligation referred to in Article 1 no restriction on competition shall be imposed on the supplier other than the obligation not to supply the contract goods to users in the contract territory.

2.   No restriction on competition shall be imposed on the exclusive distributor other than:

(a) the obligation not to manufacture or distribute goods which compete with the contract goods;

(b) the obligation to obtain the contract goods for resale only from the other party;

(c) the obligation to refrain, outside the contract territory and in relation to the contract goods, from seeking customers, from establishing any branch and from maintaining any distribution depot.

3. Article 1 shall apply notwithstanding that the exclusive distributor undertakes all or any of the following obligations:

(a) to purchase complete ranges of goods or minimum quantities;

(b) to sell the contract goods under trademarks or packed and presented as specified by the other party; ·

(c) to take measures for promotion of sales, in particular:

— to advertise,

— to maintain a sales network or stock of goods,

— to provide customer and guarantee services,

— to employ staff having specialised or technical training.

ARTICLE 3

Article 1 shall not apply where:

(a) manufacturers of identical goods or of goods which are considered by users as equivalent in view of their characteristics, price and intended use enter into reciprocal exclusive distribution agreements between themselves in respect of such goods;

(b) manufacturers of identical goods or of goods which are considered by users as equivalent in view of their characteristics, price and intended use enter into a non-reciprocal exclusive distribution agreement between themselves in respect of such goods unless at least one of them has a total annual turnover of no more than 100 million ECU;

(c) users can obtain the contract goods in the contract territory only from the exclusive distributor and have no alternative source of supply outside the contract territory;

(d) one or both of the parties makes it difficult for intermediaries or users to obtain the contract goods from other dealers inside the common market or, in so far as no alternative source of supply is available there, from outside the common market, in particlar where one or both of them:

1. exercises industrial property rights so as to prevent dealers or users from obtaining outside, or from selling in, the contract territory properly marked or otherwise properly marketed contract goods;

2. exercises other rights or take other measures so as to prevent dealers or users from obtaining outside, or from selling in, the contract territory contract goods.

ARTICLE 4

1. Article 3(a) and (b) shall also apply where the goods there referred to are manufactured by an undertaking connected with a party to the agreement.

2. Connected undertakings are:

(a) undertakings in which a party to the agreement, directly or indirectly:

— owns more than half the capital or business assets, or

— has the power to exercise more than half the voting rights, or

— has the power to appoint more than half the members of the supervisory board, board of directors or bodies legally representing the undertaking, or

— has the right to manage the affairs;

(b)   undertakings which directly or indirectly have in or over a party to the agreement the rights or powers listed in (a);

(c)   undertakings in which an undertaking referred to in (b) directly or indirectly has the rights or powers listed in (a).

3.   Undertakings in which the parties to the agreement or undertakings connected with them jointly have the rights or powers set out in paragraph 2(a) shall be considered to be connected with each of the parties to the agreement.

ARTICLE 5

1.   For the purpose of Article 3(b), the ECU is the unit of account used for drawing up the budget of the Community pursuant to Articles 207 and 209 of the Treaty.

2.   Article 1 shall remain applicable where during any period of two consecutive financial years the total turnover referred to in Article 3(b) is exceeded by no more than 10 per cent.

3.   For the purpose of calculating total turnover within the meaning of Article 3(b), the turnovers achieved during the last financial year by the party to the agreement and connected undertakings in respect of all goods and services, excluding all taxes and other duties, shall be added together. For this purpose no account shall be taken of dealings between the party to the agreement and its connected undertakings or between its connected undertakings.

ARTICLE 6

The Commission may withdraw the benefit of this Regulation, pursuant to Article 7 of Regulation 19/65, when it finds in a particular case that an agreement which is exempted by this Regulation nevertheless has certain effects which are incompatible with the conditions set out in Article 85(3) of the Treaty, and in particular where:

(a)   the contract goods are not subject, in the contract territory, to effective competition from identical goods or goods considered by users as equivalent in vew of their characteristics, price and intended use;

(b)   access by other suppliers to the different stages of distribution within the contract territory is made difficult to a significant extent;

(c)   for reasons other than those referred to in Article 3(c) and (d) it is not possible for intermediaries or users to obtain supplies of the contract goods from dealers outside the contract territory on the terms there customary;

(d)   the exclusive distributor:

1.   without any objectively justified reason refuses to supply in the contract territory categories of purchasers who cannot obtain contract goods elsewhere on suitable terms or applies to them differing prices or conditions of sale;

2.   sells the contract goods at excessively high prices.

ARTICLE 7

In the period July 1, 1983 to December 31, 1986, the prohibition in Article 85(1) of the Treaty shall not apply to agreements which were in force on July 1, 1983 or entered into force between July 1, and December 31, 1983 and which satisfy the exemption conditions of Regulation 67/67 (JO 1967, 849).

The provisions of the preceding paragraph shall apply in the same way to agreements which were in force on the date of accession of the Kingdom of Spain and of the Portuguese Republic and which, as a result of accession, fall within the scope of Article 85(1) of the Treaty.

ARTICLE 8

This Regulation shall not apply to agreements entered into for the resale of drinks in premises used for the sale and consumption of drinks or for the resale of petroleum products in service stations.

ARTICLE 9

This Regulation shall apply *mutatis mutandis* to concerted pratices of the type defined in Article 1.

ARTICLE 10

This Regulation shall enter into force on July 1, 1983.

It shall expire on December 31, 1997.

This Regulation shall be binding in its entirety and directly applicable in all Member States.

Done at Brussels, June 22, 1983.

COMMISSION REGULATION 2349/84 OF JULY 23, 1984
On the Application of Article 85(3) of the Treaty to Certain Categories of Patent
Licensing Agreements
(OJ 1984, L219/15)

ARTICLE 1

1. Pursuant to Article 85(3) of the Treaty and subject to the provisions of this Regulation, it is hereby declared that Article 85(1) of the Treaty shall not apply to patent licensing agreements, and agreements combining the licensing of patents and the communication of know-how, to which only two undertakings are party and which include one or more of the following obligations:

1. an obligation on the licensor not to license other undertakings to exploit the licensed invention in the licensed territory, covering all or part of the common market, in so far and as long as one of the licensed patents remains in force;

2. an obligation on the licensor not to exploit the licensed invention in the licensed territory himself in so far and as long as one of the licensed patents remains in force;

3. an obligation on the licensee not to exploit the licensed invention in territories within the common market which are reserved for the licensor, in so far and as long as the patented product is protected in those territories by parallel patents;

4. an obligation on the licensee not to manufacture or use the licensed product, or use the patented process or the communicated know-how, in territories within the common market which are licensed to other licensees in so far and as long as the licensed product is protected in those territories by parallel patents;

5. an obligation on the licensee not to pursue an active policy of putting the licensed product on the market in the territories within the common market which are licensed to other licensees, and in particular not to engage in advertising specifically aimed at those territories or to establish any branch or maintain any distribution depot there, in so far and as long as the licensed product is protected in those territories by parallel patents;

6. an obligation on the licensee not to put the licensed product on the market in the territories licensed to other licensees within the common market for a period not exceeding five years from the date when the product is first put on the market within the common market by the licensor or one of his licensees, in so far as and for as long as the product is protected in these territories by parallel patents;

7. an obligation on the licensee to use only the licensor's trade mark or the get-up determined by the licensor to distinguish the licensed product, provided that the licensee

is not prevented from identifying himself as the manufacturer of the licensed product.

2.   The exemption of restrictions on putting the licensed product on the market resulting from the obligations referred to in paragraph 1(2), (3), (5) and (6) shall apply only if the licensee manufactures the licensed product himself or has it manufactured by a connected undertaking or by a subcontractor.

3.   The exemption provided for in paragraph 1 shall also apply where in a particular agreement the parties undertake obligations of the types referred to in that paragraph but with a more limited scope than is permitted by the paragraph.

ARTICLE 2

1.   Article 1 shall apply notwithstanding the presence in particular of any of the following obligations, which are generally not restrictive of competition:

1.   an obligation on the licensee to procure goods or services from the licensor or from an undertaking designated by the licensor, in so far as such products or services are necessary for a technically satisfactory exploitation of the licensed invention;

2.   an obligation on the licensee to pay a minimum royalty or to produce a minimum quantity of the licensed product or to carry out a minimum number of operations exploiting the licensed invention;

3.   an obligation on the licensee to restrict his exploitation of the licensed invention to one or more technical fields of application covered by the licensed patent;

4.   an obligation on the licensee not to exploit the patent after termination of the agreement in so far as the patent is still in force;

5.   an obligation on the licensee not to grant sub-licenses or assign the licence;

6.   an obligation on the licensee to mark the licensed product with an indication of the patentee's name, the licensed patent or the patent licensing agreement;

7.   an obligation on the the licensee not to divulge know-how communicated by the licensor; the licensee may be held to this obligation even after the agreement has expired;

8.   obligations:
  (a)   to inform the licensor of infringements of the patent,
  (b)   to take legal action against an infringer,
  (c)   to assist the licensor in any legal action against an infringer,
provided that these obligations are without prejudice to the licensee's right to challenge the validity of the licensed patent;

9.   an obligation on the licensee to observe specifications concerning the minimum quality of the licensed product, provided that such specifications are necessary for a technically satisfactory exploitation of the licensed invention, and to allow the licensor to carry out related checks;

10.   an obligation on the parties to communicate to one another any experience gained in exploiting the licensed invention and to grant one another a licence in respect of inventions relating to improvements and new applications, provided that such communication or licence is non-exclusive;

11.   an obligation on the licensor to grant the licensee any more favourable terms that the licensor may grant to another undertaking after the agreement is entered into.

2.   In the event that, because of particular circumstances, the obligations referred to in paragraph 1 fall within the scope of Article 85(1), they shall also be exempted even if they are not accompanied by any of the obligations exempted by Article 1.

The exemption provided for in this paragraph shall also apply where in an agreement the parties undertake obligations of the types referred to in paragraph 1 but with a more limited scope than is permitted by that paragraph.

ARTICLE 3

Articles 1 and 2(2) shall not apply where:

1.   the licensee is prohibited from challenging the validity of licensed patents or other industrial or commercial property rights within the common market belonging to the licensor or undertakings connected with him, without prejudice to the right of the licensor to terminate the licensing agreement in the event of such a challenge;

2.   the duration of the licensing agreement is automatically prolonged beyond the expiry of the licensed patents existing at the time the agreement was entered into by the inclusion in it of any new patent obtained by the licensor, unless the agreement provides each party with the right to terminate the agreement at least annually after the expiry of the licensed patents existing at the time the agreement was entered into, without prejudice to the right of the licensor to charge royalties for the full period during which the licensee continues to use know-how communicated by the licensor which has not entered into the public domain, even if that period exceeds the life of the patents;

3.   one party is restricted frm competing with the other party, with undertakings connected with the other party or with other undertakings within the common market in respect of research and development, manufacture, use or sales, save as provided in Article 1 and without prejudice to an obligation on the licensee to use his best endeavours to exploit the licensed invention;

4.   the licensee is charged royalties on products which are not entirely or partially patented or manufactured by means of a patented process, or for the use of know-how which has entered into the public domain otherwise than by the fault of the licensee or an undertaking connected with him, without prejudice to arrangements whereby, in order to facilitate payment, the royalty payments for the use of a licensed invention are spread over a period extending beyond the life of the licensed patents or the entry of the know-how into the public domain;

5.   the quantity of licensed products one party may manufacture or sell or the number of operations exploiting the licensed invention he may carry out are subject to limitations;

6.   one party is restricted in the determination of prices, components of prices or discounts for the licensed products;

7.   one party is restricted as to the customers he may serve, in particular by being prohibited from supplying certain classes of user, employing certain forms of distribution or, with the aim of sharing customers, using certain types of packaging for the products, save as provided in Article 1(1)(7) and Article 2(1)(3);

8.   the licensee is obliged to assign wholly or in part to the licensor rights in or to patents for improvements or for new applications of the licensed patents;

9.   the licensee is induced at the time the agreement is entered into to accept further licences which he does not want or to agree to use patents, goods or services which he does not want, unless such patents, products or services are necessary for a technically satisfactory exploitation of the licensed invention;

10.   without prejudice to Article 1(1)(5), the licensee is required, for a period exceeding that permitted under Article 1(1)(6), not to put the licensed product on the market in territories licensed to other licensees within the common market or does not do so as a result of a concerted practice between the parties;

11.   one or both of the parties are required:

(a)   to refuse without any objectively justified reason to meet demand from users or resellers in their respective territories who would market products in other territories within the common market;

(b)   to make it difficult for users or resellers to obtain the products from other resellers within the common market, and in particular to exercise industrial or commercial property rights or take measures so as to prevent users or resellers from obtaining outside, or from putting on the market in, the licensed territory products which have been lawfully put on the market within the common market by the patentee or with his consent; or do so as a result of a concerted practice between them.

ARTICLE 4

1. The exemption provided for in Articles 1 and 2 shall also apply to agreements containing obligations restrictive of competition which are not covered by those Articles and do not fall within the scope of Article 3, on condition that the agreements in question are notified to the Commission in accordance with the provisions of Commission Regulation No. 27, as last amended by Regulation 1699/75, (O.J. 1975, L172/11) and that the Commission does not oppose such exemption within a period of six months.

2. The period of six months shall run from the date on which the notification is received by the Commission. Where, however, the notification is made by registered post, the period shall run from the date shown on the postmark of the place of posting.

3. Paragraph 1 shall apply only if:

(a) express reference is made to this Article in the notification or in a communication accompanying it; and

(b) the information furnished with the notification is complete and in accordance with the facts.

4. The benefit of paragraph 1 may be claimed for agreements notified before the entry into force of this Regulation by submitting a communication to the Commission referring expressly to this Article and to the notification. Paragraphs 2 and 3(b) shall apply *mutatis mutandis.*

5. The Commission may oppose the exemption. It shall oppose exemption if it receives a request to do so from a Member State within three months of the transmission to the Member State of the notification referred to in paragraph 1 of the communication referred to in paragraph 4. This request must be justified on the basis of considerations relating to the competition rules of the Treaty.

6. The Commission may withdraw the opposition to the exemption at any time. However, where the opposition was raised at the request of a Member State and this request is maintained, it may be withdrawn only after consultation of the Advisory Committee on Restrictive Practices and Dominant Positions.

7. If the opposition is withdrawn because the undertakings concerned have shown that the conditions of Article 85(3) are fulfilled, the exemption shall apply from the date of notification.

8. If the opposition is withdrawn because the undertakings concerned have amended the agreement so that the conditions of Article 85(3) are fulfilled, the exemption shall apply from the date on which the amendments take effect.

9. If the Commission opposes exemption and the opposition is not withdrawn, the effects of the notification shall be governed by the provisions of Regulation No. 17.

ARTICLE 5

1. This Regulation shall not apply:

1. to agreements between members of a patent pool which relate to the pooled patents;

2. to patent licensing agreements between competitors who hold interests in a joint venture or between one of them and the joint venture, if the licensing agreements relate to the activities of the joint venture;

3. to agreements under which one party grants to the other party a patent licence and that other party, albeit in separate agreements or through connected undertakings, grants to the first party a licence under patents or trade-marks or reciprocal sales rights

for unprotected products or communicates to him know-how, where the parties are competitors in relation to the products covered by those agreements;

4. to licensing agreements in respect of plant breeder's rights.

2. However, this Regulation shall apply to reciprocal licences of the types referred to in paragraph 1(3) where the parties are not subject to any territorial restriction within the common market on the manufacture, use or putting on the market of the products covered by these agreements or on the use of the licensed processes.

ARTICLE 6

1. As regards agreements existing on March 13, 1962 and notified before February 1, 1963 and agreements, whether notified or not, to which Article 4(2)(ii)(b) of Regulation No. 17 applies, the declaration of inapplicability of Article 85(1) of the Treaty contained in this Regulation shall have retroactive effect from the time at which the conditions for application of this Regulation were fulfilled.

2. As regards all other agreements notified before this Regulation entered into force, the declaration of inapplicability of Article 85(1) of the Treaty contained in this Regulation shall have retrocactive effect from the time at which the conditions for application of this Regulation were fulfilled, or from the date of notification, whichever is the later.

ARTICLE 7

If agreements existing on March 13, 1962 and notified before February 1, 1963 or agreements to which Article 4(2)(ii)(b) of Regulation No. 17 applies and notified before January 1, 1967 are amended before April 1, 1985 so as to fulfil the conditions for application of this Regulation, and if the amendment is communicated to the Commission before July 1, 1985 the prohibition in Article 85(1) of the Treaty shall not apply in respect of the period prior to the amendment. The communication shall take effect from the time of its receipt by the Commission. Where the communication is sent by registered post, it shall take effect from the date shown on the postmark of the place of posting.

ARTICLE 8

1. As regards agreements to which Article 85 of the Treaty applies as a result of the accession of the United Kingdom, Ireland and Denmark, Articles 6 and 7 shall apply except that the relevant dates shall be January 1, 1973 instead of March 13, 1962; and July 1, 1973 instead of February 1, 1963 and January 1, 1967.

2. As regards agreements to which Article 85 of the Treaty applies as a result of the accession of Greece, Articles 6 and 7 shall apply except that the relevant dates shall be January 1, 1981 instead of March 13, 1962; and July 1, 1981 instead of February 1, 1963 and January 1, 1967.

3. As regards agreements to which Article 85 of the Treaty applies as a result of the accession of the Kingdom of Spain and of the Portuguese Republic, Articles 6 and 7 shall apply except that the relevant dates shall be January 1, 1986 instead of March 13, 1962; and July 1, 1986 instead of February 1, 1963, January 1, 1967 and April 1, 1985. The amendment made to these agreements in accordance with Article 7 need not be notified to the Commission.

ARTICLE 9

The Commission may withdraw the benefit of this Regulation, pursuant to Article 7 of Regulation No. 19/65, where it finds in a particular case that an agreement exempted by this Regulation nevertheless has certain effects which are incompatible with the conditions laid down in Article 85(3) of the Treaty, and in particular where:

1.   such effect arise from an arbitration award;
2.   the licensed products or the services provided using a licensed process are not exposed to effective competition in the licensed territory from identical products or services or products or services considered by users as equivalent in view of their characteristics, price and intended use;
3.   the licensor does not have the right to terminate the exclusivity granted to the licensee at the latest five years from the date the agreement was entered into and at least annually thereafter if, without legitimate reason, the licensee fails to exploit the patent or to do so adequately;
4.   without prejudice to Article 1(1)(6), the licensee refuses, without objectively valid reason, to meet unsolicited demand from users or resellers in the territory of other licensees;
5.   one or both of the parties:
   (a)   without any objectively justified reason, refuse to meet demand from users or resellers in their respective territories who would market the products in other territories within the common market; or
   (b)   make it difficult for users or resellers to obtain the products from other resellers within the common market, and in particular where they exercise industrial or commercial property rights or take measures so as to prevent resellers or users from obtaining outside, or from putting on the market in, the licensed territory products which have been lawfully put on the market within the common market by the patentee or with his consent.

ARTICLE 10

1.   This Regulation shall apply to:
   (a)   patent applications;
   (b)   utility models;
   (c)   applications for registration of utility models;
   (d)   'certificats d'utilitè' and 'certificates d'addition' under French law; and
   (e)   applications for 'certificates d'utilitè' and 'certificats d'addition' under French law;
equally as it applies to patents.
2.   This Regulation shall also apply to agreements relating to the exploitation of an invention if an application within the meaning of paragraph 1 is made in respect of the invention for the licensed territory within one year from the date when the agreement was entered into.

ARTICLE 11

This Regulation shall also apply to:
1.   patent licensing agreements where the licensor is not the patentee but is authorized by the patentee to grant a licence or a sub-licence;
2.   assignments of a patent or of a right to a patent where the sum payable in consideration of the assignment is dependent upon the turnover attained by the assignee in respect of the patented products, the quantity of such products manufactured or the number of operations carried out employing the patented invention;
3.   patent licensing agreements in which rights or obligations of the licensor or the licensee are assumed by undertakings connected with them.

ARTICLE 12

1.   'Connected undertakings' for the purposes of this Regulation means:
   (a)   undertakings in which a party to the agreement, directly or indirectly:
      —   owns more than half the capital or business assets, or

    — has the power to exercise more than half the voting rights, or
    — has the power to appoint more than half the members of the supervisory board, board of directors or bodies legally representing the undertaking, or
    — has the right to manage the affairs of the undertaking;
    (b) undertakings which directly or indirectly have in or over a party to the agreement the rights or powers listed in (a);
    (c) undertakings in which an undertaking referred to in (b) directly or indirectly has the rights or powers listed in (a).
    2. Undertakings in which the parties to the agreement or undertakings connected with them jointly have directly or indirectly the rights or powers set out in paragraph 1(a) shall be considered to be connected with each of the parties to the agreement.

ARTICLE 13

    1. Information acquired pursuant to Article 4 shall be used only for the purposes of this Regulation.
    2. The Commission and the authorities of the Member States, their officials and other servants shall not disclose information acquired by them pursuant to this Regulation of the kind covered by the obligation of professional secrecy.
    3. The provisions of paragraphs 1 and 2 shall not prevent publication of general information or surveys which do not contain information relating to particular undertakings or associations of undertakings.

ARTICLE 14

This Regulation shall enter into force on January 1, 1985.
It shall apply until December 31, 1994.
This Regulation shall be binding in its entirety and directly applicable in all Member States.
Done at Brussels, July 23, 1984.

COMMISSION REGULATION (EEC) NO. 556/89 OF NOVEMBER 30, 1988
on the application of Article 85(3) of the Treaty to certain categories of know-how licensing agreements

ARTICLE 1

    (1) Pursuant to Article 85(3) of the Treaty and subject to the provisions of this Regulation, it is hereby declared that Article 85(1) of the Treaty shall not apply to pure know-how licensing agreements and to mixed know-how and patent licensing agreements not exempted by Regulation (EEC) No. 2349/84, including those agreements containing ancillary provisions relating to trademarks or other intellectual property rights, to which only two undertakings are party and which include one or more of the following obligations:
    1. an obligation on the licensor not to license other undertakings to exploit the licensed technology in the licensed territory;
    2. an obligation on the licensor not to exploit the licensed technology in the licensed territory himself;
    3. an obligation on the licensee not to exploit the licensed technology in territories within the common market which are reserved for the licensor;
    4. an obligation on the licensee not to manufacture or use the licensed product, or use the licensed process, in territories within the common market which are licensed to other licensees;

5.   an obligation on the licensee not to pursue an active policy of putting the licensed product on the market in the territories within the common market which are licensed to other licensees, and in particular not to engage in advertising specifically aimed at those territories or to establish any branch or maintain any distribution depot there;

6.   an obligation on the licensee not to put the licensed product on the market in the territories licensed to other licensees within the common market;

7.   an obligation on the licensee to use only the licensor's trademark or the get-up determined by the licensor to distinguish the licensed product during the term of the agreement, provided that the licensee is not prevented from identifying himself as the manufacturer of the licensed products;

8.   an obligation on the licensee to limit his production of the licensed product to the quantities he requires in manufacturing his own products and to sell the licensed product only as an integral part of or a replacement part for his own products or otherwise in connection with the sale of his own products, provided that such quantities are freely determined by the licensee.

(2)   The exemption provided for the obligations referred to in paragraph 1(1)(2) and (3) shall extend for a period not exceeding for each licensed territory within the EEC 10 years from the date of signature of the first licence agreement entered into by the licensor for that territory in respect of the same technology.

The exemption provided for the obligations referred to in paragraph 1(4) and (5) shall extend for a period not exceeding 10 years from the date of signature of the first licence agreement entered into by the licensor within the EEC in respect of the same technology.

The exemption provided for the obligation referred to in paragraph 1(6) shall extend for a period not exceeding five years from the date of the signature of the first licence agreement entered into by the licensor within the EEC in respect of the same technology.

(3)   The exemption provided for in paragraph 1 shall apply only where the parties have identified in any apprpriate form the initial know-how and any subsequent improvements to it, which become available to the parties and are communicated to the other party pursuant to the terms of the agreement and for the purpose thereof, and only for as long as the know-how remains secret and substantial.

(4)   In so far as the obligations referred to in paragraph 1(1) to (5) concern territories including Member States in which the same technology is protected by necessary patents, the exemption provided for in paragraph 1 shall extend for those Member States as long as the licensed product or process is protected in those Member States by such patents, where the duration of such protection exceeds the periods specified in paragraph 2.

(5)   The exemption of restrictions on putting the licensed product on the market resulting from the obligations referred to in paragraph 1(2), (3), (5) and (6) shall apply only if the licensee manufactures or proposes to manufacture the licensed product himself or has it manufactured by a connected undertaking or by a subcontractor.

(6)   The exemption provided for in paragraph 1 shall also apply where in a particular agreement the parties undertake obligations of the types referred to in that paragraph but with a more limited scope than is permitted by the paragraph.

(7)   For the purposes of the present Regulation the following terms shall have the following meanings:

1.   'know-how' means a body of technical information that is secret, substantial and identified in any appropriate form;

2.   the term 'secret' means that the know-how package as a body or in the precise configuration and assembly of its components is not generally known or easily accessible, so that part of its value consists in the lead-time the licensee gains when it is communicated to him; it is not limited to the narrow sense that each individual

component of the know-how should be totally unknown or unobtainable outside the licensor's business;

3. the term 'substantial' means that the know-how includes information which is of importance for the whole or a significant part of (i) a manufacturing process or (ii) a product or service, or (iii) for the development thereof and excludes information which is trivial. Such know-how must thus be useful, i.e. can reasonably be expected at the date of conclusion of the agreement to be capable of improving the competitive position of the licensee, for example by helping him to enter a new market or giving him an advantage in competition with other manufacturers or providers of services who do not have access to the licensed secret know-how or other comparable secret know-how;

4. the term 'identified' means that the know-how is described or recorded in such a manner as to make it possible to verify that it fulfils the criteria of secrecy and substantiality and to ensure that the licensee is not unduly restricted in his exploitation of his own technology. To be identified the know-how can either be set out in the licence agreement or in a separate document or recorded in any other appropriate form at the latest when the know-how is transferred or shortly thereafter, provided that the separate document or other record can be made available if the need arises;

5. 'pure know-how licensing agreements' are agreements whereby one undertaking, the licensor, agrees to communicate the know-how with or without an obligation to disclose any subsequent improvements, to another undertaking, the licensee, for exploitation in the licensed territory;

6. 'mixed know-how and patent licensing agreements' are agreements not exempted by Regulation (EEC) No 2349/84 under which a technology containing both non-patented elements and elements that are patented in one or more Member States is licensed;

7. the terms 'licensed know-how' or 'licensed technology' means the initial and any subsequent know-how communicated directly or indirectly by the licensor to a licensee by means of pure or mixed know-how and patent licensing agreements; however, in the case of mixed know-how and patent licensing agreements the term 'licensed technology' also includes any patents for which a licence is granted besides the communication of the know-how;

8. the term 'the same technology' means the technology as licensed to the first licensee and enhanced by any improvements made thereto subsequently, irrespective of whether and to what extent such improvements are exploited by the parties or the other licensees and irrespective of whether the technology is protected by necessary patents in any Member States;

9. 'the licensed products' are goods or services the production or provision of which requires the use of the licensed technology;

10. the term 'exploitation' refers to any use of the licensed technology in particular in the production, active or passive sales in a territory even if not coupled with manufacture in that territory, or leasing of the licensed products;

11. 'the licensed territory' is the territory covering all or at least part of the common market where the licensee is entitled to exploit the licensed technology;

12. 'territory reserved for the licensor' means territories in which the licensor has not granted any licences and which he has expressly reserved for himself;

13. 'connected undertakings' means:
    (a) undertaking in which a party to the agreement, directly or indirectly;
        — owns more than half the capital or business assets, or
        — has the power to exercise more than half the voting rights, or
        — has the power to appoint more than half the members of the supervisory board, board of directors or bodies legally representing the undertaking, or
        — has the right to manage the affairs of the undertaking;

(b)   undertakings which directly or indirectly have in or over a party to the agreement the rights or powers listed in (a);

(c)   undertakings in which an undertaking referred to in (b) directly or indirectly has the rights or powers listed in (a);

(d)   undertakings in which the parties to the agreement or undertakings connected with them jointly have the rights or powers listed in (a): such jointly controlled undertakings are considered to be connected with each of the parties to the agreement.

ARTICLE 2

—(1)   Article 1 shall apply notwithstanding the presence in particular of any of the following obligations, which are generally not restrictive of competition:

1.   an obligation on the licensee not to divulge the know-how communicated by the licensor; the licensee may be held to this obligation after the agreement has expired;

(2)   an obligation on the licensee not to grant sub-licences or assign the licence;

3.   an obligation on the licensee not to exploit the licensed know-how after termination of the agreement in so far and as long as the know-how is still secret;

4.   an obligation on the licensee to communicate to the licensor any experience gained in exploiting the licensed technology and to grant him a non-exclusive licence in respect of improvements to or new applications of that technology, provided that:

(a)   the licensee is not prevented during or after the term of agreement from freely using his own improvements, in so far as these are severable from the licensor's know-how, or licensing them to third parties where licensing to third parties does not disclose the know-how communicated by the licensor that is still secret; this is without prejudice to an obligation on the licensee to seek the licensor's prior approval to such licensing provided that approval may not be withheld unless there are objectively justifiable reasons to believe that licensing improvements to third parties will disclose the licensor's know-how, and

(b)   the licensor has accepted an obligation, whether exclusive or not, to communicate his own improvements to the licensee and his right to use the licensee's improvements which are not severable from the licensed know-how does not extend beyond the date on which the licensee's right to exploit the licensor's know-how comes to an end, except for termination of the agreement for breach by the licensee; this is without prejudice to an obligation on the licensee to give the licensor the option to continue to use the improvements after that date, if at the same time he relinquishes the post-term use ban or agrees, after having had an opportunity to examine the licensee's improvements, to pay appropriate royalties for their use;

5.   an obligation on the licensee to observe minimum quality specifications for the licensed product or to procure goods or services from the licensor or from an undertaking designated by the licensor, in so far as such quality specifications, products or services are necessary for:

(a)   a technically satisfatory exploitation of the licensed technology, or

(b)   for ensuring that the production of the licensee conforms to the quality standards that are respected by the licensor and other licensees, and to allow the licensor to carry out related checks;

6.   obligations:

(a)   to inform the licensor of misappropriation of the know-how or of infringements of the licensed patents, or

(b)   to take or to assist the licensor in taking legal action against such misappropriation or infringements, provided that these obligations are without prejudice to the licensee's right to challenge the validity of the licensed patents or to contest the secrecy of the licensed know-how except where he himself has in some way contributed to its disclosure;

7. an obligation on the licensee, in the event of the know-how becoming publicly known other than by action of the licensor, to continue paying until the end of the agreement the royalties in the amounts, for the periods and according to the methods freely determined by the parties without prejudice to the payment of any additional damages in the event of the know-how becoming publicly known by the action of the licensee in breach of the agreement;

8. an obligation on the licensee to restrict his exploitation of the licensed technology to one or more technical fields of application covered by the licensed technology or to one or more product markets;

9. an obligation on the licensee to pay a minimum royalty or to produce a minimum quantity of the licensed product or to carry out a minimum number of operations exploiting the licensed technology;

10. an obligation on the licensor to grant the licensee any more favourable terms that the licensor may grant to another undertaking after the agreement is entered into;

11. an obligation on the licensee to mark the licensed product with the licensor's name;

12. an obligation on the licensee not to use the licensor's know-how to construct facilities for third parties; this is without prejudice to the right of the licensee to increase the capacity of its facilities or to set up additional facilities for its own use on normal commercial terms, including the payment of additional royalties.

(2) In the event that, because of particular circumstances, the obligations referred to in paragraph 1 fall within the scope of Article 85(1), they shall also be exempted even if they are not accompanied by any of the obligations exempted by Article 1.

(3) The exemption provided for in paragraph 2 shall also apply where in an agreement the parties undertake obligations of the types referred to in paragraph 1 but with a more limited scope than is permitted by that paragraph.

ARTICLE 3

Articles 1 and 2(2) shall not apply where:

1. the licensee is prevented from continuing to use the licensed know-how after the termination of the agreement where the know-how has meanwhile become publicly known, other than by the action of the licensee in breach of the agreement;

2. the licensee is obliged either:

(a) to assign in whole or in part to the licensor rights to improvements to or new applications of the licensed technology;

(b) to grant the licensor an exclusive licence for improvements to or new applications of the licensed technology which would prevent the licensee during the currency of the agreement and/or thereafter from using his own improvements in so far as these are severable from the licensor's know-how, or from licensing them to third parties, where such licensing would not disclose the licensor's know-how that is still secret; or

(c) in the case of an agreement which also includes a post-term use ban, to grant back to the licensor, even on a non-exclusive and reciprocal basis, licences for improvements which are not severable from the licensor's know-how, if the licensor's right to use the improvements is of a longer duration then the licensee's right to use the licensor's know-how, except for termination of the agreement for breach by the licensee;

3. the licensee is obliged at the time the agreement is entered into to accept quality specifications or further licences or to procure goods or services which he does not want, unless such licences, quality specifications, goods or services are necessary for a technically satisfactory exploitation of licensed technology or for ensuring that the production of the licensee conforms to the quality standards that are respected by the licensor and other licensees;

4.   the licensee is prohibited from contesting the secrecy of the listed know-how or from challenging the validity of licensed patents within the common market belonging to the licensor or undertakings connected with him, without prejudice to the right of the licensor to terminate the licensing agreement in the event of such a challenge;

5.   the licensee is charged royalties on goods or services which are not entirely or partially produced by means of the licensed technology or for the use of know-how which has become publicly known by the action of the licensor or an undertaking connected with him;

6.   one party is restricted within the same technological field of use or within the same product market as to the customers he may serve in particular by being prohibited from supplying certain classes of user, employing certain forms of distribution or, with the aim of sharing customers, using certain types of packaging for the products, save as provided in Article 1(1)(7) and Article 4(2);

7.   the quantity of the licensed products one party may manufacture or sell or the number of operations exploiting the licensed technology he may carry out are subject to limitations, save as provided in Article 1(1)(8) and Article 4(2);

8.   one party is restricted in the determination of prices, components of prices or discounts for the licensed products;

9.   one party is restricted from competing with the other party, with undertakings connected with the other party or with other undertakings within the common market in respect of research and development, production or use of competing products and their distribution, without prejudice to an obligation on the licensee to use his best endeavours to exploit the licensed technology and without prejudice to the right of the licensor to terminate the exclusivity granted to the licensee and cease communicating improvements in the event of the licensee's engaging in any such competing activities and to require the licensee to prove that the licensed know-how is not used for the production of goods and services other than those licensed;

10.   the initial duration of the licensing agreement is automatically prolonged by the inclusion in it of any new improvements communicated by the licensor, unless the licensee has the right to refuse such improvements or each party has the right to terminate the agreement at the expiry of the initial term of the agreement and at least every three years thereafter;

11.   the licensor is required, albeit in separate agreements, for a period exceeding that permitted under Article 1(2) not to license other undertakings to exploit the same technology in the licensed territory, or a party is required for periods exceeding those permitted under Articles 1(2) or 1(4) not to exploit the same technology in the territory of the other party or of other licensees;

12.   one or both of the parties are required:

(a)   to refuse without any objectively justified reason to meet demand from users or resellers in their respective territories who would market products in other territories within the common market;

(b)   to make it difficult for user or resellers to obtain the products from other resellers within the common market, and in particular to exercise intellectual property rights or take measures so as to prevent users or resellers from obtaining outside, or from putting on the market in the licensed territory products which have been lawfully put on the market within the common market by the licensor or with his consent;

or do so as a result of a concerted practice between them.

ARTICLE 4

(1)   The exemption provided for in Articles 1 and 2 shall also apply to agreements containing obligations restrictive of competition which are not covered by those Articles and do not fall within the scope of Article 3, on condition that the agreements in

question are notified to the Commission in accordance with the provisions of Commission Regulation No. 27 and the Commission does not oppose such exemption within a period of six months.

(2)   Paragraph 1 shall in particular apply to an obligation on the licensee to supply only a limited quantity of the licensed product to a particular customer, where the know-how licence is granted at the request of such a customer in order to provide him with a second source of supply within a licensed territory.

This provision shall also apply where the customer is the licensee and the licence, in order to provide a second source of supply, provides for the customer to make licensed products or have them made by a sub-contractor.

(3)   The period of six months shall run from the date on which the notification is received by the Commission. Where, however, the notification is made by registered post, the period shall run from the date shown on the postmark of the place of posting.

(4)   Paragraphs 1 and 2 shall apply only if:

(a)   express reference is made to this Article in the notification or in a communication accompanying it; and

(b)   the information furnished with the notification is complete and in accordance with the facts.

(5)   The benefit of paragraphs 1 and 2 may be claimed for agreements notified before the entry into force of this Regulation by submitting a communication to the Commission referring expressly to this Article and to the notification. Paragraphs 3 and 4(b) shall apply *mutatis mutandis*.

(6)   The Commission may oppose the exemption. It shall oppose exemption if it receives a request to do so from a Member State within three months of the transmission to the Member State of the notification referred to in paragraph 1 or of the communication referred to in paragraph 5. This request must be justified on the basis of considerations relating to the competition rules of the Treaty.

(7)   The Commission may withdraw the opposition to the exemption at any time. However, where the opposition was raised at the request of a Member State and this request is maintained, it may be withdrawn only after consultation of the Advisory Committee on Restrictive Practices and Dominant Positions.

(8)   If the opposition is withdrawn because the undertakings concerned have shown that the conditions of Article 85(3) are fulfilled, the exemption shall apply from the date of notification.

(9)   If the opposition is withdrawn because the undertakings concerned have amended the agreement so that the conditions of Article 85(3) are fulfilled, the exemption shall apply from the date on which the amendments take effect.

(10)   If the Commission opposes exemption and the opposition is not withdrawn, the effects of the notification shall be governed by the provisions of Regulation No. 17.

ARTICLE 5

(1)   This Regulation shall not apply to:

1.   agreements between members of a patent or know-how pool which relate to the pooled technologies;

2.   know-how licensing agreements between competing undertakings which hold interests in a joint venture, or between one of them and the joint venture, if the licensing agreements relate to the activities of the joint venture;

3.   agreements under which one party grants the other a know-how licence and the other party, albeit in separate agreements or through connected undertakings, grants the first party a patent trademark or know-how licence or exclusive sales rights, where the parties are competitors in relation to the products covered by those agreements;

4.   agreements including the licensing of intellectual property rights other than

patents (in particular trademarks, copyright and design rights) or the licensing of software except where these rights or the software are of assistance in achieving the object of the licensed technology and there are no obligations restrictive of competition other than those also attached to the licensed know-how and exempted under the present Regulation.

(2)   However, this Regulation shall apply to reciprocal licences of the types referred to in paragraph 1(3) where the parties are not subject to any territorial restriction within the common market on the manufacture, use or putting on the market of the products covered by the agreements or on the use of the licensed technologies.

ARTICLE 6

This Regulation shall also apply to:
1.   pure know-how agreements or mixed agreements where the licensor is not the developer of the know-how or the patentee but is authorised by the developer or the patentee to grant a licence or a sub-licence;
2.   assignments of know-how or of know-how and patents where the risk associated with exploitation remains with the assignor, in particular where the sum payable in consideration of the assignment is dependent upon the turnover attained by the assignee in respect of products made using the know-how or the patents, the quantity of such products manufactured or the number of operations carried out employing the know-how or the patents;
3.   pure know-how agreements or mixed agreements in which rights or obligations of the licensor or the licensee are assumed by undertakings connected with them.

ARTICLE 7

The Commission may withdraw the benefit of this Regulation, pursuant to Article 7 of Regulation No. 19/65/EEC, where it finds in a particular case that an agreement exempted by this Regulation nevertheless has certain effects which are incompatible with the conditions laid down in Article 85(3) of the Treaty, and in particular where:
1.   Such effects arise from an arbitration award;
2.   the effect of the agreement is to prevent the licensed products from being exposed to effective competition in the licensed territory from identical products or products considered by users as equivalent in view of their characteristics, price and intended use;
3.   the licensor does not have the right to terminate the exclusivity granted to the licensee at the latest five years from the date the agreement was entered into and at least annually thereafter if, without legitimate reason, the licensee fails to exploit the licensed technology or to do so adequately;
4.   without prejudice to Article 1(1)(6), the licensee refuses, without objectively valid reason, to meet unsolicited demand from users or resellers in the territory of other licensees;
5.   one or both of the parties:
   (a)   without objectively justified reason, refuse to meet demand from users or resellers in their respective territories who would market the products in other territories within the common market; or
   (b)   make it difficult for users or resellers to obtain the products from other resellers within the common market, and in particular where they exercise intellectual property rights or take measures so as to prevent resellers or users from obtaining outside, or from putting on the market in the licensed territory products which have been lawfully put on the market within the common market by the licensor or with his consent;
6.   the operation of the post-term use ban referred to in Article 2(1)(3) prevents the licensee from working an expired patent which can be worked by all other manufacturers;

7. the period for which the licensee is obliged to continue paying royalties after the know-how has become publicly known by the action of third parties, as referred to in Article 2(1)(7), substantially exceeds the lead time acquired because of the head-start in production and marketing and this obligation is detrimental to competition in the market;

8. the parties were already competitors before the grant of the licence and obligations on the licensee to produce a minimum quantity or to use his best endeavours as referred to in Article 2(1)(9) and Article 3(9) have the effect of preventing the licensee from using competing technologies.

ARTICLE 8

(1) As regards agreements existing on 13 March 1962 and notified before 1 February 1963 and agreements, whether notified or not, to which Article 4(2)(2)(b) of Regulation No. 17 applies, the declaration of inapplicability of Article 85(1) of the Treaty contained in this Regulation shall have retroactive effect from the time at which the conditions for application of this Regulation were fulfilled.

(2) As regards all other agreements notified before this Regulation entered into force, the declaration of inapplicablity of Article 85(1) of the Treaty contained in this Regulation shall have retroactive effect from the time at which the conditions for application of this Regulation were fulfilled, or from the date of notification, whichever is the later.

ARTICLE 9

If agreements existing on 13 March 1962 and notified before 1 February 1963 or agreements to which Article 4(2)(2)(b) of Regulation No. 17 applies and notified before 1 January 1967 are amended before 1 July 1989 so as to fulfil the conditions for application of this Regulation, and if the amendment is communicated to the Commission before 1 October 1989 the prohibition in Article 85(1) of the Treaty shall not apply in respect of the period prior to the amendment. The communication shall take effect from the time of its receipt by the Commission. Where the communication is sent by registered post, it shall take effect from the date shown on the postmark of the place of posting.

ARTICLE 10

(1) As regards agreements to which Article 85 of the Treaty applies as a result of the accession of the United Kingdom, Ireland and Denmark, Articles 8 and 9 shall apply except that the relevant dates shall be 1 January 1973 instead of 13 March 1962 and 1 July 1973 instead of 1 February 1963 and 1 January 1967.

(2) As regards agreements to which Article 85 of the Treaty applies as a result of the accession of Greece, Articles 8 and 9 shall apply except that the relevant dates shall be 1 January 1981 instead of 13 March 1962 and 1 July 1981 instead of 1 February 1963 and 1 January 1967.

(3) As regards agreements to which Article 85 of the Treaty applies as a result of the accession of Spain and Portugal, Articles 8 and 9 shall apply except that the relevant dates shall be 1 January 1986 instead of 13 March 1962 and 1 July 1986 instead of 1 February 1963 and 1 January 1967.

ARTICLE 11

(1) Information acquired pursuant to Article 4 shall be used only for the purposes of the Regulation.

(2) The Commission and the authorities of the Member States, their officials and other servants shall not disclose information acquired by them pursuant to this Regulation of the kind covered by the obligation of professional secrecy.

(3) The provisions of paragraphs 1 and 2 shall not prevent publication of general information or surveys which do not contain information relating to particlar undertakings or associations of undertakings.

ARTICLE 12

This Regulation shall enter into force on 1 April 1989.
It shall apply until 31 December 1999.
This Regulation shall be binding in its entirety and directly applicable in all Member States.
Done at Brussels, 30 November 1988.

Index

COMMERCIAL EXPLOITATION OF
INTELLECTUAL PROPERTY